THE FRENCH PRESIDENTIAL ELECTIONS OF 1988

The French Presidential Elections of 1988

Ideology and Leadership in Contemporary France

Edited by

JOHN GAFFNEY

Department of Modern Languages
Aston University

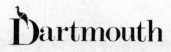

Published by
Dartmouth Publishing Company Limited
Gower House
Croft Road
Aldershot
Hants GU11 3HR

Gower Publishing Company
Old Post Road
Brookfield
Vermont 05036
USA

British Library Cataloguing in Publication Data
The French presidential elections of 1988: Ideology and
leadership in contemporary France
  1. France. Presidents. Elections.
  I. Gaffney,- John. 1950-
324. 944

ISBN 1-85521-059-2

Printed in Great Britain by
Billing & Sons Ltd, Worcester

Contents

Acknowledgements

This book is the product of a research project organised by members of the Department of Modern Languages at Aston University. I should like to thank the Department for its support, the Aston members of the group for their co-operation and David Bell of Leeds University and George Jones of the European Business School, London, for joining the project and contributing to the book.

I want to extend thanks to the following people in France for their help: Pierre Boussel, Jean Canet, Véronique Delahaye, Martine Desailly, Renée Frégosi, Franck Lessay, Henri Malberg, Michel Rodinsen and Antoine Wæchter; and to Jean-Louis Lemaire whose help during the election campaign itself was extremely valuable.

Wendy Firmin and Gillian Rex of the Department of Modern Languages, Aston, were very helpful in providing extensive video recordings and documentation and I should like to extend thanks to them, and to Peter Morris of the University of Nottingham for his helpful comments on the draft of my introductory chapter.

Finally, everybody in the group wishes to thank Catherine Bate for her invaluable secretarial expertise, and equally invaluable patience, in the preparation of the manuscript.

Main Abbreviations

BNP	Banque Nationale de Paris
CDS	Centre des Démocrates Sociaux
CERES	Centre d'Etude, de Recherche et d'Education Socialistes
CFDT	Confédération Française Démocratique du Travail
CFTC	Confédération Française des Travailleurs Chrétiens
CGC	Confédération Générale des Cadres
CGPME	Confédération Générale des Petites et Moyennes Entreprises
CGT	Confédération Générale du Travail
CIR	Convention des Institutions Républicaines
CNCL	Commission Nationale de la Communication et des Libertés
CNPF	Conseil National du Patronat Français
EMS	European Monetary System
FGDS	Fédération de la Gauche Démocrate et Socialiste
FN	Front National
FO	Force Ouvrière
LO	Lutte Ouvrière
MPPT	Mouvement pour un Parti des Travailleurs
MRG	Mouvement des Radicaux de Gauche
MRP	Mouvement Républicain Populaire

OAS	Organisation de l'Armée Secrète
PCF	Parti Communiste Français
PME	Petites et moyennes entreprises
PR	Parti Républicain
PS	Parti Socialiste
PSD	Parti Social-démocrate
PS (SFIO)	Parti Socialiste (Section Française de l'Internationale Ouvrière)
PSU	Parti Socialiste Unifié
RPF	Rassemblement du Peuple Français
RPR	Rassemblement pour la République
SIVP	Stages d'Initiation à la Vie Professionnelle
SMIC	Salaire Minimum Interprofessionnel de Croissance
SNAC	Syndicat National des Associations de Commerçants
UDF	Union pour la Démocratie Française
UDR	Union des Démocrates pour la République
UNETT	Union Nationale des Entreprises de Travail Temporaire
UNR	Union pour la Nouvelle République
URC	Union du Rassemblement et du Centre

Part One: The Background

1 Introduction: Presidentialism and the Fifth Republic

JOHN GAFFNEY

On 8 May 1988 François Mitterrand was reelected as the sixth President of the French Fifth Republic.[1] At 8.50 pm that day he made the following declaration:

> My dear compatriots, the results known at the moment I speak indicate that you have chosen to place your confidence in me. I shall continue, therefore, to carry out the mission, the greatness and weight of which I have known for seven years, but which, renewed, obliges me still more to do what I must to rally all the French people who wish it.
>
> I will act, that is the least I can say, true to the principles of the Republic. Liberty, equality and respect for others, the refusal of exclusions, which we call fraternity, still nourish the hopes of men. There are too many difficulties, too much anguish, too much uncertainty for too many of our people in our society for us to forget that the first duty is that of national solidarity. Each according to his means must contribute to the well-being of all.
>
> Throughout this presidential campaign, I told you that it was only through social cohesion that France would be able to spread throughout the world, and in the Europe we must build, the benefits of its economy, its technology, its culture, in a word, its genius.
>
> But everything begins with the young. That is our soundest asset. I want to commit the thrust of our efforts to the creation of equality of opportunity for them, and through education, through the training of the mind and hands, the jobs which will put at last the greatest number of our businesses into the competition of the modern world, and with the means to win.
>
> Finally, and because the very life of humanity depends upon it, I shall serve passionately in your name the cause of the underdeveloped countries, of disarmament and of peace.
>
> And so, because it is a pressing issue, I intend that the government to be formed in the next few days, in France and in its overseas territories, should undertake to heal the wounds and establish the dialogue necessary to success.
>
> My dear compatriots, to each woman and man, whatever your vote was, I offer my fraternal greeting. From the bottom of my heart, I thank those women and men who gave their vote to me, those

women and men who helped me so much. I know what it represents for them and for France, our beloved country, this their victory. As another millenium approaches, as a stage or as a symbol, a new period in our history is beginning.

How can I express to you my feelings at this serious and solemn moment? Let me say it again: let us love France and serve her. Long live the Republic and long live France.[2]

It is clear from this declaration, irrespective of Mitterrand's own personal style, that the presidency of the Republic is treated here with a legitimacy surpassing that of all other political posts, and the electing of the President treated as the fundamental political act within the Fifth Republic. It is this extraordinary conception of the presidency, and its relation to the rest of the political process, which is the underlying theme of this book.

The results of the election were as follows:

First round (% of votes cast), 24 April 1988:[3]

Raymond Barre	(UDF)	16.54%
Pierre Boussel	(MPPT)	0.38%
Jacques Chirac	(RPR)	19.96%
Pierre Juquin	(Rénovateurs)	2.10%
Arlette Laguiller	(LO)	1.99%
André Lajoinie	(PCF)	6.76%
Jean-Marie Le Pen	(FN)	14.38%
François Mitterrand	(PS)	34.11%
Antoine Waechter	(Ecologists)	3.78%

Second round (% of votes cast), 8 May 1988:

Jacques Chirac	45.98%
François Mitterrand	54.02%

Two days after his victory, and following the resignation of the Prime Minister, Jacques Chirac, François Mitterrand asked Michel Rocard (PS) to form a government. Rocard's new government was announced on 12 May. On 14 May, Mitterrand dissolved the National Assembly. After the legislative elections of 5 and 12 June, in which the Socialists and their allies gained 63 extra seats but failed to obtain an absolute majority, François Mitterrand once again asked Michel Rocard to form a government, thus inaugurating a new period of political realignments, the motor of which was the creation of new political boundaries which would allow parties and personalities of the centre to govern with the Socialists, a realignment which was desired by national opinion (as expressed in opinion polls) and reflected in Mitterrand's substantial majority of 8 May.[4]

From this series of events, it is clear that as an organising principle of French political life, the presidential elections are of crucial significance. The assumed supreme importance of the presidency was, of course, affirmed in 1958 when de Gaulle, the last Prime Minister of the Fourth Republic, became the Fifth Republic's first President rather than its first Prime Minister. After him, Georges Pompidou, Valéry Giscard d'Estaing and François Mitterrand all, when President, considered themselves to be the head of the executive, Pompidou and Giscard d'Estaing in particular extending the role and apparent powers of the presidency to the point where it became the main architect of government policy. Through both constitutional provision and acquired practice, it became clear that the powers of the President in favourable political circumstances were wide. Between 1958 and 1986, the presidency of the French Republic was arguably the strongest political post (relative to country) in the Western world.

The power of the President in political life and over governmental activity decreased sharply between 1986 and 1988, this demonstrating, for the first time, the constraints placed on such power in less auspicious circumstances. This diminution was the result of the election of a National Assembly in March 1986 whose majority was politically hostile to the President. The 1986 legislative elections, in fact, 'reduced' the President to his role as prescribed by the *letter* of the 1958 Constitution, the *constitutional* demarcation of powers between the President, government and parliament becoming relatively clear for the first time.[5] Given the hostile majority in the National Assembly, and the hostile government which was formed from that majority, it became evident in 1986 that, constitutionally, the powers of the President were, in fact, extremely limited. Symbolically, moreover, just as hitherto the President's status had been enhanced by the fact that the government and majority of the Assembly had been 'his', his *status* was now radically diminished because the election of the Assembly from which the 1986 Chirac government was formed inevitably appeared to be a form of public sanction of the popularly elected President of 1981. Nevertheless, the paradox remains, and is clearly illustrated by the example of the 1988 presidential elections and their consequences: the actual influence of the presidency (and the presidential election itself) on political life, and its effect upon national political activity, cannot be overestimated. This political post, the ultimate powerlessness of which was demonstrated after 1986, remains the organising principle of political activity and, of course, the ultimate prize sought by France's major politicians. Before analysing the reasons for this paradoxical and intriguing state of affairs, let us state and comment briefly upon the powers of the President as prescribed by the Fifth republican constitution.

The powers of the President of the Republic are set out in *Titre II* (articles 5-19) of the 1958 Constitution. The President of the Republic is the Head of State, and, therefore, in terms of protocol, the most senior political figure in the country. The President has a general secretariat and a military secretariat. There is a certain ambiguity regarding his military role. The President is the head of the armed forces (and as such controls the nuclear strike force) and presides over the senior councils and committees of national defence. The government, however, is responsible for the nation's defence. The President represents France at summit conferences and signs international treaties (many international agreements and laws, however, in the present period, fall outside his jurisdiction, given that they are often not, strictly speaking, treaties).

The President also appoints the Prime Minister (who need not be a member of the National Assembly) and, on the Prime Minister's proposal, the other Ministers. The President cannot force the Prime Minister or government to resign, the government being responsible not to the President but to parliament. He can, however, dissolve the National Assembly and call for new legislative elections (but cannot repeat this procedure in the year following a dissolution). He also presides over the Council of Ministers.[6] The powers of the President vis-à-vis the calling of referendums are described in Article 11 of the Constitution, and do not, contrary to popular opinion, give the right to an arbitrary presidential call for a referendum.[7]

Article 16 of the 1958 Constitution confers state of emergency type powers on the President (although the government and National Assembly continue to sit throughout the time that Article 16 is in force). De Gaulle, however, is the only President to have invoked Article 16 (in 1961, when, in the context of the Algerian crisis, he was threatened by a military putsch), but, although accused of having let it run for longer than was necessary, he nevertheless did not use it to create any threat to the regime or to the Constitution itself.

The President also names (although subsequently has no control over) three of the nine members of the Constitutional Council (including its president). He can also submit government bills to the Constitutional Council for a ruling on their constitutionality.

We can conclude from this overview that the near-totality, if not indeed the totality, of these attributes could be interpreted as, or else could become, merely formal and ceremonial, rather than directly political powers, and few of them suggest an unambiguous political power such as that exercised by the Presidents between 1958 and 1986.

There remains one other constitutionally prescribed power, the interpretation and application of which has been the source of considerable ambiguity. It concerns the question of *arbitrage*. According to Article 5, the President is the *'arbitre'* of the nation. This is open to etymological interpretation as to whether the President is empowered to act as an arbitrator *between* the various political forces or whether, with different implications, he has an arbitrary right to *take* decisions in the name of the nation. Although the first meaning is the more credible one, it is the second (which would seem to stretch etymology to the limits of credibility) which most political observers and actors have subscribed to (see Chapter Two for further discussion of this).

Nevertheless, irrespective of this permanent potential source of arbitrary intervention, the President's powers are both prescribed and limited: with a government responsible to parliament, France is essentially a parliamentary, not a presidential, regime; and the ascendancy of the Prime Minister and his government over the President in terms of government policy and legislation between 1986 and 1988 was a clear demonstration of the relativity of the President's power.

Given both the 1958-1986 and the 1986-1988 experiences, we can say that, depending on 'opinion', as expressed in legislative elections and in the governments formed as a result of these, the political influence of the President may exceed or else be strictly limited to the powers prescribed by the Constitution. The President of the Fifth Republic does not, in fact, have markedly greater powers than the Presidents of the Third Republic.[8] What distinguishes the President of the Fifth Republic are two factors: acquired practice, as we have seen, and the constitutional amendment of 1962.[9]

In 1962, General de Gaulle effected an amendment to the 1958 Constitution which introduced the election of the President of the Republic by direct universal adult suffrage, a revision which was approved by a national referendum.[10] The amendment did not, however, change any of the *powers* of the President as laid down in the 1958 Constitution. It reaffirmed, nevertheless, for all the Presidents who were to come after de Gaulle, the supreme 'legitimacy' of the President over all other political actors. We can make three points here.

First, and quite simply, the 1962 amendment meant that the President was the only nationally plebiscited figure in the polity.[11]

Second, this 'national' authority has been enhanced by the media, arguably in response to public opinion, and its general treatment of the President as the most significant actor in French political life - and of presidential campaigns as the most significant act of French political life. Given such media and public attention, moreover, the presidential campaigns themselves lend to the presidency a further authority in terms of the electing of a President as being, at its least extreme, a public desire for a particular governmental orientation, at its most, a legitimation of a particular governmental programme. Over and above this, Prime Ministers in the Fifth Republic, with the exception of Jacques Chirac (as Prime Minister of both Valéry Giscard d'Estaing and François Mitterrand), have behaved as if their greatest loyalty and obedience was to their President rather than to the National Assembly to which they were constitutionally responsible.[12]

Third, in spite of the fact that the government is responsible to parliament, the *majorité* supportive of that government in the Fifth Republic has always perceived itself and behaved (the exception being, once again, the 1986-1988 government - and to a much lesser degree Chaban-Delmas' 1969-1972 government) as the President's rather than the Prime Minister's majority. The clearest illustrations of this were, in the first place, the legislative elections which were triggered by presidential elections (1981 and 1988), and, in the second, those which were the result of appeals by the President to the electorate to reaffirm his authority *through* legislative elections (1962, 1967, 1968). This phenomenon of National Assembly allegiance to the President is directly linked to the latter's near-mystical relation to the nation, given the plebiscitary form of his election.[13]

We can see that, irrespective of the prescribed powers of the President as laid down by the 1958 Constitution, a whole series of factors has enhanced the de facto influence of the President. One of these is the fact that the support for a President (as measured by votes cast) has always exceeded the national popularity of the party from which the President has emerged (the 'crisis' legislative elections of 1968 are arguably an exception to this rule), and, moreover, has been instrumental in the increase in national popularity of the party itself; de Gaulle and Pompidou for the Gaullists, Valéry Giscard d'Estaing for the UDF confederation, and François Mitterrand for the Socialists. We can say, therefore, that the presidency has become the organising principle, not only of political life generally, but of the political parties themselves.[14]

We can add to these observations the fact that, paradoxically, since de Gaulle, the developing lack of precision on the part of presidential candidates in relation to proposed governmental programmes has, in fact, enhanced presidential authority within the polity. François Mitterrand in 1988 is perhaps the best illustration of this. His programme, delivered in his *Lettre à tous les Français,* was both highly personalised and relatively imprecise vis-à-vis proposed legislation, this being presented as the domain of the government which would be formed after the election of the President, and the detailed elaboration of which was, as it were, beneath presidential concern. 1988, however, showed Mitterrand making a virtue of necessity, given that the 1986-1988 period had already demonstrated the relative political weakness of the presidency in this area. The implicit message of François Mitterrand in the 1988 election campaign, therefore, was that, after his election, he would allow a new government to govern with an independence from the President enjoyed by no government hitherto *except* the Chirac government of 1986-1988 which had divested Mitterrand of the near-totality of acquired presidential power. In 1988, therefore, we can say that both the President's popularity and his authority were based, in part, upon his clear intention to *restrict* his own powers to those prescribed by the 1958 Constitution while reasserting his influence over the whole process of political activity.[15]

We can therefore make four points regarding the Fifth Republic presidency which will have a particular relevance for the significance of the French presidency in the political life of France in the late 1980s and the 1990s.

1) Between 1986 and 1988, the French tolerated and were even sympathetic to *cohabitation,* even though polls suggested that they preferred a regime with the President in overall control, that is to say, with a sympathetic majority in the National Assembly and a sympathetic government. Nevertheless, the *cohabitation* period, albeit in extreme form, demonstrated for the first time the respective powers of the President and the government, in particular those of the President vis-à-vis the Prime Minister. In a word, the Prime Minister had become de facto as well as de jure head of government. The *choice* of Prime Minister by the President (which would reflect his own interpretation of the nation's wishes and needs, as well as the political arithmetic in the National Assembly) meant, however, that the President's power remained considerable, and his authority to dissolve the National Assembly a major factor in the political process.

2) The French generally and the French political class particularly have always regarded and continue to regard the presidency as the real political prize, as well as the most prestigious office, in the Republic. Between 1986 and 1988, even though Jacques Chirac exercised his constitutional rights to the full

and dominated governmental activity to the relative exclusion of the President, the premiership was never regarded (as it had been in the Third and Fourth Republics), either by political actors or by the French people (or, indeed, by Jacques Chirac), as a new and permanent site of overall power which could replace the presidency in political importance. Moreover, in the Fifth Republic, the Prime Minister's standing has always been overshadowed by that of the President, and in the case of the 1988 presidential elections - the first in which a President and Prime Minister had confronted one another in such an election - the Prime Minister in office (Chirac) lost decisively to the sitting President (Mitterrand).

3) However strong the Prime Minister became in terms of his majority in the Assembly, the President still retained an unassailable legitimacy because of the manner of his election, a legitimacy which conferred the right to redraw the political map through dissolution in an attempt to return a President's majority.[16] We can add here, over and above our earlier remarks concerning the preeminence of political allegiance to the President, that such legitimacy was further enhanced by the fact that, generally speaking, the parties' presidential *candidates* were dominant figures within their parties, taking significant precedence over the individuals who *might* become the parties' preferred Prime Minister.[17]

4) Throughout the 1986-1988 period of *cohabitation*, the incumbent President saw his popularity soar, leaving that of his rivals way behind. Such a phenomenon suggests more than anything else that, depending upon the constitutional conduct of the incumbent (i.e., that he exercise his *arbitrage* in a way which was not reminiscent of MacMahon[18]), the presidency would retain its legitimacy within public opinion as well as its political preeminence, even though, as we have seen, in 1988, Mitterrand's proposals were less clear than those of any major presidential candidate since 1965.

We can see, therefore, that the 1958 Constitution, and de Gaulle's own prestige, conferred a particular set of powers, a particular status, and a particular influence upon the presidency, but that it was the 1962 constitutional amendment which increased dramatically (for those who came after de Gaulle) the *potential* political influence of the President of the Republic.

None of these points directly concerns the constitutional power of the President. They each, however, raise major questions concerning the nature of the popularity and resulting political influence of the presidency and its place in French political culture. Popularity sufficient to do what? Be what kind of President? Legitimacy to exercise what kind of authority? During the main period of *tontonmania* (Mitterrand's phenomenal popularity) in 1987 and 1988, it was never clear whether this popularity was based upon Mitterrand's discreet and patient exercise of limited authority in a difficult period, which would itself legitimate his unassailable credentials to adopt a strong political role after 1988; whether the constraining of the President's power was itself the cause of approbation, which meant that the French were implicitly in favour of Mitterrand's stance as a kind of symbolic near-apolitical constitutional monarch; whether the nature of the sympathy created, however strong, would affect the status of the reelected President's political authority; whether the popularity was a specifically personal issue (Mitterrand as more 'presidential' than Chirac); or involved a wider view concerning Mitterrand's 'right' to subsequently redraw or attempt to redraw the political map.

These questions also raise many others, particularly those concerning the nature of political allegiance itself, and the persona of individuals as a focus for political activity. They also take us beyond the dubious analytical value of popularity as measured by the opinion poll or the plebiscitary election, and beyond the examination of the question of the distribution of power within the institutions (essentially that of Matignon's and the Elysée's power vis-à-vis each other), and towards questions concerning the nature of political legitimacy itself in France, and the myths and beliefs which underpin the notion of national leadership.

All the presidential elections since 1965 have been very much popular elections.[19] 1988 was the fifth time since 1965 that a President had been elected by direct universal adult suffrage. In 1962, such *recours* to a person in a manner which would recapitulate the popular approval of and national rally to de Gaulle in 1958 was inscribed into the Republic through the constitutional amendment (itself plebiscited by referendum) so that, henceforward, the President of the Republic would be elected by direct universal adult suffrage. This had a dual and contradictory effect. First, the disenchantment of heroic leadership through its institutionalisation meant that contenders for power (and this included de Gaulle in 1965) were now part of the institutional political process. Second, it heightened significantly the political effect of individual claims to authority vis-à-vis political institutions and practice, affording all candidates the opportunity to create for themselves the kind of popularity which, hitherto, had been exclusive to de Gaulle. As a consequence, as we have seen, possession of the presidency became the Republic's organising political principle, and all political groups, to differing degrees and at different times, responded to this. Each elected President, moreover, whether his 'power' increased or diminished, informed the shape or dimension of presidentialism in the Fifth Republic and its relationship to the parties and to French politics more generally. Let us summarise here what the election of each of the individuals to the presidency represented in terms of the regime itself:

1965. Election of de Gaulle (Charles de Gaulle v. François Mitterrand). De Gaulle and his Republic consolidated by direct popular vote. Reaffirmation of the political supremacy of the presidency. Foundations laid for Mitterrand's subsequent claim to the presidency.

1969. Election of Pompidou (Georges Pompidou v. Alain Poher). Reaffirmation of the dominance of Gaullism and the right, but demonstration that a change of President did not threaten the Republic. Reaffirmation of the political supremacy of the presidency.

1974. Election of Giscard d'Estaing (Valéry Giscard d'Estaing v. François Mitterrand). Reaffirmation of the dominance of the right, but demonstration that change from Gaullist dominance did not threaten the

Republic. Reaffirmation of the political supremacy of the presidency.

1981. Election of Mitterrand (François Mitterrand v. Valéry Giscard d'Estaing). Affirmation that *alternance* between right and left within the Republic did not threaten the Republic. Reaffirmation of the political supremacy of the presidency.

1988. Election of Mitterrand (François Mitterrand v. Jacques Chirac). Reaffirmation of the presidency as a stabilising factor in the political development of the Republic. Nuanced reaffirmation of the political supremacy of the presidency. Affirmation of increased political autonomy of Prime Minister and government from the President.

This idea of individuals raised to supreme office as part of what was effectively a consolidating process affects interpretation of the relation within the Fifth republican system between the presidency, the political parties and the French electorate. What became increasingly clear from the 1965, 1969, 1974, 1981 and 1988 presidential elections was that, in spite of the continuing strong presence of the parties at all levels of political activity, the development of presidentialism in that context, and the latter's 'domestication' by virtue of having to become part of a stable cyclical process within a party system, the Fifth Republic did not simply move back to control by the parties after the Algerian crisis[20] had been resolved and the state strengthened. Instead, it experienced developmentally the influential relation of Presidents both to the polity and to society as a whole. The developing presidentialism of the Fifth Republic saw the parties regaining their strength, but this according to the manner in which they adapted to presidential contests. More fundamentally, the parties themselves were changing in their organisation, orientation, and eventually their ideologies, and were responding to the exigencies both of presidential contests, as they perceived them, and of the wider political culture. And, paradoxically, between 1986 and 1988 the diminution or putting into context of the actual powers of the President saw the dramatic reaffirmation of the President's symbolic status, the political consequences of such reaffirmation being in part responsible for the reelection of the incumbent President.

We can say, therefore, that the Fifth Republic has witnessed, not the simple domestication of what we might call charismatic authority, but a cultural reorientation to this phenomenon in institutional form. This has affected the political parties in terms of their relation both to the National Assembly, local elections and political activity more generally, and to the creation, from within their ranks, of presidential candidates. Between 1958 and 1988 the Gaullist and Socialist parties (to differing degrees at different times) had a major advantage here in that they each became large electoral parties and, more significantly, in that their leaders were undisputed leaders, that is to say, were perceived as being the heroic, visionary leaders of a great national awakening. The manner and modalities of party orientation to presidentialism, however, are of crucial importance in any understanding of the way presidentialism functions within the polity: *how* the cultivation of *présidentiables* takes place, and the effect of this upon the political party in particular and the polity in general, are perhaps the keys to an understanding of French presidentialism in the Fifth Republic.

One of the consequences of such cultivation of *présidentiables* for the political parties (perhaps a politically debilitating one) is that they and their potential presidential candidates are now in a permanent presidential election campaign. A great deal of party (and related governmental) activity takes place in relation to this, as, of course, do the actions and resulting fortunes of individuals within, or in a relation to, the parties or the government. Because of this, a good deal of the energies of the parties is directed towards the presidency (with all the increased power this affords to king-makers or breakers). We can take as an example of this at the individual level Michel Rocard, whose political life has been dictated by the presidential elections from 1969 onwards, and his relation to the organised left in the context of his presidential pretensions. Jacques Chirac's political life too has been nothing other than a quest for the presidency of the Republic, a quest which has involved him in breaking one potential President (Chaban-Delmas), making another (Giscard d'Estaing in 1974), radically influencing the Gaullist movement (after 1977), becoming twice Prime Minister, and twice a candidate for the presidency, the first time to break the President he had earlier helped to power (Giscard d'Estaing in 1981), the second to become the sole leader of the right (1988). The *effects* of these and other political quests, however, have been nothing less than the redefinition of political life in the Fifth Republic. Valéry Giscard d'Estaing's political manœuvring between 1967-1974 was, perhaps, the first major (and successful) example of this. And since Giscard, France has seen a gallery of second-rank leaders developing their political careers, and expending the energies of their political parties, in relation to a manœuvring for the next (or next but one) presidential election.[21] Such a situation has had major effects upon political life in the Fifth Republic, the best illustration in the late 1980s being the paralysing effect upon the French right of the rivalries of its several pretenders to right and centre-right leadership.

In order to identify the constituent elements necessary to this cultivation of presidentialism, we need to return to the founder of Fifth republican presidentialism to see what the legacy which informed subsequent developments actually was. Individual claims to potentially presidential status take place not only in what we might call a strictly political context (who enjoys power within a political party at a particular time) but also within a personal, symbolic context which involves the potentially presidential stature or perceived stature of certain individuals in relation to the exigencies of a presidential persona. This is not to say that all presidential candidates try to be 'like' de Gaulle, far from it; the point is rather that de Gaulle's treatment of the presidency, institutional, symbolic, political, and personal, constituted the conditions, if not the parameters, of subsequent claims to the presidency itself.

De Gaulle's political career involved the exemplification of a myth and the creation (subsequently institutionally legitimated) of a privileged relation between a leader and the people. Briefly, we can say that the myth involved a particular interpretation of the relationship State/Republic/France, a valorisation of the idea of the nation, and the relation of *l'homme providentiel*

11

to this last. The legendary figure who exemplified the myth was de Gaulle himself who was depicted, and who depicted himself, as (and here we see the nature of the relation between the leader and the people) returning to save France, *within* republicanism with the *help of* the nation. This is, of course, a hard act to follow. It is, however, what all subsequent main presidential candidates have done in one form or another; all have created a relationship with the people in the context of a personal vision of the relation between a mythical France, State, and Republic.

It is true that attempts have been made to render the presidency less 'enchanted'; Defferre in 1964 as potential candidate, and Poher in 1969 as actual candidate, are perhaps the best examples of this. Even those who have been successful have attempted, both as candidate and President, to disenchant the presidency. Pompidou, Giscard and Mitterrand, essentially through their presidential style, or rather through certain aspects of it, have attempted to domesticate, as it were, in a fundamental manner, the *grandeur* of the office, while maintaining their authority and *sens de l'Etat*. All of them, however, have had to use, or have been beaten or overtaken by, the exigency of some form of the greatness which de Gaulle brought to the presidency. Valéry Giscard d'Estaing's presidency is an interesting case in point. At one level he humanised and 'Americanised' the presidency. At another he was generally perceived as behaving during his presidency in an almost monarchical manner. At yet another, he became vulnerable to accusations of having abused his power and of being only too much like ordinary people in that he accepted 'gifts' (a euphemism for bribes, or rewards for services rendered). At the other extreme, François Mitterrand, the Machiavellian schemer, the old fox, was, as it were, overwhelmed (in a positive sense) by the misnamed *tontonmania* of 1987 and 1988. His reputation in this period had not been that of a jovial uncle but one of a respected father-figure, reminiscent of de Gaulle himself, and evoking the idea that his concerted personal undertaking was to sustain the dignity and integrity of the Republic founded and personally maintained by his old rival, de Gaulle. Any figure in the Fifth Republic who tries to domesticate the presidency is in danger either of seeming inadequate to the role model or else of being overtaken by a Gaullian figure. And whatever new qualities candidates and Presidents have brought or tried to bring to the presidency, all incumbents or pretenders have been vulnerable to this trait of greatness ascribed to the presidency of the Republic.

As we have suggested, political parties are not in a necessary opposition to the idea of allegiance to a leader. They too have myths which leaders have drawn upon: François Mitterrand, exploiting Socialism's myths and expanding upon those which accord with allegiance to a personal leader (essentially, Socialist millenarianism), and Jacques Chirac, capitalising upon Gaullism's post-war RPF rally heritage and attempting to adapt governmental Gaullism to it, are the best examples of this. Nevertheless, throughout the Fifth Republic the distrust of parties (largely a legacy of the Third and Fourth Republics), in and out of power, has also been a discursive resource which has inevitably undermined parties and concomitantly increased the personal status of

Presidents, reduced the weight of the party machine vis-à-vis presidential pretenders, challenged intra-party ideologies vis-à-vis extra-party ones, and so on.[22] To understand the complexity of the presidential phenomenon within Fifth republican political culture we need, therefore, to look at how organisations have responded to individuals, and how individuals have in their turn responded to organisations, how organisations have supported individuals in terms of the organisations' own discourse and traditions, and how individuals have deployed the myths fundamental to organisations, how parties and individuals have responded to electorates far wider than their traditional ones, how the media has reacted to these developments, and how significant corporate interest groups have responded to this part-presidential, part-party system. The following chapters address these various issues.

By 1988, partly *because* the Fifth Republic had weathered so many social and political changes, many of the fears concerning the Republic's ability to cope with change within it, and with challenges to it, had played themselves out. The electorate, moreover, had become accustomed to presidential elections. All political organisations were also used to them, and used to the behavioural norms and organisational exigencies of a presidential election, as were campaign managers, publicity agencies and, of course, the media. By 1988, moreover, the Republic was at a stage where several candidates had stood for the presidency more than once (among the main candidates, Giscard d'Estaing, Jacques Chirac, and François Mitterrand). And, as we have noted, the Republic was entering a stage where many individuals were using the presidential election in order to enhance their position, not for that election itself, but for a subsequent election, possibly seven, even fourteen, years into the future.[23]

By the mid-1980s, one of the effects of what we might call the developing consensus concerning the Republic was the centrist convergence of much of the activity, many of the policies, and most of the claims of the main political actors. This meant, however, that a significant margin was left on the extremes of the political spectrum which allowed movements and individuals to exploit, by means of the presidential election and its highly personalising effect upon the political scene, the contestatory tradition in French politics, and to canalise the discontent of sections of the population who were the victims of a) the economic crisis b) France's modernisation process and c) the centripetal effect of presidentialism itself. The gap on the right was filled by Jean-Marie Le Pen whose candidacy, campaign and support in the presidential elections of 1988 called into question the depth of consensus and the strength of the Republic's institutions to combat threats to it. The Le Pen candidacy is analysed in detail in Chapter Seven. Here we can make three points: 1) it was, in part, the Fifth republican system itself, through its form of election of the President, which allowed Jean-Marie Le Pen to gain such a high profile in French political life;[24] 2) the media treatment of politics, and of presidentialism in particular, enhanced, as we have seen, the personalisation of this combative strain in French politics; 3) the Le Pen vote, in fact, strengthened in certain respects the consensual politics advocated by Mitterrand, and gave it a focus and a solidity, especially in terms of the political centre and the post-election prospects of its leading figures.

On the left, the developing presidential credibility of François Mitterrand had moved the non-communist left, often unbeknown to itself, towards the centre (see Chapter Two). The problem for the non-socialist left, essentially the Communist Party, was that, by allowing Mitterrand to represent its *presidential* interests in 1965 and 1974, it was unable to impose itself successfully on the political scene. The decline of the Communist Party is, in part, a result of this failure to become a presidential party in a political system in which the presidency and the presidential election had become so influential in political life generally. The ultra-left candidates, such as Arlette Laguiller, undoubtedly gained national recognition as a result of the presidential system, but the acquisition by the PS of the presidential representation of the left meant that the whole of the left was ultimately forced to increase the stature of Mitterrand (in 1965, 1974, 1981 and 1988) in order either to put the left into power or to impede the right's retention or regaining of power.

In this context of a developing centripetalism, the need for candidates to distinguish themselves from one another accentuated the personal rivalries involved, and emphasised the distinguishing personal visions and character traits of candidates and potential candidates. Both of these factors enhanced further the personalised nature of the presidential contest. The paradox here was that the 1988 presidential election was one where confrontation had to be (for reasons we shall discuss below) kept to a minimum until the very last minute. Let us now turn our attention to the 1988 election.

We should remember first that *cohabitation* existed (in the form of the two-year, relatively smooth, working relationship of President Mitterrand and Prime Minister Chirac), and had not been condemned by the electorate (which was, after all, responsible for it), and that the spirit of *cohabitation* (people of good sense all working together for the good of France), irrespective of the perceived awkwardness of the political conjuncture, was now in some sense consensual. The need for Chirac and Mitterrand to maintain a certain respectful cooperation was heightened because a prolonged confrontation between the Republic's President and Prime Minister would have diminished France's international status, and doubtless harmed the status of both the President and the Prime Minister in the eyes of the public, thus bringing both offices into a disrepute from which only anti-system personalities or groups would have profited.

Doctrinal developments also contributed to the lack of acerbity between candidates. The 'new realism' of the PS (1983-1986), the relative failure of neo-liberalism (1986-1988), the relative marginalisation of the PCF, and relative threat of the FN (from 1981), and the personal openness of the main protagonists with one another, for example, François Mitterrand with Jacques Chirac, Michel Rocard with Raymond Barre and with Simone Veil, strengthened the notion of a consensus, the unnecessary fracturing of which would have harmed any candidate seen as having called it into question for the purposes of personal advantage.

At this level of interpersonal relations, however, the consensual constraint not only placed further emphasis upon the perceived distinguishing personal qualities of all the individuals concerned; it also created very complex situations in terms of the political manœuvring constitutive of political life. Any action could, moreover, have a whole series of reactions which might be contrary to the intention of the original one. What, for example, would have been the effect if François Mitterrand had done *too* good a public relations job on Jacques Chirac in terms of upgrading his status vis-à-vis Raymond Barre (Chirac's rival for the leadership of the right and, arguably, a more dangerous second round election opponent to Mitterrand), and contributed to the transformation of Chirac, the careerist politician, into Chirac, the statesman worthy of the presidency? Did the centre-right, economically sound, style of Chirac's Finance Minister, Edouard Balladur, detract from or enhance Raymond Barre's similar status? Was the presence of Charles Pasqua, Chirac's Interior Minister, and on the extreme right of his party, a help or a hindrance to Jean-Marie Le Pen's presidential challenge? The possible permutations of the actions of the political actors upon one another are infinite. Let us just schematise some of these constraints in the period preceding the run-up to the first-round election of 24 April.

François Mitterrand could attack no-one. In particular, he could not attack Jacques Chirac, his Prime Minister, for fear of calling into question the integrity of the Republic (and, as we have suggested, the maintenance of Jacques Chirac's popularity was necessary to limit that of Raymond Barre). The Socialist Party was itself under similar constraints, and had been since 1986: it could not attack the Prime Minister of its own President too forcefully, nor be seen to undermine to any great extent the *cohabitation* experiment willed upon France by the French electorate. By the same token, Mitterrand could not use the PS as his oppositional voice to his own government. And if, in the period preceding the 1988 elections, he became too associated with the PS, he would risk all the capital he had built after 1986 as a non-partisan President of all the French.

For very similar reasons, Jacques Chirac, as a Prime Minister who wished to transcend his partisan party status, could not attack François Mitterrand, and needed, moreover, to cultivate a responsible image which would enable him to represent the right as its credible presidential candidate. Nor could Chirac be critical of Raymond Barre, given that, whichever of the two reached the second round of the presidential elections, he would need to take the other's first-round vote with him, and that any major disagreements would undermine not only both candidates' second-round possibilities but also their first-round status. Both Chirac and Barre, therefore, needed to remain true in some sense to a kind of rightist *discipline républicaine*, not only after but also before the 24 April first-round vote, in order to remain credible as presidential candidates. For Barre, moreover, any attacks upon Chirac or his government also meant that he risked the danger of the RPR machine mobilising against him, or else the electorate disapproving of him as a *diviseur* of the right.

In terms of his campaign vis-à-vis François Mitterrand, Raymond Barre was constrained to limit any critical onslaught in the same way as he was with Chirac: just as Chirac was the Prime Minister, so Mitterrand was the President, and Barre, a defender of the Fifth Republic's institutions, could not undermine the holders of the executive office to the point where he might be seen to question the integrity of the regime. There was also, of course, the question of Barre's far greater affinity with Mitterrand's style and his disdain for Chirac. Finally, Barre knew that it was possible that, in some way or another, he might work with Mitterrand if the latter were reelected President (see Chapter Six).

A similar moderation applied on the left. The PCF for its part could not appear too hostile to François Mitterrand for fear of its own electorate voting for him anyway (and the PCF leadership would have to recommend a Mitterrand vote in the second round). The PS could not attack the PCF too forcefully for fear of upgrading the latter's status as a leftist alternative to itself, as had been the case in the pre-1981 period, and, in a leftist version of the relation between Chirac and Barre, for fear of losing the PCF's supporters' votes in the second round.

Pierre Juquin, the dissident Communist candidate, was unable to launch too many broadsides against François Mitterrand, as he needed to present himself as the bridge between the 'new'-communist and the non-communist left. Moreover, Juquin and André Lajoinie (the PCF's candidate) had to avoid consistent direct confrontation with one another for fear of turning themselves into an irrelevant political sideshow, and, in the case of the PCF, in order not to legitimise the Juquin candidacy by conferring upon it some kind of alternative communist status (see Chapter Eight).

For the ecologist candidate, Antoine Waechter, it was judicious to refrain from attacking any of the main candidates because of the relatively composite nature of his electorate, an electorate he hoped to consolidate in the post-electoral period.

Arlette Laguiller and Pierre Boussel, the two ultra-left candidates, were, because of their extreme position, able to attack all the other candidates. However, because they were both Trotskyist candidates (although only Boussel's MPPT was in the Fourth International), their campaigns represented more than anything else the apparently eternal division of the ultra-left. Moreover, Laguiller's candidacy had come to be perceived by the public as an expected feature of the presidential campaign - and the ultra-left an extremely marginal phenomenon in the political culture. And any attacks directed at *all* the other candidates did not constitute a specific attack upon anyone.

Even the non-runners and second-rank leaders were constrained in both their support and their criticisms. In particular, François Léotard, leader of the PR, a constituent element of the UDF, who supported Raymond Barre, could not undermine Jacques Chirac too much as he would have to work with the RPR whatever happened. Léotard, moreover, doubtless unofficially wanted a Jacques Chirac victory over Raymond Barre in order to remove one of his main rivals for the leadership of the post-1988 centre-right. It is clear, however, that he did not anticipate such a strong Le Pen vote in the first round, a vote which would force him into an uncomfortable alliance with a very right-orientated second round Chirac campaign.

In fact, the only candidate whose attacks had any significant effect upon the electoral fortunes of the other candidates was Jean-Marie Le Pen, who was able, with political impunity, to voice his criticisms of all other candidates, and, in particular, of Jacques Chirac whose first-round vote he clearly reduced. The strength of his support on 24 April, moreover, dismayed the centre-right, enhanced Mitterrand's status, shattered Chirac's virile image, and mobilised the non-socialist left in favour of Mitterrand.

Paradoxically, however, one of the results of these many constraints was not the diminishing of the presidential contest in the terms we have been discussing, but the enhancing of its most salient features, in particular, its personalised quality and the idea of a personally perceived vision of, and mission for, France. Given that candidates were constrained not to *say* too much, the perception of what they *were* became even more important.[25] Although, as we have noted, the prevailing political situation of *cohabitation* placed considerable limitations upon individuals in terms of direct or explicit attacks upon one another at *either* a political or a personal level, it therefore also enhanced the persona and personal qualities of the candidates over and above the explicit ideas (programmes and policies) they expressed and advocated. Because there were several main candidates, who were all relatively close both ideologically and in terms of the electorate they were trying to capture, they had to present themselves even more as being 'alone' in the supra-partisan, Gaullian sense, thus emphasising further the most salient feature of Fifth republican presidentialism. This phenomenon was also given prominence, again paradoxically, by the sudden personal antagonisms which erupted once all the main candidates had declared themselves by the end of March 1988. By then, with only four weeks of campaigning left after Mitterrand had declared his candidacy, the perceived personal qualities and character traits of the candidates became the main, arguably the only, feature of the campaign. In terms of policies, the main candidates had similar views on the economy, on Europe, on economic realism, on industrial modernisation, on research, and on the state's institutions. Thus, the personal image of the candidates became heightened still further. As we have argued, however, this notion of image, and of the cultural relationship of a national leader or potential leader to the political institutions and to the wider culture, becomes much more complex and profound than has been generally assumed.

In the context of our analysis, let us examine in more detail the closing stages of the first-round campaign for the presidency of the Republic, and comment upon the events and the significance of the campaign for the second round which saw the decisive victory of François Mitterrand over Jacques Chirac, a victory which inaugurated the long-term political realignments of the post-1988 period in the political life of the Fifth Republic.

The first point to make concerning the presidential elections of April-May 1988 was that they bore out the theory that such elections continue to be the major organising principle of French political life: the energies devoted to them (by the parties), the attention directed at them (by the media and the electorate), their effects upon the immediate and longer-term political fortunes of individual political personalities, their influence upon potentially major political realignments, their triggering of legislative elections and a new National Assembly and government, and their further nuancing of the respective roles within the Republic of the Fifth Republic's institutions, and the President's place within these, are all evidence of this. Second, not only in terms of presidential power, the parties, and the National Assembly, but also in terms of: the relationship of the media to politics, and to presidentialism more specifically; the relationship of political ideologies to the ideas and myths informing the wider political culture; and the implications of the elections for French political sociology (especially as regards the *Front National* vote), the presidential elections of 1988 turned out to be extremely interesting, significantly more interesting than was anticipated by most observers, or than could be deduced from the immediate politically paralysing context described above.

Initial interest, such as it was, in the months preceding the first-round voting of 24 April 1988, was focused upon just two factors.

The first concerned the effects of François Mitterrand's late declaration of his candidacy (22 March), six weeks after Raymond Barre's declaration and over two months after Jacques Chirac's. The late declaration had effects upon Chirac's and Barre's campaign, both of them having to shadow box until Mitterrand declared. Raymond Barre, in particular, suffered as a result, given that his was, exclusively, what we might call a second-round campaign, that is to say, a campaign which tried to give the impression that the only real contest was the one between Barre and Mitterrand. We should also note that Mitterrand's late declaration enhanced his own sphynx-like presidential image. The overall result was a relatively desultory campaign until 22 March. Conversely, not only the tardiness of Mitterrand's declaration but also his style of campaign when he did declare (involving a concerted attack upon the political 'cliques' and 'clans') triggered a violent eleventh-hour clash (thrown into higher relief by the earlier desultoriness) between Mitterrand himself and Chirac who had, by this time, become his most likely second-round opponent.

The second point of interest before 24 April, linked to the first, was the question of the *report des voix* between Jacques Chirac and Raymond Barre. Initially, this had been assumed to be a question of how many of Jacques Chirac's votes would go to Raymond Barre in the second round (and, by extension, how many of François Mitterrand's potential votes might also). As Chirac overtook Barre in the polls in February, this question of the *report des voix* not from Chirac to Barre but from Barre to Chirac took on a further element of interest given: a) that Jacques Chirac's campaign was seen to have deliberately undermined that of Barre, and; b) that Chirac's relatively prime ministerial discourse and style was, from January, radicalising rightwards and flirting with themes close to those of the *Front National*, abhorrent to Barre and much of his support. Nevertheless, these developments created only restricted media interest given that Chirac's relative ascendancy only seemed to confirm further the outcome of 8 May: the reelection of François

Mitterrand.

This situation of limited interest and relative ennui was transformed on the evening of 24 April (and was to be transformed again in the second week of the two-week second round campaign). The transformation was not directly related to the expected outcome of the campaign - Mitterrand's victory - nor even to the necessary conflictual alliance between Raymond Barre and Jacques Chirac between rounds one and two. Neither of these assumptions (even though the second, Barre's support for Chirac, was put under considerable strain) was in much doubt: François Mitterrand would probably win,[26] and the *code de bonne conduite* between Barre and Chirac would remain intact for the duration of the second-round campaign. The interest in the campaign and the assessment of its immediate, medium and longer-term effect upon French political life were transformed by three quite unexpected factors.

The first, greeted with generalised consternation, was Chirac's relatively low vote (19.96%). He had been credited with 24% in some polls before the closing of polls one week before round one. Such a low vote not only affected his chances of rallying the traditional right's vote in a respectable showing against François Mitterrand in the second round but also damaged the credibility of Chirac as the leader of the right and the credibility of organised Gaullism as a viable force in French politics.

The second factor, which was equally unexpected, was Jean-Marie Le Pen's relatively high vote (14.38%) which put him on a par with Raymond Barre and Jacques Chirac, changing overnight the idea of the *trois grands* of the first round into *quatre*. Until then, media coverage had invariably been divided into two: between François Mitterrand, Jacques Chirac and Raymond Barre, on the one hand; and the lesser candidates, on the other. Le Pen's vote was, as he himself claimed, and as all concurred, a political earthquake. There were two aspects to this: first, the simple reality of an extreme right-wing candidate polling four and a half million votes in a national election in a Western democracy, and the concomitant national and international interest such an unexpected phenomenon occasioned; second, the effects this would or might have upon both the immediate prospects of the right (whether the traditional right could resist implosion after such an event), and its longer-term prospects in terms of future alliances, especially at local level. (A third, more minor aspect was the rhetorical advantage given to Le Pen in his claims of a pre-24 April media conspiracy against him.)

It is worth stressing the point here that the Le Pen vote caught all observers off guard. This not only has implications in terms of the lessons to be drawn from the confounding of media and opinion poll predictions (a confounding of specialist opinion which was to be repeated in the legislative elections that followed the presidential elections), but also raises questions concerning the status of political observation *when* the unexpected occurs. Few (observers or actors) knew *how* to respond in the face of this astounding result, thus adding to the generalised feeling of confusion and consternation.

The third factor of interest was related to the first and second and has implications for our earlier discussion of the mythical or visionary personal nature of presidentialism in Fifth republican politics. It involved the question of how Jacques Chirac, in a high-profile campaign with massive media exposure over a period of a fortnight, would respond to the first two factors: how he would, even could, campaign against François Mitterrand after achieving such a surprisingly low first-round vote and in the context of a first-round rival (Le Pen) who had polled so many votes, votes he needed if he was to win an honourable defeat, let alone a victory.

The first impression of the first round voting of 24 April, therefore, was that there were two 'winners' and two 'losers', the two winners being François Mitterrand and Jean-Marie Le Pen, the two losers, Jacques Chirac and Raymond Barre.[27]

In terms of the campaign after 24 April for the second round, the electoral arithmetic was such that, in order to win, François Mitterrand needed all of the left's vote (that is, his own first round vote plus that of the PCF, Arlette Laguiller, Pierre Juquin and Pierre Boussel), the near-totality of the ecologist vote, some of Raymond Barre's vote and some of Le Pen's. The PCF gave its support 'sans aucune illusion' on Wednesday 27 April. Laguiller and Juquin also called for a François Mitterrand vote. Antoine Waechter and Pierre Boussel gave no recommendation to their voters but in subsequent interviews gave a clear impression that Mitterrand was their choice. It is interesting to point out here that, irrespective of the recognition by the other candidates of the left that most of their voters would probably vote for François Mitterrand in any second round contest, the transforming situation of a strong Le Pen vote created a kind of reflex; in such a situation, no left candidate could be seen to be either encouraging, by neutralism, the election of a candidate with an ambivalent relation to the extreme-right, or weakening a reelected Mitterrand faced with what all of them considered to be the threat of neo-fascism (see Chapter Four).

For Chirac, the electoral arithmetic was such that he needed the near-totality of the vote of the, now, 'three' rights (his own, Barre's and Le Pen's), and some of the abstentionist vote (estimated for round two as a potential maximum of 5% of the electorate, that is, approximately, one quarter of the first round abstentionists).

The difference between the two candidates in terms of how they responded to the need to win over certain key voters was marked. Mitterrand, as we shall see below, could appeal to the republican centre (Barre's or Waechter's vote) while assuming that the vote of the rest of the left was a given, either automatically or as a 'stop Le Pen' vote, and that some of Le Pen's vote would be his as a result of the fact that it was a) a working class vote and b) an anti-Chirac vote rather than an anti-Mitterrand one.[28] Jacques Chirac's problem was infinitely more complex than Mitterrand's, and raises the question not only of whether both electorates (the centre and the extreme-right) *could* be appealed to simultaneously, but of whether Jacques Chirac even tried (see Chapter Five).

Formally, and as expected, Raymond Barre, in correct response to the previously established code of good conduct, appeared with Jacques Chirac within an hour of the unofficial results of the first round results and gave him his support, calling upon his electorate to do the same. Nevertheless, he made a point on this very public occasion of saying that he assumed that the Gaullist candidate would refuse all 'extremisms' (i.e., an appeal in any form to Le Pen's support). The Chirac and Barre campaign *comités de soutien* immediately fused as had been planned.[29] On the Wednesday following the first round Sunday voting, Valéry Giscard d'Estaing also gave his support to Jacques Chirac in a television broadcast.[30] All leading centrists gave their formal support to Chirac's campaign as evidence of their respect for agreements previously entered into. In spite of these formalities, however, the Le Pen vote had transformed the nature of these previously agreed allegiances. What had been, in many cases, at best a formal, contractual support was now not even that. Centrists could only be less than wildly enthusiastic in their demonstration of support for Jacques Chirac, given the two factors of his own low vote and Le Pen's threateningly strong vote. Despite this evident lack of convinced support, the question remains, however, of the extent to which Jacques Chirac concerned himself with the cultivation of his actual or potential centrist support. Up to a point, he simply assumed it as Mitterrand assumed the PCF and ultra-left vote, banking on the fact that the formal agreements would survive a fortnight while he attempted to capture the Le Pen vote. Culturally, however, the hostility of the centre (and its supporters), as well as that of many Gaullists, to the extreme-right was equal to that of the left's. In such a situation only one of the two rights outside Gaullism could be properly appealed to, and the result was, as we shall see, the formal assumption (and ignoring) of centrist support, and the concerted appeal to the extreme right. This was, therefore, a complete reversal of the good conduct code. The strategy adopted by Jacques Chirac (ignoring the centre and going for the 'hard' right) might have been a possible one if the Le Pen vote had not been so great, notional overtures to ultra-rightist themes having often been seen as tactically necessary to the centre-right in the context of the Fifth republican presidential system. It is arguable, moreover, that this was always Chirac's intended post-24 April strategy. The scale of Le Pen's victory, however, changed the implications of such a strategy, pushing many centrist politicians and voters towards the centre-left and François Mitterrand.[31]

The difficulty of the situation was compounded for Chirac at a personal level, given the fact that, although many Barre and Le Pen voters would vote for him as a vote against Mitterrand, many were as hostile to him as, say, Arlette Laguiller's 2% of the electorate were to François Mitterrand. Beginning a two-week campaign to gain a necessary 30% increase in his vote, a 30% which was as 'contractual' as were, say, Laguiller's votes for François Mitterrand, further diminished Jacques Chirac's personal presidential status. The twin facts that these two necessary groups of voters (Barre's and Le Pen's) were not only in many cases hostile to Chirac personally, as well as to one another, but were electorates almost as numerically significant as Chirac's, undermined both his personal status and his claim truly to represent the right in the second round. And, as we have suggested, a clear defeat would further deprive him, and Gaullism too, for the first time since 1958, of its ability to dominate the right in the post-1988 period.[32]

Within Gaullism itself, the first round vote and its consequences were to have significant effects. The 'earthquake' caused by Le Pen created fault lines not only across the 'civilised/uncivilised' right divide, and across the UDF, and between the UDF and the RPR, but across the RPR itself. One of Gaullism's main political and politico-cultural assets since 1958 had been the nuances of ideology within it. Not only in the 1950s and 1960s, with Louis Vallon, Jacques Debû-Bridel, René Capitant and others, but also in the 1980s with figures such as Philippe Séguin and Michel Noir, the RPR had been able to encapsulate an extremely wide range of philosophies and politico-cultural dispositions (far wider than, say, those within the British Conservative Party), a situation which had enabled 'satellites' (the PR, for example) to approach congruously, profit politically from, and contribute to this range. The appeal by Jacques Chirac to Jean-Marie Le Pen's voters (via a sensitivity to the latter's campaign themes) withdrew from Gaullism such polyvalence, and the silence of figures such as Séguin and Noir[33] during the second round only exacerbated this idea. This paralysing effect, both within Gaullism's leftist radical element, and upon the centrism in its UDF ally, was increased still more when Jacques Chirac's campaign was further radicalised rightwards by the interventions of Charles Pasqua in the second week of the round-two campaign (see below).

Immediately after the first-round campaign, the centrist Simone Veil (whose anti-racist credentials were impeccable) publicly announced that if Jacques Chirac were to go for the Le Pen vote in a concerted way, he would lose more centrist votes than he would gain from the extreme-right. Such a comment, Raymond Barre's *mise en garde* of 24 April, the gathering (local) centrist move towards François Mitterrand, and the neutralising of the RPR 'left', are evidence that it was generally anticipated that Chirac's second-round campaign *would* involve an appeal to the extreme-right. As we shall see, Le Pen's own response at the end of the first week of the two-week second round campaign would diminish Chirac's leadership status still further,[34] while the projection of Mitterrand, now (because of Le Pen's vote) as a personification of a Republican Front, continued (in spite of Le Pen's refusal to adequately support Chirac).

We can say, therefore, that even though he was to stand against François Mitterrand in the second round in a bid to destroy Raymond Barre's pretensions to a position as the right's most presidential figure, and to assert his own exclusive leadership of the right, the first round of the presidential election seriously harmed Jacques Chirac in terms of his *personal* claim to lead the right after 8 May (and concomitantly enhanced the status of other contenders for that position, in particular that of Valéry Giscard d'Estaing).

The end of the first week was characterised by several factors. We can comment on six of them here.

The first was the confrontation on 28 April between Jacques Chirac and François Mitterrand in the now traditional television debate between the two remaining presidential candidates (see Chapter Three). Most observers agree that these debates make little difference to voting behaviour. This is gross over-simplification. Polls taken immediately after the debate suggested that François Mitterrand was the 'winner' of the debate. Given the 8 May result, we might conclude from this that most voters had already chosen their candidate. We can, however, ask four questions here concerning the significance of the debate: a) what might have been the effect of one of the two candidates making a significant error in the debate (of style, of fact, of presentation, and so on); b) what might have been the effect if a candidate had not lived up to his perceived image, if, say, Chirac had managed to make Mitterrand seem old or unstatesmanlike, or if Mitterrand had made Chirac seem a stooge of the ultra-right; c) what might have been the effect if the initial margin between the two candidates had been much narrower; and, d) how can the political significance or effect of a television programme watched by an estimated 25 million people be discounted?

The second factor to bear in mind was the relative inter-round mobilisation of the totality of the left (typified by the trade unions' sudden involvement in the campaign (see Chapter Ten) as a result of the strong Le Pen vote), and this in spite of a decade of accusations by the PCF and ultra-left that Mitterrand was capitalism's fool. This not only lent to the campaign something of the classical left republicanism characteristic of nineteenth and twentieth century French politics, but also meant that such a development took place, paradoxically, in the context of the most 'centrist' leftist candidacy of the Fifth Republic. The Sunday (1 May) at the end of the first week of the second round campaign saw large demonstrations both by the trade unions and by the FN: the unions' explicit support for Mitterrand and the Front's explicit humiliation of Chirac, through Le Pen's depiction of him as the 'candidat résiduel', only further enhanced the status of Mitterrand as a bulwark against fascism, while portraying Chirac as little more than its hapless tool.[35]

The third factor was the very strong turn-outs (and media coverage) at the rally meetings organised by the two second-round candidates. Good illustrations of these were Chirac's spectacular rally meeting (involving special lighting and so on) on the Friday evening of the first week (attended by Raymond Barre), and Mitterrand's rally at Lille where, to tumultuous acclaim from the thousands of Socialists present, he made clear his intention to open his post-election government towards the centre.

The fourth factor was that by the end of the first week of the second-round campaign, neither candidate was specifying any more clearly than they had before 24 April what their future policies would be. Rather, both were accentuating the projection of a *style* of politics; in the case of both candidates the issues of the campaign had become not only those of what kind of government, what kind of National Assembly, what kind of *septennat*, but even of what kind of France each represented or personally advocated.

The fifth factor was the increased focus upon Michel Rocard at this time. Such implicit association of him with Mitterrand's campaign suggested a) a definitive change in Mitterrand's outlook (they had been rivals within the left for many years), b) the notion that it was presidential office itself which had changed him or made him more responsive to the desires of the people (Rocard had remained immensely popular in public opinion from the late 1970s), and c) that Mitterrand now had the *governmental* credibility which he had been deprived of since 1986 and which his first-round campaign had, through necessity or choice, been lacking (the implication was that Rocard would become his Prime Minister). Moreover, Rocard's many pronouncements after 24 April were widely reported and suggested a 'dream ticket', the uniting of the two main rivals of the non-communist left, who also happened to be the two most popular politicians in France.

The sixth important factor, especially in the context of François Mitterrand's frequent reference to *ouverture*, was the fact that not only had the pro-Chirac centre been relatively silent, but also certain figures (including Valéry Giscard d'Estaing's ministers, Stoléru, Durafour, Giroud, and Dorhlac) had publicly associated themselves, along with a local, and developing national, rally of centrist support, with François Mitterrand,[36] taking further the idea of a growing movement of support for his candidacy. Such declarations by prominent figures of the centre-right transformed Mitterrand's more neutral and contractual support into a kind of rally not only to him but to the defence of (a new interpretation of) the Republic which only he could effect.

As we have indicated, the second week of the round-two campaign was to see a further transformation of the situation, again not in terms of political outcomes, but in terms of public attention, media response to events, and, arguably, the longer-term effects of the presidential election upon French politics. The second week was, in fact, characterised by a series of events which were to electrify the French public, which the daily newspaper *Libération* was to headline on the Saturday of the second week as the *Coups d'éclat permanent,*[37] and which involved a never-before-seen assault upon opinion via a series of dramatic media events.

The first coup was the declaration by the Interior Minister, Charles Pasqua, that 'on essentials the National Front draws its inspiration from the same preoccupations, the same values, as the majority'.[38] By the Monday of week two of the second round, this had been reported in all newspapers and in the media. One of the results, apart from its quite dramatic radicalisation of the Chirac campaign's discourse,[39] was the fierce intensification of political debate and an increasing reference to 'values', and the interventions of major centrist politicians demanding that Jacques Chirac respond immediately to counter the claims of his lieutenant. Chirac did not respond however. Through his silence not only the left of the RPR but even its mainstream, Pompidolian tradition, as represented by Balladur, was paralysed, leaving only the style of Gaullism's RPF heritage, and, given that there was a significant left-wing tradition within that movement, not even all of that.

The second coup on Wednesday 4 May, four days before the second-round vote, was the most dramatic of all. For three years Marcel Carton, Marcel Fontaine and Jean-Paul Kauffmann had been held hostage in the Lebanon. The television channel, *Antenne 2*, had, for three years, announced at the beginning of every main news bulletin the number of days the three had been held. Since their capture, media rumours, often involving politicians, had abounded regarding attempts to release them (and this to a far greater extent than in similar cases in the UK or US). The importance attached to the attempt to gain the hostages' freedom may be judged from the fact that observers had, in fact, accredited some of Le Pen's vote to the government's failure to secure their release. In the course of Wednesday's 8.00 pm news it was stated that the hostages might have been released. Minutes later it was confirmed that this was indeed the case. From this moment, the release took over all the main television channels, most of them cutting planned programmes and devoting the rest of the evening to the release of the three. And the generalised perception was that the deliverance of the hostages was the work of the Prime Minister, Jacques Chirac, and his team, only days before the second round of the election of the President of the Republic.

The third coup came the following day while the morning's newspapers devoted huge coverage to the news from the Lebanon. At the moment the newspapers' ten-page spreads on the release of Carton, Fontaine and Kauffmann were hitting the news-stands, there came radio and television reports, swamping all other programmes, as they had the previous evening, of the dramatic rescue of the Ouvéa hostages in the French Pacific island territory of Nouvelle Calédonie. Just before the presidential elections, Kanak separatists on Nouvelle Calédonie had taken several French gendarmes hostage. This event, while affronting public opinion and embarrassing Mitterrand, had been expected to be resolved by some form of negotiation after 8 May. The rescue itself was reminiscent of the SAS's ending of the Iranian Embassy siege in London in 1980.[40] Once again media coverage was extensive, equalling that of coverage of the release of Carton, Fontaine and Kauffmann, and further underlining the Prime Minister's involvement and the President's position as an impotent bystander. Raymond Barre's response, involving reference to his regret concerning the loss of life, was perhaps a significant signal of disapproval of the episode to voters of the centre and an implicit suggestion that the rescue was an event motivated by electoral rather than humanitarian considerations.[41] Nevertheless, for the moment, once again, as with the release of the Lebanon hostages, Chirac seemed to have demonstrated that he was a strong Prime Minister who could get things done.

Linked to these events, in the context of the dramatic arrival of the FN in presidential politics with Le Pen's four and a half million votes, there was, if not a mounting feeling of potential violence reminiscent of many of France's earlier trials, such as the period of the Algerian crisis, then at least the suspicion that two strains within French political culture now confronted one another, the one humanist and conciliatory, the other virile and nationalistic.

These three events, Pasqua's 'valeurs' declaration, the release of the hostages in the Lebanon, and the rescue of the French gendarmes, created, by themselves, a near-saturation of the media in the days running up to the weekend of 7-8 May.

The fourth coup of Friday 6 May was less dramatic. It was the publication of the government's figures concerning the overseas deficit, which was down, and manufacturing production, which was up. This news, probably of crucial importance in a 'normal', undramatic situation, was, nevertheless, overshadowed by the other events. Its addition to them, however, suggested that there was little that a Chirac government could not do, its dramatic diplomatic and military successes now underscored by its domestic, 'governmental' ones.

The fifth coup, the announcement of the release of Dominique Prieur,[42] came on the same day, 6 May, with all its further appeals to a French nationalist sentiment and to the idea that a Chirac government could get things done, rectify the mistakes of others, and demonstrate what resolute governmental action by a strong leader could achieve.

The sixth coup was the 100,000 strong 'Rally for the Fifth Republic' - reminiscent of the 1968 rally in favour of de Gaulle in response to the student uprising of May - on the evening of 6 May in the Place de la Concorde. The media had suggested that the rally would be a failure. In the event, it was an impressive demonstration of Chirac's ability to mobilise support.

The official campaign for the second round ended on that Friday at midnight. The voting took place on the following Sunday, and Mitterrand was reelected as the President of the Republic. Let us make some concluding points related to these dramatic closing days of the campaign, and to their significance for the presidency of the Republic's preeminent political status in French political culture.

Observers have argued that Chirac's series of *coups*, like the television debate of the previous Thursday, had little effect on the electorate, possibly increasing Chirac's vote by 1%, but also providing a further mobilisation of a 'republican' and leftist vote for Mitterrand. In terms of other, perhaps in the longer term more significant, effects, we can, however, make two points: the first is that the presidential elections themselves had become, by 1988, major media, especially television, events. The *coups* not only increased this already extensive coverage to almost total saturation but also turned the elections into even more of a television spectacular; the second point is a similar one to our earlier observations concerning the effect (or non-effect) of events upon voting intentions. If the *coups* had little effect in 1988, it should be noted that they have set a precedent which, in a future election, could raise the tension of a highly publicised national campaign to critical proportions, and thus provoke considerable reactions in national opinion. We should also note that the campaign *coups* were closely associated not only with a presidential candidate but also with an incumbent government. In the future, all political actors and campaign teams will be aware of the 1988 precedent. It may be the case that the *coups* made little difference to the 8 May vote. This does not mean that such attempts at the precision-bombing of an electorate will be abandoned in future. It could equally mean that efforts will be made to *refine* the technique in the future, with all the implications that this will have for the media's relation to the democratic process.

Given that the *coups* of the campaign were, as we have seen, major media events, the role of television in the campaign and its contrastive relation to previous presidential campaigns calls for brief comment here (see Chapter Three for more detailed examination of this).

The presidential election had become a national phenomenon not only because of its personalised nature but also through the national media - especially television - coverage of it; it was now, to a significant degree, a media 'event', involving an army of commentators and interviewers. This was particularly true of the television coverage of 24 April and 8 May which turned the comments upon the results into marathon *'soirées electorales'*. In this context, it is true to say that, just as in British or American elections, such a situation favoured the leading contenders, the President and the Prime Minister benefiting from their respective offices and media coverage of government and state issues. *Cohabitation* had also created a novel situation where television coverage of government activity had to take account of the fact that the President and the Prime Minister were rivals for the presidency. Also, by 1988, there were several more television channels than there had been in 1981, the fifth channel, *La 5*, in particular, introducing a significant competitive edge to its coverage - especially concerning the release of the hostages - and forcing TF1, A2 and FR3 to meet the challenge by increasing their own reports on such events.

It is also true that, by 1988, campaign headquarters and organisers had become acutely sensitive to the media and had tailored their campaigns in many respects to the exigencies of television coverage. Jacques Chirac and Jean-Marie Le Pen in particular had introduced a chatshow format and mock-up television studio into some of their publicity material. All the candidates in 1988, moreover, timed their rally speeches to coincide with the 8.00 pm news in order that clips could be shown before the end of the news. The back-drops of these rally meetings, moreover, especially Mitterrand's, were designed with the television cameras in mind; and the speakers (again, Mitterrand in particular) employed a style (leaning on the rostrum and speaking quietly) conducive to the small screen rather than to the mass rally. It is also worth pointing out that newspaper and television journalists were courted by the campaign teams, accommodated to and treated extremely well, in some cases lavishly, this being something of a new departure in the relationship between politicians and the media.

Finally, according to Michèle Cotta, who is perhaps the most famous and influential French television journalist, neither from Matignon nor from the Elysée had there been, in 1988, and this was apparently the first time this had happened, telephone calls to the television channels, making suggestions, criticising or applying pressure of some kind.

Whatever the effects of all of these developments in the longer term, the result of the 8 May election was the reelection of François Mitterrand as President of the Republic with 54% of the national vote. We can make two series of conclusions, the first involving direct comment on the presidential elections themselves, the second, their effects upon the post-8 May period.

The first point to note is that the increase in Mitterrand's vote over his 1981

27

showing was a national one, capturing 13 departments which might be called traditionally right-wing (Chirac took 3 'left-wing' departments).[43] This orientation of the political map towards Mitterrand, however, should be taken not as a victory of the left over the right, but as a significant change, in fact, in French voting patterns. Mitterrand's victory was, in part, a victory for the centre. Only 54% had voted for both candidates combined in the first round. Therefore, we can say that François Mitterrand's victory was the victory of a) a person, b) a person against another person, and c) the idea of a political opening from the centre-left to the centre.[44] We should also note that it was in part a centrist, anti-Le Pen and anti-Chirac vote (and an extreme-right anti-Chirac vote) which put François Mitterrand back in the Elysée (more than 30% of Le Pen's voters abstained or voted for Mitterrand on 8 May).

This result also raises the question of the effect of presidential elections on the political centre and of the position of centrism within the wider political culture. The centre has enjoyed a walk on, walk off part at every major election of the Fifth Republic and every moment of apparent political realignment. 1988 suggested a more fundamental and lasting shift of national political power to the centre. And it is clear that Michel Rocard's appointment was made in direct response to this. He became the Prime Minister of the much discussed 'opening' advocated by Mitterrand during his campaign. Given the electoral system itself, the divisions within French society, and the many extended political alliances at local level, however, the translation of a centrist sentiment into political reality was an extremely problematic issue. The bipolarisation encouraged by the Fifth republican electoral system militates against this development, and the creation of the URC (UDF and RPR), in order to avoid a Socialist landslide in the legislative elections which followed Mitterrand's reelection, put a further brake upon its successful implementation.

The results of the legislative elections (the failure of the PS to gain an overall majority) renewed the possibility of an immediate bipolarisation, but, paradoxically, also revived the longer-term possibility of a political realignment to the centre. The presidential election campaign had itself encouraged this for several reasons: a) the victor had demonstrated clearly throughout the campaign that he hoped for an opening to the centre; b) the PS had not opposed this development and had demonstrated between 1983 and 1986, when in government, that its policies were moderate centre-left policies; c) elements within the non-Gaullist UDF (and especially Raymond Barre) had moved towards a potential independence from the RPR because of Chirac's low vote, because of the RPR's ambivalent attitude to the FN, and, of course, because of the prospects of sharing power with the Socialists. The strong Le Pen vote had also given a depth to centrism by suggesting that a republican front of sorts was necessary to counter the extreme-right and to support a government committed to solving the social problems which had given rise to much of Le Pen's support. It is also worth noting that a renewed discussion of republicanism itself and republican values had been developing throughout the 1980s, and was heightened dramatically between the two rounds of the presidential election. This generally sympathetic consensual climate had been reflected in the immediate aftermath of Mitterrand's election and in the refusal of triumphalism on the part of leading Socialist Party personalities (and the inclusion of several second-rank centrists in Rocard's government). It was also clear, however, that the developing realignments would take place over a considerable period of time as groups and personalities, between the PS on their left and the RPR on their right, defined themselves, their role and orientation, and began tentatively to ensure that they and their potential gains were not swept away by a sudden bipolarisation of the polity.

On the question of the representation of political movements via presidential candidates, we should also address here the question of whether the presidential campaign itself had specific effects upon the 'lesser' candidates. It is true that a candidate such as Arlette Laguiller,[45] the only woman candidate in 1988, even though she was the object of much less attention than the 'big' candidates, received a national exposure during the presidential campaign normally reserved for major national political actors. One nevertheless has to ask whether in her case such inscription into the normative parameters of the political system has not institutionalised the ultra-left, making it acceptable, harmless and, for many, something of a joke. It is clear also that the bad campaign and result of Pierre Juquin harmed considerably the infant 'reorientation' of organised political communism. The ecologist candidate on the other hand did well and was thus able to counter the PS's attempt to absorb the ecologist movement. All these minority candidates, however, were stonewalled by the Le Pen vote of 24 April and had little choice but to more or less efface themselves and call for unconditional support for Mitterrand as a kind of anti-fascist republican figure. The point here is that the presidential elections are arguably not only a litmus test of the relative strengths and weaknesses of particular strands within the polity, but instrumental in the creation or accentuation of those strengths and weaknesses, the rise to national popularity of the PS in the train of Mitterrand's rise to power being perhaps the most extreme example of this.

Let us conclude with several remarks concerning the immediate, medium and longer-term effects of the presidential elections of 1988 on French political life.

The presidential election had three immediate consequences for the political parties, all of which will have longer-term effects upon the polity. The first is that all political organisations, especially those which can entertain the possibility of gaining the presidency, will increase significantly their preoccupation with candidates for the presidency and, with this, the presidential stature of such candidates. This will in turn lead to the accentuation of leadership struggles within political organisations and the influence of perceived presidential qualities upon such struggles.[46]

The second effect is of a doctrinal or ideological nature. The relative orientation of parties towards presidentialism, and the 'decline' of traditional ideologies and of allegiances to, say, socialism as an elaborated doctrine, are indisputable. These developments have, however, paradoxically accentuated and revivified preoccupation with 'values', both within organisations and on the wider political stage. This means, therefore, that, within the context of presidentialism, all political organisations will address the questions of 'what they stand for', particularly in terms of the notion of the Republic and republicanism. Political organisations will witness, therefore, not, as many observers have claimed, an emptying of doctrine and an end of ideology but a reorientation to it and, in fact, a reevaluation of political ideas and their relation to political traditions on the one hand and to contemporary French society on the other.

The third effect is also of an organisational nature. In terms of the presidential election campaign itself, the question is raised as to how political organisations should organise. Should the right have presented three major candidates? Did the Raymond Barre/Jacques Chirac 'primary' assist the presidential chances of both by creating a potentially wider electorate? Or did the rivalry between them simply increase the standing of Jean-Marie Le Pen? Over and above this, how should political organisations organise for each round of the campaign? Raymond Barre's campaign was clearly, and unsuccessfully, a 'round two' campaign; Jacques Chirac's, by the same token, was patently a 'round one' campaign. François Mitterrand's was arguably a 'round three' campaign, that is, a campaign for rounds both one and two, in the context of a redefinition of politics after the second round of the campaign, a redefinition which was deliberately ill-defined, and which did not focus particularly upon attacks on his adversaries.

The campaign and its aftermath also triggered a series of second rank rivalries within the parties. In the case of the Gaullists, these involved (with implications for the leadership of the Gaullist movement itself) Alain Juppé, Philippe Séguin, Jacques Toubon and, with particular significance for the potential radicalisation of Gaullism, Charles Pasqua. In the FN, the campaign saw a significant rivalry between Bruno Mégret (the 'left' of the FN), Le Pen's campaign organiser, and the late Jean-Pierre Stirbois, the leader of the party's 'right' and the number two of the party. In the PS, the campaign's aftermath triggered a personal contest for the leadership of the party between Pierre Mauroy and Laurent Fabius which was presented as a battle for the soul of the party itself, and a series of individual rivalries within government, involving particularly Lionel Jospin and Michel Rocard.

In the days following the election of François Mitterrand and the nomination of Michel Rocard as his Prime Minister, it became clear that up to 40 rightist MPs would be necessary to the stability of the new government. Such a scenario, which would have put the government at the mercy of the good will of, most notably, Valéry Giscard d'Estaing, must have been foreseen. The extent of François Mitterrand's victory was a further encouraging reason to dissolve the National Assembly in the hope of gaining 'his own' solid majority. The Assembly returned to parliament as the result of the legislative elections of June did not, however, involve an overall majority for the PS, and those who stood as non-PS supporters of the President did extremely badly. The reasons for this can be summarised as follows: 1) It was clear that François Mitterrand's victory was not a PS one and therefore would not necessarily be reflected in the legislative elections. 2) The right was still strong nationally. Even Chirac had polled 46% of the national vote against Mitterrand, and the discipline of the RPR and UDF, in forming the URC for the legislative elections and drawing upon the RPR/UDF local support in the context of the prevailing electoral system, was an effective tactic. 3) François Mitterrand's interventions and indications that he did not want a large Socialist majority demobilised the left's support to a certain extent. 4) As a result of the confusion and demobilisation of the left and the search for a centre, which was precluded by the nature of the voting system, the abstention rate was very high.

The essential question after the second-round voting of the legislative elections of June 1988 was whether significant elements of the centre-right could develop a politically credible parliamentary and local reality sufficient to lay the foundations of a centre-left/centre-right *alternance* in French political life. This would probably involve the re-introduction of some form of proportional representation (introduced by the PS for the 1986 legislative elections but changed back to the *scrutin majoritaire* for the 1988 legislative elections).

We can conclude by raising two questions concerning the presidentialism of the Fifth Republic. The first is the question of whether presidentialism, and the Fifth republican system more generally, 'hides' or 'creates' socio-political reality. Did the system and the developing 'consensus' conceal a social reality which exploded in 1988 with the 14.5% Le Pen vote, or did the presidential election, with its personalisation of power and the idea that a 'leader' (in this case, Le Pen) could canalise the discontent of a significant section of the population, in a sense 'create' the three rights?

The second point is related to this and concerns the notion of the identity of this political France and the extent to which it responds to, the extent to which it creates, the prevailing system; whether, apart from a small group 'organising', for better or worse, the 'modernisation' of France and its most clear manifestation, the single market of 1992 (see Chapter Nine), there are developing two Frances: the first a France which profits from, or else is unharmed by, and accepts with varying degrees of compliance or enthusiasm, the developing modernisation of the French economy; the second a France which does not accept it, or else is not reassured by it, and which entered the 1988 *septennat*, the 1988 legislature and France's commitment to 1992 with hostility, fear, or dismay.

The chapters contained in this volume, by taking as their focus the circumstances surrounding the main political act of the Fifth Republic, the presidential election, are a contribution to this continuing discussion.

NOTES

1. The official declaration was made in the *Journal Officiel* of 12 May 1988 in the form of a proclamation by the Constitutional Council.

2. Mes chers compatriotes, les résultats connus à l'heure où je m'exprime m'apprennent que vous avez choisi de m'accorder votre confiance. Je continuerai donc d'exercer la mission dont j'ai déjà pu éprouver pendant sept ans la grandeur et le poids, mais qui, renouvelée, m'oblige plus encore à faire ce que je dois pour rassembler tous les Français qui le voudront.

   J'agirai, c'est bien le moins, dans la fidélité aux principes de la République. La liberté, l'égalité et le respect des autres, refus des exclusions qu'on nomme aussi fraternité, n'ont pas fini d'entretenir l'espérance des hommes. Il y a trop d'angoisse, trop de difficultés, trop d'incertitudes, pour trop des nôtres dans notre société pour que nous oublions que le premier devoir est celui de la solidarité nationale. Chacun selon ses moyens doit concourir au bien de tous.

   Je vous ai dit, au long de cette campagne présidentielle, que c'est dans la cohésion sociale que réside la capacité de la France à faire rayonner à travers le monde, et d'abord dans l'Europe à construire, son économie, ses technologies, sa culture, bref son génie.

   Mais tout commence par la jeunesse. Voilà notre ressource la plus sûre. Je veux consacrer le principal de notre effort à lui procurer l'égalité des chances, par l'école, par la formation de l'esprit et des mains aux métiers qui placeront enfin le plus grand nombre de nos entreprises dans la grande compétition moderne, avec les atouts pour gagner.

   Enfin, puisque la vie même de l'humanité en dépend, je servirai passionnément en votre nom le développement des pays pauvres, le désarmement et la paix.

   Et sans plus tarder, car l'urgence est là, j'entends que le gouvernement qui sera bientôt mis en place recherche, dès les prochains jours, en métropole et outre-mer, les apaisements et les dialogues nécessaires.

   Mes chers compatriotes, à chacune et chacun d'entre vous, quelles qu'aient été ses préférences, j'adresse un salut fraternel. Je remercie du fond du cœur celles et ceux qui m'ont apporté leurs suffrages, celles et ceux qui m'ont tant aidé. Je sais ce que représente pour eux et pour la France, notre patrie si chère, cette victoire qui est la leur. A l'approche d'un autre millénaire, étape ou symbole, s'ouvre une période nouvelle de notre histoire.

   Comment vous dire les sentiments qui sont les miens en cette heure grave et solennelle. Je le répète : aimons la France et servons la. Vive la République et vive la France.

3. There were 38.32 million French eligible to vote in the 1988 presidential elections (a larger and younger electorate than in 1981). 20.33 million, a significant majority, of this electorate were women, and half of the electorate were below the age of 42.

4. In 1986 the PS and its allies had 214 seats. In the 1988 elections this was increased to 277 (12 seats short of an overall majority).

5. It is worth stressing that the demarcation of powers would still not have become clear in 1986 had Mitterrand resigned from the presidency, following the right's victory in the legislative elections.

6. Under Article 9 of the Constitution, the President presides over the Council of Ministers and has control of its agenda. Chirac as Prime Minister was able to overcome this, however, by holding unofficial meetings from which the President was excluded.

7. Article 11: Le président de la République, sur proposition du gouvernement, pendant la durée des sessions ou sur proposition conjointe des deux Assemblées, publiées au

Journal officiel, peut soumettre au référendum tout projet de loi portant sur l'organisation des pouvoirs publics, comportant approbation d'un accord de Communauté ou tendant à autoriser la ratification d'un traité qui, sans être contraire à la Constitution, aurait des incidences sur le fonctionnement des institutions. Lorsque le référendum a conclu à l'adoption du projet, le président de la République le promulgue dans le délai prévu à l'article précédent.

8. On the question of presidential power, Nicolet has argued that the President in the Third Republic had significantly more power, particularly in foreign affairs, than has generally been assumed, see C. Nicolet, *L'Idée republicaine en France* (Paris, Gallimard, 1982).

9. It is arguable that, without the 1962 amendment, the Prime Minister would, over time, have become the most significant political actor in the polity. The Constitution remains, however, open to diverse interpretations. Some observers believe the Fifth Republic's Constitution to be an extremely sophisticated document concerning the distribution of power. I take Wright's view that it remains a 'constitutional morass', see V. Wright, *The Government and Politics in France* (London, Hutchinson, 1978) p. 24.

10. De Gaulle was elected as the first President of the Republic according to the rules of Article 6 of the 1958 Constitution, that is, by an electoral college (essentially MPs, senators, municipal councillors, mayors, and regional councillors) of about 80,000 people.

11. The President is a national figure not only because of the strong electoral participation in presidential elections but because candidates must be nominated by 500 elected representatives drawn from at least thirty departments.

12. Notwithstanding their allegiance to the President, Prime Ministers Debré, Pompidou, Chaban-Delmas, Fabius, and Rocard, all expressed varying degrees of disagreement with their President at different times. Ironically, such disagreement simply underlined the potential *presidential* status of these Prime Ministers.

13. In spite of his being elected by the electoral college, this was also true of de Gaulle in 1958, given that the referendum on the Fifth Republic's Constitution in September 1958 was akin to a personal plebiscite.

14. Personal allegiance is less of an organising principle of the smaller parties, Jean-Marie Le Pen's FN being an exception to this rule.

15. This was not the case in Mitterrand's campaigns in 1974 or 1981. We should stress, nevertheless, that the 110 propositions of 1981 were a presidential campaign programme rather than a party one, and, to the extent that they implied a legislative programme, probably were of little significance in the campaign; and in 1974 the recent Common Programme of Government signed with the Communists was completely ignored.

16. Valéry Giscard d'Estaing made a possibly fundamental tactical mistake in not dissolving the Assembly after his election in 1974.

17. The PCF and UDF were exceptions to this rule in 1988: the PCF made it very plain that its candidate, André Lajoinie, was clearly subordinate to the party leader; the UDF supported Raymond Barre partly *because* he had very little influence within the UDF.

18. MacMahon, President of the Third Republic between 1873 and 1879, abused the spirit of the Constitution by unnecessarily dissolving the Assembly in 1877. The victory of his opponents in the ensuing elections confirmed the Assembly's ascendancy over the President for the duration of the Third Republic.

19. See Notes 10 and 13.

20. The Algerian War ended in 1962.

21. The only party to have attempted to diminish the significance of the presidential elections is the PCF. Such a strategy only served to diminish the party's own significance.

22. The status of the parties is further diminished by the fact that the support enjoyed by any one political party would never be enough to secure the election of that party's candidate.

23. The use of the elections by second-rank leaders as an essential moment in their political manœuvring is now a widespread phenomenon. The clearest example of this, however, was Mitterrand's own candidacy in 1965.

24. Le Pen's profile had been helped significantly by the FN's successes in the 1984 European elections and the 1986 legislative elections. Many of his four and a half million votes on 24 April 1988, however, were clearly personal votes.

25. Paradoxically, in such a situation, language, *petites phrases*, connotations, and *sous-entendu* take on an inordinate significance.

26. François Mitterrand's first-round vote was also less than many of the final opinion polls had forecast. In some he had been credited with 38%, and privately assumed that 35% was the desirable score necessary in order to cruise home in the second round. The first round score was 34.11%.

27. In minor terms, Waechter was also a 'winner', the PCF a 'loser'. Interestingly, even this initial assessment of winners and losers was to change again, Raymond Barre's status subsequently profiting from the idea of a candidate who had done badly because of his personal integrity and refusal of opportunistic calculation, and Jean-Marie Le Pen's immediate political influence being drastically reduced by the legislative elections which followed Mitterrand's (generally unexpected) dissolution of Parliament.

28. Many Le Pen supporters loathed Jacques Chirac, and the extreme-right's hostility to Gaullism goes back to the early years of the Fifth Republic, if not to 1940.

29. We can note here that this conflation of Barre and Chirac's *comités de soutien* was a symbolic gesture with no organisational logic to it, given especially that Barre's *comités* had been organised badly and were themselves a confused composite of Barre's REEL support and the campaign headquarters of the UDF parties.

30. Giscard's support for Chirac, however, was as ambiguous in the second round as it had been for Barre in the first, and his warning to Chirac to change his language and style at Chirac's penultimate second-round rally at Clermont-Ferrand was, in fact, a damning indictment.

31. The clearest indication of the centre's collapsing support for Chirac was the centrist, ex-Giscard Minister, Lionel Stoléru's affirmation that he would vote for Chirac but 'le 9 mai je suis libre'. He was simply affirming clearly what most centrists believed privately. Stoléru subsequently entered Rocard's government.

32. This shift was also reflected in the legislative elections of June in which the UDF, for the first time, held marginally more seats than the RPR (one or two more, in fact, depending on how one identifies UDF MPs).

33. It was Michel Noir who had asserted, when an RPR minister in Chirac's government, that it was better to lose an election than to lose one's soul (by associating with the FN).

34. Le Pen's comportment after 24 April was designed to give the deliberate impression that, for him, 8 May and Chirac's political fortunes were totally unimportant, whereas the aftermath of 8 May was all-important.

35. Trying to ascertain the figures of participation for these meetings and meetings like them is notoriously hard. The FEN-CFDT rally attracted between 10,000 and 30,000 participants, the CGT and FN rallies between 30,000 and 100,000 each.

36. A whole stream of non-partisan support, in the form of petitions, declarations and so on, and involving doctors, Nobel prize winners, ecologists and, as we have seen, the trade unions, developed after 24 April (largely in reaction to Le Pen's vote), further crediting to Mitterrand the status of a guardian of a threatened humanist tradition of tolerance.

37. This is a pun on Mitterrand's anti-Fifth Republic book published in 1965, *Le coup d'État permanent*.

38. 'Sur l'essentiel le FN se réclame des mêmes préoccupations, des mêmes valeurs, que la majorité'. This declaration, part of an interview, had been published in *Valeurs Actuels* the previous Thursday but had only gained major national prominence through television and newspaper reporting of it at the beginning of the second week of the campaign.

39. We should note here that Pasqua's declaration was significant because its reference is one of sympathy, not to the FN's voters, but to the FN itself, that is, to the party, its views and its ideology, and not simply to the values of its electorate. Pasqua subsequently modified his view, claiming that he had been quoted out of context. The effect of the modification was nothing compared to the effect of the initial declaration.

40. Interestingly, the effect of this action not only made Mitterrand seem powerless, but also withdrew much of Le Pen's exclusive claim to a virile nationalism. When interviewed at this time, it was clear that Le Pen was annoyed by Chirac's successes.

41. It is true to say that, although there was initially a certain degree of suspicion, the notion that some of the hostage-takers had been executed in cold blood only surfaced later.

42. Dominique Prieur had been one of the two French spies found guilty by a court in New Zealand of involvement in the blowing up of the Greenpeace vessel, *Rainbow Warrior*, in July 1985, in which one person was killed.

43. It is worth stressing that the increase in Le Pen's first round vote was also remarkable by its being a national one.

44. According to exit polls conducted on 8 May, 53% of respondents were in favour of legislative elections being called. Polls also indicated that 33% wanted Michel Rocard as Prime Minister. His nearest rival was Valéry Giscard d'Estaing with 17%.

45. It should also be noted that Laguiller's campaign literature was significantly more personalised in 1988 than in 1981.

46. Given the President's growing distance from interference in government, the question is also raised as to whether the qualities perceived as being required by a potential Prime Minister are now different, requiring different personal strategies and

relationships within political parties.

2 François Mitterrand: from Republican contender to President of all the French

ALISTAIR M. COLE

> 'Ever since 1962, when it was decided that the President of the Republic would be elected by universal suffrage, I knew that I would be a candidate'.
> **François Mitterrand**[1]

No commentator can fail to be surprised by the element of paradox surrounding the long relationship between François Mitterrand, the Fifth Republic and presidentialism. Mitterrand's political spurs were earned as a non-Socialist, neo-Radical minister during the Fourth Republic, when he held ministerial office on eleven occasions. Mitterrand strongly opposed the creation of the Fifth Republic in 1958, condemned it as a *coup d'état,* and campaigned for a 'no' vote in the constitutional referendum of September 1958.[2] His initial opposition to de Gaulle was predicated upon the idea that the republican form of government had been betrayed by the 1958 events.

Despite his fierce opposition to de Gaulle's October 1962 referendum introducing the direct election of the presidency, Mitterrand was one of the first politicians to recognise its importance. His conversion to the new rules of political competition imposed by the direct election of the presidency was of fundamental significance, and his strategic aim gradually became clearer: to use the Fifth Republic and the new rules of the game introduced by the presidential election to restructure the left as the only plausible opposition to Gaullism. This would involve supplanting the old Socialist Party, *Section Française de l'Internationale Ouvrière* (SFIO), by an organisation more attuned to the new realities of political competition and to the need to organise around an attractive presidential candidate. Such an organisation would have to reduce the importance of the *Parti Communiste Français* (PCF), whose continuing domination of the left prevented any prospect of the left as a whole gaining power, because of the fear it inspired amongst most non-Communist voters. In addition, a new Socialist Party would have to fight off the alternative opposition to Gaullism provided by the centrists.[3]

The presidential factor provided the main source of cohesion for those political clubs which formed the *Convention des Institutions Républicaines* (CIR) in 1964, a kind of mini-party whose major objective was to promote Mitterrand as a candidate for the 1965 presidential election. At this stage, Mitterrand continued to regard himself as a republican, rather than a socialist; indeed, the ideological roots of Mitterrandism in the early Fifth Republic were Radical rather than Socialist, and the genealogy of most of the political clubs within the CIR can be traced to Radicalism. After the failure of the bid by the Socialist mayor of Marseille, Gaston Defferre, to stand as a presidential candidate for the 1965 presidential election backed by a Socialist-Centre-Christian Democratic federation (which would have excluded the PCF), François Mitterrand was able to impose his presidential candidacy for the 1965 election on the main parties of the left: the PCF, the SFIO and the PSU.[4] These parties supported Mitterrand partly because they were afraid to put up candidates themselves, for fear that their score in the presidential contest (which was suspected of promoting personality at the expense of party programmes) would be inferior to that which they could expect to obtain in legislative elections (in which the PCF and the SFIO could rely on well-tested organisations and deputies with proven grass-roots support). Moreover, the main left-wing parties refused to regard the direct presidential election as a legitimate exercise, fearing that it would be transformed into a plebiscite in favour of de Gaulle's leadership at their expense, and to the detriment of parliamentary government.

The 1965 presidential election represented a watershed in the development of the Fifth Republic. The 1965 contest was the first time that a President had been directly elected in France since Louis Napoleon in 1848, a historical parallel which led many on the left to equate direct election with the danger of dictatorship. The only previous presidential election in the Fifth Republic had occurred in 1958, when de Gaulle was overwhelmingly elected by the electoral college established in the 1958 constitution, composed of 80,000 local, departmental and national elected officials. De Gaulle's October 1962 referendum replaced this system of indirect election with one which involved a direct appeal to the electorate, over the heads of the intermediaries represented by parliament and the political parties. His initial calculation was that through direct election he would be able to plebiscite the French people in favour of his leadership (as he had done in four referendums from 1958 to 1962), and would need only one ballot for his overwhelming reelection. However, the decline in de Gaulle's standing from its exceptional levels of 1958-1962, the gradual revival of the left after 1962, and the use of a second-ballot electoral system in the presidential election, forced de Gaulle to a second ballot against Mitterrand in 1965.[5] De Gaulle's failure to secure reelection on the first ballot surprised many observers and shocked the General, but perhaps of greater importance was the fact that Mitterrand, backed by a broadly based left-wing coalition, clearly outdistanced the centre candidate, Jean Lecanuet, to provide a more credible opposition to Gaullism. The first fifteen years of the Fifth Republic (1958-1973) witnessed the non-Communist left (Socialists, left-wing Radicals, political clubs) and the centrists (Christian Democrats, right-wing Radicals and old-style Conservatives) contest for the privilege of being the main non-Communist force to oppose the Gaullist majority, a contest from which the non-Communist left (Mitterrand's PS) had clearly emerged victorious by 1974, despite the hiccup represented by the 1969 presidential election (see below).

Mitterrand's performance in 1965, first in forcing de Gaulle to a second ballot, then in obtaining 45.5% of votes cast in the run-off against him, was of primordial importance in explaining the future development of the left. Two main conclusions could be drawn from Mitterrand's performance. Firstly, his presidential bid coincided with an important step towards the presidentialisation of the party system, since the major forces of the non-Communist left (CIR, SFIO, Radicals, political clubs) were cajoled to join together in the *Fédération de la Gauche Démocrate et Socialiste (FGDS)*, the 'small federation' that backed Mitterrand's 1965 candidacy. The impact of the election was fully confirmed after the event, in so far as Mitterrand, the 'presidential' leader of the left, dominated the FGDS throughout its existence (1965-1968) rather than Guy Mollet, the official leader of the SFIO, which remained the most powerful organisation within the Federation.

Secondly, the bipolar confrontation between left and right on the second ballot strengthened the non-Communist left at the expense of the PCF. The emergence of the presidential election as the Fifth Republic's *decisive* election meant that to be credible a party had to be able to field a presidential candidate who stood a chance of victory. The non-Communist left proved it could do this in 1965: Mitterrand was able to capture support from voters beyond the pale of the left on the second ballot, whereas a Communist candidate, struggling against deep-seated anti-Communism, would have stood no chance of being elected, or even of equalling the left's combined first-round vote.

The presidential election thus opened an important and credible political space between Communism and Gaullism which the non-Communist left was potentially well-placed to occupy: that of leadership of the anti-Gaullist forces within the country. Mitterrand calculated that strength in presidential contests would have an influence on the overall party system, and on the performance of particular parties in legislative elections. The potential strength of the non-Communist left depended upon its various forces maintaining their unity, which, in practice, however, proved difficult. Nevertheless, despite internecine pressures and the collapse of the FGDS in the wake of the events of May-June 1968, the formation of the *Parti Socialiste* (PS) from 1969-1971 provided the organisational framework for the fusion of various groups into a genuinely new political party, which gradually established itself as the most dangerous opponent of the right. The process of socialist unification culminated in 1974, virtually effacing the divisions caused by the Algerian war and the advent of the Fifth Republic.[6]

Mitterrand's 1965 performance created a new and dual image for him: that of presidential leader of the left and that of proponent of the alliance between the non-Communist left and the PCF. This 'presidential stature' gave Mitterrand immense authority, and enabled him to impose his leadership on the non-Communist left at the expense of Mollet and the SFIO. Mitterrand led the FGDS at the 1967 and 1968 legislative elections, on both occasions in alliance with the PCF. Despite temporary discredit for his intempestive statements during the May '68 crisis and the poor FGDS showing in the June 1968 legislative election, Mitterrand regained the initiative in 1969, after the SFIO candidate Gaston Defferre's disastrous performance (5.1%) in the 1969 presidential election on a strongly anti-Communist ticket. Mitterrand was left as the only plausible 'presidential' leader, and alliance with the PCF as the only realistic strategy.[7] Mitterrand took control of the PS at the congress of Epinay in June 1971, committed the party to allying itself with the PCF, and signed a Common Programme of Government in June 1972 with the PCF.[8] The PS remained bound to the PCF by the Common Programme until September 1977, when the parties failed to agree on terms for updating their programme. A looser form of electoral alliance persisted in the 1978 and 1981 legislative elections, but this owed more to mutual electoral self-interest than it did to any profound agreement over policy.[9]

Socialist-Communist Relations, 1971-1988

During the decade from 1971 to 1981, when he was First Secretary of the PS, Mitterrand was obsessed by the need to reverse the balance of power on the left between Socialists and Communists in the former's favour, since he regarded PS domination of the left as the essential precondition to the left's winning an election. Despite the potential advantage that the presidential election gave to the new PS over the PCF, the latter remained, until 1978, the larger party as measured in terms of votes at legislative elections. Mitterrand was determined to reduce the PCF to being a marginal force on the extreme left, and to build a great Socialist Party which would be able to expand its natural boundaries of support well beyond those of the old SFIO, both on its left (from the ashes of a marginalised PCF), and on its right (by attracting support from centrist and floating voters willing to back the PS as the only alternative to the right). Mitterrand's priority throughout the 1970s was thus to reduce the PCF's importance. Paradoxically, his pursuit of this strategic aim led to the PS adopting a neo-revolutionary language throughout much of the 1970s and committing itself to radical measures in the 1972 Common Programme, which, on the surface, seemed likely to alienate moderate anti-Gaullist voters. This was, however, the necessary price to pay for attracting PCF voters to the PS, a process which began in 1973, gathered pace in 1978, when the PS became the leading party of the left for the first time in the Fifth Republic, and had become a major political phenomenon by 1981, when the party profited from the dynamic caused by Mitterrand's presidential election victory to secure an absolute parliamentary majority.[10]

Despite the gradual drift of ex-Communist voters to the PS, the continuing strength of the PCF, which polled over one-fifth of votes cast in the 1973 and 1978 legislative elections, prevented the left-wing parties from obtaining an overall parliamentary majority during the 1970s. The alliance with the PCF continued to scare many centrist-inclined and even pro-Socialist voters away from Mitterrand's PS, since they feared that it would be a hostage to the PCF in any united left-wing government. It was only in the June 1981 legislative elections, after Mitterrand had been elected as President in May, that PS domination of the left became indisputable and hesitant voters seeking a change were willing to confide their support in the PS without fearing that a left-wing government would be dominated by the PCF. The PS performance in the 1981 legislative elections was integrally related to Mitterrand's victory in the preceding presidential contest, since the electorate was anxious to confirm the choice it had made by electing Mitterrand in the decisive presidential battle. This appeared to testify to the underlying presidentialism of the political system, from which the PS now profited. From that moment onwards, the crucial political significance of the respective strengths of the PS and PCF began to decline in importance.

The decline of the PCF eased the pressure which the party's political importance had previously exercised upon the PS; as long as the PCF had represented around one-fifth of voters, the PS had perpetually feared losing face with the Communist electorate, both in terms of party programmes (the PS had to attempt to appear to be as 'radical' as the PCF) and ideology (the Socialists were constrained to refute continually the PCF's charge that they were a 'Social-democratic' party). The PCF's decline enabled the PS to appeal more openly for support from non-Socialist voters in the centre without fearing the consequences of being labelled as 'Social-democratic'. In addition, once widespread disillusionment over the left's attempts to implement its reform programme in 1981-1982 had set in, the weakness of the PCF made it easier for the Socialists to change course and adapt their policies.[11] The weakening of the PCF rapidly gathered pace during Mitterrand's first seven-year presidential term (1981-1988): the party declined to 11.2% of votes cast in the 1984 European election, 9.8% in the 1986 legislative elections, and 6.8% on the first ballot of the 1988 presidential election, before rallying somewhat in the legislative elections of June 1988 (11.2%).[12]

The Presidentialisation of François Mitterrand's Socialist Party, 1971-1986

Mitterrand's presidential stature was of considerable importance in explaining why he was able to capture control of the PS at the congress of Epinay in 1971: he was its only plausible presidential candidate, whereas the old-guard represented by Guy Mollet, the SFIO leader since 1946, continued to resist the 'decisive' presidential election. Such resistance incited powerful forces within the SFIO to prefer Mitterrand to Mollet. The only other convincing presidential candidate on the non-Communist left had been Gaston Defferre, but his severe setback in 1969 effectively ended his presidential ambitions, and he rallied to Mitterrand at the congress of Epinay.

Although in 1971 the PS recruited its own 'providential' leader in Mitterrand, it would be misleading to reduce the post-1971 party to that of a mere appendix of Mitterrand's presidential ambitions. The 1971 PS was formed after a process of 'fusion' on the left, and its component elements only gradually became forged into a coherent political party. Mitterrand's supporters were originally in a minority and he was not at liberty to ignore rival factions within the PS. From 1971 to 1974, Mitterrand's margins of manoeuvre within the PS were narrow, since he depended upon the support of alliance partners to assure his control over the party: in particular Pierre Mauroy, the powerful number two, who officially controlled the party organisation; Gaston Defferre, the mayor of Marseille, and (until 1973) the left-wing CERES faction. Only after his triumphant defeat in the 1974 presidential election was Mitterrand able to govern the PS in a more presidential manner and pay less attention to internal party constraints (see below). In addition, from 1972 to 1974 Mitterrand's PS was firmly tied into the alliance with the PCF based around the Common Programme, which undoubtedly limited the extent to which the party could develop its own policies.

Despite these reservations, it became clear during the 1970s that Mitterrand's presidential status had had a fundamental impact on the organisation of the PS. The presidentialisation of the PS gathered pace well before Mitterrand's victory. In fact, the vital turning point might be traced to the 1974 presidential campaign. Mitterrand's 1974 campaign effort was concentrated neither on the official PS organisation, nor on the PS-PCF Common Programme. On the contrary, Mitterrand's 1974 platform watered down the radical commitments of the Common Programme and replaced them with a series of vague policy preferences. Moreover, the 1974 campaign largely by-passed the official PS organisation, and Mitterrand preferred to rely on his own personally-appointed advisers in his Paris headquarters and his delegates in the federations. It was the presidential logic of the political system which encouraged Mitterrand to play down the party's programmatic commitments during the 1974 campaign: to stand a chance of victory, Mitterrand had to broaden his appeal beyond the ranks of the left, and attempt to unite as broad as possible an electorate around his challenge on the second ballot. In addition, the personalisation encouraged by the presidential election enabled the candidate to portray himself as being above party and to fudge programmatic commitments.

By running a close second to Valéry Giscard d'Estaing on the second ballot of the 1974 presidential election (49.3% against 50.7%), Mitterrand confirmed that the bipolarisation stimulated by the second ballot of a presidential election gave the left serious chances of victory, and illustrated that Socialist leadership was a condition *sine qua non* of the left's accession to power. From the autumn of 1974 onwards, the impact of Mitterrand's presidential performance made itself felt in a number of different non-presidential contests: legislative by-elections (especially those of September 1974), departmental elections (1976) and municipal elections

(1977).[13] The impetus provided by the presidential election, together with the far-reaching changes taking place in French society, consolidated PS leadership of the left after 1974 at the PCF's expense.[14] The PCF immediately realised the dangers represented by Mitterrand's 1974 performance on the internal balance of power between the left-wing parties: after a series of manoeuvres from 1974 to 1977 destined to weaken the PS, the PCF finally responded to its loss of leadership on the left by breaking off the alliance over the Common Programme with the PS, on the pretext that the Socialists were unwilling to agree to proposed PCF ameliorations to the programme. In the legislative elections of 1978 and 1981, left-wing unity was reduced to mutual withdrawal agreements in favour of the best placed left-wing candidates on the second ballot.

From 1974 onwards, presidentialism dominated the PS. Mitterrand governed the PS in a largely presidential manner and created a 'dual circuit of legitimacy'[15] within the party leadership, by appointing delegates to parallel the work of the official National Secretariat, the party's main executive organ. These delegates were responsible only to Mitterrand, and allowed him to keep himself informed on all of the party's main policy areas and activities without having to rely on the official organisation. Their existence recalled that of the presidential advisers in the *Secrétariat Général de l'Elysée*, whose function is to supervise and scrutinise government departments and to advise the President.

Further evidence of the extent to which presidentialism dominated the PS internally after 1974 could be found in the intra-party rivalries created between potential candidates for the party's presidential nomination. Although Mitterrand's suzerainty over the party was scarcely called into question from 1971 to 1978, this situation changed after the left's defeat in the 1978 legislative elections (a defeat which, in retrospect, must have appeared fortuitous to Mitterrand). Mitterrand was challenged after 1978 by Michel Rocard, the candidate most favoured by the opinion polls to win the 1981 presidential election for the PS. Mitterrand eventually fought off Rocard's challenge at the 1979 party congress, and consolidated his control over the party organisation by expelling Rocard and his erstwhile ally Mauroy from the leadership.[16] Despite Rocard maintaining his challenge to Mitterrand until late in 1980, the latter's control over the PS leadership ensured that he secured the PS nomination for the 1981 presidential election. The lesson of the Mitterrand-Rocard conflict from 1978 to 1980 was that, despite the impact of presidentialism, the PS retained at least one fundamental role: the party selected its own candidate, which could not be imposed upon it against its will, whatever the opinion polls said. This meant that Mitterrand, the favourite of the party, rather than Rocard, the favourite of public opinion, represented the PS in the 1981 presidential election. Thus, the party's sense of its self-sufficiency placed limits on the extent to which it would allow presidentialism to dictate what presidential strategies it should adopt. Notwithstanding this, the Rocard phenomenon illustrated how far down the presidential path internal party rivalries had gone.

Mitterrand's 1981 campaign called into question a number of truisms frequently voiced about the presidential election. Firstly, his campaign platform, the '110 propositions', contained a large number of detailed policy commitments which were inspired by the party's Socialist Project of 1980. The rationale behind this bold programme was as much political as ideological, and two types of explanation explain this paradox. Firstly, Mitterrand's '110 propositions' could not be entirely dissociated from the internal party manoeuvres which had taken place within the PS since the 1979 Metz congress in the attempt to block Rocard's route to the presidential nomination. The PS had adopted its Socialist Project in early 1980 as the basis of a presidential platform for 1981. The object of the Socialist Project, drawn up by Jean-Pierre Chevènement, the leader of the left-wing CERES faction, was, by committing the party to a far-reaching series of social and economic reforms, to make it virtually impossible for the moderate Rocard to stand as a candidate. Having publicly supported this project, it would have been difficult for Mitterrand totally to disavow it, although his presidential platform greatly modified its provisions.

A second explanation is more convincing. In the 1981 presidential election, Mitterrand was for the first time faced by a separate Communist candidate, the PCF General Secretary, Georges Marchais. Since the breakdown of the Common Programme in September 1977 the PS and the PCF had been fighting a bitter battle for supremacy on the left, which the 1978 legislative elections had not really settled. Mitterrand needed to attract as many Communist voters as possible to his standard from the first-ballot, not only to strengthen the PS at the PCF's expense, but also because the extent of his first-ballot lead over the PCF candidate Marchais would determine how successfully he could convince undecided voters that he was genuinely independent of the PCF. This situation had not arisen in 1974, since Mitterrand was already assured of Communist support, and his main preoccupation had been to reassure hesitant voters that his programme was a moderate one. In 1981, by contrast, Mitterrand stood on a programme offering radical change, and eventually tempted a fraction of 1978 PCF voters to vote 'usefully' for him from the first ballot, rather than for the Communist, Marchais, who stood no chance of being elected. In fact, Mitterrand (25.85%) emerged with a ten point lead over Marchais (15.3%), whereas only two percentage points had separated the PS from the PCF in 1978. Paradoxically, this rallying to Mitterrand of ex-Communist support on the first round made him an acceptable candidate in the run-off to centrist voters dissatisfied with President Giscard d'Estaing, since it proved his independence from the PCF and his domination of the left.[17]

The policies outlined in Mitterrand's '110 propositions' repeated the main demands of the old left, which had not substantially changed from the 1972 Common programme: extensive nationalisations in industry, primacy of the Plan in industrial policy, consumer-led economic reflation stimulated by massive increases in public spending, priority given to fighting unemployment, decentralisation, increased worker rights and so on. A further novelty of the 1981 campaign was that Mitterrand made greater use of the official PS organisation than in 1974, although his Paris headquarters and support committees in the provinces continued to force the PS somewhat into the background.

By 1981, the PS had been firmly subordinated to Mitterrand's leadership. Mitterrand relinquished his formal control over the PS in January 1981, when he became presidential candidate, in favour of one of his young protégés, Lionel Jospin, who, as First Secretary of the party from 1981 to 1988, loyally executed Mitterrand's wishes and rallied the PS behind the President. The election of an absolute PS majority in the 1981 legislative elections led to parallels being drawn with the period between 1962 and 1974, when the Gaullist UNR/UDR had acted as a majority party which supported the President unquestioningly and had had little input into government policy. Prominent PS leaders initially refused to accept the idea that the PS should unquestioningly subordinate itself to the executive, as the Gaullist Party had done, and insisted that the party should find new institutional channels within which it could make its influence felt on government decisions. To a limited extent, such new institutional channels did come into existence during the first Mitterrand presidency (1981-1988). During 1981-1982, President Mitterrand met with representatives of the PS leadership on at least three occasions weekly, to discuss proposed legislation, or party-government relations. Such formalised meetings between a President and his party leaders to discuss policy were unprecedented in the Fifth Republic's history. These early contacts between the President and his party lieutenants became rarer after the Algerian generals affair in November 1982 and especially after the economic u-turn of March 1983.[18] Nonetheless, Lionel Jospin, the PS leader, continued to meet at least weekly with the President throughout Mitterrand's first presidency.

Despite the evidence that the PS had a somewhat greater input into policy than had previously been the case with the presidential party during the Fifth Republic, the party's importance must not be exaggerated. There were several reasons which could explain the party's subordination to the President. Firstly, Mitterrand's early actions as President clearly reasserted the pattern of presidential supremacy that had characterised the Fifth Republic under previous Presidents (see next section). Secondly, the governmental system was largely dominated by Mitterrandists, the President's own supporters, although Pierre Mauroy, who was Mitterrand's first Prime Minister from 1981 to 1984, did not belong to the President's faction. Potential conflict between different institutions (presidency, government, parliamentary party, and PS executive) was thus, in theory, minimised. However, the sheer extent to which Mitterrand's supporters dominated created new problems: Mauroy's authority as Prime Minister from 1981 to 1984 was frequently undermined by individual ministers appealing directly to Mitterrand to back them against Mauroy. The replacement of Pierre Mauroy by Laurent Fabius as Prime Minister in July 1984 completed the virtual domination exercised by the Mitterrandists over the institutional machinery.[19] Notwithstanding this, each of the party's other major factions (Mauroy's supporters, Rocard's supporters, and CERES) was represented in the government throughout most of the period, as well as in the official PS leadership, which minimised the chances that an opposition faction would attempt to transform the party into a campaigning body opposing government policy (as occurred with the British Labour Party under the 1974-1979 Labour governments).[20] The logic underpinning this convergence was that of presidentialism: the effective concentration of real power and patronage in the presidency incited each of the party's factions to fall into line behind President Mitterrand's choices, except in a few well-publicised instances.

The party's initial hostility to its transformation into a *parti de godillots* (a party of bootlickers) was vented at its Valence congress in October 1981 when prominent PS leaders called upon the government to step up the pace of the left's reform programme, and demanded a greater voice for the party in deciding government policy. The negative impact that this congress left on public opinion made Mitterrand determined to limit the party's autonomy and bring it into line with the government. At the party congresses of 1981 (Valence), 1983 (Bourg-en-Bresse), and 1985 (Toulouse), Mitterrand insisted that the party's role was, above all, to support the government, rather than to propose alternative policies or to urge the government to go further than it intended. Despite the early declarations of independence made by certain PS leaders, the party generally fell into line, especially after the economic u-turn of 1982-1983 when growing unpopularity forced the PS to close ranks with the government. Nonetheless, leading PS politicians continued to pressure the government to adopt symbolic Socialist measures that would offset the disappointment they felt with the government for abandoning its economic policies. The education bill of 1984, promoted by the Minister of Education, Alain Savary, which attempted to place stricter controls on mainly Catholic private schools, and thus to satisfy the deeply ingrained anti-clerical sentiment that continued to exist within the PS, was one example of this. The disastrous outcome of this bill (which provoked an intense popular mobilisation against Mauroy's government in the name of freedom) and the advent of Laurent Fabius's government in July 1984, effectively buried the last vestiges of independent party influence. The supremacy of executive government in the Fifth Republic (which limited the autonomy PS deputies could display), and Mitterrand's preservation of the essentials of presidential power until 1986, usually reduced the PS to the status of an impotent observer, whose main function was a propaganda one: to support government policies in the country and to prepare for elections. Finally, the subordination of the party was indispensable in enabling Mitterrand to portray himself as President of all the French people, rather than merely as a Socialist President. This necessity became all the more pressing as the left-wing governments became more unpopular after 1982.

François Mitterrand and the Institutions of the Fifth Republic, 1981-1986

In order to understand the nature of the changes which occurred to the French presidency during the period of '*cohabitation*' from 1986 to 1988, when the Socialist President Mitterrand coexisted with the right-wing government headed by Jacques Chirac, we need to outline here the institutional pattern of Mitterrand's first presidency as it operated during its fully active phase from 1981 to 1986.

The development of the PS in the decade preceding Mitterrand's 1981 victory had been extremely paradoxical: despite the advantage of having a presidential leader at the helm, and despite acceptance and exploitation of the political situation created by direct election of the President, the PS had steadfastly refused to accept the 'executive presidency' such as it had evolved under de Gaulle, Pompidou and Giscard. In party programmes and congress resolutions throughout the 1970s, the PS demanded a restoration of Parliament's authority, and a new equilibrium between the presidency, the government and parliament. Indeed, even for Mitterrand (who claimed not to lament the passing of the Fourth Republic with its weak executive authority) the reinforced presidential function after 1962 retained a taint of illegitimacy.[21]

Despite Mitterrand's often-repeated opposition to the monarchical character of the Fifth Republic's institutions, his 1981 presidential platform, the '110 propositions', arguably contained no constitutional proposals which were directly aimed at challenging the supremacy of the French President. Although candidate Mitterrand promised to reduce the presidential mandate from seven to five years, and paid vague respect to the idea of reinforcing the powers of parliament, these limited proposals were not respected. In fact, there was little immediate evidence to suggest that, once elected President, Mitterrand seriously called into question the model of the 'executive presidency' that had evolved since de Gaulle.

Immediately after his 1981 victory, Mitterrand dissolved the National Assembly and called upon voters to elect an absolute PS majority, in order to 'give him the means to govern'. The crushing PS majority returned in June 1981 thus owed its existence to Mitterrand. Once this majority had been elected, Mitterrand insisted that his '110 propositions' were to act as 'the charter of the government's action', and that PS deputies must not overstep the limits of this programme. The pattern of presidential supremacy was thus reasserted by Mitterrand's early activities.

Mitterrand not only named the Prime Minister, as stipulated by the constitution, but had a decisive influence on the nomination of the other ministers, ensuring that Mitterrandists were placed in a majority of the important strategic positions. Despite this, the new President declared his intention of allowing the government to govern, and initial indications hinted that, once he had defined the broad parameters of governmental policies, Mitterrand would be willing to allow Mauroy's second government

47

(1981-1983) to pursue its ambitious reform programme without excessive presidential interference. In addition, there was evidence that the intervention of the Elysée in arbitrating interministerial disputes would be less commonplace than under Giscard.[22] However, after the left's major economic u-turn in March 1983, and the nomination of Mauroy's third government, Mitterrand's presidency moved into a more directly interventionist phase. Tight control of the economy became the government's virtually exclusive consideration after 1983, and throughout Mauroy's third government (March 1983 to July 1984) Mitterrand supervised the conduct of government affairs far more closely than had previously been the case.[23] It should be pointed out, however, that the major economic decisions taken by Mitterrand were forced upon him, firstly by Mauroy in June 1982 (the decision to freeze wages and salaries for a four month period), and secondly by a powerful alliance between Mauroy, and the Minister of Finance, Jacques Delors, in March 1983 (involving the decision to remain within the European monetary system and the adoption of an economic austerity package).

Although Mitterrand introduced no successful reforms to limit the powers of the President during the first five years of his presidency, he claimed to have altered the Fifth Republic's constitutional practice and to have restored control of government to the government.[24] The move away from the all-powerful presidency, which certain commentators discerned during the early period of Mauroy's premiership, became more apparent under Laurent Fabius who replaced Mauroy as Mitterrand's second Prime Minister in July 1984. It might be argued that Mitterrand initially left a greater degree of manoeuvre to Fabius than to Mauroy in an attempt to prepare the groundrules for *cohabitation*, the institutional situation whereby a Socialist President would have to coexist with a right-wing government, which Mitterrand knew was almost certain to be produced after the 1986 legislative elections. The new Prime Minister was in greater overall control of the coordination of government policy, and the Elysée's interventions were less erratic and unpredictable than they had been under Mauroy. However, several examples illustrated that when conflicts between the Prime Minister and the President emerged, the latter retained his ascendancy.[25] The more supple operation of the presidency between 1984 and 1986, together with the Socialists' ideological and policy evolution (which culminated at the congress of Toulouse in 1985, when the PS declared itself, at last, to be a 'Social-democratic' party), facilitated the transition to *cohabitation* after March 1986, and made Mitterrand's eventual victory possible in 1988.

François Mitterrand and *Cohabitation*, 1986-1988

The defeat of the PS in the 1986 legislative elections was the first time that an incumbent President had failed to secure the return of a parliamentary majority favourable to him; at one stroke the political base for the executive presidency - the existence of a parliamentary majority to back the President - was removed. Until 1986, French presidential power in the Fifth Republic had always owed more to the accumulated practices of the presidential incumbents, and to the legitimacy conferred by direct election, than to the President's strict constitutional powers (see Chapter One). A detailed analysis of *cohabitation* lies outside of the scope of this chapter; we can, however, illustrate here how Mitterrand exploited *cohabitation* to his own political advantage by defining a new role for the French President.

Although no-one could deny Mitterrand's right to remain as President until the end of his seven year mandate in 1988 (he could not be forced to resign), the fact that France had voted unambiguously for the right in 1986 could not be ignored. By naming Jacques Chirac Prime Minister (rather than experimenting with a non-partisan, 'technocratic' government), Mitterrand respected the democratic logic that control of the government must be confided to the winners of the latest election. Indeed, by naming the head of the majority coalition in the National Assembly as Prime Minister, Mitterrand appeared to create a new constitutional precedent in French politics: that the leader of the majority party or coalition had a tacit right to be called upon to form a government. That indispensable principle of most parliamentary regimes had never previously been applied in France's semi-presidential regime. It must be pointed out, however, that Mitterrand's nomination of Michel Rocard (who was not PS leader) as Prime Minister in May 1988, after the former's reelection as President, reverted to the older presidential practice whereby the main legitimacy of the Prime Minister's function stemmed from the fact that he had been named by the President.

After March 1986, Chirac's will prevailed largely unchallenged by Mitterrand in most major areas of policy, except in foreign policy and defence, where the constitution gives specific powers to the President. Even in these traditionally presidential sectors, Chirac exercised considerable influence. Although Mitterrand was clearly frustrated by his limited ability to influence government legislation, his political astuteness persuaded him that any openly *partisan* interference in government policy would be counter-productive.

Mitterrand's response to this new situation was to accept his loss of executive authority, to attempt to turn it to his own advantage, and to fight off Chirac's early efforts to force him to resign. From the outset, Mitterrand positioned himself as *Président de tous les Français,* and he claimed to speak in their name when he condemned particular government policies as being against the national interest. He did not contest Chirac's right to determine government policy, but periodically reasserted his own right to challenge policy by claiming, as Head of State, to express the interests of the French nation as a whole, rather than any specific fraction of it. Mitterrand's primary objective in stressing his role as President of all the French people was to promote consensus across the left/right boundary, in an attempt to efface the electorate's memory of the left's unpopularity from 1982 to 1986, and to promote a new image of the President as a figure above the political fray. The successful exploitation of this new image of the President was a precondition for Mitterrand being able to rehabilitate himself with public opinion. It was a task Mitterrand performed with consummate skill. The praise the President bestowed on selective members of Chirac's government in 1987 illustrated this, since it not only helped to create tensions within the government, but also made Mitterrand appear to public opinion as a reasonable, bipartisan figure. In fact, Mitterrand was careful to intervene only in those areas in which he could attract the support of a majority of the population: either by refusing to sign government decrees (such as over privatisations, employment policy, flexible working, or electoral reform), or by making public his reservations over government policies (for example over the Nationality Act, and university reform).

The executive president was thus transformed into the arbiter president, the constitutional justification for which lay in article 5 of the 1958 constitution (see Chapter One). By proclaiming his opposition to certain controversial government policies, and by refusing to countersign a number of government decrees (an act which most commentators agreed was permitted by the constitution), a widespread feeling developed that Mitterrand was preventing the government from going too far, and thereby safeguarding the cohesion of society. The idea that the most sacred duty of the President was to defend social and national cohesion and promote consensus was a new departure in Mitterrand's exploitation of presidentialism, but it was one which fitted in well with his loss of executive power and his attempt to portray himself as the President of all the French people. When Mitterrand criticised government policies, he was careful not to refer to the divisive idea of Socialism but to consensual notions which were likely to be supported by a majority, such as national independence (over privatisations), the Republic (over electoral reform), or pluralism (over the privatisation of TFI).

In May 1986, Mitterrand envisaged his arbiter function as follows:

> The French people have got the impression that they have gained an arbiter in me... . It is my duty to act in those essential areas which form part of the presidential domain, as defined by the constitution. In addition, in exercising my arbitral function, I must represent all those people who form part of a minority, and all those categories of people who are liable to suffer from injustice. [26]

Far from being a disinterested, objective referee, Mitterrand as arbiter thus had a duty to defend minorities and the underprivileged in society. This was a means of consolidating his left-wing electorate. However, the insistence with which Mitterrand claimed to speak in the name of all the French also represented an attempt to establish his position as being above the political fray, in order to attract 'legitimist' and centre-right voters repelled by Chirac's confrontational style. The perception that Mitterrand was not actually hindering Chirac's government from pursuing its policies was important in restoring a degree of confidence in Mitterrand amongst RPR and UDF voters, which had been virtually non-existent until 1986. Part of his new credibility thus came from the right and the centre-right, which conferred a new source of legitimacy onto the presidency as a bipartisan institution representing the superior interests of the French nation and people, above those of particular factions, parties or even governments. The diffusion of such a positive image was of considerable political advantage to Mitterrand.

Moreover, Jacques Chirac as Prime Minister could do little to contest Mitterrand's right to speak in the name of all the French people: it was essential for him not to question the authority of the presidential function which he hoped shortly to occupy, whereas the public opinion polls confirmed early on that the politician with the responsibility for deliberately ending *cohabitation* would be severely sanctioned by the electorate. Mitterrand's self-portrayal saw him recover popularity ratings not seen since his first year in office. Throughout the period from March 1986 to October 1987, Mitterrand averaged 54% of positive responses in the polling organisation IFOP's monthly satisfaction rating, as against 32% of negative responses. This success was all the more remarkable in so far as between 1983 and 1985 Mitterrand had consistently been the most unpopular President in the Fifth Republic, and had descended below Giscard's previous record of unpopularity (35% satisfied) on twenty-three different occasions.[27]

Despite proclaiming himself an arbiter, Mitterrand's clear intention was to discredit certain government policies (without preventing the government from governing), and thereby undermine Chirac's image before the 1988 presidential election. Mitterrand's support of the student protest movement of November-December 1986 marked the apogee of his interpretation of what an arbiter's role should be: that of defending minorities and the underprivileged, albeit in the name of 'all the French people'. In fact, a subtle change in tactics could be observed from early 1987 onwards. After January 1987, Mitterrand was less prompt to criticise unpopular government actions, or to refuse to sign government decrees, and more willing to let the government govern in the domestic arena. It was not in Mitterrand's interests to transform *cohabitation* into a new left-right confrontation. He learned from experience that when *cohabitation* enjoyed widescale public confidence (as from April to December 1986), both he and Chirac benefited. When the main antagonists of *cohabitation* fell out too publicly (as over the student strikes of November-December 1986, and the public sector strikes of January 1987) both suffered in public opinion at the expense of Raymond Barre, the alternative, anti-*cohabitation* presidential candidate. Both Chirac and Mitterrand thus came to recognise that they shared an interest in the survival of *cohabitation* until the 1988 presidential election. Rather than attempt to undermine publicly the Chirac government, Mitterrand preferred to allow the government to discredit itself by its own divisions, while continuing to remind public opinion that he was not responsible for government policy.

As the presidential campaign approached, the image of the arbiter president was increasingly complemented by that of *Tonton Mitterrand* (Uncle Mitterrand), in whose hands France's unity was secure. In reality, *Tonton* was a misnomer; the real image was that of the father of the nation whose primary objective was to promote consensus across the left/right divide. And the preparatory stages of his 1988 presidential campaign (when he had not yet declared himself to be a candidate) portrayed Mitterrand as the father of the nation in a number of senses. The *génération Mitterrand* poster campaign in early 1988 portrayed him as father of a generation, that of the entire French nation from young to old which had been reunified under his presidency. Mitterrand as father was above the fray, offering kind, but firm leadership of the French people, who together formed one family. That family might divide itself along ideological lines, between left and right, but as father of the family Mitterrand alone had sufficient authority to ensure that order and consensus reigned. Mitterrand's ability to cast himself in this new light was integrally related to *cohabitation*, which had illustrated that the left and right shared the same viewpoint on many of the great problems facing France.

A number of precedents in twentieth century French history (Clemenceau, Pétain, de Gaulle) suggested that the father-figure met with success when a generalised feeling of insecurity, powerlessness and antipathy towards politicians prevailed amongst many French people. Indeed, one of the great successes of Mitterrand's self-portrayal as father of the nation was to make the electorate forget that the President himself was the representative *par excellence* of the scheming politician. However, the comparison with his forebears must not be pushed too far. Mitterrand's paternalistic image had little in common with the authoritarianism of Pétain in 1940, or the austerity of de Gaulle in 1958. It must be stressed, however, that the development of what can only be called Mitterrand's personality cult in 1986-1988 did take place in a context of an increasing distrust of politicians and a considerable pessimism over France's future. In order that Mitterrand should benefit from his paternal image, his supporters were more than willing to organise a personality cult, and to extol the qualities of 'the Leader' to the virtual exclusion of the policies he was proposing.

By 1988, François Mitterrand's political career in the Fifth Republic had demonstrated his capacity to adapt to changing political circumstances. He was one of the first politicians to respond with shrewd acceptance of the new 'rules of the game' implied by the presidential election. His status as presidential leader of the left for most of the period after the first direct election of the President in 1965 was of immense political benefit to him. During the 1970s, it enabled him to construct a new Socialist Party which, unlike its predecessor, the SFIO, was itself a product of the new political conditions of the Fifth Republic. Despite the PS's theoretical opposition to presidential institutions, and despite the variety of the factions which composed it, it gradually became a subordinated instrument of Mitterrand's will, especially after the left's victories in 1981. Once elected President, Mitterrand initially accepted, de facto, the executive presidency which had been established by his three predecessors. Nonetheless, as his seven-year mandate progressed, a new definition of the presidency began to emerge whereby the President was less anxious to immerse himself in every aspect of government policy and keener to portray himself as being 'above' the political fray. This evolution began during the premiership of Laurent Fabius (1984 to 1986), but reached its culmination during the period of *cohabitation* (1986 to 1988), when Mitterrand had lost the essence of his executive power. As his real power waned, so his symbolic status soared, carrying him back to the Elysée in May 1988, and the beginning of his second seven-year term.

NOTES

1.   'Dès 1962, c'est-à-dire depuis qu'il a été décidé que l'élection du président de la République aurait lieu au suffrage universel, j'ai su que je serais candidat'. François Mitterrand, *Ma part de vérité* (Paris, Fayard, 1969).

2.   See F. Mitterrand, *Ma part de vérité* (Paris, Fayard, 1969).

3.   The anti-Gaullist Conservatives, right-wing Radicals and remnants of the Christian Democratic *Mouvement Républicain Populaire* (MRP) of the Fourth Republic were usually labelled 'centrist' from 1962 onwards.

4.   Gaston Defferre was the first Socialist personality to recognise the importance of the new presidential system for an attempted realignment and modernisation of the party system. After pressure from the journal *L'Express*, which had named a Mr X (which, it soon transpired, was Defferre) as the ideal candidate to confront de Gaulle, Defferre declared his intention in 1963 to stand against de Gaulle for the presidency in 1965. His decision took the SFIO leader, Guy Mollet, who was constrained to support the initiative, by surprise. Defferre's bid failed for two principal reasons. Firstly, he made his presidential candidacy conditional on the creation of a 'large federation' composed of the SFIO, the MRP and the Radical Party. This ambitious initiative foundered over whether the word Socialist should appear in the title and over the issue of reform of the church schools, upon which the SFIO could not agree with the other parties. Secondly, both Mollet's SFIO and the PCF (against whom Defferre's initiative was aimed) were determined to sabotage Defferre's bid. Realising the insuperable obstacles he faced, Defferre withdrew his candidacy, and left the way open for Mitterrand.

5.   The system, first used in 1965, provided for two ballots. To be elected on the first round, a candidate needed to obtain 50% (+1) of the votes and at least 25% of registered voters. Should no candidate have fulfilled these requirements, the two leading candidates contested a second ballot run-off two weeks later at which the candidate with a majority was declared elected.

6.   The main components of the new Socialist Party (with their dates of joining in brackets) were: the Socialist Party (SFIO), which traced its roots back to 1905 (1969); Mitterrand's CIR (1971); Alain Savary's *Union des Clubs pour le Renouveau de la Gauche* (UCRG, 1969); Jean Poperen's *Union des Groupes et des Clubs Socialistes* (UGCS,1969) and the minority of the *Parti Socialiste Unifié* (PSU) which followed Michel Rocard into the PS after Mitterrand's 1974 campaign (1974).

7.   The 1969 presidential election was also the occasion which launched Michel Rocard, then PSU leader, into a long presidential orbit. Rocard polled 3.7%, not far short of Defferre's 5.1%.

8.   At the Epinay congress in 1971, Mitterrand (with 15% of party mandates) allied with the SFIO minority based around Mauroy and Defferre (30%) and the left-wing ginger group CERES (8.5%). A common determination to rid the new party of Mollet's influence united these opposing factions. The defeated minority was composed of Mollet (the SFIO leader since 1946) in alliance with Alain Savary, the PS leader from 1969 to 1971 (34%), and Jean Poperen (12%).

9. Under the second ballot electoral system used for legislative elections, taking into consideration the bipolar manner in which it has operated throughout most of the Fifth Republic, it would have been electorally disastrous for the PS and the PCF to maintain their candidates against each other on the second ballot and allow the election of right-wing candidates on a minority of the vote. This does mean that the second ballot system is by definition bipolar. See A. Cole and P. Campbell, *French Electoral Systems and Elections since 1789* (Aldershot, Gower, 1989).

10. The balance between the two parties during these legislative elections was as follows:

	PCF	PS+MRG
1973	21.4	18.9
1978	20.6	24.9
1981	16.1	37.7

    The inclusion of the left-Radicals (MRG) within the Socialist total gives a more accurate picture than the PS figure alone, since in each election the PS withdrew in a number of constituencies in favour of the MRG. The MRG represented that fraction of the Radical Party which split in 1972 to support the PS, the PCF and the Common Programme. That the PS was able to associate itself with the PCF was facilitated by the continuing existence of a well established Marxist tradition within the French Socialist movement, which was best expressed during the 1970s by the left-wing CERES faction.

11. A detailed analysis of the changing policies of the 1981 to 1986 left-wing governments lies outside of the scope of this study. See D. Bell and B. Criddle, *The French Socialist Party: The Emergence of a Party of Government* (Oxford, Clarendon Press, 1988).

12. The author suspects that this temporary rallying of the PCF, which is limited to a strengthening of its existing bastions, is a conjunctural factor (contingent on Mitterrand's centrist-style presidential campaign and his call for an opening to the centre), rather than a structural reversal of the party's long term decline.

13. In each of these contests the PS progressed at the PCF's expense, although this was not always immediately apparent (for example in 1977). During this period the PS established a 28-31% average in the opinion polls, whereas the PCF stagnated at around 19-21%. See R. Johnson, *The Long March of the French Left* (London, Macmillan, 1981).

14. On changes in French society, see H. Mendras, *La deuxième révolution française* (Paris, Gallimard, 1988).

15. The expression is Roland Cayrol's: 'La direction du Parti Socialiste: organisation et fonctionnement', *Revue Française de Science Politique*, 28, 2 April 1978.

16. The leadership was dominated by a new generation of Mitterrandists, the *sabras*, whose political experience had been limited to the post-1971 party. Mitterrand relied on such politicians to forge a PS which was totally loyal to him. The two most prominent *sabras* were Lionel Jospin (party leader from 1981 to 1988) and Laurent Fabius (Prime Minister from July 1984 to March 1986).

17. See Cole and Campbell, *op. cit.*, Chapter Eight.

18. On the complicated question of relations between the party and the President, see, *inter alia*, J. Charlot, 'Le président et le parti majoritaire: du gaullisme au socialisme', *Revue Politique et Parlementaire*, 905, August 1983; J. Lhomeau 'Le gardien laisse sa marque' in 'Bilan du septennat. L'alternance dans l'alternance', *Le Monde: Dossiers et Documents*, 1988. Socialist deputies initially revolted against Mitterrand's proposed general amnesty for the rebellious officers of the French army in Algeria who had

attempted to forestall Algerian Independence in 1961. The PS parliamentary group eventually fell into line.

19. PS leader Lionel Jospin was coopted by Mitterrand in January 1981. Mitterrand's trusted allies controlled the parliamentary party (P. Joxe, then A. Billardon) and the presidency of the National Assembly (L. Mermaz). Fabius's replacement of Mauroy as Prime Minister in July 1984 completed Mitterrandist supremacy.

20. There were occasional resurgences of the factional disputes that had characterised the PS before 1981 (by Chevènement's CERES in 1983 to 1984 to protest against the new economic policy, and by Michel Rocard, who resigned from Fabius's government in April 1985 in ostensible protest against the government's adoption of proportional representation for the 1986 legislative elections).

21. Six months before the 1981 election, Mitterrand defined the Fifth Republic as a 'popular monarchy which is not even popular'. Cited in C.Nay, *Les sept Mitterrand* (Paris, Grasset, 1988).

22. During the 'state of grace' from 1981 to 1982 the role of the Prime Minister in settling interministerial disputes increased considerably. There was a steep increase in the number of interministerial committees chaired by the Prime Minister to iron out disputes between government departments, and a corresponding decline in the number of interministerial councils, which, chaired by the President or a member of the President's staff, had played a role of unprecedented importance under Giscard d'Estaing.

23. The nomination of two 'superministers' personally supervised by Mitterrand (the Minister of Finance, Jacques Delors, who had responsibility for carrying out the new economic policy, and the Minister for Social Affairs and National Solidarity, Pierre Bérégovoy) testified to the lessening of Mauroy's authority as Prime Minister after March 1983. These two 'superministers' worked in close collaboration with Mitterrand.

24. In September 1987, Mitterrand claimed: 'Working in collaboration with Pierre Mauroy and then Laurent Fabius, I attempted to fulfil my duty in such a way that the President presides, the government governs and parliament legislates. I have protected the major functions performed by the President, in particular the concentration on great national issues, which stem from the constitution, and especially from article 5.' (cited in 'Le Bilan du septennat', *op. cit.*, p. 37).

25. For example, Mitterrand resented Fabius' assertion of his independence from the Elysée early after assuming office - *lui c'est lui, moi c'est moi* - as well as his failure to control the Greenpeace affair (Summer 1985), and his criticisms of the President for receiving the Polish leader, General Jaruzelski, in December 1985. Mitterrand responded by refusing to accede to Fabius' demand that he, Fabius, should lead the PS campaign in the 1986 legislative elections.

26. 'Les Français ont l'impression d'avoir gagné avec moi un arbitre, d'avoir retrouvé une fonction arbitrale. Je dois à la fois marquer des domaines essentiels, ceux qui relèvent des pouvoirs du président de la République definis par la constitution. Et pour tous ceux qui sont minoritaires, je dois exercer ce pouvoir arbitral, représenter les categories de Français qui pourraient souffrir d'un manque de justice.' (cited in H. Portelli 'Les conquêtes tranquilles du premier ministre', *Projet*, 202, December 1986).

27. 1986-1987 figures from J.-L. Parodi, 'La France de la cohabitation: Profil de l'année politique (1986-1987)', *Pouvoirs,* 44, 1988. Figures for 1983-1985 from O. Duhamel and J. Jaffré, *Le nouveau Président* (Paris, Seuil, 1987) p. 81.

INDICATIVE BIBLIOGRAPHY

Bell, D., and Criddle, B., *The French Socialist Party: The Emergence of a Party of Government* (Oxford, Clarendon Press, 1988).

Charlot, J., 'Le Président et le parti majoritaire: du gaullisme au socialisme' *Revue Politique et Parlementaire,* 905, August 1983.

Cole, A., *Factionalism in the French Socialist Party, 1971-1981* (Oxford University, Unpublished D.Phil thesis, 1985).

Daniel, J., *Les Religions d'un Président* (Paris, Grasset, 1988).

Duhamel, O., and Jaffré, J., *Le nouveau Président* (Paris, Seuil, 1987).

Gaffney, J., *The French Left and the Fifth Republic* (London, Macmillan, 1989).

Giesbert, F., *François Mitterrand, ou la tentation de l'Histoire* (Paris, Seuil, 1977).

July, S., *Les années Mitterrand* (Paris, Grasset, 1986).

Le Monde, Bilan du septennat 1981-1988. L'alternance dans l'alternance (Paris, supplément aux dossiers et documents du *Monde,* 1988).

Mitterrand, F., *Ma part de verité* (Paris, Fayard, 1969).

Mitterrand, F., 'Journal sur les institutions', *Pouvoirs,* 45, 1988.

Nay, C., *Les sept Mitterrand* (Paris, Grasset, 1988).

Parti Socialiste, 'Les '110 propositions' de François Mitterrand', *Le Poing et la Rose,* 91, 1981.

Pfister, T., *La vie quotidienne à Matignon au temps de l'union de la gauche* (Paris, Hachette, 1985).

Part Two: The Actors

3 Television and the presidential elections April-May 1988

SUSAN HAYWARD

> 'Up until now I've voted for Mitterrand with my eyes shut, now I plug my ears too!' **Guy Bedos**[1]

This playful remark, made by Guy Bedos in April a few days before the first round of the presidential elections, was soon to become common currency in Paris and elsewhere in France. In a campaign which relied heavily upon a form of slogan-packing more suited to the sales marketing of fast-food than to political ideology, Bedos was not incorrect to point to the ludic (some might say, ludicrous) nature of the election, an election which many commentators felt was fought less on ideological grounds or 'real issues' that on the basis of personalities.

Personality politics is not a new phenomenon. However, the advent of television has brought in its wake a more extended theatre and repertoire. The number of actors on stage and therefore visible to a mass audience is greater than at any other time in political history. It is obvious too that, because television is an entertainment media, its effect on political personages will be one of mediatisation - whether perceived as good or bad, politicians have had fame or notoriety thrust upon them. In much the same way as the stars of the silver screen before them, they are stars of the small screen and subject to the same scrutiny as their predecessors. The United States was the first country to exploit television as an instrument of mass communication capable of mediatising political events, starting in earnest in the mid-1950s. France did not lag far behind, but, because television was at that time completely state controlled, the exploitation of the medium was more evidently politicised. Indeed, it was de Gaulle who first perceived of television as the instrument *par excellence* for putting across the presidential image and message to the greatest number of the electorate (by 1962, the number of television sets in France had more than quadrupled, from 800,000 to four million).

Studies have revealed that although television does not make an election, it does greatly contribute to reinforcing the individual voter's opinions of a particular candidate.[2] Whilst not evidently a decisive factor in the outcome of an election, nonetheless, television has influenced the modalities of elections: because television is an instrument of mass communication, it has become the main arena where the election is fought out, and this fight has to be battled out in a way that is consistent with the exigencies of this particular media. In this regard, television has fundamentally altered the way a political campaign is constructed and the way in which it is understood by the electorate. Since television's primary function is to entertain and inform (inform, but in an entertaining way), its impact upon elections has been to transform some of their essential characteristics. Increasingly, hustings and meetings - the old style of electioneering - have diminished in significance (with the exception of the PCF). The electorate, for the most part, stays at home and television relays the campaign into their homes. The formatting of election campaigns must, as I have said, bow to the exigencies of television; this essentially means their being transformed into spectacle. Because politics have become personalised, the way in which the rivalries between the various political personalities is now played out have changed: where once the posturing (in the sense of an ideological stance) of a candidate was all important, now it is the positioning of the *self* in the public eye that matters; and to create an image suited to television, a candidate must pay scrupulous attention not only to positioning, but also to the *mise-en-scène* of his or her campaign and to his or her morphology. These three terms are crucial to an understanding of how television has changed the modalities of elections and as such require an explanation.

Making the Image: Positioning, Mise-en-scène and Morphology of the Candidate

The first term, **positioning**, operates on both the political and the personal level. Political positioning refers to a candidate's political beliefs, personal positioning to his or her personal qualities. In order to be successful, a candidate's positioning has to be simple (that is, not confused or contradictory) and be *seen* to be answering to the expectations of the electorate. In this respect, the electorate (or the assumptions about the electorate) creates the image to which a candidate is expected to match up. Good positioning relies on four factors, some relating more to the political, others more to the personal, and they are: simplicity, allure, credibility and distinctiveness.[3] As we shall go on to show, at least two of the main presidential candidates (Jacques Chirac and Raymond Barre) failed to meet some of these criteria.

These key terms need a brief explanation. 1) Simplicity means simplicity of the message. It is evident that the viewing electorate will only retain a little of what is said during a televised debate or election broadcast; it is, therefore, vital to decide beforehand what that 'little' will be. Interestingly, in the 1988 presidential election, the very format of the election broadcasts (each evening the election broadcast addressed only one topical or political issue) should have meant that all candidates observed this first golden rule of positioning. However, despite this simple format, a tendency on the part of some candidates to be verbose (Jacques Chirac) or too detailed (Raymond Barre) meant that they ran the risk of losing the electorate's attention. 2) To have the prerequisite allure, the candidate's positioning must correspond to the concerns and attitudes of the electorate. The success of the Jean-Marie Le Pen campaign in the first round attests to a correct reading of some four million voters' preoccupations. Unemployment and immigration were key concerns to some 14% of the voting public - concerns to which Jean-Marie Le Pen's quick-fire slogans (for example: three million immigrants = three million unemployed, get rid of the former and France will be free of the latter) appeared to provide realistic answers. 3) Credibility can only be assured provided the stand of the candidate is consistent with his or her past actions. However, inconsistency, too much self-satisfaction and not enough humility could be fatal here as we shall observe when we examine how Jacques Chirac attempted to establish his credibility, and, more specifically, re-establish his credibility in the final stages of the second round of the election. 4) Finally, a candidate must have qualities which distinguish him or her from the other opposing candidates: greater aptitude, greater understanding, more experience and so on. On this particular issue of difference, it is worth noting that, of the main candidates, only two - François Mitterrand and Jean-Marie Le Pen (who, as I shall explain later, became a main candidate after the fact) - were able, but for very different reasons, to play this card of distinctiveness.

The second aspect of television's legacy to election campaigns is *mise-en-scène*, the staging of events by political personalities in order to gain television coverage. *Mise-en-scène* falls into two categories. The first is the construction of pseudo-events designed to coincide with news coverage, and takes the form of impromptu walk-abouts, visits by candidates to disaster areas, schools and so on. The second is the construction, real this time, of a backdrop or stage for the political rallies held by the various candidates. Again, these rallies will be timed to coincide with news coverage.[4] The first category is the cheapest form (economically speaking) of free publicity and one which Mitterrand put to extraordinary effect in 1981: whilst Valéry Giscard d'Estaing spent a fortune on staging meetings, François Mitterrand, who had (by far) fewer financial resources than his rival, went on numerous 'solitary' walk-abouts. In this respect, economic exigencies served François Mitterrand's image well: reality (few resources) created the myth of a dignified, solitary statesman not concerned with nor needing razzmatazz to explain his political and personal positioning to the electorate. Interestingly, Raymond Barre adopted this campaign style for his 1988 presidential bid. However, its adoption did not serve him well: the solitary image projected this time served only to reinforce perceptions of Raymond Barre as aloof and out of touch with the electorate. Raymond Barre had refused to mediatise his candidacy. However, television - because its technology evolves so rapidly - forces change in campaign styles from election to election (it is also true that the electorate expect something different). By sticking to the old style of electioneering, Raymond Barre did little to dispel the image of the stuffy, old-fashioned professor which the electorate had formed of him.

The second category of *mise-en-scène*, political rallies, creates a media event which is expensive but which obtains free television coverage. Neither François Mitterrand (so different were his financial circumstances from 1981) nor Jacques Chirac spared any expense in the 1988 campaign. For François Mitterrand's inaugural campaign speech at Rennes (8 April 1988), Jack Lang (at that time the former Minister of Culture) enlisted the talents of the architect Christian de Pavillon.[5] The *mise-en-scène* at Rennes was deliberately designed to echo the long tradition of republican values in much the same way as the *Grandes machines* paintings (post-1789) of David and Delacroix (notably, *Liberty leading the people*) were the first representations of the new-born *République*. In fact, reference to Delacroix' painting was quite intentional, the *mise-en-scène* (for this and all subsequent rallies) looking for all it was worth like a gigantic tricolore flag. The floor space and long stairway to the podium were in blue and the background made up of 46 red, white and blue flags so designed to appear as if they were flying in the wind in a manner directly reminiscent of the flag held by Liberty in Delacroix' painting. The podium (in tricolore) placed François Mitterrand centrally within the red, white and blue of France's national colours thus signifying that he was the natural and legitimate heir to that long tradition of republican values. Later in this chapter we shall see how his election broadcast reflects this same conflation of meaning.

Jacques Chirac's *mise-en-scène* for his rallies was a mock-up of a television studio. In this mock-up studio, Chirac sat up on stage, relaxed and holding the microphone, and fielded questions invited from the floor. The audience of supporters were treated more to a television chat show than to a traditional rally. Conceptually more modern and high-tech than Mitterrand's *mise-en-scène*, it certainly reflected the candidate's voluntarist image of dynamism. Given Jacques Chirac's profound mistrust of television, this intertextuality (television referring to television) is not without interest. It is well documented that Chirac's televisual image is that of an aggressive politician.[6] The idea behind the mock-up studio was to make the simulacrum of television signify or stand for real television. News coverage of his rallies (i.e., television filming the simulacrum, with all the complex meaning that that entails) would reveal Jacques Chirac as the great communicator, in fact the smiling, relaxed Prime-minister candidate of his posters.

In both instances the spectacle gets more attention than what is said, the peripheral becomes the substance; presented as they are as news items, they provide an excellent example of how television mediates reality, how it constructs a reality and ultimately controls our interpretation. In exchange, the candidates use the media to make sure the electorate receive the desired meaning: 'my candidacy means this' - in Jacques Chirac's case: 'We will go further because I am modern and dynamic'; in François Mitterrand's: 'France will be united because I am the legitimate heir of all republics past'.

The third aspect of image making, the **morphology of the candidates**, is a particularly televisual phenomenon and addresses the issue of the signification (different levels of meaning) of facial gestures, body movement and dress code. I shall go into greater detail on this aspect of image making below but will cite here one example by way of illustration of what is meant by morphology; it is François Mitterrand's notoriously badly cut, ill-fitting, old-fashioned jacket which he wears when he is at Latché, his country residence and rural retreat. The jacket seems anachronistic until we stop to consider that two of the key planks to his campaign are 'continuité' and 'rassembler'. On a first level of signification, his jacket denotes the past (because of its outmodishness), on a second, it connotes rural France and a return to the roots (because it is associated with Latché where François Mitterrand meets up with old friends and those who work his farm),[7] but because it is worn by the *actual* President of the Republic it becomes a sign of mythological proportions whereby we apprehend the meaning of François Mitterrand as the site of France, past and present. He is both the past and present generations - all generations united in one - he *embodies* the 'génération Mitterrand'.[8] The 'Father earth', patriarch of a generation, will guarantee France its unity and continuity.

Indeed, François Mitterrand's entire television campaign reflects this desire to be seen as the only candidate who can unite France. His diversified image shows the multi-dimensionality of the President-candidate. This seeming paradox of unity and diversity must be seen in the light of his above-mentioned planks of 'continuité' and 'rassembler'. The image not only demonstrates that he has depth, more importantly still it signifies that he is the locus of the many aspects of France: all France united in one person. Over the weeks of the official campaign, he is seen on the television screen masterfully revealing, but with the greatest naturalness, the many images which construct his persona; he is the patriarch (*Père de la patrie, Père de la nation, Petit-père des peuples, Grand-père de l'Europe*), the gentleman farmer, the man of letters, humanist, philosopher, teacher, lawyer - so many images, all modestly displayed. A first indication that the multi-dimensional image is the one he would project is clearly implied in the subliminal message of the video clip made for him by Jacques Séguéla for the first round of the presidential election. The clip is a photo-montage of 800 images and lasts 90 seconds. For marketing purposes 'montage' is a very effective visual method of getting a message across subliminally. 'Montage' is based on the Eisensteinian principle of collision editing: one image is juxtaposed to the next and the collision of the two meanings of the separate images creates a third meaning. In Séguéla's clip an excitingly fast-edited photo-montage, with an appropriate sound and music track, links together images starting with those of the Revolution, proceeding all the way through images of great moments in France's political, social, technological, sporting and cultural history, ending on a shot of François Mitterrand and Helmut Kohl holding hands. The whole montage is summed up by the last image which is of François Mitterrand's election poster - a dignified profile of François Mitterrand, and inscribed beneath 'La France unie'. The overall message is clear, François Mitterrand is the legitimate site for this great republican heritage and the man who can unite France in all its diversity. His credentials as *homme d'Etat* are irreproachable.

If during the election campaign period François Mitterrand disclosed the many facets of his being, a similar disclosure did not occur for his two major opponents Raymond Barre and Jacques Chirac (a point I shall return to later in this chapter). The very difference between the style of the three initial declarations of the candidates' intention to run for the presidency point to the President-candidate's distinctiveness. The modesty of François Mitterrand's almost inadvertent 'oui' in response to a reporter's question in an interview on *Antenne 2*'s evening news (22 March 1988), because of its surprise value - both in form and content - was a masterful stroke of mediatisation against Jacques Chirac's own televised declaration. The timing of the declaration itself was unexpected, although it is clear from the unusually high audience rating for *Antenne 2* on that evening (57% of the total viewing audience as opposed to its more normal rating of around 26%) that the general public were anticipating a *coup médiatique* of some sort; unexpected also was the tone (described by some newspapers as almost virginal 'le oui d'un jeune marié'.[9] The natural, unforced disclosure of his candidacy measured strongly against the steeliness of Jacques Chirac's televised performance and, too, compared more than favourably with the tone of Raymond Barre's benign professorial declaration. Jacques Chirac's performance had none of the *naïveté* or ingenuousness of his Socialist opponent. It was, in fact, a formal declaration filmed at Matignon and not a live interview with a journalist (as was the case with François Mitterrand), and it took three takes before he was satisfied. The first take was judged too hard, the second seemed acceptable, but a third take was made just for safety's sake.[10] The surprise factor of François Mitterrand's 'oui' also had the mediatic effect of dramatising what was already known. Speculation had long since been rife that the President would run for a second term, and with Jacques Chirac standing higher in the polls than Raymond Barre (SOFRES poll, 4 February 1988) and increasing his lead (SOFRES poll, 21 March 1988) there could be little doubt that François Mitterrand would feel obliged to run against a candidate whom he considered unworthy of the presidency.

The Official Presidential Election: Round One

The official election campaign started on 8 April 1988. Jacques Chirac had announced his candidacy almost a full three months before (16 January 1988), Raymond Barre a full two months (8 February 1988). François Mitterrand, by withholding disclosure of his candidacy until a very late date, played the card of avoiding too much media exposure as a presidential candidate and of obtaining the maximum as a President. The longer and the more a candidate is visible, the more chances exist to erode his or her positioning or image. There were other tactical reasons for this delay, the most significant being to give Jacques Chirac enough time to overtake Raymond Barre in the polls - a run-off in the second round between Raymond Barre and François Mitterrand would be a much closer race according to all predictions. The delay would, therefore, eliminate the stronger opponent. Furthermore, by the time the official campaign opened, Jacques Chirac would already be in danger of over-exposure; giving fresh vigour or new dimensions to an already much seen image would prove very difficult. François Mitterrand stood to gain a great deal through his unforthcomingness.

As far as the television coverage of the official campaign was concerned there were two radical changes from previous coverages. Both were the result of audiovisual legislation voted during the period of the Chirac government (1986-1988). The first change altered considerably the viewing patterns of the television audience during election time. The commission in charge of matters audiovisual, the *Commission nationale de la communication et des libertés* (CNCL), had - in keeping with Jacques Chirac's electoral promise of 1986 - overseen the privatisation of TF1 (France's first and most prestigious television channel). This meant that France's television was now firmly balanced in favour of the private sector, since (by 1987) only two out of the six existing channels belonged to the public sector. The official campaign - that is to say the election broadcasts - would, therefore, only be carried on the two state channels: A2 and FR3. For the first time since television had been involved in the coverage of the presidential election campaign, the electorate were free to choose between either American series on TF1 and M6, or a game show on *La 5*, or the presidential hopefuls. The interest of the television viewing public in the 1988 presidential election campaign for the first round dropped from a reasonable 17% of the total viewing public on the first two nights to a mere 9%. The second round sustained a more creditable interest at 13%.

The second change implemented by the CNCL also marks a greater spirit of *ouverture*. All candidates presenting themselves for election would be entitled to equal access to the state channels for their election broadcasts. In the past, air time was proportional to the percentage of votes received by a candidate at the last presidential election. Thus, for example, for the first time ever, Arlette Laguiller of *Lutte Ouvrière*, who grossed 2% of the vote in 1981, had as much time to present her candidacy as did the *grands candidats* whom she so vigorously denounced. This *décrispation* certainly gave the oxygen of publicity to small political parties and it would not be unreasonable to speculate that the ecology candidate, Antoine Waechter, profited by this. In presidential election campaigns heretofore, the voice of the Greens had been unheard. Presently, with fifteen minutes at his disposal for every slot he was allocated, Antoine Waechter had the time to present his programme - the ecology party was allowed to mediatise its political meaning.

The CNCL established the following rules for the televising of the campaign: each candidate on the opening and closing dates of the first round (11 and 22 April respectively) would be entitled to five minutes; between these two dates each candidate would be entitled to four slots of fifteen minutes, each one to be broadcast three times. These election broadcast slots could be made up of as much as 40% film footage (e.g. video-clips of the candidate in action or the photo-montage video-clip analysed earlier), but the tricolore could not be used, nor any combination of red, white and blue, nor indeed any part of the national anthem, *la Marseillaise,* on the sound track and, finally, no archival footage without the consent of those involved. The intention behind the need for consent was to prevent the campaign - at least from the point of view of the election broadcasts - from becoming a finger pointing exercise to earlier statements of opponents.[11] One of the spots could be shot outside the television studios, but no shots of the public places where the candidates exercised their functions could be screened. The film crew would be chosen by the respective candidates from a list of filmmakers established by the *Société française de production.*

A comparison between the first round election broadcast spots of the front-running candidates on just one day points, once again, inexorably towards François Mitterrand's ability to show himself as distinctive. Both Raymond Barre and Jacques Chirac position themselves in relatively similar ways and in conformity to the traditional, normative practices of an election broadcast - that is to say: a brief introduction either via a short clip or an introductory statement by a well-known personality, followed by an interview of the candidate on a particular topic by a journalist of his choosing (the only woman candidate, Arlette Laguiller, elected not to be interviewed), an interview which can be interspersed with 'testimonies' from appropriate members of the public.

François Mitterrand's opening clip of one minute and twenty seconds portrays, as we have already stated, two centuries of republican France (1789-1988). The next section, on this particular day, is an interview on the issue of Europe. The interview is conducted by a woman journalist, Marie-Laure Augry (François Mitterrand's appeal to women voters had not escaped the President-candidate's notice), and is very brief (lasting one minute and thirty-two seconds). It is followed by more film footage, this time showing François Mitterrand in action over Europe, with sound clips from various speeches. These images are visually sandwiched on the screen between two key words which change every few seconds. This section lasts three minutes nine seconds, thus leaving only a further nine minutes, out of the fifteen allowed, for dialogue. The introductory clip, as we have seen earlier, constructs François Mitterrand as the natural site for the heritage of France's republican past and present. The second filmed section is equally astutely conceived in that it allows the President-candidate to proffer his own 'testimonies' to his presidency. And the dynamism of the images, thanks to a quick editing style, is clearly intended to engage the viewers' attention in a more active way than that of the ordinary run of the mill 'testimonies' of a businessman or teacher, for example, which proliferate in other election broadcasts. It is the anti-pedestrianism of this film footage as well as the fast moving photo-montage of the initial clip which make François Mitterrand's election broadcast memorable, because remarkable in its difference.

In terms of positioning, Raymond Barre's television campaign caused him to fall between two stools. This does not necessarily explain his poorer showing in the results than previously predicted. It does, however, help to show what went wrong in his campaign. Firstly, Raymond Barre insisted repeatedly that he did not want to run a campaign on 'le Look'; he would be none other than himself. He also insisted that he was going to address the issues (especially economic where he certainly had more political credibility than his two main rivals) and indeed, in discussing problems and solutions in the light of 'l'après-8-mai' with his interlocutor, he made extensive references to all sorts of different figures and statistics. Furthermore, in terms of personal positioning, he projected the image of the honest broker. The slogan attached to him in this context was 'Barre: du sérieux, du solide, du vrai'. And in interviews of him in his political broadcast spot he is seen admitting to the fact that during his premiership, the success of his policies in certain areas notwithstanding, he failed to counter other problems. On the issue of both the political and the personal positioning, then, Raymond Barre tries to create the image of 'l'homme d'Etat', the man of integrity, and 'l'homme naturel'. However, these three caps fit François Mitterrand (as President he is the Head of State, as President-candidate he takes responsibility for the unpopularity or errors of some of his policies, and in his television appearances he makes it abundantly clear that he is being himself). Secondly, Raymond Barre's inability to project a dynamic image (for example his delivery is slow and ponderous) leaves him looking stuffy, out-moded - a man of the past. His seriousness (evoked through facial expressions and a deep censorial voice) and his solidity (whatever the camera frames of his person, his face or his body - whichever way, he fills the screen) create the image of the 'loved, but severe father-figure'. But once again, the role of the patriarch is not there for him to adopt, François Mitterrand has already fully projected his image as 'Père de la patrie', 'Père de la nation', 'Petit-père des peuples' and 'Grand-père de l'Europe' - in terms of patriarchy the President-candidate has cornered the market. Finally, on the issue of political positioning, there is little to distinguish Raymond Barre's economic theories on the one hand ('relancement de l'économie', 'taxe professionnelle') from those of Jacques Chirac, and, on the other, his proposals for fighting unemployment ('formation, investissement, recherche, innovation') from those of François Mitterrand (see Chapter Nine). In other words, Raymond Barre's campaign failed, televisually at least, because he was unable to project a positioning which would distinguish him from the two other front-runners.

Jacques Chirac's early campaign trail might well have been original enough (the roving mock television studio), although the implicit narcissism (creating his own television crew and set to televise himself) was not devoid of running the risk of presenting an image of arrogant auto-satisfaction. In fact, TF1 and A2 took a very firm stance on this self-promotioneering and refused to use any film footage that was not shot by their own camera crew. On a more abstract level of mediatisation, the circularity of the intertextual reference (television referring to television) was also not unproblematic because it begged the question: 'of the two televising activities (carried out by either Chirac's crew or TF1/A2 crews) which one, in the end, is real?'. This in turn begs the question 'is there anybody *real* there?'. And in point of fact, shortly after François Mitterrand had joined the race, Jacques Chirac decided to abandon this simulacrum and focus his attention on television purely and simply. In a similar attempt at media-hype, Chirac attempted to garner the young voters by throwing a mass meeting *soirée pour la jeunesse* (10 April 1988). This was a media-staging event worthy of Hollywood, with its huge welcoming photograph of a young Jacques Chirac adorning the massive marquee and looking for all it was worth like an entry for a James Dean look-alike competition.[12]

The brashness of these stagings is far from being in evidence in the Prime-minister-candidate's election broadcast spots. A far more traditional format is followed: image of the candidate (the photograph of his poster) plus slogan 'Nous irons plus loin ensemble', followed by dialogue with a journalist. Even his out-of-studio clip is traditionally constructed: Jacques Chirac in his home region, Corrèze, doing rural things. If Jacques Chirac adopted this tempered positioning it was because his most crucial difficulty in terms of image projection throughout the campaign was the issue of his credibility on both the personal and the political level. On the personal level, his aggressive, impetuous, tough-guy image would not project well on television. He had already experienced failure on that count.[13] In other words, Jacques Chirac could not be Jacques Chirac on television. Dissimulation on television is quickly perceived as such by the spectator because the camera will reveal it - or rather the candidate's morphology will reveal it (Jacques Chirac's famous frozen smile, 'sourire-rictus', for example). On the political level, there are two aspects to Jacques Chirac's credibility. The first is positive but limiting, the second inconsistent and therefore ambiguous. In the first instance, Jacques Chirac and his government had made security and law and order a popular issue. These were on their general election platform for the legislative elections of 1986, and, by 1988, they could point to their success in this area. Jacques Chirac was identified with that success and it was his ace card. However, candidates standing for election to the presidency must do battle on more than just one front. The objectives targeted must be numerous. Running a campaign on a single observable success will not suffice and will only serve to show up the limitations of the candidate. Furthermore, as we have already seen in the case of François Mitterrand, in order to appeal successfully to the electorate, the image candidates present of themselves must be multi-dimensional. In aligning himself with this one success, Jacques Chirac ran the serious risk of limiting his image to one facet only: the tough law-and-order man.

In the second instance, again with regard to his credibility, Jacques Chirac's governmental policy since March 1986 had often been contradictory, earning him the image of *l'homme 'virevoltant'*.[14] Catching policies on the wing or grasping at straws, whichever way the Prime-minister's leadership of the government was read, his image was ambiguous and lacked mettle. In an attempt to counter this image, Jacques Chirac's election broadcasts presented, for the most part, a lengthy litany of personal political successes in the economic and social spheres. If his first image, the law and order man, was credible, this attempt to be all things to all people was not exempt from the danger of causing incredulity. The electorate is never easily persuaded that a politician has all the answers, and Jacques Chirac's efforts to project himself as the problem-solving Prime-minister-candidate brought his image perilously close to one of smug self-satisfaction. It also led him into making promises he could not fulfil (for example his *coup médiatique* that he had clinched the deal to bring the next World Cup Football to France was nothing more than a *coup* and his impetuous claim was categorically denied by the International Football Federation;[15] and it earned him François Mitterrand's withering sarcasm that his Prime-minister's electoral promises made him resemble a 'distributeur automatique' and a 'jackpot!' [the pun was doubtless intended]).

Despite confident predictions of the outcome of the first round, the night of the election results for the first round, 24 April 1988, in terms of television coverage, was not without its surprises. But before elaborating on this point, the staging of the coverage itself merits description. Of the three television channels covering the election, TF1, A2 and FR3, we shall focus on the two major ones (only 1% of the viewing audience watched the election on FR3). TF1 opted in its run-up to 8.00 pm (when the first reading of the polls is announced) to play the card of suspense 'On peut dire qu'il y aura de très grosses surprises, sans trahir ce que sera le verdict...' ('without stating the outcome, we can say that there will be some very big surprises') - echoing the 'faux-suspens' of the pre-election campaign (will he, won't he join the race?). On A2, indirect criticisms were directed at TF1's decision to interrupt the coverage of the election first with advertisements and then later with a film. As if to underscore their own seriousness, A2's studio *mise-en-scène* was a mock-up of the National Assembly, both inside (the foreground was in the shape of a rotunda) and out (the background consisted of pillars and the outline of the façade of the Assembly). The walls of TF1's studio, by way of contrast, were entirely tiled with small square mirrors which gave a glittery glamour to the studio but which nonetheless had a distorting effect on the reflections of the various personalities (political and media alike) in the studio.

The format followed by both channels, after the initial announcement of the poll results, was for a round table debate by and between politicians and political analysts interspersed with interviews of the candidates at their headquarters and declarations to journalists by members of the candidates' election teams. Another important feature of the post-result debate was that once politicians had finished their input on one channel they would go over to the other one, thus ensuring equal air time. A2 added a circle of personalities from different sectors ranging from Yves Saint-Laurent to Harlem Désir and including Daniel Cohen-Bendit. TF1 included a new element in election coverage by setting up a series of what they termed 'Duels', that is verbal duels between representatives of opposing political factions.

The astonishing aspect of the coverage, however, was the prime position, in terms of debate, given to Jean-Marie Le Pen. On both channels, his election result was the first to be commented on. On TF1 Michèle Cotta singled it out as the first surprise (the second one being, according to her analysis, Jacques Chirac's very low score). On A2, Bernard Rapp and Paul Amar agreed that the result obtained by Jean-Marie Le Pen was 'un des événements de cette soirée'. And indeed, it becomes such. Jean-Marie Le Pen was the first candidate to make his election result speech, but, more significantly, he was the first candidate to be interviewed by journalists of the two channels. The phenomenon of his election result was the only event which spiced the otherwise fairly uneventful debate on the two channels (with the major contribution coming from a veritable slanging match between the Communist leader, Georges Marchais, and Bruno Mégret of the FN, repeated since they switched channels at the same time).

Jean-Marie Le Pen could rightfully claim a victory, and one achieved against all odds. Apart from his election broadcasts, the media had all but marginalised him.[16] And it was perhaps apposite that, on both channels, most of the attention was focused on his shock result of 14.3%. This result brought him within two points of Raymond Barre's and, with hindsight, the television channels should have placed him among the 'grands candidats' (Barre, Chirac and Mitterrand) as opposed to the 'petits candidats'. Where television coverage was concerned, Jean-Marie Le Pen was forced into a low profile campaign. The attempt to silence him, if such was the case, assuredly misfired. And it is interesting to note that it was the two candidates who fought their campaign on a low profile, one from choice (François Mitterrand), the other from necessity (Jean-Marie Le Pen), who could be deemed to have come out of the first round victorious.

So much of the television coverage of the results was given over to the relative success of Jean-Marie Le Pen that the success of the actual overall winner seemed, paradoxically, to be almost of less importance. On both channels, François Mitterrand's result was low profiled even though his result (although predicted) was an equally remarkable event given his unpopularity in 1986. This is not to say that the low profiling might not have been what François Mitterrand wanted; his campaign had been relatively low profile and both he and his party had decided that there should be no gloating in the event of success - modesty and conciliation were to be the order of the day. And the brevity of François Mitterrand's speech decried any hint of self-satisfaction.[17]

Jean-Marie Le Pen's unprecedented result makes it clear that television, because he had so little access to it, does not make an election. Under-exposure, provided the image projected is clearly defined, can in fact be to a candidate's advantage. François Mitterrand's campaign tactics admirably proved that point. Conversely, over-exposure on television, as was the case for Jacques Chirac (in both rounds), did not ultimately reap any benefit but served rather to muddle the image he sought to project. And, finally, an ostrich attitude to the use of television's mediatisation powers, as exemplified by Raymond Barre might well have cost him the run-off in the second round against François Mitterrand. It would seem clear from the above, therefore, that television has an important role to play where image making is concerned. Candidates who can position themselves well are more likely to profit from this media than those who cannot. And it could be argued that, in this respect, television has contributed not inconsiderably to the trivialisation of ideological debate. However, the immediate objection which that argument raises is that television is a popular cultural media, and therefore the inevitable outcome, once politics engages with the media, is politics as political spectacle. Television, then, shapes the modalities of an election, but it does not, as yet, foreclose the outcome. At the very most, studies have revealed that television may help floating or undecided voters in making their decision and that often, with this specific category of up to 4% of any electorate, it is the televised debate between the two main presidential contenders which most helps them come down in favour of one or the other.[18] France is one of the few Western countries to follow this formerly exclusively American electoral practice. Since the presidential election of 1974, when it was first adopted in France, tradition has placed the debate in the second round. And it is to the second round and the debate that we should now turn our attention.

The Official Campaign: Round Two

If the most mediatic event in round two has now become the debate, it is because the two previous ones (1974 and 1981) set a precedent of verbal swordsmanship where the rapier wit of one could cause humiliation for the other (as in 1974 when Valéry Giscard d'Estaing trounced François Mitterrand); or the dexterous skill of one could undo the apparently unassailable superiority of the other (as occurred in 1981, when François Mitterrand out-manœuvered the incumbent Giscard d'Estaing who was favourite to win not just the debate, but also the election - in the end he lost both).

The importance of the debate, therefore, would not be underestimated either by the two candidates, nor indeed by the television audience. The debate was shown live on the two major channels TF1 and A2 and it drew the same percentage of spectators as did coverage of the first round election results: 75% of the viewing audience watched both these media events. In fact voter turn-out and audience interest in the election coverage at the crucial moments (results, debate) point to a much greater interest in the presidential election that was originally being touted by media and poll experts.

Before turning to the actual debate, one or two points need to be made concerning the role of television journalism in the shaping of these election debates. Firstly, there is a strong symbiosis between journalists and politicians and, as a result, the nature of the debate can be quite limited and not related to the concerns of the electorate but more related to what the politicians and therefore journalists (because they cover what politicians do and say) consider to be important. Secondly, journalists have a tendency to cut debates up according to certain themes, and in this respect their way of organising debates is similar to the organisation of national news; and as with news, a reality is constructed but it is not real reality. Thus, as with the first point, the political agenda is fixed not according to what might preoccupy the electorate but according to what journalists and politicians think is important or think preoccupy the electorate. For example, in this 1988 debate between Jacques Chirac and François Mitterrand only half as much time was devoted to education and unemployment as was to immigration and security and yet those last two issues had been tackled with success under Jacques Chirac's government, so were less overriding in importance than the first two, neither of which had been dealt with successfully by any government since François Mitterrand's election to office in 1981 (parenthetically, then, the 'solved' issues were worthy of more debate than the unsolved). Thirdly, television journalism is institutional and as such has a tradition of presenting politics as a duopoly. Thus in elections, journalism will show itself, above all, capable only of transparence on a duopolist or bi-partisan position. So, for example, in the first round of the presidential election the focus was concentrated mainly on the Barre/Chirac duel and, then, in the second round on the left/right duel. The media is, therefore, as responsible as the politicians for closing the debate (i.e., limiting it to a duopoly), and it was noticeable, and remarked upon by such different protagonists in the election as Pierre Boussel and Jean-Marie Le Pen, that as candidates became increasingly unlikely to get to the second round so they became marginalised by the media. And it might be said, in contradiction with his own view that it was a conspiracy, that Jean-Marie Le Pen was marginalised far more because he was not part of the bi-polarity than because his style was not conform with political institutional practices.[19]

The extent of the journalistico-political symbiosis finds its most apposite metaphor in the fact that the televising of the debate became a news item in and of itself on the 8.00 pm news on the very evening of the debate. The total mediatisation of this political event (where, for example, is there any regard for the tradition that the presidential election places the candidates 'face à l'électorat'?) is summed up in the journalist's last comments, said in all seriousness: 'une tension règne, digne d'un combat de gladiateurs - comme si l'avenir de la France ne tenait qu'à une émission de télévision.' ('Tension reigns, worthy of a gladiator fight - as if the future of France depended on one single television programme.')

Prior to the actual debate, fixing a date presented the opportunity for a show of muscle-flexing on both sides: first Jacques Chirac said he wanted the debate to take place in the first week and as soon as possible. François Mitterrand, who had overseas engagements, agreed to the first week but on condition that it be Thursday (the date of his return). He declared that Thursday would be preferable to Friday, because a Friday meeting would be too late for official opinion polls to be published (no official opinion polls can be published in the second week). Jacques Chirac countered with a new date at the beginning of the second week, and in support of this suggested change of venue pointed to the date of publication of the *Journal officiel* (Friday, 29 April 1988) in which would appear officially the names of the two candidates. A second-week meeting would prevent public opinion from being polled on the performance of the two candidates in the debate which would be completely counter to convention and tradition. Eventually, Thursday, 28 April was agreed. François Mitterrand scores a first victory over his opponent.[20]

Next came the negotiations over the studio decor, the shape of the table, the number of cameras and the types of shots that would be allowed. We learn from the afore-mentioned 8.00 pm news item that it took five hours to agree on the first two. Three cameras would be permitted and only single shots would be allowed, no two shots. The use of single shots meant that the camera would focus only on the person speaking, there would be no cut away to see the reaction of the other candidate nor would there be any shots of the two together at the same time in a shot (i.e., no two shots). 'On est là pour honorer la démocratie' pronounced Serge Moati (the producer responsible for the televising of François Mitterrand). In effect, in withholding permission to use shots habitually associated with the shooting of dialogues or debates, the politicians were trying to prevent television from mediatising the event (making it a televised spectacle). The decision on the shots ran counter to the idea of a debate having anything to do with dialogue or exchange of ideas and could have reduced the actual debate to a series of visually very boring partisan election broadcasts. As we shall see, however, this did not happen. Nonetheless, this proscription clearly demonstrated the power ascribed to television.

The televising of the debate proper started up with a full shot (the only one until the end) of all involved: journalists Michèle Cotta (of TF1) and Elie Vannier (of A2) facing the camera, and to their left and right the respective candidates face to face over a table. The background decor was a sombre blue and the table red. To this very dignified *mise-en-scène* was added a musical score reminiscent of *Star Wars*! Let battle commence! Michèle Cotta set out the guidelines and rules and the topic areas. There were to be four sections to the debate and each candidate, added Elie Vannier, would be timed in order to ensure parity within each section. He went on to say that as journalists they would feed the questions to ensure that the debate addressed issues that the telespectator was concerned about (however, as we have already pointed out, this did not occur). Overall, the *mise-en-scène,* with the two opponents facing each other and the two journalists acting as arbiters to ensure fair play and equal time with their timing-clocks, was not dissimilar to the staging of a world chess championship. Certainly, it had all the solemnity of such an occasion. However, as we shall see, although justice may have been observed, the debate bore more resemblance to a heavyweight boxing match, low blows and all.

Obviously the point of a debate is to score off your opponent through reasoned argument or the presentation of irrefutable facts which damn your opponent's stance. Furthermore, use of language by the debaters will be precisely chosen for maximum effect, generally speaking either to privilege one's own position over the opponent or to minimise the importance of the adversary and his or her opinion. Since there are rules to a debate, these must be seen to be respected. Finally, given that the journalists are putting precise questions, it will be important for answers or discussion to bear a reasonably close relation to them.

According to an opinion poll, 42% of the people questioned thought that François Mitterrand came out the winner, 33% named Jacques Chirac and 18% saw no difference.[21] Almost a ten point gap separates the two. If we now go on to analyse the performance of the two candidates, the reason for François Mitterrand's victory will become clear. The debate was divided into four sections; section 1 was devoted to affairs of the state and state institutions, section 2 to Europe and to economic and social problems, section 3 to society, section 4 to foreign affairs and defence. At the end of the debate, each candidate would be allowed to draw a three-minute conclusion.

In the **first section** of the debate, François Mitterrand scored nine times off his opponent and Jacques Chirac two. The most important hit occurred over the situation in New Caledonia. The journalist, Elie Vannier, asks François Mitterrand what are his thoughts about two propositions put forward by the *Conseil des ministres* (to establish a mediating body and to dissolve the FLNKS, the separatist Kanak movement). François Mitterrand replies that he can have no thoughts on the matter because 'Monsieur le Premier ministre' has said nothing to him. François Mitterrand scores by showing up Jacques Chirac's lack of respect for the Constitution and pointing to his impulsive authoritarianism. Jacques Chirac tries to hit back but is unsuccessful. Furthermore he runs over his allotted time, refuses to allow the journalists to stop him and throws in a statement that all was peaceful in New Caledonia until just before the elections, insinuating that the trouble was instigated. François Mitterrand, who is calm and reason itself, hits back firmly with a lesson in history and scores again. Jacques Chirac again tries to come back but François Mitterrand puts a halt to this section: 'Arrêtons les paradoxes et continuons' ('Let's stop quibbling and move on'). And he is not finished. Told by the journalists that he has another minute and a half he retorts 'Je préfère ne pas avoir parlé une minute et demie de plus pour dire des choses aussi irréelles et *injustes* que celles qui viennent d'être prononcées.' ('I prefer not to have spoken one and a half minutes more if to do so would mean saying such false and *unjust* things as have just been said') (Mitterrand's stress).

Part of François Mitterrand's tactics becomes clear in this section. One method is to allow Jacques Chirac enough rope to hang himself. Another is to claim the role of the teacher of history and to assume the role of arbiter (all seen in the above illustration). A further method is to show how unworthy he finds his opponent and takes the form of dismissive gestures, phrases or glances (he looks to his left off-screen to an imaginary audience). On this latter point it is worth quoting just one example from this section because it is revealing. Jacques Chirac plays the tactic of comparing his record on crime and unemployment with that of the Socialists (sounding remarkably like Le Pen's balance-sheet rhetoric, he claims that there were 600 crimes per day more under the Socialists, 600 less per day under his government; unemployment up by 500 per day under the Socialists, down by 500 per day under his). To this François Mitterrand replies 'Laissez-moi vous conseiller de ne pas tomber dans ces schémas un peu trop simplistes' ('Let me advise you to not fall into these rather simplistic diagrams'). The patriarch-politician advises the aspiring pretender-son on his tactics. The dismissiveness implicit in 'laissez-moi' rather than the more courteous 'permettez-moi' coupled with the equally dismissive evaluation 'trop simplistes' amounts to a double-barrelled castigatory remark by a professor to his inadequate student. In summation, the teacher-father-arbiter dresses down the student-son.

In this first section, then, François Mitterrand positions both himself and his opponent. Aware that the election is being fought on the issue of personalities, he elects to fight the debate at the level of personal positioning. And he effectively bi-polarises personalities. Jacques Chirac has misread the game and his attempts to fight the debate by bi-polarising political stances and records will simply not succeed. Firstly, because as a debate tactic it is old hat and regressive (as François Mitterrand frequently points out during the debate); secondly, because if any political debate is to be engaged it must be in relation to the post-presidential election period - that is to say, new ideas must enter into the arena (again it is François Mitterrand who makes the point 'mais ce qui m'intéresse, la seule chose qui m'intéresse c'est l'après 8 mai' ('but what interests me, the only thing that interests me is after 8 May'), implying simultaneously that there is no uncertainty as to who will be there after that date).

Throughout the debate François Mitterrand's performance is one of confidence. On the level of discourse it is marked by a number of forms of interaction but perhaps the most important one is the use of interruption where he far exceeds Jacques Chirac (by 65% to 35%). This actually has a positive effect televisually in that it enlivens the debate; but, more significantly, it clearly demonstrates François Mitterrand's assumption of his superiority. A second aspect in terms of discourse is the ironic use of epithets. François Mitterrand insists on calling Jacques Chirac *monsieur le Premier Ministre*. Instead of ignoring it, Jacques Chirac falls into the trap and tells his opponent 'Permettez-moi de vous dire que, ce soir, je ne suis pas le Premier Ministre et vous n'êtes pas le Président de la République [...] vous me permettrez donc de vous appeller monsieur Mitterrand' ('Permit me if you will to tell you that, this evening, I am not the Prime Minister and you are not the President of the Republic [...] you will, therefore, permit me to call you Monsieur Mitterrand'). Jacques Chirac's decision to respectfully call on François Mitterrand to stop the use of epithets would indicate that he is remembering a similar event in the 1981 televised debate and that he may even be hoping to turn it to his advantage. On that occasion, it was François Mitterrand who refused to address Valéry Giscard d'Estaing as *monsieur le Président*. Monsieur Mitterrand was called to order by Giscard d'Estaing and told to show proper respect for the presidency. François Mitterrand refused and scored by showing up Giscard d'Estaing's pomposity. This time, by reversing the taunting tactic, the President-candidate scores by getting a reaction from his opponent: the subtext to Jacques Chirac's remonstration at the use of epithets is that, in this debate, both he and François Mitterrand are equals; the subtext to the President-candidate's use of the epithet is that the Prime-minister-candidate is not his equal. And François Mitterrand's ironic retort to Jacques Chirac, said in all dignified seriousness, bar the little smile on the lips, shows that he knows he has scored 'Mais vous avez parfaitement raison, monsieur le Premier Ministre'.

This type of retort also points to another difficulty presented to Jacques Chirac by his opponent. By agreeing, or by stating that there is no point each candidate saying how poorly the other has done during their mandate, or by admitting that, whilst some of his proposals were not liked, at least he did not seek to implement them if the French did not want them, François Mitterrand cannot be pinned down. He makes himself totally elusive, *insaisissable*, to the complete frustration of his opponent.

On the morphology of the two candidates, François Mitterrand's gently ironic smile on the lips (to which he often draws his opponent's - and the audience's - attention 'j'ai souri à cette expression') contrasts with Jacques Chirac's frozen open-mouthed smile. Jacques Chirac's gestures are frequent, voluble and numerous. They range from opening wide his arms, putting his hands palm down on the table, shuffling his papers, pointing with index and thumb touching at the tips, placing either an open hand (or hands) fingers outstretched (or touching at fingertips) or again a clenched fist on his chest and, finally, though not often, putting his hands together at the fingertips. François Mitterrand's are far fewer and his hands are often at rest, held together, on the table: he too puts his hands together at the fingertips but he also very frequently rubs his hands together rolling them around each other ending with the left hand holding the right; he very rarely points his index and his only other gesture is a dismissive one from the right hand. One final point on their hand gestures, Jacques Chirac uses his pen to strike off items on his pieces of paper and does so noisily and with vigour: left hand on the paper, strong gesture with the pen. François Mitterrand can be observed using his pen to write. Clearly, Jacques Chirac's gestures show him to be restless, somewhat agitated (fairly incessant movement of arms and hands), aggressive (through his pointing and via the pen), needing to control (shuffling papers, striking off items) and to impose or assert the self (the frequent pointing to himself). François Mitterrand's lack of agitation show him to be the calm elder statesman, his hand rolling and hand holding point to satisfaction with the self, as does the dismissive gesture of the right hand. Finally the presence of the pen is a masterly stroke. This must be the pen with which the *Lettre à tous les Français* was written!

To return now to the specifics of the debate: in **section two**, Jacques Chirac changes tactics and starts to put questions to his opponent. The protocol that should have been observed was that the journalists were the ones whose role it was to put the questions. The reason for this change represents an attempt to take control of the direction of the debate. Jacques Chirac may also be remembering the debate of 1974 when Giscard d'Estaing used this tactic to excellent effect against François Mitterrand. At that time, by answering or attempting to answer questions, François Mitterrand was seen to be jumping through Giscard d'Estaing's hoops. The net result was a flummoxed Socialist candidate; in 1981, François Mitterrand refused to be called on by Giscard d'Estaing to answer questions. This time, however, he does not attempt to stop his opponent, thereby showing his willingness (at least) to engage in dialogue which would presumably have the effect of making the debate less stilted. But for those spectators with a memory of the two earlier debates, this acceptance will also be read as François Mitterrand's refusal to be threatened by Jacques Chirac's debating tactics.

Having got François Mitterrand to accept his questioning, Jacques Chirac fails to come through with any powerful punch to disarm his adversary. Instead, he puts a series of duopolist questions: on the issue of taxes, he asks, will you follow a right or a left-wing policy? on the issue of nationalisation, he queries, in a catch-22 manner, if nationalisation was seen as the right policy by the Socialists how can he as a Socialist candidate approve of privatisation, will he not have to go back to nationalisation if he is to be true to his political colour? and so on. On the first question François Mitterrand replies by giving his opponent a lesson in fiscal policy, and scores. Irritated, Jacques Chirac reacts by getting tough: he points to the misery François Mitterrand's government caused to the thousands of pet owners, who are either poor or old, by doubling the VAT on cat and dog food. François Mitterrand comes back playfully by evoking something 'que j'ai entendu naguère: vous n'avez pas le monopole du cœur des chiens et des chats' ('something I heard ages ago: you haven't got the monopoly of cats' and dogs' hearts') and adds that in fact the increase was of one and a half percent not double and that in exchange a corresponding one and a half percent was taken off 'produits alimentaires, c'est-à-dire les produits de première nécessité pour les humains' ('food products, that is to say products of prime necessity for human beings'). The irony is consumate. The reference to the heart harks back to the 1974 debate when Giscard d'Estaing turned the tables on François Mitterrand by telling him what arrogance he displayed in believing he had 'le monopole du cœur des Français'. The fact that Jacques Chirac's monopoly is tied up with cats and dogs makes François Mitterrand's response very funny, as does the little lesson in fiscal policy (c'est-à-dire), and of course the President-candidate scores. Whilst the second question, on nationalisation, is being rather falteringly phrased by Jacques Chirac (he seems to lose the thread of his thoughts), it causes a little chuckle from François Mitterrand. The response of the President-candidate is just simply dismissive: he has already stated his position, the answer is no, because there cannot be 'un remue-ménage permanent' ('a constant upheaval').

At the end of this section, Jacques Chirac again insists on carrying on and refuses to be stopped by the journalists. However, as he is trying to pull off a point at the end, he once more stumbles over his words and ends rather feebly: 'chaque... chômeur... compte... vous savez'.

In total for the whole debate, François Mitterrand scores 18 points off his opponent, and Jacques Chirac 3. Jacques Chirac obtains two hits in section one and one in section three; after that, nothing, and for the very dramatic reason that Mitterrand stops him dead in his tracks in **section three** over the issue of terrorists. Already weakening at the end of section two, this time Chirac almost has the stuffing knocked out of him. Chirac starts to set up a trap by implying that the President is guilty of *laxisme* on the issue of terrorists. Mitterrand indignantly replies that he has never released or pardoned a terrorist. Chirac, believing he has snared his opponent, throws in the punch line: when you were elected, Ménigon and Rouillan were released; we eventually caught them and put them back in prison, in the meantime they had assassinated Georges Besse (Director of Renault) and General Audran. Outraged, Mitterrand immediately makes it clear that a foul has been played: 'Vous en êtes là? [...] C'est triste. Et pour votre personne et pour votre fonction [...] C'est indigne de vous !'('You will stoop to this? [...] That's sad. Both for your person and for your role [..] It's shameful of you!'). He reminds the Prime-minister-candidate of the tradition, upon the election of a new President, of amnesty for prisoners with less than a six months sentence which explains Rouillan's release, and as for Nathalie Ménigon, her release was the result of a legal decision (therefore nothing directly to do with the Head of State). But François Mitterrand is not finished and discloses an *in camera* discussion he had with his Prime-Minister Jacques Chirac over the Gordji affair (Wahid Gordji, an Iranian interpreter, was accused of several bombing attacks in Paris in 1986 and was being detained for trial. However, without any reasons being supplied, he was subsequently released in 1987, without trial, and sent back to Teheran). François Mitterrand accuses Jacques Chirac of having sent Gordji back to Iran after having told him in his office that the file on Gordji held overwhelming proof of his complicity in the spate of terrorist attacks in Paris. Jacques Chirac retorts by calling François Mitterrand to order on protocol which he has broken by revealing a private conversation. He then demands that Mitterrand repeat these allegations looking him straight in the eye. 'Dans les yeux, je le conteste' comes the President-candidate's fulminating reply. Chirac has to admit defeat: 'Passons, je ne joue pas au poker'; his planned trap having completely back-fired.

Chirac is virtually out for the count. In the last section he makes two further - one has to say feeble - duopolistic attempts to get at his opponent, but both times it is Mitterrand who scores. In the end it is François Mitterrand who has the *tonus* and mettle so much vaunted by Jacques Chirac.

The debate did nothing to harm Mitterrand's standing in the polls, but did little to enhance Chirac's position. In fact a comparison between poll figures for 15 April 1988 (Mitterrand: 52%; Chirac: 48%) and 30 April 1988 (Mitterrand: 56%; Chirac: 44%)[22] indicates a gain of four points over that period for the President-candidate, pushing his lead over Jacques Chirac to a massive 12 points.

With only ten days left before the second round, Jacques Chirac was, therefore, desperately in need of vote-catching. Just three days prior to polling day, Chirac pulled out three *coups médiatiques*. On 5 May, news that the three journalist hostages in Lebanon were freed was released. On 6 May, news was released of an assault in New Caledonia on the Kanak hostage-takers by the military which resulted in the freeing of the 23 hostages. And, finally, on 7 May, the news of Dominique Prieur's (the secret police agent who participated in the blowing up of Rainbow Warrior in New Zealand) repatriation was released. These three media events provided Jacques Chirac with a total of 17 minutes and 40 seconds of free publicity on the 8.00 pm television news on one channel alone (TF1). If they did help his electoral chances, in the final instance, it was by almost four percent in relation to the last poll taken. However, given that Jacques Chirac's standing in the polls, since early March 1988 and up to the penultimate poll of 15 April 1988, had been between 45 and 48%, it is more realistic to suppose that the debate disappointed some of his less committed supporters (thus explaining his low standing on 30 April 1988) who, nevertheless, returned in sufficient numbers to raise his final polling figure to 45.97%.

In conclusion, it would be fair to say that television did not help Jacques Chirac's campaign. But equally it must be said that he misunderstood how to use it in the light of the supreme goal in sight: the presidency of France. Certain errors can be pinpointed. Firstly, in his own election broadcasts, he should have thought through more clearly what image he wanted to present to the electorate and he should at the same time have ascertained what image the electorate wanted for its future President. In his election broadcasts, the Prime-minister-candidate remained prime-ministerial and it was acutely visible that he was not relaxed nor true to his self. His movements throughout the campaign, covered by television news, showed him to have extraordinary energy, and his last *coups médiatiques* proved that he could achieve extraordinary results. However, what his actions and movements apparently did not reveal - and, in this respect, this is precisely where he failed to convince the majority of the electorate - was that, he, Jacques Chirac, was a statesman.

Television cannot make a politician a statesman, but it can reveal that person as being such if the role is correctly assumed and acted out. All along the campaign trail, François Mitterrand kept the modest profile of a statesman carrying on with his duties and attending to the necessities of the campaign without polemicising (with the one exception in the debate, he launches no direct attacks against his opponents). Low visibility, careful positioning of the self, the convincing presentation of a multi-dimensional image, calm reassurance and clearly stated respect for the French. The electors, gratified with his *image de marque*, duly elected him President of the Republic for a second mandate (by 54.02%). In being re-elected, François Mitterrand made political history. He became the first Frenchman to be elected President twice by universal suffrage.

NOTES

1. 'Jusqu'ici j'ai voté Mitterrand les yeux fermés, maintenant, en plus, je me bouche les oreilles!', *Le Monde*, 5 May 1988.

2. See J. Blumler and D. McQuail, *Television in Politics: Its Uses and Influences* (London, Faber & Faber, 1968) pp. 51-138; A. Ranney, *Channels of Power: The*

impact of Television on American Politics (New York, Basic Books Inc., 1983) especially Chapters 3-6.

3. For this section on image-making, I am indebted to Denis Lindon's very useful study on positioning in *Media-Pouvoirs*, 9, January-March 1988, pp. 117-124.

4. This marks an interesting break with tradition and shows the importance attributed to television and live coverage. Political rallies used to be later (because of French eating habits). Now much of the television coverage of rallies comes in 'hot', to the 8.00 pm news especially.

5. It was Christian de Pavillon who staged François Mitterrand's now famous hommage to Jean Jaurès et al. at the Pantheon in 1981.

6. See the article in *Le Monde,* 18 February 1988, p. 12: 'L'obsession télévisuelle des candidats à l'Elysée.'

7. Latché in turn has a series of connotations associated with the mythology of the presidency. Since Colombey-les-deux-Eglises and de Gaulle's presidency, all candidates or incumbent candidates have adopted the tradition of a 'rural' retreat and with the exception of this last election the tradition has been to declare one's candidacy for the presidency from that retreat.

8. See Séguéla's analysis of his poster design, *Le Monde*, 22 January 1988.

9. *Le Monde*, 24 March 1988.

10. *Le Monde*, 18 February 1988.

11. The RPR in the legislative elections of 1986 had shown a clip of François Mitterrand declaring that unemployment figures during his presidency would never exceed three million, a promise he could not keep. In point of fact, a few days prior to the campaign (25 March 1988), the CNCL modified its ruling on consent stating that sound archives could be freely accessed for election purposes and added that, to give all candidates equal opportunity of access, this change in the ruling would not take effect until 18 April. There is little doubt that the RPR and the organisers of Jacques Chirac's campaign managed to bring pressure to bear on the CNCL to change the ruling, and with the clear purpose of inserting some sound recordings which would at least point to some inconsistencies on the part of the President-candidate. (see *Le Monde,* 15 April 1988).

12. This particular *mise-en-scène* was not without its resemblance to an earlier stunt involving the pop-singer Madonna ('J'aime Madonna!' shouted Jacques Chirac, greeting her on the stage). These appeals to the youth of France came as a result of advice from Chirac's daughter who told him he needed to project a positive, young image to the young first-time voters.

13. *Le Monde* (18 February 1988) documents Jacques Chirac's inability to project well on television. It is also worth pointing to the newspaper documentation surrounding the famous Chirac-Fabius televised debate in 1985. Chirac went through a media-training session worthy of a professional boxer. In fact, the debate was described in the press as a boxing match.

14. *Le Monde*, 21-22 February 1988.

15. *Le Monde*, 21-22 February 1988.

16. See *Le Monde*, 23 March 1988 and 29 March 1988.

17. This image of modest, no-triumphalism was repeated on the evening of the second round results, 8 May 1988.

18. See Blumler and Quail, *op. cit.*.

19. See Thierry Pfister's very good article on the relationship between politicians and journalists in *Media-Pouvoirs*, 9, January-March 1988, pp. 135-140.

20. The Mitterrand entourage were concerned that a late date might advantage Chirac and for at least two reasons. Firstly, there would not be enough time to counter allegations or bits of disinformation and, secondly, although official polls are prohibited in the last week of either round, unofficial or secret polls are not proscribed. And Charles Pasqua as Minister of the Interior had access to the *Renseignements généraux*, a police controlled polling institute (see *Le Monde*, 15 March 1988).

21. *Le Monde*, 2 May 1988.

22. See *Le Monde*, 15 and 30 April 1988 respectively.

INDICATIVE BIBLIOGRAPHY

Blumler, J. G. and McQuail, D., *Television in Politics: Its Uses & Influence* (London, Faber and Faber, 1968).

Brusini, H. and James, F., *Voir la vérité: le journalisme de télévision* (Paris, PUF, 1982).

Fiske, J. and Hartley, J., *Reading Television* (London, Methuen, 1978).

Hartley, J., *Understanding News* (London, Methuen, 1982).

Labbé, D., *François Mitterrand : essai sur le discours* (Grenoble, La pensée sauvage, 1983).

Masterman, L., (ed.), *Television Mythologies* (London, Comedia, 1984).

Mermet, G., *Démocrature: comment les médias transforment la démocratie* (Paris, Aubier, 1987).

Missika, J.-L., and Wolton, D., *La Folle du logis: la télévision dans les sociétés démocratiques* (Paris, Gallimard, 1983).

Ranney, A., *Channels of Power: The Impact of Television on American Politics* (New York, Basic Books, 1983).

Rolot, C. and Ramirez, F., *Choisir un président*, (Paris, Ramsay, 1987).

Smith, A., *The Politics of Information* (London, Macmillan, 1980).

4 La France unie?
François Mitterrand

ALISTAIR M. COLE

'Every individual always exercises all of
the power which has been bestowed upon
him.' **Thucydides**

'The Institutions of the Fifth Republic? I
have adapted to them because they have
been accepted by the French people.'
François Mitterrand[1]

Whenever he was asked by journalists whether he intended to stand for
reelection in 1988, Mitterrand's message had scarcely varied since March
1986: he had no personal desire to stand as a candidate, but could not totally
exclude that eventuality, depending on his assessment of the needs of France.
However, Mitterrand's auto-personality cult, and the propagation of his image
as father of the nation, by himself and his supporters, were clearly intended to
rally support for the idea of a new presidential bid. His public uncertainty as to
whether he would be a candidate in 1988 was aimed both at neutralising the
campaigns of his rivals, and at creating a powerful movement of support
within the country for his renewed candidacy.

Throughout 1987 and early 1988, political commentators were obsessed
with whether Mitterrand would decide to stand again, or whether he would
desist in favour of Michel Rocard, his only serious rival for the Socialist Party
(PS) nomination. Despite Mitterrand's renewed popularity as the arbiter
President, three main reasons might have caused him to hesitate before
declaring anew his candidacy. Firstly, the difficulty of being reelected after a
seven-year mandate could not be underestimated. De Gaulle had been forced to
a second ballot in 1965 - against everybody's expectations - and had even
considered resigning because he was backed by a minority of the overall
electorate. Giscard had failed to be reelected despite being the overwhelming
favourite six months before polling day. Mitterrand's popularity as the arbiter
President of *cohabitation* was considerable by comparison to his ratings as the
executive President for most of the 1981-1986 period (especially between
1983-1985), but not particularly outstanding in terms of previous Presidents
of the Fifth Republic. Moreover, according to every opinion poll during
cohabitation, and the results of cantonal by-elections, the left remained in a

minority in terms of voting intentions in a legislative election (although not in the presidential contest).[2]

Secondly, the campaign itself might be difficult for Mitterrand, especially if, as most commentators assumed, it forced him to descend from his pedestal as paternal leader and to defend more precise policy options.[3] The Chirac camp counted on this effect to lead to a traditional bipolar left-right campaign. However, *cohabitation* had given Mitterrand the prestige of executive power, without his having to bear the responsibility for government decisions. Mitterrand's status as President of all the French would probably enable him to avoid the campaign turning around a comparison of his governments' records between 1981-1986 with that of the 1986-1988 conservative administration, which would resurrect the old left-right cleavage. (Moreover, criticisms of his first two governments' records could even be turned to Mitterrand's advantage: unlike Chirac, Mitterrand was willing to recognise that the left had made mistakes, and that there were decent ministers within the present government, in order to stress that only he could bring about a political realignment of the type the polls indicated the electorate favoured.)

Thirdly, there were a number of subsidiary reasons for doubt. Political commentators wrote numerous articles on the 'age of the captain', or on Mitterrand's desire for retirement in his adopted *Landes* department in South-west France. However, Mitterrand's 'maturity' corresponded well with the image he portrayed in 1987-1988 of father of the nation. Amongst the other reasons evoked for Mitterrand's hesitation was his obsession with his place in history: an electoral defeat would tarnish Mitterrand's record in the history books. However, these considerations were almost certainly outweighed by Mitterrand's obsessive habit of comparing himself with de Gaulle, and by his determination to leave the PS as the natural party of government, as an un-ideological centre-left party that could occupy a widened political space between the extreme left and the centre. Ultimately, Mitterrand's decision as to whether or not to stand again decided upon one overriding factor: would he win? By March 1988 he had become convinced that he would defeat Jacques Chirac, who had established a commanding lead over his conservative rival Raymond Barre in the opinion polls.

Notwithstanding his possible motivations for hesitation, solid reasons existed to persuade Mitterrand that he should declare his candidacy. Firstly, the political setting for the 1988 campaign was more favourable to him than in any of his previous presidential election campaigns. In 1965, even the most charitable observer considered it unlikely that Mitterrand would force de Gaulle to a second ballot (although he did). In 1974, Mitterrand stood as the candidate of the united left alliance, supported not only by the PS, but by the PCF and the major trade union federations. Although this provided him with a solid basis of support (43.3%) on the first round, the PCF's backing for Mitterrand alienated too many centrist and floating voters on the second ballot run-off against Giscard d'Estaing for him to stand a chance of victory, since these electors were not convinced that Mitterrand was sufficiently independent of the PCF.[4] Finally, when Mitterrand declared his candidacy for the 1981 presidential election in November 1980, the opinion polls predicted a large victory for the outgoing President Giscard d'Estaing.[5]

The political circumstances in 1988 were far more favourable to Mitterrand. The right was divided between three candidates - Chirac, Barre and Le Pen - who, as a result of their intense rivalries, seemed intent on facilitating Mitterrand's task should he decide to stand again. Moreover, the decline of the PCF had removed one of the right's traditionally powerful arguments: the fear of Communism, which, in 1965, 1974, and even in 1981, had scared a proportion of centrist-inclined voters away from backing Mitterrand on the second ballot, had greatly diminished. Finally, within the left there was no serious rival to Mitterrand (see below on Michel Rocard).

For many non-Socialist voters, Mitterrand, as the arbiter President of *cohabitation*, had come to embody the spirit of tolerance, compromise and consensus.[6] Indeed, taking into account his dual experience as the man who presided over the left's ideological transformation from 1981 to 1986, and as the arbiter President of *cohabitation*, Mitterrand was better-placed than his main rival, Jacques Chirac, to rule over a nation in which the distinction between left and right had become blurred, and to pose as the unifier of the French people. Chirac could scarcely hope to portray this image of national unifier on account of his long standing opposition to the left, his flirtation with Le Pen's *Front National* electorate, and his confrontational style. Finally, Mitterrand was probably the only candidate who could genuinely aspire to create a new political compromise based on an opening of his future presidential majority towards the centre, and a weakening of left-right bipolarisation. Both Barre (who refused any form of *cohabitation* and had pledged to dissolve the National Assembly) and Chirac (who would automatically have a parliamentary majority if elected President) remained committed to different versions of the 'majoritarian' logic, whereby, if elected President, they could govern effectively only if they could count upon a majority of their own supporters within the National Assembly.[7]

The obvious contender for the vital centrist political space that Mitterrand was positioning himself to occupy was Raymond Barre, but he was constrained by his own vigorous opposition to the idea of *cohabitation*, a position he had cultivated since well before March 1986 in the name of preserving the presidential institutions of the Fifth Republic (see Chapter Six). Barre's past intransigence over *cohabitation* in fact made any public compromise with the left impossible in 1988, since this would involve the necessity of agreeing to some form of future *cohabitation*. Barre's stance reinforced Mitterrand's claim to be the only politician who offered voters the prospect of some form of future cooperation between moderate Socialists, centrists and 'open-minded' centre-right politicians.

In the light of his strong position, why did Mitterrand hesitate before finally announcing his decision to stand again on 22 March? Such hesitation was an integral part of his campaign strategy. That Mitterrand actually exercised the presidential function gave him an inherent advantage over his rivals, since he was able to situate himself 'above the fray', and was relatively confident that his rivals would not dare criticise the President in office. Presidential incumbency might, of course, have proved a double-edged sword: two previous Presidents, de Gaulle and Giscard d'Estaing, had postponed their election campaigns until the latest moment, and then had had to face concerted campaigns against their records in government and descend from their Elysée pedestal. However, Mitterrand had an added advantage, since he had not exercised power for the previous two years, which made it less likely that he would be effectively criticised on his governments' records.

What might be labelled as Mitterrand's 'pre-campaign' lasted for the first three months of 1988. It was characterised by three main features. Firstly, Mitterrand managed gradually to introduce the idea that he would stand again as a candidate without any serious loss in electoral support, as measured by the polls. This was achieved by promoting and consolidating his image as the President of all the French, and as the only (non-declared) candidate who could be trusted to maintain France's unity. He was helped in this task by his right-wing opponents, who were proving their unsuitability for the presidency by their internal rivalries. Mitterrand was thus the great victor of the 'pre-campaign', despite the fact that his rivals had occupied the limelight of public attention.

Secondly, Mitterrand's hesitation coincided (purposefully) with the crucial period in the run-up to the presidential election in which Chirac overtook Barre as the candidate most likely to meet Mitterrand on the second ballot. This evolution suited Mitterrand since, according to most polls, Barre would have been a more formidable opponent on the second ballot. Thirdly, Chirac's early declaration (in January 1988) polarised opinion for or against his candidacy, and thus left Mitterrand as the only genuine practitioner of *cohabitation* before the election, and the only real 'consensus' politician who offered the prospect of broader-based governments after the 1988 election. However, the phoney war induced by Mitterrand's calculated hesitation could not last forever, and by mid-March, opinion polls were showing the first signs of public irritation with his failure to make his decision known. The implicit candidate became an explicit one on 22 March. We must now turn our attention to the conduct of Mitterrand's short campaign and to the programme he presented to the French people.

La France Unie? Mitterrand's First-Ballot Campaign

Mitterrand's campaign declaration of 22 March placed him in harmony with previous Presidents, de Gaulle (in 1965), and Giscard d'Estaing (in 1981), who had both attempted to renew their presidential mandates. In fact, even President Pompidou, who died in office in 1974, had envisaged standing again in the presidential election originally scheduled for 1976. Each President has justified his decision to stand again by the argument that France must be saved from the dangers that his adversaries' victory would involve. However, before Mitterrand, no President had yet won two direct presidential elections.[8]

Mitterrand's 1988 campaign bore few similarities to his campaign of 1981. The fact that Mitterrand had presided over France during the period which witnessed the transformation of the nature of French socialism from 1981 to 1986, as well as his coexistence with the right from 1986 to 1988, had illustrated the President's adaptability. His adaptability acted as an important political advantage during the period of *cohabitation*. While *cohabitation* enabled Mitterrand to conserve (indeed, to increase) his audience amongst left-wing voters, who saw him as the only safeguard against misgovernment by the right, the impression that Mitterrand was allowing the right-wing government to govern, in a period of continuing economic difficulties during which an institutional crisis might have had damaging consequences for the nation, increased the respect with which he was viewed by moderate conservative voters.[9]

Mitterrand's recovery in public opinion since March 1986 had been partially based upon his appeal to the diffused feeling within the electorate that all ideological solutions had been tried and failed. In the course of his short campaign, Mitterrand drew upon his richly varied experiences between 1981-1988, in order to portray himself as being the only candidate who could offer a synthesis of the various policies that had been adopted, under left and right, during his first seven-year presidency. He thus attempted to respond to the large consensus on most aspects of policy which, after the contrasting experiences of 1981-1986 Socialist and 1986-1988 Conservative governments, now prevailed amongst two-thirds of French voters.[10]

Mitterrand 88 was also the candidate who, in his campaign discourse, which called for an opening of the new presidential majority to the centre and centre-right, implicitly refused the old Fifth Republic pattern of bipolarisation between the left and the right. Although Mitterrand was careful not to commit himself to future alliances too firmly in advance, the implicit promise of his 1988 campaign was that his election would be followed by a political realignment, and that a new presidential majority backing Mitterrand would have to comprise not only the PS, but also those politicians in the centre and centre-right who were willing to support the new President.[11]

Mitterrand surprised many commentators by the vigour of his entry into the campaign, when he implicitly accused Chirac of governing France in the interests of one 'faction'. In reality the tactical manœuvre was clear enough. By frontally attacking the 'RPR-State', Mitterrand was not provoking a new left-right bipolar battle, as certain commentators claimed, but (in conjunction with his moderate programme) was attempting to appeal to all good-willed republicans who were willing to believe that the Chirac government was dangerous for democracy, including those unable to support a Socialist programme. Mitterrand borrowed the theme of the 'impartial State' from Raymond Barre's campaign in a clear attempt to appeal to those centre-right electors who were unhappy with the extent to which Chirac's RPR dominated the government and the administration, who despaired of Barre's ability to defeat Chirac on the first round, and who, Mitterrand hoped, would probably prefer him to Chirac on the run-off.[12] There could have been little clearer evidence that Mitterrand considered it virtually certain that Chirac would be his second-ballot adversary. In order to maximise his chances of being reelected, Mitterrand had to avoid the campaign being reduced to a classic left-right battle, such as Chirac was preparing, not least because opinion polls continued to suggest that the left (PCF, PS) remained in a minority within the country at large. The central objective of his campaign declaration, which sought to cultivate the divisions that existed within the right-wing electorate, was precisely to blur the distinction between the moderate left and the centre-right electorates, both of which had cause for dissatisfaction with Chirac. That Mitterrand had chosen the right tone to launch his campaign was confirmed in the opinion polls: the announcement of his candidacy was not accompanied by a fall-off in voting intentions.[13] His dramatic entry into the campaign forced Chirac on the defensive.

As well attempting to build bridges with centre-right voters alienated by Chirac and disappointed with Barre, Mitterrand's declaration was also intended to reassure his left-wing electorate by adopting a clear, offensive language. These two constituencies meant that Mitterrand varied between two different campaign discourses, according to which fraction of the electorate he was trying most to woo. Nonetheless, the first, centrist-inspired discourse generally prevailed. Mitterrand's objective of opening his future presidential majority to the centre-right was implicit in his campaign slogan of *la France Unie*, which held forth the prospect of a broader based government being formed after his victory, composed not only of Socialists, but of centre-right politicians as well.[14]

The second great offensive of Mitterrand's campaign, after the declaration of his candidacy on 22 March, was the publication of his *Letter to All the French People* in nine national and regional daily newspapers on 7 April 1988.[15] The letter format symbolised the personalised nature of Mitterrand's campaign, even more so than his previous campaigns of 1974 or 1981. It was a direct communication between the providential leader and 38,000,000 French electors, rather than a party programme or manifesto, such as the '110 propositions' of 1981 had been. Policies were largely replaced in Mitterrand's letter by *priorities,* which future governments would have the responsibility of translating into legislation. In terms of policy substance, the letter made few specific promises, probably because the cumulative experience of the 1981-1986 left-wing governments and the 1986-1988 conservative administration had been to discredit detailed policy manifestos,[16] and Mitterrand's letter reflected the electorate's loss of faith with programmatic panaceas for the problems of France. Mitterrand's letter broadly called for the maintenance of the social and economic status quo, unlike his '110 propositions' of 1981, which had promised a 'break' with capitalism. Only a modest number of reforms were proposed, most of which the other candidates would have agreed with in principle. Mitterrand pledged that, if reelected, his first priority would be given towards expanding education and training, ensuring that the French welfare system (*la sécurité sociale*) was safeguarded, and that a minimum income for all French citizens was introduced. The only 'radical' reform which distinguished Mitterrand's proposals from those of Barre or Chirac was the reintroduction of the wealth tax, which, from the polls, appeared to be a popular measure. Mitterrand did not call into question most of the Conservative government's 1986-1987 reform programme, in particular its important privatisation programme of nationalised industries, although, unlike Chirac or Barre, he envisaged no further returns of state enterprises to the private sector.

Only minor details distinguished the candidates in terms of economic policy, undoubtedly because both the Socialists after 1983 and the RPR/UDF after March 1986 had led broadly similar anti-inflationary macro-economic policies. Mitterrand pledged that there would be no return to the 1981-1982 period, when the triumphant Socialists had attempted to push through a radical programme of social and economic reform, before being abruptly forced to change their policies after only one year in office.[17] Indeed, Mitterrand recognised that neither the 1981-1986, nor the 1986-1988 administrations had been able to control unemployment, whereas both could take credit in reducing inflation. The absence of controversial reforms was justified above all by the 1992 rendezvous because national unity was indispensable to prepare France for the single European market: 'The period which separates us from the creation of the single European market is too short for us to take the risks involved in overhauling the economy once again'.[18] In so far as it sought to preserve the status quo in most areas, Mitterrand's *Letter* might be considered as an attempt to attract centre-right support to his presidential bid. The core of his message was that national unity constituted the only means of preparing France for future competition and that he, François Mitterrand, offered the best perspective that this unity would be maintained.

Mitterrand's *Letter* was also interesting in that it appeared to commit the President-candidate to exercise a more limited interpretation of presidential power should he be reelected than had been the case between 1981 and 1986. Mitterrand clearly underlined in the text that the role of the President was no longer to define the details of the government's legislative programme ('the President must not govern'), but to outline broad orientations and preferences:

> I believe and I hope that whatever future majorities govern in France there will be a return neither to the absolute President of the early Fifth Republic, who in fact exercised all powers, nor to the 'impotent' President of the Fourth Republic, who had no power.[19]

Mitterrand reaffirmed presidential supremacy in matters of defence and foreign policy, but limited the President's role in domestic policy to that of 'defining the great choices', leaving the Prime Minister with the responsibility of forming a government and coordinating government policy. Mitterrand confirmed that his new Prime Minister would be given responsibility for naming a government composed of 'republicans'; and that the eventual dissolution of the National Assembly would occur only if 'the Prime Minister considers that he is being prevented from governing', a formula full of ambiguity.[20] The extent to which Mitterrand's *Letter* would act as a guide for future action in this area was uncertain. As was pointed out in Chapter Two, Mitterrand, throughout his political career before being elected as President in 1981, had consistently proclaimed the need to reduce the powers of the 'elected Monarch'. During the 'active' phase of his first seven-year term (1981-1986), however, presidential supremacy was never really in doubt.

Mitterrand's campaign strategy, as expressed in the theme of *La France Unie* and repeated with moderate stress in his *Letter*, represented an attempt to use the theme of national unity to efface the left-right conception of political divisions that had traditionally prevailed in the France of the Fifth Republic, and thus to secure support from centre and centre-right, as well as left-wing electors on the first ballot, and thereby to make himself the favoured candidate on the second round. The candidate who succeeded in uniting as broad as possible a coalition of electors around his name on the first ballot would enjoy a greatly enhanced chance of victory on the run-off. However, Mitterrand's courting of the centre-right electorate, at the expense of his more traditional left-wing base, increased the problems he faced in mobilising his own Socialist Party behind his presidential bid. The complicated relations maintained between President Mitterrand and the PS during the 1988 campaign must now occupy our attention.

François Mitterrand and the Socialist Party

By excluding the PS from a positive role during most of the campaign, and by burying traditional Socialist policies in his *Letter to All the French People*, Mitterrand succeeded in disillusioning and demobilising many Socialist activists and voters alike. The party approached the 1988 campaign after a difficult two-year period in opposition. *Cohabitation* had meant that, since March 1986, the PS had been unable or unwilling to criticise Chirac's government too directly: it could not afford to jeopardise Mitterrand's position as President, or his chances of reelection, both of which depended upon the successful duration of *cohabitation* until 1988. The PS was, moreover, searching for a new identity, after the ideological transformation it had undergone during its period in government from 1981-1986. Therefore, due to the combined effects of the 'culture of government' and *cohabitation*, the PS could no longer act as a traditional party of opposition. Since March 1986, however, neither had it been a real party of government. The result of these various pressures was that the PS that was curiously silent throughout the period of *cohabitation* and was chiefly preoccupied with not doing anything which might embarrass Mitterrand.[21]

Moreover, the pressures of the presidential election had harmed the party's internal cohesion. Throughout the *cohabitation* period (March 1986 to April 1988), the PS had been threatened with serious internal divisions over who would be its presidential candidate. Michel Rocard had made clear his intention to stand as a presidential candidate 'whatever happens' back in 1985, when he resigned as Agriculture Minister from Laurent Fabius' government, ostensibly because of his opposition to the introduction of proportional representation for the 1986 legislative elections, but in fact in order to position himself for the presidential election. The threat of a separate Rocard candidacy was diminished at the PS congress of Lille, in April 1987, at which the party's main factions came to an agreement over the mode of procedure they should follow in relation to the thorny issue of the presidential nomination.[22] In return for the final motion containing no mention of the party's desire for a new Mitterrand candidacy, which had originally been proposed by the Mitterrandist leadership, Rocard agreed to respect 'party discipline', which the PS leadership interpreted as a tacit commitment not to oppose Mitterrand should he decide to stand, and not to force the issue before the President had made his decision.

Nonetheless, Rocard did not formally disavow his previous assertion that he would be a candidate 'whatever happens' until Mitterrand's declaration that he would stand in March 1988. Despite the agreement at the congress of Lille, Rocard's launching of a renewed bid for the PS nomination during the summer of 1987 raised the prospect that the party would be seriously divided in 1988, and, even at this late stage, the possibility that a separate Rocard candidacy might split the party could not be totally excluded. However, by January 1988, press rumours began to appear that Rocard and Mitterrand had concluded a deal whereby, in return for standing down, Rocard would be named by Mitterrand to a senior post in government and a prominent role in the campaign.[23] The objective bases for a Rocard candidacy simply did not exist in 1988. Unlike in 1978-1980, Michel Rocard was shown to be a less attractive candidate than Mitterrand in all opinion polls. Once Mitterrand had succeeded in restoring confidence in his leadership amongst conservative, as well as left-wing voters, Rocard never stood a chance of securing the PS nomination, unless Mitterrand had decided not to stand. Nonetheless, Rocard performed a useful role for Mitterrand: that of a reserve presidential candidate, paradoxically taking the pressure off Mitterrand to declare his intentions until the latest possible moment.

That the PS, which, in theory, was a democratic party responsible for selecting its own presidential candidate, was so totally paralysed while awaiting Mitterrand's decision, revealed the extent to which the party continued to be subordinated to the President's influence. Moreover, it confirmed how far the impact of presidentialism had in fact emptied the idea that the party controlled who would be its presidential candidate of any real meaning. For although the PS leadership overwhelmingly backed Mitterrand, it had little influence on the President's decision whether or not to stand for reelection. To this extent, the comparisons frequently made between the French PS and the US Democratic Party, as organisations which exist primarily to select presidential candidates, is somewhat misleading, since in the Democratic Party potential candidates for the presidency have to prove themselves in a testing primary procedure.[24]

A distinction might be drawn between 1981 and 1988 in order to illustrate how far the process of presidentialisation had gone by 1988. During the struggle between Mitterrand and Rocard for the 1981 PS nomination, control of the PS leadership had been the crucial element which enabled Mitterrand to secure the PS candidacy, despite Michel Rocard's more favourable standing in the opinion polls. As a party of opposition which had yet to capture the presidency, the PS retained the power to determine who should be its presidential nominee in 1981. By 1988, however, after seven years of PS subordination to Mitterrand as President of the Republic, the PS had become a virtual irrelevance in terms of the presidential nomination, and the sole criteria which were really important were whether Mitterrand would decide to stand again, and, to a lesser extent, what Rocard's reaction to this would be.

Mitterrand's apparent hesitations left the PS in a difficult situation since the party was forced to launch its 1988 presidential campaign without knowing which candidate it would be backing.[25] However, once Mitterrand declared his candidacy, the party was pushed firmly into the background and had less input into Mitterrand's campaign than ever before. Of course, any serious presidential candidate had to appear as being 'above party', and Mitterrand had proved no exception in 1965, 1974 or 1981. In 1988, however, two additional reasons explained the party's marginalisation which had not existed in the previous elections: Mitterrand's new status, and his determination to extend his parliamentary majority well beyond the PS. A precondition of the 'opening to the centre' was felt to be the relegation of the PS to a minor role in the campaign.

The party's marginalisation during the campaign was illustrated on numerous occasions.[26] Mitterrand originally ordered that the Socialist symbol, the rose inside a clenched fist, was not to be used in his campaign propaganda material, a gesture which prompted party leader Jospin to 'take several days holiday' to coincide with Mitterrand's first public meetings. Moreover, relations between the PS leadership and Mitterrand's campaign headquarters at *Avenue Franco-Russe* were never good, and deteriorated steadily throughout the campaign. Finally, Mitterrand's *Letter to All the French People* bore little relation to the PS' own *Propositions pour la France*. The debate over the PS *Propositions* had clearly illustrated the fact that widespread hostility existed within the party towards the idea of alliances with the centre, although in the *Propositions* the PS leadership stopped short of calling for an automatic dissolution of the National Assembly in the event of a PS victory in the presidential election.[27] When Mitterrand publicly ventured the opinion that 'there are some excellent people in the present government' in his first campaign meeting at Rennes (9 April 1988), he received an incredulous reception. As the campaign progressed Mitterrand relentlessly drove home the same message, which was amplified in between the two rounds.

Before 24 April, Mitterrand was the only candidate certain to go through to the second round. This enabled him to dispense with the traditionally mobilising, partisan, first-round campaign, and to concentrate entirely on securing as broad a base as possible for the second round. Indeed, rather than upon policy, Mitterrand based his campaign on his presidential stature, and on eventual alliances after the first round, or following a presidential victory.

Nonetheless, his ambiguous message possibly overestimated the extent to which older notions of left and right had become outdated. While Mitterrand remained convinced that the second ballot had to be the focus of his campaign (and therefore emphasis had to be placed on the 'opening towards the centre'), it became evident during the last week of the first ballot campaign that too low a score on the first round might jeopardise his chances for the decisive run-off. During the last week before the first ballot, therefore, Mitterrand campaigned more openly as a centre-left candidate and allowed the PS a more prominent public role.[28]

Why Mitterrand Won

Mitterrand's first-ballot total of 34.09% was below the range that had been predicted by most opinion polls (37-40%). Nonetheless, he polled a considerably higher proportion of the vote than Giscard in 1981 (28,31%), and he was nearly 15% ahead of his nearest rival Jacques Chirac, whereas most commentators had considered that the leading right-wing candidate would have to be no more than 10% behind Mitterrand on the first ballot to stand a chance of victory on the second round. The first ballot thus left Mitterrand as the great favourite to win on the second round. That Mitterrand virtually equalled the combined support obtained by Chirac and Barre in 1988 (36.48%) suggested that the bipolar pattern of party support which had existed since 1981, whereby the bulk of the electorate selected either a centre-left PS or a centre-right UDF-RPR coalition, remained a reality, despite Le Pen's breakthrough (14.39%).[29]

The composition of Mitterrand's first round electorate illustrated that the President represented a better cross-section of French society than any other candidate. Two 'exit polls' (CSA, BVA) carried out on the first ballot gave slightly contradictory results.[30] Nonetheless, both converged in their main conclusions. The sociological composition of Mitterrand's first-round electorate is outlined in Table 1, whereas Table 2 illustrates how the 1986 legislative election vote was divided between different candidates on the first round of the 1988 presidential election. Two distinct elements could be identified in Mitterrand's 1988 first-ballot vote, a 'core' left-wing electorate, and a smaller non-Socialist one. We shall consider these electorates in turn.

The first lesson to be drawn was that a fraction of those voters who had supported the PS in 1986 refused to back Mitterrand on the first ballot in 1988: according to CSA, only 75% of those 1986 PS voters who voted on 24 April supported Mitterrand, whereas 25% voted for other candidates.[31] Nonetheless, the bulk of Mitterrand's first-round vote was provided by a core PS electorate, and he also picked up sizeable minorities of 1986 PCF, extreme left and Ecologist voters on 24 April which underlined the predominantly left-wing character of his first round electorate. Notwithstanding this, the demobilisation of a fraction of 1986 Socialist voters on the first ballot in 1988 was undeniable. This demobilisation could be explained mainly by the unwelcome ambiguity of Mitterrand's centrist-style campaign for many left-wing voters, and to some extent by the availability of alternative left-wing candidates. However, the attraction exercised by Le Pen and the other right-wing candidates on a small minority of 1986 PS voters must not be ignored.[32]

Table 1
Sociological Composition of the First Round Candidates' Electorates

	Ex.Left	Lajoinie	Mitterrand	Waechter	Barre	Chirac	Le Pen
Total	4	7	34	4	17	20	14
Men	4	7	33	4	15	18	19
Women	5	5	35	6	18	20	11
18-24	5	6	36	6	18	12	17
25-34	7	9	41	6	11	14	15
35-49	5	5	33	4	16	18	18
50-64	3	7	33	2	17	24	14
Over 65	2	7	30	1	23	26	11
Farmer	1	7	30	3	17	22	20
Bus/Commerce	1	3	21	2	20	26	27
Professions/ *Cadre Supérieur*	1	3	29	4	24	26	11
Cadre Moyen	6	4	36	6	18	15	15
Clerical Worker	6	6	38	5	16	15	14
Ind. Worker	6	15	40	2	8	8	21
Housewife	4	4	28	5	17	26	16
Unemployed	8	11	36	3	8	17	17

Source: CSA exit poll

Table 2
The evolution of electoral support, 1986-1988

Vote 16 March 1986	Vote 24 April 1988						
	Ex.Left	Lajoinie	Mitterrand	Waechter	Barre	Chirac	Le Pen
Extreme Left	48	12	16	7	6	3	8
PCF	10	73	13	1	0	0	3
PS	6	2	75	6	4	2	5
Ecologist	4	1	10	47	25	7	6
UDF-RPR	0	0	2	2	35	46	15
FN	0	0	2	1	4	3	90
Abstention	6	8	38	7	17	11	13
Too Young	2	2	34	6	18	13	19

Source: CSA exit poll.

The second component of Mitterrand's first round vote was composed of a non-Socialist, presidential, previously undecided or 'legitimist' vote.[33]

Mitterrand performed particularly well amongst those voters who had abstained in 1986, but voted in 1988 (38% compared to only 11% for Chirac, 13% for Le Pen, and 17% for Barre), as well as amongst certain social categories which were traditionally hostile to the left, such as the over-50s, farmers and businesspeople.[34] However, Mitterrand attracted most support from those social categories which had consistently been the most important elements within the Socialist electorate since the party's revival in the 1970s: low and medium status clerical workers, industrial workers, the under 35s, non-practising Catholics (41%) and atheists (42%).[35] Indeed, he made several spectacular gains within these categories by comparison with the first ballot of the 1981 presidential election, gains which corresponded to the steep decline of the PCF's audience in between the 1981 and 1988 elections.[36]

To summarise these figures, we can say that Mitterrand attracted the bulk of his electorate from those categories of the population which had traditionally been most favourable to the left, but he also garnered significant support from 'legitimist' voters, who were anxious, above all, to support the President of the Republic. However, as Table 2 illustrates, he did not perform particularly well on the first ballot amongst those right-of-centre voters who had already backed the UDF-RPR coalition in 1986, and only 2% of those voting in both elections crossed over to Mitterrand. The significance of this was considerable: despite Mitterrand's extensive campaign in the direction of centre-right voters, he was unable to capture more than marginal support on the first ballot from voters who had already backed the right in 1986. This confirmation that left and right continued to constitute electoral realities probably presaged ill for Mitterrand's chances, if reelected, of durably attracting centre-right politicians (with different electoral constituencies) to serve in his governments.

The first week of the two week second-ballot campaign saw the televised duel between Mitterrand and Chirac on 28 April 1988. Mitterrand emerged with the advantage, after cleverly exploiting his presidential incumbency to demarcate Chirac - whom he addressed throughout as *monsieur le Premier Ministre* - as challenger (see Chapter Three). And the campaign really came to life during the final few days, as the result of a bewildering series of events triggered by Chirac (see Chapter One).

Mitterrand's final score (54,02%) was in the middle range of the results the polls had been predicting (52-57%). The results of the first ballot had clearly distinguished between the two finalists by way of the sociological bases of their support. The great simplification of the second round, which reestablished an apparently straightforward contest between left and right, allowed such comparisons to be pushed even further. The sociological composition of the two finalists' electorates is outlined in Table 3.[37]

Mitterrand's electoral strongholds on the second ballot of the 1988 presidential election, were remarkably similar to those of 1981: industrial workers, low and medium status clerical workers, the under 35s, atheists (74%), and non-practising Catholics (56%). By contrast, Chirac's electorate heavily over-represented those social categories traditionally associated with the right in France: farmers, businesspeople, practising Catholics (67%), the liberal professions, and the over-65s.[38]

Table 3
The Mitterrand and Chirac Electorates Compared

	Mitterrand	Chirac
Men	57	43
Women	52	48
18-24	57	43
25-34	69	31
35-49	52	48
50-64	49	51
Over 65	46	54
Farmers	36	64
Business/Commerce	35	65
Professions/*Cadres Supérieurs*	45	55
Cadres Moyens	58	42
Clerical Workers	64	36
Industrial Workers	74	26
Retired	47	53
Housewives	55	45
Unemployed	60	40

Table 4
Vote Transfers between the 1st and 2nd Rounds [39]

1st Round	Mitterrand		Chirac	
	BVA	CSA	BVA	CSA
Extreme Left	91	-	9	-
Lajoinie	93	100	7	0
Mitterrand	99	100	1	0
Waechter	79	78	21	22
Barre	14	13	86	87
Chirac	3	2	97	98
Le Pen	26	22	74	78
Abstentionists	65	65	35	35

The key to Mitterrand's victory lay in the complex pattern of vote transfers between the first and second round (see Table 4). Mitterrand was the recipient of excellent transfers of first ballot votes from the extreme left, Ecologist and Communist candidates: the traditional left-wing theme of 'republican defence' was exploited to favour an exceptional degree of left-wing mobilisation in reaction against Le Pen's first round vote, and Chirac's attempts to attract Le Pen's voters. Nonetheless, even if, on the second ballot, Mitterrand had attracted every vote cast for a left-wing candidate on the first round, and none had abstained, this would have been insufficient to assure him of victory, since the left had been in a first round minority (45.23%).[40] Moreover, even if four-fifths of the Ecologist, Antoine Waechter's, first-round voters had transferred to Mitterrand, and none had abstained, this would still have left him well below the 50% barrier (48.2%). Even if the high degree of left-wing and ecologist solidarity with Mitterrand is acknowledged, it is clear that Mitterrand's victory depended on second round votes from three different sources: first ballot abstentionists, and those who voted for Barre or Le Pen on 24 April.

Mitterrand profited on the second ballot from a favourable distribution of votes from first-ballot abstainers who were receptive to the theme of 'republican defence', but the limited increase in the number of valid votes cast on the second ballot (around 500,000) undoubtedly meant that this gain would have been insufficient to give Mitterrand a majority. In fact, the 4-5% which gave Mitterrand victory came from voters who had backed Barre or Le Pen on the first round. A minority of Le Pen's first-ballot support transferred to Mitterrand on the run-off (22% [CSA] or 26% [BVA] of those who voted on the second round). These 'Lepeno-Mitterrandists' were overwhelmingly ex-left-wing voters from popular social strata (industrial or clerical workers), who sided with Le Pen over immigration and security issues, but the left in terms of social justice and anti-conservatism.[41] Finally, Mitterrand captured the support of 13-14% of Barre's first round total that voted on 8 May. Nonetheless, Barre's first round electorate transferred far more solidly to Chirac on the second ballot in 1988 than Chirac's first ballot voters had done to Giscard d'Estaing on the run-off in 1981, or, arguably, than Chaban-Delmas's electors had switched to Giscard on the second round in 1974.[42]

Mitterrand's second round total thus extended largely beyond the ranks of the left. From the above evidence, the heterogeneity of Mitterrand's second-ballot coalition was obvious. His reelection as President paid tribute to his capacity to unite a broad second-ballot coalition around his candidacy, ranging from the extreme left to elements of the centre-right, and, indeed, extreme-right. To this extent, his constant positioning as President of all the French people during the preceding two years had paid dividends, whatever the differing motivations of the various fractions of his second-round electorate were.

The margin of Mitterrand's reelection was greater than that of any President since de Gaulle in 1965. But it was precisely the heterogeneity of this second ballot electoral coalition which was likely to cause Mitterrand problems in the future. According to the exit-poll conducted by BVA, a substantial percentage of those electors who backed Mitterrand on the run-off declared their vote to be a negative one, intended primarily to bar the way to Chirac, rather than express confidence in Mitterrand's personality or ideas.[43] Moreover, the different components of Mitterrand's second-ballot coalition held differing expectations of what his new *septennat* would achieve, or should attempt to achieve. Mitterrand had clearly managed to mobilise against the danger represented by Chirac, but it was difficult to speak of a completely unified *rassemblement* supporting the President on the basis of ideas he had canvassed during the campaign.

Analysis of the complicated period which began with Mitterrand's reelection as President lies outside of the boundaries of the present study.[44] Nonetheless, it seemed clear that his composite coalition would be difficult to manage, whatever political circumstances prevailed. Whether the electoral coalition which came together to reelect President Mitterrand on the second ballot could hold together (and if so for how long), and whether his presidential victory would eventually succeed in provoking a lasting realignment in French politics, based on closer cooperation between the Socialists and the centre, were the salient questions which remained unanswered in the immediate aftermath of Mitterrand's reelection.

NOTES

1. 'Les institutions ? Je m'en accommode, puisqu'elles ont été acceptées par les Français', *Paris-Match*, March 1984.

2. The poll in this paragraph is from O. Duhamel and J. Jaffré, *Le nouveau Président* (Paris, Seuil, 1987), and J.-L. Parodi, 'Sept ans de restructuration de l'opinion', *L'élection présidentielle 1988* (Paris, *Le Figaro*/Etudes Politiques, 1988).

3. In fact, the convergences between the three main candidates' programmes in 1988 were more remarkable than their divergences. Conflict over policy was less important than during any previous presidential election in which Mitterrand had been a candidate.

4. See P. Lindon and D. Weill, 'Pourquoi M. Giscard d'Estaing a-t-il gagné?', *Le Monde*, 22 May 1974.

5. See H. Machin and V. Wright, 'Why Mitterrand Won: The French Presidential Elections of April-May 1981', *West European Politics*, 5, 1, January 1982.

6. J.-L. Parodi, 'La France de la cohabitation. Profil de l'année politique 1986-1987', *Pouvoirs*, 44, 1988.

7. See Duhamel and Jaffré, *op. cit.*, Chapters Ten and Twelve.

8. De Gaulle had been indirectly elected as President of the Republic in December 1958 by an electoral college composed of 80,000 local, departmental and national elected officials.

9. See J.-L. Parodi, 'Sept ans de restructuration de l'opinion', *L'élection présidentielle 1988* (Paris, *Le Figaro*/Etudes Politiques, May 1988).

10. See Duhamel and Jaffré, *Le nouveau Président, op. cit.*, Chapter Two, for details of this consensus.

11. Mitterrand's announcement in his *Letter to All the French People* (see below) that he would form a government composed of 'republicans' should he be reelected; along with the attempts made by Rocard to attract centre and centre-right politicians to serve in his governments, provide evidence to support this view.

12. See S. July, 'La campagne turbo', *Libération*, 23 March 1988, and, 'La diagonale de Mitterrand', *Libération*, 24 March 1988.

13. See J.-M. Colombani, 'Les réactions des Français à la candidature Mitterrand', *Le*

Monde, 25 March 1988.

14. Depending upon their political stances, most commentators tended to interpret Mitterrand's promise of an opening to the centre either as the prelude to the emergence of a new-style presidency, based on less executive domination and broader parliamentary alliances, or else as a clever electoral fraud to disguise Mitterrand's real objectives - facilitate his reelection, and recover and restore the powers of the presidency.

15. F. Mitterrand, 'Lettre à tous les Français', *Libération*, 7 April 1988. Mitterrand's letter was published in three national dailies - *Le Monde, Libération, Le Parisien* - and in six regional dailies - *la Montagne, l'Est Républicain, le Télégramme de Brest, la Depêche du Midi, le Provençal* and *Sud-Ouest*. The total operation cost 10,000,000 francs.

16. See Duhamel and Jaffré, *op. cit.*, pp. 27-57 for evidence to this effect.

17. See D. Bell and B. Criddle, *The French Socialist Party: The Emergence of a Party of Government* (Oxford, Clarendon Press, 1988) for discussion of Socialist policies during the 1981-1986 governments.

18. 'Le délai qui nous sépare du grand marché européen est trop court pour que soit pris le risque de bouleverser à nouveau le paysage économique'.

19. 'Je pense et j'espère que, quelles que soient les majorités futures, on ne retournera ni au Président "absolu" des débuts de la Vᵉ République, maître en fait de tous les pouvoirs, ni au Président "soliveau" de la IVᵉ République qui n'en avait aucun'.

20. '*le Premier ministre constate qu'on l'empêche d'agir...*.' The ambiguity of this phrase was such that it did not actually commit Mitterrand to naming a government which would seek a vote of confidence from the National Assembly, although it was interpreted in that sense by most commentators and François Mitterrand's political opponents.

21. See A. Cole, 'Le parti socialiste et la cohabitation', *Aston Contemporary Trends in France*, 3, February 1988.

22. See A. Cole, 'French Socialists at Lille: the PS Congress of 3-5 April 1987', *Modern and Contemporary France*, 30 July 1987.

23. See, for example, B. Mazières, 'Rocard: le réserviste du président', *L'Express*, 5 February 1988; D. Molho, 'Rocard fait comme si...', *Le Point*, 25 January 1988.

24. See J. Gaffney, 'Socialism and Presidentialism in France', *West European Politics*, 11, 3, pp. 42-46.

25. In January 1988, the PS adopted its programme, *Propositions pour la France,* in the hope that the PS candidate would at least pay lipservice to it, although the party entertained few illusions that either Mitterrand or Rocard would take any notice of it. The PS' own campaign ran from January until Mitterrand's March declaration.

26. See E. Dupin, 'Les socialistes remettent une touche de rose dans la campagne', *Libération*, 21 April 1988; L. Sichler, 'Mitterrand: pas facile de réinventer la France', *L'Evénement du Jeudi*, 14-20 April 1988.

27. At the PS National Convention which adopted the *Propositions...*, on 16-17 January 1988, two competing left-wing amendments, which included the demand for an automatic dissolution of the National Assembly in the case of victory in the presidential

election, received respectively 20.95% (Jean Poperen), and 17.33% (Chevènement's *Socialisme et République*). Party leader Jospin was determined not to attempt to tie Mitterrand's hands too firmly in advance of the election campaign. T. Bréhier, 'Les socialistes offrent une image d'unité sur leur programme', *Le Monde*, 19 January 1988.

28. See Dupin's article cited in footnote 25. This was symbolised by Mitterrand allowing the party to use its traditional symbol - the rose inside the clenched fist - in its final propaganda material before the first ballot.

29. On the 1981 and 1986 elections, see A. Cole and P. Campbell, *French Electoral Systems and Elections since 1789* (Aldershot, Gower, 1989), Chapter Eight. The emergence of the FN considerably complicated this neat schematisation, since strategy to adopt towards the Front seriously divided the other two right-wing formations (UDF and RPR) and dominated Chirac's second ballot campaign.

30. CNRS-BVA-*Le Monde* poll published in *Le Monde*, 27 April 1988. CSA-RFI, *le Parisien*, *l'Evénement du Jeudi* et *la Vie* poll published in *Libération*, 27 April 1988. *Cadre Supérieur* might loosely be translated as executive; *cadre moyen*, as mid-level management/medium status clerical worker.

31. This figure underestimated the number of PS 'defectors', since it did not include PS 1986 voters who abstained on the first-ballot in 1988. These exit polls (*sondage sortie des urnes*) are conducted by random testing as voters leave the polling booths.

32. Most of the 25% of 1986 PS voters who backed candidates other than Mitterrand on 24 April supported either the extreme-left, ecologist or PCF candidates (together 14%), but a sizeable minority switched over to Le Pen (5%), Barre (4%), or Chirac (2%).

33. By 'legitimist' vote, we mean that fraction of the electorate primarily anxious to support the President of the Republic, above any specifically political considerations. This might account for Mitterrand's good performance amongst the over-50s, and 1986 abstentionists.

34. By way of comparison, the PS had polled 25% amongst the 50-64 age cohort in 1986, and 23% amongst the over-65s. Amongst farmers, the party had obtained 18%, and amongst businesspeople 14%; BVA-Bull exit poll cited in G. Grunberg, 'Quelques éléments pour un sociologie du vote', *Intervention*, 18, 1986

35. *Industriel-commerçant* = businesspeople, *agriculteur* = farmer, *employé* = low status clerical worker; *cadre moyen* = mid-management, medium status clerical worker. All figures from CSA poll cited above, except that for atheists and non-practising Catholics, which is derived from G. Michelat and M. Simon, 'Les catholiques et l'élection' in *L'élection présidentielle: le nouveau contrat de François Mitterrand* (Paris, *Le Monde*, May 1988). Michelat and Simon distinguish between believing, non-practising Catholics (35% for Mitterrand) and non-believing, non-practising Catholics (41% for Mitterrand).

36. For example, Mitterrand gained 12% amongst the under-35s by comparison to 1981, 6% amongst industrial workers, and 14% amongst atheists, all categories which had previously given strong support to the PCF. Figures cited in P. Perrineau, 'Le socialisme... un électorat qui fait son chemin', *L'élection présidentielle 1988* (Paris, *Le Figaro*/Etudes Politiques, May 1988).

37. CSA-RFI, *le Parisien*, *l'Evénement du Jeudi* and *la Vie* exit poll, conducted amongst a representative sample of 4,199 voters having already voted. Cited in E. Dupin, 'Contrôle d'identité pour 16,7 millions d'électeurs de Mitterrand', *Libération* 10 May 1988.

38. Figures for religion and vote for both candidates are from the Bull-BVA-CNRS-*Le Monde* exit poll, published in *Le Monde*, 11 May 1988.

39. BVA exit poll, *Le Monde*, 11 May 1988; CSA exit poll, *Libération*, 10 May, 1988. BVA classed Laguiller, Boussel and Juquin as Extreme Left. CSA distinguished between Laguiller, whose voters split 94/6 in favour of Mitterrand, and Juquin (99/1). Neither poll takes account of second-ballot abstentions.

40. The great limitation of the exit polls is that they cannot measure the behaviour of those first round voters who abstained on the second ballot. This means that, by this technique, we do not know how many voters of a particular first round candidate (e.g. Le Pen or Barre) abstained on the run-off.

41. See N. Mayer, 'L'"effet Le Pen" s'est nourri de l' "effet premier tour" ' in *Le Monde*, *L'élection présidentielle*, *op. cit.* . See also Dupin 'Contrôle d'identité...' *op. cit.* .

42. See J. Charlot, 'Le séisme du 8 mai et la nouvelle donne politique', *L'élection présidentielle 1988*, (Paris, *Le Figaro*/Etudes Politiques, May 1988). According to Charlot, who uses figures from another polling organisation IFRES, Barre voters split 84% for Chirac, 6% for Mitterrand, with 10% abstentions. This figure is difficult to reconcile with those given by CSA or BVA, even though these latter polls take no account of abstentions. Nonetheless, whichever version is accepted, Barre's voters transferred more solidly to Chirac than did Chirac's to Giscard in 1981 (71.5%, 15.5% for Mitterrand, 13% abstentions) and, arguably, Chaban-Delmas' to Giscard in 1974 (79.5%, 11% for Mitterrand, 9.5% abstentions).

43. BVA exit poll, *op. cit.*, 26% of Barre's first-round electors who opted for Mitterrand declared that the motivation for their vote was 'bar the route to Chirac'. These corresponding figures for the other first-round candidates were: Le Pen (27%), Waechter (29%), extreme left (28%), abstentionists (31%), Lajoinie (42%).

44. The nomination of Michel Rocard as Prime Minister, the failure of Rocard's attempts to persuade more than a handful of centre-right politicians to join his first government, Mitterrand's dissolution of the National Asssembly within five days of his reelection, the failure of the PS to obtain an overall majority in the legislative elections of 14-21 June 1988, despite its status as the largest party, and the constitution of a minority Socialist government under Michel Rocard's leadership which initially failed to attract support from any of the centrist parties, constituted the first main developments in this rapid sequence of political events.

INDICATIVE BIBLIOGRAPHY

The following material has been consulted in preparing this chapter, in addition to many of the sources listed at the end of Chapter Two. For reasons of space, individual articles are not cited.

L'Evénement du Jeudi (26 January-3 February, 25 February-2 March, 10-16 March, 17-23 March, 24-30 March, 7-13 April, 14-20 April, 21-27 April, 28 April-4 May, 5-11 May, 12-18 May, 19-25 May, 26 May-1 June 1988).

L'Express (5 February, 11 March, 18 March, 1 April, 15 April, 29 April, 6 May, 13 May, 19 May 1988).

Habert P., and Ysmal C., *L'élection présidentielle 1988* (Paris, *Le Figaro*/Etudes Politiques, May 1988).

Goguel F., *et al.*, '5 clés pour le 2ᵉ tour', *Le Journal des Elections*, 1, April-May 1988.

Goguel F., *et al.*, 'Les marges de manœuvre du Président', *Le Journal des Elections*, 2, May 1988.

Libération (21 January, 22 February, 8, 15, 17, 18, 23, 24, 26-27 March, 2-3, 5, 7, 8, 9-10, 11 19, 20, 21, 25, 26, 27 April; 5, 6, 9, 10, 11, 12, 13, 14-15, 18, 26 May, 3, 4-5, 6 June 1988).

Le Monde (23, 24, 25, 26 March, 15, 20, 26, 27 April, 5, 10, 11 May 1988).

Le Monde. L'élection présidentielle: le nouveau contrat de François Mitterrand (Paris, supplément aux dossiers et documents du *Monde*, May 1988).

Le Nouvel Observateur (29 January-4 February, 4-10 March, 18-24 March, 25-31 March, 8-14 April, 15-21 April, 22-28 April, 29 April-5 May 1988).

5 A hunger for power: Jacques Chirac

DAVID S. BELL

> 'I will be a candidate. There is no doubt about that.' **Jacques Chirac**

Despite his well-defined public persona, Jacques Chirac is a paradoxical figure. He is a Gaullist moulded in Pompidou's technocratic entourage, yet he is an old-fashioned party manager: a local politician with national ambitions. As a personality Chirac seems 'jamais à l'aise dans l'immobilité... le sourire est souvent crispé, la démarche raide, la voix saccadée... le ton cassant...' and these images are well implanted in the public mind; he is also 'aimable, attentif aux autres, généreux, fidèle, plein d'humour et d'humanité'. Few politicians in France have been saddled with epithets as easily as Chirac, despite his acute intelligence and a compassionate personality.[1]

In addition to Chirac's problem of image he also had problems of political choice. His career has been one of rapid upward strides in which he gained high office with relative ease at a startlingly young age. It is, however, the nature of this career and its peculiarities which both made Chirac the right's front runner in 1988 and detracted from his effectiveness as a presidential candidate. Thus, in order to place the 1988 elections in context, it is necessary to review the outlines of Chirac's career. Chirac's 'hunger for power', as one biography was entitled, reminds the observer that the race for the Elysée between the three principal contenders, Mitterrand, Barre, and Chirac, had been running since 1977 and Chirac's ambition dates back well before that.

Chirac was born in Paris in 1932, into the family of a prosperous banker from the Corrèze. He attended the Louis-le-Grand secondary school, then the Institute d'Etudes Politiques, and entered the Ecole Nationale d'Administration in 1954. He graduated in 1959 after military service in Algeria and six months officers' training.

Chirac's educational record was brilliant but essentially non-political, although (perhaps under the young Michel Rocard's influence) he had Socialist leanings, and he does appear to have been briefly attracted by the Communist Party. National service in Algeria seems to have made him an *Algérie française* enthusiast but, in the early 1960s, he leant increasingly towards the Gaullists; in April 1962 he joined the government secretariat. In November of 1962 he entered Prime Minister Pompidou's private office in the Matignon and started to rise rapidly. In 1962 began the patronage relationship in which Pompidou trusted Chirac with a succession of promotions into key posts (Chirac clearly respects Pompidou's memory more than the General's).

In 1967, Chirac, against seemingly impossible odds, became deputy for Ussel in the Corrèze, a district which was strongly left-wing and which was won against the left-wing trend. Chirac used his position in government to channel grants, projects and contracts into the constituency: in the typical Radical manner he became a councillor for Sainte-Féréole in 1965 and president of the departmental council in 1970, implanting himself firmly in local affairs.

At the same time, at national level, Chirac became junior Minister for Employment from 1967-8, an appointment which turned out to be crucial because it enabled him to play a leading part in the negotiations with the unions during the general strike of May 1968. At these 'Grenelle' negotiations, Chirac displayed a talent for conciliation which was vital to Pompidou's policy of keeping the workers apart from the students, and hence containing the discontent. In the reshuffle after the June 1968 elections Pompidou was ousted, but Chirac was made junior Finance Minister (responsible for the budget), a post which brought him into contact with Giscard d'Estaing (with whom he did not get on). Chirac, however, continued to keep in very close touch with Pompidou. After Pompidou's election to President, Chirac was promoted and was made Minister for Relations with the Parliament from 1971-2. However, the talent for painstaking consensus and the patience which were evident in 1968 were not conspicuous in that post (he also lacked the essential background experience in the National Assembly) and he made no impact. From 1972-4 he was Minister of Agriculture.

Representing as he did, a rural constituency, Chirac made full use of this short tenure of the Ministry of Agriculture and developed a lasting reputation as the farmer's friend by means of tough talk in Brussels and some timely reforms. It is likely that at this stage Chirac was being marked out for higher promotion (perhaps to Prime Minister) as indicated by his promotion to Minister of the Interior in March 1974. Pompidou's unexpected death in April of the same year ended his prospect of continuing ascent of the Gaullist hierarchy. The 1974 elections were, however, crucial. Pompidou's death had left the Gaullist party leaderless. Jacques Chaban-Delmas, the Gaullist candidate for the presidency, was a weak candidate, and the left, united behind Mitterrand, appeared within sight of victory.

It was Chirac who organised the startling coup which led 43 Gaulllist deputies to declare support for Giscard d'Estaing rather than for the Gaullist, Chaban-Delmas. Giscard came ahead of Chaban-Delmas on the first ballot and hence, in part at least, owed his very narrow victory over Mitterrand in 1974 to Chirac who was rewarded with the post of Prime Minister. However, Giscard's view of the Matignon's role as a subordinate post to the Elysée was very different from Chirac's more traditionally Gaullist view of the Prime Minister as the coordinator of the government's programme. Chirac was kept out of the inner policy-making circles, often humiliated, and his instructions to ministers often whimsically countermanded - Chirac became a *laisser pour compte*. Moreover, Giscard's liberal social reforms were not to the taste of the Gaullist Party, and Chirac himself wanted more ambitious action to counter the effects of the oil price rise recession. Although an economic package to reflate was introduced in 1975, the differences between President and Prime Minister continued to grow. Chirac resigned at the end of August 1976.

Chirac returned to the Assembly in a by-election in November 1976 and started a long war between the Gaullists and the centrists which, with its hot and cold interludes, continued to divide the right until 1988. In November 1976, Chirac also reorganised the Gaullist Party into the *Rassemblement pour la République* (RPR) and was elected its president. The strengthening of the Gaullist Party, its war against Giscard's supporters, as well as Chirac's half-hearted support for the government, did much to undermine the right-wing majority.

It was in 1977, as part of this continuing internal war on the right, that Chirac flung himself into the battle of the newly-created position of Mayor of Paris against Giscard's close confidant, Michel d'Ornano. Chirac was elected Mayor after a debilitating internecine fight on the right. This conflict between the Gaullists and the Giscardians, however, continued into the legislative elections of 1978. At these elections, the RPR retained its position as the dominant partner in the majority (with 158 seats to the UDF's 138) but Chirac, in a campaign of hostility to the Community, lost this hegemonic position in the European elections of 1979 (RPR 16.3%, UDF 27.6%). The RPR's base was shrinking and, worse, it was the UDF which was picking up the floating voters. There was, in the meantime, a continuous battle in the Assembly between the RPR and Barre's government: in 1979, for example, the RPR refused to vote for the budget. The incessant attacks on Barre's government were, of necessity perhaps, essentially negative. Chirac's inability to provide a positive programme was made worse by the deliberate decision to bury the Gaullist past of the RPR and concentrate on the new leadership.

Chirac's hostility to Giscard continued into the 1981 presidential elections. On the eve of the second ballot, when Giscard needed every vote, Chirac (who had polled only 17.99% in the first ballot) commented 'chacun devra voter selon sa conscience. A titre personnel... je ne puis que voter pour M. Giscard d'Estaing' ('Each person must vote according to their conscience. Personally, ... I can only vote for Mr. Giscard d'Estaing'). Chirac's lukewarm endorsement, and his refusal to mobilise the RPR behind Giscard, were elements in the right's defeat in 1981. The weakened RPR nonetheless emerged from the Socialist landslide as the biggest party on the right and Chirac was the dominant figure in it. Yet it is significant that despite the disarray within the centre-right, it was Barre who, in 1984, emerged in the opinion polls as the front runner in the presidential race. In addition, the *Front National* emerged as a threat. The rise of the FN both divided the right, into those who wanted to have nothing to do with Le Pen and those who accepted the possibility of an alliance, and ate into traditional conservative support. Hence, although Chirac benefited from the unpopularity of the Socialists in 1986 because he headed the largest party on the right, he was not the most obvious '*présidentiable*'.

In sum, Chirac had shown, before 1988, the talent to salvage the dwindling Gaullist Party but had not shown any ability to attract an electorate beyond the RPR faithful. Worse, Chirac had been responsible for intensifying the divisions on the right, twice profiting from the splits he had created or exacerbated in his own camp. For the right there was the further paradox that, since 1984, the centrist Raymond Barre had led Chirac in the polls as the right's presidential choice and was also consistently shown by the polls to have a much better chance of defeating Mitterrand in the run-off.

Cohabitation: (i) Strategy

On 19 March 1986, the left was heavily defeated in the legislative elections which returned an Assembly majority of the right (excluding the FN: 292 deputies to 285), a right in which Chirac's RPR was still the biggest party. A war then opened on two fronts: Prime Minister against President and Prime Minister against Barre supporters in the UDF. Balladur, Chirac's 'Prime Minister', urged Chirac to undertake the *'cohabitation'* experiment of a Conservative government and Socialist President as double or quits: if it worked, Chirac might go on to be President, but it could also break him. The position was delicate. Public opinion wanted *cohabitation* to continue until 1988, liked to see politicians cooperating, and did not want an open war at the summit of the state. Balladur described the situation as a 'Mexican stand off'; a 'high noon' in which whoever drew first would lose. The political art would consist in forcing on the adversary the blame for any disharmony; but this was a game at which Mitterrand, in the Socialist alliance with the Communists in the 1970s, had already proved an adept.

Mitterrand was unable to make Chirac abandon any of his reforms, and although Mitterrand had few constitutional powers he manœuvred the symbolic and representative functions of the office with skill. For example, although Chirac tried to move into the so-called presidential *domaine réservé* of foreign affairs, it probably did not do him much good. Foreign Minister Raimond affirmed that foreign policy from 1986-8 was Chirac's but it was still *perceived* as a presidential responsibility.[2] Moreover, the fear of the President's resignation (in which case victory by Raymond Barre seemed certain) prevented Chirac from pressing Mitterrand too far.

Chirac's action in government was immediate and energetic because there had to be visible results before 1988. This haste led to the attempt to use ordinances for some measures in order to avoid the time-consuming need for parliamentary debate. The procedure for ordinances gave Mitterrand a chance to object by refusing to sign privatisation bills and electoral law changes. Chirac, however, swept aside the wealth tax, removed price controls, reduced taxes on businesses, lowered interest rates, eliminated the tax on video recorders, and annulled the contracts on the fifth and sixth television channels. This vigorous and impressive action was straight from the right's free-market, liberal manifesto, but was not especially popular. Chirac's strategy at this point seems to have been twin-tracked, based on creating an economic revival, through a laissez-faire programme, and on enticing FN voters back behind the mainstream right through tougher law and order and anti-immigration measures. Chirac's impetuosity and the lack of time for measures to work led to mistakes.

Mitterrand, who had been counted out in 1986, saw his popularity begin to rise as he successfully dissociated himself from Chirac's inevitable blunders. In November 1984, *Figaro Magazine*'s popularity rating had put Mitterrand's standing at 27% 'satisfied', the worst result for any Fifth Republic President, but by mid-1987 the polls made Mitterrand an easy winner in the presidential elections. Even confrontation, when it came, was to benefit Mitterrand: the President chose the ground, that of affirming his continuing social conscience. In particular, the President was able to dissociate himself from the education reform bill which brought students on to the streets in the winter of 1986, and from the subsequent mishandling of the demonstrations and strikes. Chirac then abandoned the more radical aspects of his programme. When Mitterrand turned to praising the government (certain ministers and some select measures) this too redounded to his benefit.[3]

Mitterrand's astute use of the minimal presidential powers (those of a constitutional monarch) contributed to the enormous increase in his popularity, and by the time Chirac realised the problem it was too late. Moreover, Mitterrand had grasped that if the 1988 presidential elections could be won by a Socialist they would be won in the centre, and had accordingly repositioned himself. Chirac had been overly impressed by the size of the right's victory in 1986 and had made an initial appeal to the FN and the hard-core RPR support rather than to the centre.

Chirac lacked the skill to manœuvre out of his own political constituency. In this his weakness resembled more traditional boss politics and the party machine, than Fifth Republic conservatism. On the one side he was effectively trapped by Le Pen who ate into the RPR electorate and, during 1986-1988, prevented Chirac from winning over FN voters. On the other side, Chirac's handling of the UDF in the government visibly played up divisions between the other rivals on the right. Many of Barre's supporters stayed out of office, but the principal point of pressure was François Léotard, leader of the *Parti Republicain* (PR) who had ambitions of his own. With his close collaborators, Léotard tried to make his party the free-market dynamo within the right. For Chirac, Léotard, who was also a '*présidentiable*', deprived Barre of support and enabled *cohabitation* (which Barre opposed) to go ahead with UDF support. Chirac, having paved the way for Léotard's ambition was later forced into conflict with him on several occasions. Thus, *cohabitation* within the right was as conflictual as between Mitterrand and Chirac. Léotard, who was denied the defence portfolio, had difficulties as Minister of Culture in getting the audio-visual law through the Assembly and Senate in July 1986 (Chirac's close supporter, Jacques Toubon, had to help out). The RPR's power over the budget, over nominations (particularly to the television authority, the CNCL) and the difficulties of the 1986-7 winter demonstrations and strikes caused the UDF to close ranks against RPR pressure. The UDF did, more or less, stay in government where it, and Léotard's group in particular, prevented Raymond Barre from being overtly critical of Chirac's record during his tenure of the Matignon.

Cohabitation: (ii) Image

Chirac did benefit to a limited extent from *cohabitation* and from the legitimacy of holding the Prime Minister's office. However, the effect was weak and not what the RPR had hoped for. It was what J.-L. Parodi called the *'quand même'* factor rather than genuine enthusiasm:'Il a quand même mis de l'ordre, nous avons un taux d'inflation qui est quand même minime.'[4]

Two years' *cohabitation* enabled Chirac to try to be the unifier and to reduce his aggressive image somewhat: he appeared, by 1988, less of a one-man-band, less impetuous and more relaxed. *Cohabitation* also promoted Chirac's team which enabled implications to be made during the campaign that Barre was a loner. Balladur and Pasqua, in particular, but also Séguin, Barzach and Noir, all became popular ministers.

Hence Chirac's government began to be seen in a more favourable light before the elections: in December 1987, 61% thought things were getting worse, and only 21% thought they were getting better. But in April 1988, the gap had narrowed to 39%. Although the Chirac government's record was not regarded more favourably than the Socialists', it had the strong support of the conservative electorate.[5] Although 31% thought the Socialist governments had performed better than Chirac's (the *cohabitation* government rated only 27% positive with 31% don't knows), this gap in appreciation had been reduced from 16% in March 1987; the positive rating was 51% from Barre's supporters, 54% from the UDF electorate and 69% from the RPR supporters.[6] Balladur's status as Finance Minister was not exceptional but was probably high enough to prevent Barre from overcoming Chirac's lead through the deployment of the 'Barrist' issues of unemployment and growth; although it was also a generalised pessimism or scepticism about miracle cures which aided Chirac here. More significantly, Chirac's period in office was seen as positive neither on the most pressing problem (unemployment 14% negative opinions), nor on living standards (15% negative), nor on business (12% negative,) nor on immigration (13% negative), although he was credited for his struggle against terrorism (16% positive). It was not, therefore, on the economy but on the fight against crime where Chirac was clearly ahead: he was 9% ahead of Barre on this issue and 5% ahead of Mitterrand.[7] This lead, however, was also weak.

But in 1988 Chirac's image still suffered from a damaging series of negative points despite the *cohabitation* period. He was criticised for promiscuous promises ('il multiple les promesses et il ne pourrait pas les tenir') by 36% of voters (and 25% of the right), and for clientelism ('il mettrait l'Etat au service de ses amis politiques') by 18% of voters (7% of the right). Despite *cohabitation* Chirac was still seen as 'aggressive' (26%), 'far from ordinary people's preoccupations' (24%), and 'sectarian' (69%). At the beginning of the campaign, 21% (40% of the right) thought that Chirac was of presidential stature, and only 9% (4% of the right) disagreed.[8] Chirac, through *cohabitation*, made some progress with the under 25s (his rating went up by 18%), with public service workers (up 15%), with senior managers (up 14%), and even in the left's electorate (up 9%).[9] Unfortunately Chirac's support was still confined essentially to the hard core of conservative RPR opinion and he was unable to capitalise on the right's popularity in local elections (of about 58%) because of the poor, intra-right transfer of votes. Overall, the government's two-year record was considered not nearly good enough. In reality the beneficiary from *cohabitation* was Mitterrand: if Chirac had the authority, Mitterrand had the popularity.

The Campaign

The effective beginning of the Chirac campaign was his (earlier than planned) declaration of candidature on 16 January. This declaration immediately (and for the first time since 1984) put Chirac ahead of Barre in the polls, a position he retained thereafter, although Barre, who remained personally popular, did prevent Chirac's position from strengthening appreciably after January.

Chirac's campaign was based partly on the government's achievements (which conveniently left Barre out of the reckoning), and a new low-key style was developed which eschewed personal attacks. The campaign portrayed a modern, youthful but statesman-like Prime Minister: a relaxed but open and attentive Chirac. Poster campaigns (*Il rassemble, Il écoute, Il construit*) tried to promote the same image and presented a sun-tanned and relaxed Chirac in an attempt to efface the general perception of Chirac as 'the bulldozer'. The centre pieces were a series of well-organised travelling shows until these were abandoned (in panic) in mid-April to concentrate on television appearances. The new approach emphasised discussion. In carefully chosen places, Chirac developed the campaign themes in 'discussions' with four or five (carefully selected) 'ordinary' people. As an example, in the *gymnase* Pierre-de-Coubertin, packed with RPR activists, Chirac conversed with the mother of a large family, a small shopkeeper, a restaurant owner, and the heads of two local associations. Chirac sat at ease in a swivel armchair (backed by giant video screens of himself).

Mitterrand's delaying of his own descent into the election arena extended the 'primary' between Chirac and Barre on the right, but the President's declaration of his candidacy on 22 March and his reference to the 'bands' and 'bandits' (in control) evoked an immediate reply. This was a difficult issue for Chirac, who was attacked by Barre for the same reasons. He countered by an attack on the vagueness of the presidential programme and asked 'ten questions'. Amongst these ten were 'Will you re-establish proportional representation, create a unified lay education service, annul the laws on crime and immigration [passed by the Chirac government], amnesty terrorists, continue privatisation and respect the wish expressed [in a referendum] by our citizens in New Caledonia?'

Mitterrand's reply came in the form of the long rambling *Letter to All the French People*, intended to dispose of Chirac's argument that he had run out of ideas, or was vague and had nothing to offer other than *'immobilisme'*. Chirac's attacks, therefore, were effectively countered, whereas the RPR repost to hostile critics of the *'Etat RPR'* was to publish a 'black book' of Socialist nominations during 1981-1986. This was more aggressive than convincing; Chirac had no difficulty in enthusing partisans, but again met the problems of appealing to an electorate which was wider than long-standing supporters (the opposite problem to Mitterrand who had to enthuse Socialists in 1988).

However, Chirac's difficulty of having to appeal to both the centrist floating vote and FN partisans caused a drift rightward. Chirac's attempt to use the immigration issue was not only unsuccessful but also confirmed centrist fears and led to further mistakes. Chirac attempted to maintain a fine wire-drawn distinction between the FN leaders (with whom there could be no deals), and the voters. In Marseille, Chirac was imprudent enough to state that, although he did not approve of racist sentiments, he 'understood' them: 'la politique de refoulement aux frontières des étrangers en situation irrégulière continuera sans faiblir si je suis élu ... les réactions de xénophobie auxquelles nous assistons parfois sont le fruit du laisser-aller socialiste des années précédentes. Les réactions, je ne puis pas les admettre mais je peux tout à fait les comprendre' ('The policy of expelling illegal immigrants will continue unabated if I am elected... the xenophobic reactions we sometimes see are the fruit of the Socialists' laxity in previous years. I do not condone such reactions but I can quite understand them'). Chirac promised to 'solve' the immigration problem in five years, and in an RPR brochure it was stated that 'les problèmes provoqués par l'immigration ne trouvent leur solution que si notre pays renforce la conscience de son identité. Il faut avoir le courage de réformer le code de la nationalité...' ('The problems caused by immigration will only be solved if our country reinforces its awareness of its identity. We must have the courage to reform the Nationality Code'). Admiral Philippe de Gaulle was put up to point out, to FN leaders and supporters, that although the FN had never voted a confidence motion during 1986-1988, Chirac had never stated that he would dissolve the Assembly or 'qu'il rayerait le FN de la carte ...' ('or would wipe the FN off the map...').[10]

The difficulties with the centrists were not helped by the ostensibly unifying, but in reality highly divisive, proposal made by Edouard Balladur for a French Conservative Party (*'grand parti conservateur'*) and his call on the right-wing parties to 'discuss the creation of common departmental committees, a common directing committee at the national level, and the allocation of leading posts for the envisaged new confederation'.[11] This was both a spoiler for Barre's television appearance and set Léotard's PR and the UDF hierarchy at odds. The UDF had no interest in being ingested by the RPR. Chirac's tactics annoyed Barre's campaign managers and played into Mitterrand's hands.

Chirac's campaign made its mark with the traditionally conservative section of the electorate. Chirac did gain 12% amongst the 50-64 age group, 11% from those over 65, 17% more from farmers, 16% up in the shopkeepers and small business groups and 8% more from upper management. His campaign enabled him to pick up 13% from UDF sympathisers but only 4% from the large number of don't knows.

The Issues

Chirac's manifesto, *The Decade of Renewal,* published on 6 February gave space, in particular, to the family, to business and to education. Chirac promised to build France into one of the leading European nations and emphasised the need to continue the government's policies. Chirac's programme was not precise, despite the protestations to the contrary of campaign spokesman Alain Juppé, nor was it 'an exact opposite of the Socialist programme', which it resembled in outline and in many details. A convergence in the centre was, however, evident in the programmes of all the major contenders although there were differences in presentation and nuance.

Chirac stressed 'volonté de réussite' ('the will to succeed') and renewal, and the activity of the government was implicitly contrasted with the old and '*immobiliste*' President, (a style recommended by Chirac's opinion researchers).[12] Thus 'le courage, l'ardeur, la volonté' of the campaign posters were assimilated into the notions of dynamism, competitiveness and optimism.[13]

On constitutional matters, Chirac, like Barre and Mitterrand, wanted to extend the use of the referendum but opposed Mitterrand's suggestion to reduce the presidential term to five years and had a more active conception of the presidency. Chirac, of course, favoured the retention of the '*scrutin majoritaire*' in legislative elections.

On defence, the differences between candidates were at their most pronounced. Both candidates of the mainstream right concentrated on the need to modernise the French nuclear deterrent, and Chirac was sceptical about the Reagan/Gorbachev disarmament agreements. Defence Minister, André Giraud, argued that the removal of all missiles from Western Europe, the 'zero option', represented a 'Munich', and Chirac saw an American withdrawal from Europe as creating a 'dangerous' disequilibrium between the conventional arms of Nato and the Warsaw Pact. Chirac was more hawkish than Mitterrand, who was insistent on disarmament and emphasised that the choice was between 'build down' or war. Chirac also wanted France to play a bigger role in Nato.

Europe, it was agreed by the three major candidates, would be the great issue of the next presidential term. On this, Chirac was not best placed because his conversion to Europe was relatively recent: he had fought rearguard actions against the enlargement of the Community to include Spain and Portugal. He reiterated the view that France had to become 'the most dynamic of European countries by the end of the century' ('*La France en Tête*', as one section was entitled), and he presented himself as the defender of French interests. The unification of the internal market in 1992 had been put at the centre of all the programmes but Chirac's detailed knowledge (of agriculture especially) deprived him of the wider vision of Mitterrand or Barre (Chirac's neglect of the fears raised by unification in 1992 may have been one of the reasons for FN progress in rural areas).

Other foreign policy issues hardly figured, but the Third World crisis was mentioned by all the candidates. Mitterrand envisaged a 'Marshall Plan' for the Third World, and Chirac proposed a world food plan, a scheme of French youth 'volunteers for progress', as well as a coordinated solution to the less developed countries' debt problem.

Economic debate was also situated on the middle ground but this was Barre's preferred territory. Chirac's 1986 rhetorical stance about the 'minimal state' and the free market was less evident but he chose to stress the need for the freedom of business entrepreneurs as a priority through the working of market forces which would encourage individual initiative. Chirac underlined the need for quality and competitiveness (in agriculture as well as in industry), and the need to lighten tax burdens in order to create jobs. He made promises to reduce professional taxes still further,[14] and wanted to reduce company taxation progressively to 40% and eventually to 37.5% - personal income tax would also be reduced. In addition to reducing taxes and the budget deficit by 15 million francs each year, Chirac wanted to lighten the tax on inheritance, but although he made much of telecommunications and space and was lyrical about research, there were no costings (see Chapter Nine). One of Chirac's principal themes was the continuation of privatisation - though at an unspecified rate - and he brought back the old Gaullist concept of 'participation' between management and workers to be introduced in the public sector. The new poor were an issue, but Chirac rejected 'minimum wages' or a 'social wage' and talked of a guaranteed 'activity' for the jobless to be the responsibility of both national and local government.

The campaign rhetoric of 1986 often called into question the social security system but Chirac in 1988 limited his proposals to a restructuring and modernisation of hospitals. Despite the government report in 1987, the problem of financing pensions had, Chirac thought, to be left until after the elections. He was, however, more prolix on family policy and called for extra aid to three-children families to enable either the mother or the father to stay at home, family allowance increases, increased maternity leave, and help to enable professional women to continue their careers after childbirth.

As has been stated, where Chirac continued to have an impact was on law and order, nationality and immigration. Chirac wanted to increase resources for the police (which the others did not propose) and criticised the 'abuses' of the right to asylum France. Chirac also persisted with his project to reform the French nationality laws (then still under consideration by a committee). And in contradiction to Barre, who wanted a vigorous integration policy, Chirac put the accent on 'French identity', French 'values' and French culture. He argued that French distinctiveness should not disappear 'au profit de la pseudo-culture universelle que véhiculent certains médias' ('to the profit of the universal pseudo-culture propagated by certain media'). Chirac was again looking to the FN electorate for the second ballot or possibly also for the first. As the results of the first round showed on 24 April, Chirac's campaign and arguments made little impact. In order to fully understand where and why this was so, we need to look more closely at the sociology of his support.

Chirac's Electorate

Table 1
First ballot 24 April 1988 - Sociology of Support

	Laguiller & Boussel	Juquin	Lajoinie	Mitterrand	Waechter	Barre	Chirac	Le Pen
All	2	2	7	34	4	17	20	14
Men	2	2	7	33	4	15	18	19
Women	3	2	5	35	6	18	20	11
18-24	3	2	6	36	6	18	12	17
25-34	3	4	6	41	6	11	14	15
35-49	3	2	5	33	4	16	18	18
50-64	2	1	7	33	2	17	24	14
65+	1	1	7	30	1	23	26	11
Farmers	0	1	7	30	3	17	22	20
Ind. commercial bosses	0	1	3	21	2	20	26	27
Upper management & lib. prof.	1	3	2	29	4	24	26	11
Middle Managers	3	3	4	36	6	18	15	15
Employees	3	3	6	38	5	16	15	14
Workers	4	2	15	40	2	8	8	21
Housewives	3	1	4	28	5	17	26	16
Students	1	3	3	36	8	23	14	12
Unemployed	6	2	11	36	3	8	17	17
CGT	4	3	49	38	1	0	2	3
CFDT	7	6	2	70	4	2	6	3
FO	7	1	0	35	3	26	7	21

Source: Exit poll published by *Le Parisien*, 25 April 1988

The result of the first ballot came close to a humiliation for Chirac whose vote of 19.9% was lower than the combined Gaullist vote in 1981 (Chirac 17.9%, Garaud 1.33% and Debré 1.65%), and below the RPR's vote in the legislative elections of 1981 (20.8%). A party looks to a presidential candidate, freed from partisan ties, to cast more widely than the party's core vote and extend support beyond traditional allies in order to create a coat-tails effect. If Chirac gained votes during the campaign, they were probably taken mainly from Barre, but in any case, the combined votes of the two orthodox conservatives was, at 36%, far lower than the Giscard/Chirac total of 1981 (46%).[15]

Chirac, with 40% of the right's presidential vote, lagged behind the RPR which, in the 1986 legislative elections, represented about 50% of the combined conservative electorate. Unlike the RPR, Chirac's support was concentrated in the West, in Finistère, Ille-et-Vilaine and Morbihan; also Chirac had support in Alsace-Lorraine (usually centrist not RPR), and failed to poll well in the north and east where the RPR is normally strong. The structure of Chirac's electorate was similar to that of 1981 and 1979, a sign of Chirac's continuing inability to pull together the conservative electorate. Chirac, for example, failed to advance (relative to 1981) in areas like the Bas-Rhin, Haute-Loire, Meuse and Ain where Giscard was well supported. Chirac's failure is a distorted reflection of the continuing inability of the Gaullists to reestablish the hegemony over the right which they enjoyed in the early 1970s when two-thirds of the conservative electorate were Gaullist.[16]

After two years of *cohabitation* and a lavish campaign, the RPR leader came only 2.5% ahead of Barre, was not much better placed than in 1981 and had the lowest poll for the right's front runner in the Fifth Republic. Even in his own constituencies Chirac was a prophet without honour; in Corrèze Chirac's vote fell by 2.2% (it even fell in his home town of Ussel by 3.9%), and, relative to 1986, it fell in the Fifth Paris district.

Table 2 shows that Chirac's campaign made its mark with the traditionally conservative sections of the electorate and that Chirac's vote was (sociologically) the hard core of the Gaullist right. The antithesis between a populist Gaullism and conservative notability of the 1960s gave way, in the 1970s, to an RPR and UDF barely distinguishable in composition - though in 1981 Chirac's electorate was the more conservative and the UDF's had become relatively heterogeneous. In 1988, this Gaullist conservatism was accentuated. Chirac's supporters were older than Barre's, and he came ahead of Barre with upper management and farmers. Chirac's supporters located themselves firmly on the right (Barre's were on the moderate centre-right).[17] Although 45% of Barre's voters agreed with the objective of creating a multi-racial society, only 32% of Chirac's did, and 55% of Chirac's voters wanted an agreement with Le Pen whereas 51% of Barre's supporters objected to a deal with the FN.

Chirac's first ballot vote was based on two strong supports: Paris, of course, and the rural communities. About 40% of the first round farmers' vote went to Chirac, perhaps as much as a quarter of his first ballot total, and perhaps 78% of the farmers voted Chirac in the second ballot. Thus, Chirac had a high vote in the South-West, Massif-Central, Cantal, Corrèze, Creuse, Dordogne, Lozère and Aveyron - all departments with an agricultural workforce of over 17%.

Table 2
First round Vote by Religious Affiliation

	All voters	Practising	Non-Practising	Protestant	Muslim	Jewish	Catholics
R. Barre	16.5	32.7	15.8	12	-	11.6	6.8
P. Juquin	2.1	0.3	1.3	0.7	5.3	-	9.5
J.-M. Le Pen	14.4	12.2	18.9	16.3	11.9	2.1	6.3
J. Chirac	19.9	33.8	18.6	27.6	68.9	32.8	43.6
F. Mitterrand	34.1	18.8	35	31.3	1.3	44.5	0.7
P. Boussel	0.4	3.8	0.3	0.8	4.2	-	6.9
A. Waechter	3.8	3.5	3.9	5.4	-	0.9	6.9
A. Laguiller	2	0.5	2.1	-	8.4	1.9	2.5
A. Lajoinie	6.8	0.5	4	5.9	-	6.1	14.7

Source: *La Croix*, 28 April - 4 May 1988 (CSA Exit Poll)

Chirac improved on his 1981 result only in the conservative rural areas where he was already strong: in the Puy-de-Dôme, Cantal, Lozère, Avignon, Ardèche, and Haute-Loire (Massif-Central), in both Corsican departments, in the Alpes-Maritimes, Aquitaine, the West, and in Paris. However, the vote for Chirac was below the combined 1981 Gaullist vote (Chirac + Debré + Garaud) in all departments. It fell most in the Haut-Rhin (down 4.5%) in the Moselle, Rhône, Mayenne (all places where Le Pen made a good showing), and it even fell in conservative Brittany. The drop in the rural areas of Charente, Dordogne and Orne were a result of the farming crisis but were unexpected all the same.

Chirac's vote was also a 'Catholic' one. Practising Catholics voted principally for the 'civilised' (conservative and centre) right, with little or no advantage to Chirac over Barre, but the left polled at a level similar to 1978 when it did equally well (taking 38%). Le Pen's vote has become steadily less Catholic (and more non-religious) since 1984 and Protestants voted slightly more enthusiastically for the FN candidate and for Mitterrand, but Chirac was well supported by people professing a religious faith.

The Second Ballot

Consistent with Chirac's own style and the desperate situation, he applied Marshal Foch's precept: 'Mon centre est enfoncé. Mon aile droite est en déroute. Mon aile gauche ne vaut pas mieux. J'attaque'. The attack took the now stale line like that Mitterrand represented 'left wing' socialism.

Although, overall, the left had some 46% of the vote and the conservative right 30%, Mitterrand had no need to make concessions to the extreme left, and was the favourite in the polls. Chirac's first task should have been to repair the damage done to the UDF/RPR alliance by the first round 'primary'. But his second task, which was in implicit conflict with the first, was to win over those who had voted for Le Pen in the first ballot. Barre aided the healing process with a declaration of support, alongside Chirac, immediately after the results were announced but also complicated Chirac's second task by spelling out the conditions for centrist support (nor did he renege in his criticisms of the 1986-1988 *cohabitation* government). Chirac's task all along had been the difficult two-way stretch to bring together FN extremists and centrists. Mitterrand had, on the left, accomplished a similar stretch reaching from the Communists to the centre but it had taken patience, skill and ten years.

After the first ballot Barre said, 'Je compte qu'il [Chirac] défendra les objectifs auxquels nous sommes particulièrement attachés, une société ouverte et tolérante qui refuse la xénophobie, le racisme et tous les extrémismes' ('I count on Chirac to support the objectives we are particularly attached to, an open and tolerant society which rejects xenophobia, racism, and all extremisms').[18] Chirac again ruled out any deal with Le Pen in the words, 'il allait de soi qu'aucune négociation ne sera menée avec qui que ce soit...' ('it goes without saying that there will be no negotiation with anybody'). Persistent rumours of contacts between the RPR and FN were denied but in a presidential campaign no party collective endorsement could have been sought. The difficulty was that Barre had effectively blocked off any accommodation with the FN. Le Pen, in any case, had made clear that his formal backing for Chirac would require a range of major concessions and a policy of systematic discrimination against foreigners. These concessions could not have been accepted.

Le Pen decided not to make his preference known until 1 May when there would be an FN rally to commemorate Joan of Arc. Charles Pasqua, the Interior Minister, declared in the meantime that the FN and the RPR 'se réclame des mêmes préoccupations et des mêmes valeurs' ('shared the same preoccupations and the same values').[19] Crime, law and order, lower taxes, excessive bureaucracy as well as a *méfiance* concerning European unity were common points, but Le Pen had an eye on local government alliances as well as what he called 'un véritable réforme intellectuelle, morale et politique' ('truly intellectual, moral and political change').[20] There were RPR deputies who were as dismayed as the centrists at Pasqua's tactics. Le Pen's 1 May statement proposed a vote against Mitterrand but dismissed the second round as a choice between 'Le pire et le mal' ('the worst and the bad'). Chirac had not made the best of bad job and had lost on both fronts, to the centre and to the right.

Chirac's position was very weak, but RPR supporters still entertained hopes of a victory. Chirac's campaign in between ballots needed a coup to lift it out of the impossible position of also ran. It was hoped by the RPR strategists that the television debate with Mitterrand would give Chirac's chances a boost if he demonstrated his superiority. Chirac is a notoriously bad television performer, but his television confrontation with Fabius in December 1985 had confirmed his standing as leader of the parliamentary right. Mitterrand, moreover, had been wrong-footed into giving the impression of trying to avoid a debate (although Chirac had thrown away this advantage by changing his mind about the date). In the event, the viewers were treated to an ill-tempered exchange (they accused each other of lying) which, both practically and symbolically, ended two years of *cohabitation*. Mitterrand was generally thought to have 'won' by viewers by some 42% to 33% (18% undecided).[21] More importantly, Mitterrand played on Chirac's continuing inability to '*rassembler*' the authoritarian xenophobic right along with the centrist, pro-European, anti-racist right. Both Barre and Giscard were already beginning to regroup their supporters in clubs and study circles in the expectation of Chirac's defeat by Mitterrand.[22]

Chirac continued his campaign with indefatigable energy and concentrated on the 'danger' of a re-elected Mitterrand ('*le socialisme ou la liberté*') as well as on the possibility of an Assembly dissolution which would damage both the UDF and the FN because both would lose seats under the two-ballot electoral system. The FN, in fact, could hope for only one or two seats - and in the event took only one seat. Chirac, of course, could have continued to work with the Assembly majority of 1986 which had made him Prime Minister.

In the last few days of the campaign, Chirac exploited Mitterrand's principal weakness - his lack of power. Captain Prieur was returned from confinement in the Pacific to France. Chirac's government organised the release of three French hostages from the Lebanon (the President was kept well out of this process), and a spectacular operation to free captured gendarmes in New Caledonia was undertaken (see Chapter One).[23]

The Second Ballot Results

Chirac's 46% was just short of a rout. Chirac's poll was lower than the combined right's first round vote in all departments and he 'won' only 19 metropolitan departments. Chirac's vote was also the lowest for any Fifth Republic right-wing candidate under universal suffrage; it was a result which was deeply demoralising for the RPR.

Chirac's tactic of seeking the FN vote did not pay off and the second ballot rally against 'socialism' attracted neither Le Pen's voters nor Barre's supporters. Perhaps a quarter of Le Pen's voters transferred to Mitterrand on 8 May. Chirac lost voters mostly (relative to the combined right total) in the departments of Var, Vaucluse, Gard, Bouches-du-Rhône, Bas-Rhin, Haut-Rhin and Moselle. And Chirac's campaign had the perverse effect of further rallying the left's splinter groups (Juquin, Lajoinie, Waechter, Boussel and Laguiller) behind Mitterrand, and even some of Barre's (55% of Barre's voters thought that Le Pen was 'a danger to democracy'). Chirac probably lost 13% of Barre's supporters who transferred to Mitterrand on the second ballot, and Mitterrand was well ahead in such centrist fiefdoms as Vitré (Méhaignerie), Rouen (Lecanuet) and Issy-les-Moulineaux.

Chirac's second ballot vote was again a traditionally right-wing vote. He did best amongst independent workers (69%), those over 50 years of age, and practising Catholics, as well as in the categories of farmers, self-employed, small businesses, and the liberal professions. Chirac's electorate was relatively well disposed towards Le Pen (61% thought Le Pen played a 'positive role'), but the Mitterrand campaign found a response even here because a third of Chirac's voters wanted a wealth tax and a third wanted to end privatisation. In addition, Chirac's electorate shared his strong views on the nationality laws and defence but these were not distinctive election themes. Chirac again polled badly in Paris where he took only two of the eleven districts, and despite eleven years as Mayor his vote of 54.68% was lower than Giscard's 56.9% in 1974 (in 1981 Giscard polled 53.56% in Paris).

Chirac resigned as Prime Minister ten days after the polls. The question of the alliance with the FN at local elections had not been solved by the presidential elections and although Chirac's supporters still held the key positions within it, the RPR was left effectively leaderless.

* * *

Although Chirac's presidential ambitions may have started as early as 1972 (when Pompidou began to look for a dauphin), his career has been divisive and he has made powerful, and rancorous enemies. It is ironic that Chirac failed because he fought too hard with inappropriate, non-Gaullist methods. The paradox is that Chirac, who led the second-generation Gaullists, misread the lessons of the presidency, that most Gaullist of institutions. Lacking the leadership and the inspiration of the General, the Gaullist party found that it had few resources to call on other than the local popularity of its elected officials. Chirac's RPR became a conglomeration of local politicians rather than the modern conservative party it was in de Gaulle's time.

Chirac owed his election as RPR leader, as deputy for the Corrèze, and as Mayor of Paris to a number of qualities which, although they produce success at local level, are not necessarily practicable at national level where the techniques of the Radical 'arrondissmentier' are off-putting. Many local politicians in the Fifth Republic who aspire to national office have overcome this narrow outlook, but Chirac has not, and it is significant that neither de Gaulle nor Pompidou entered national life from municipal politics. As stated at the beginning of this chapter, Chirac's undertaking always had something of the old-style Radical about it, and Third Republic politics are not compatible with the presidency of the Fifth Republic.

In the presidential election of 1988, Chirac's methods were fully deployed and can be briefly outlined. Let us mention the last, first: the spectacular *coups de foudre*. Thus, the Chirac campaign ended with the release of three hostages from the Lebanon, the freeing of the 22 gendarmes captured by New Caledonian separatists, and the return of Captain Prieur to France. All of these were too obviously electorally self-serving (only days before the final ballot), and were badly handled (which undermined the Gaullist reputation for

116

competence). In addition, the return of the hostages from the Lebanon implicated the government in negotiations with hostages takers (and opened a flank to Socialist attack and Le Pen's criticism),[24] there were 19 deaths in the operation to release the gendarmes (the separatists stated that the police would have been released after the elections), and the return of the 'Rainbow Warrior' saboteur was, arguably, contrary to International law. Coups of a similar nature had occurred throughout 1987, for example, the return of two hostages and the 'repatriation' of Alain Mafart for 'medical reasons' in December 1987. The opportunistic timing of the May 1988 coups, however, threw into question Chirac's integrity.

The second aspect of Chirac's approach was its clientelism. There was an injudicious and *voyant* distribution of favours to pressure groups in the run-up to the presidential elections (see Chapter Nine). For example, the farmers, whose union leader, François Guillaume, had been made Minister of Agriculture, were treated with exemplary tenderness and received an extra subsidy of 3 billion francs in February 1988.[25] Other groups, doctors, small businesses, and the like, were given similar treatment. Chirac's campaigns at local level are said to resemble Second Empire elections with their attention to special interests. The presidential constituency, however, is the entire nation and is hence less amenable to such methods. Material interests are, of course, never far from the centre of the political stage but in a presidential election, personality, a national vision, and a sense of mission are more to the fore in winning campaigns.

Most politicians have faith in their stars, but Chirac's self-confidence spills over into *la méthode coué* which is barely distinguishable from braggadocio and self-deception. The belief, in between ballots, that he could win may have been genuine but was unrealistic and imprudently expressed. This *confiance en soi* was undamaged in Chirac's early, steady ascension; it is an infectious technique at local level where personal contact and networks of activists spread optimism, but is difficult to master in a presidential election. In particular, television 'does not love' Chirac who performs badly on this essential mass media and hence cannot communicate self-confidence convincingly to a wider audience, however genuine it might be.

Chirac is also inconsistent; this lack of fixed points is not important in a Mayor or councillor but in a presidential aspirant it is fatal. Other politicians, Mitterrand notably, but also de Gaulle, have been inconsistent but have at the same time managed to suggest a longer-term inspiration and avoid the impression that they are just tacking - *navigant à vue*. Chirac was an interventionist, state-managing Keynesian in the mid-1970s, at which point he called for the creation of a French '*travailliste*' party. However, within weeks of leaving office in 1976 he was criticising the reflation programme he had himself initiated, and in the early-1980s he was converted to a laissez-faire non-interventionism in a radically free-market mode. This too was abandoned under the pressure of events during 1986-7. Chirac's inconsistency and unconvincing rhetorical stance draw attention to the strategic shifts which a politician must inevitably undertake. The revelation, not particularly startling in itself, that Chirac was once briefly attracted by the Communist Party is damaging because, in his case, it underscores this perceived inconsistency.[26] In short, his principles appear subordinate to his ambition.

Finally there is Chirac 'the bulldozer' with a Stakhanovite capacity for work. Chirac, unlike de Gaulle and Mitterrand, is neither a writer nor an orator (his speeches are rather technocratic), but an old-fashioned glad-hander surrounded by ward-heelers who run the RPR party machine with unrivalled efficiency. The sheer energy of Chirac's campaign was extraordinary and would have exhausted a lesser politician. According to the campaign staff, Chirac met 8,000 local officials, 10,000 pressure group members, 500,000 people in public meetings, gave 190 interviews to the press, was on 20 radio and television programmes, and travelled 20,000 kms within France and 40,000 kms overseas. That was the first ballot campaign. On the second ballot campaign he held 40 meetings, six in the last six days, and visited 18 cities. At the local level, this gives the impression of ubiquity but the impact is almost lost at national level. In previous campaigns Chirac has mobilised the hard-core Gaullist vote, but, as argued, this is a diminishing asset, and the meetings do not reach the centre, floating voter, which is the aim of a presidential campaign, whether one is coming from the right or the left. The contrast here between Mitterrand's and Chirac's campaigns was stark.

Although Chirac's result was not as bad as it could have been, his future is not assured despite both his proxy leadership of the RPR, exercised through the new General Secretary, Alain Juppé, and his tenure of the Paris City Hall. There remains the question of character, real or perceived. And Chirac has yet to demonstrate the ability to come back from the politically dead which so impressed Catherine Nay about Mitterrand's career.[27]

There is also the problem of reunifying the right, and that is Chirac's biggest problem. Chirac's career until 1988 involved either internal promotion by a patron, or divisive, un-presidential victories. Chirac won purely personal victories over his own team: in 1974 over Jacques Chaban-Delmas, in 1981 over Valéry Giscard d'Estaing, and in 1988 over the best placed candidate of the right, Raymond Barre. To be the best player in your own team and to achieve this, Geoffrey Boycott-style, at the expense of your companions, is not presidential training. By 1988, Chirac had still not shown an ability to win for the conservative right, and the divisions within the camp, which were what caused its loss of the Elysée, were partly a result of Chirac's tactics.

NOTES

1. 'Unable to keep still... his smile is often strained... his movements awkward... his voice halting... his tone curt.' 'Friendly, attentive to others, generous, loyal, full of humour and humanity'. See F.-O. Giesbert, *Jacques Chirac* (Paris, Seuil, 1987), a critical but effective biography; J.-M. Cotteret and G. Mermet, *La Bataille des images* (Paris, Larousse, 1986). Giscard's 'agité' and the left's 'fascho' have stuck to Chirac very easily. Philippe Alexandre, who claims to have known Chirac over twenty-five years writes as follows: 'Chirac ... il a toujours été ainsi, sympathique, pressé,

empressé, changeant, volubile, généreux, exigeant, fidèle, superficiel, conservateur, cynique, tendre, etc. Cet homme est une collection d'adjectifs.' (p. 70). But he adds that Michel Noir said to Chirac 'Tu serais un homme d'Etat le jour où tu sauras t'arrêter quelques heures par jour pour réfléchir', *Paysage de campagne* (Paris, Grasset, 1988), p. 21; and again 'Le cœur vous serre en voyant cet homme, généreux et chaleureux, s'agiter dans tous les sens, et ainsi précipiter sa propre noyade', *ibid.*, p. 94.

2. *Le Quotidien*, 20 April 1988.

3. *Le Nouvel Observateur*, June 1986.

4. 'Even so, he has put things in order. Even so, we have a minimal inflation rate'. *Libération*, 16 April 1988.

5. *L'Express*, 15 January 1988.

6. *Le Monde*, 15 April 1988.

7. *Ibid.*.

8. *L'Express*, 4 March 1988.

9. *Le Monde*, 11 April 1988.

10. *Valeurs Actuels*, 21 March 1988.

11. *Le Monde*, 17 March 1988.

12. *Le Monde*, 18 April 1988 and *Le Monde*, 5 April 1988. See also *Le Monde*, 29 April 1988.

13. *Le Monde*, 20 April 1988.

14. *Le Quotidien*, 20 April 1988.

15. *Libération*, 27 April 1988.

16. J. Capedeveille *et. al.*, *France de gauche vote à droite* (Paris, FNSP, 1981).

17. *Libération*, 27 April 1988.

18. *Le Quotidien*, 26 April 1988.

19. *Le Monde*, 2 May 1988. Pasqua's declaration could have been made with an eye to saving the RPR City Halls in 1989 after the rout of Chirac in 1988.

20. *Figaro Magazine*, 30 April 1988.

21. IFOP *Le Monde*, 2 May 1988.

22. *Le Monde*, 2 May 1988.

23. Some voters may have switched to Le Pen on the first ballot because of the violence in New Caledonia before the first ballot, but suspicions of a deal on the hostages were fuelled by the release of Mr Mouhajer who was arrested in connection with the 1986 bombings in Paris.

24. Chirac's coups tended to be gimmicky. For example, Chirac's appeal to young voters

was garish, and included a video-montage image of the American pop singer, Madonna, superimposed over the RPR leader's face.

25. *Financial Times,* 26 February 1988. Difficult decisions, like social security reform (principally through the increase in tobacco and alcohol duties), were shelved for the election period.

26. J.-M. Cotteret and G. Mermet, *op. cit..*, p. 148.

27. In C. Nay, *Le Noir et le Rouge* (Paris, Grasset ,1981).

INDICATIVE BIBLIOGRAPHY

Alexandre, P., *Paysage de Campagne* (Paris, Grasset, 1988).

Chirac, J., *Discours pour la France à l'heure du choix* (Paris, Stock, 1978).

Chirac, J., *La Lueur de l'espérance* (Paris, Table Ronde, 1978).

Chirac, J., *Oui à l'Europe* (Paris, Albatros, 1984).

Colombani, J-M. and Lhomeau, J.-Y., *Le mariage blanc* (Paris, Grasset 1986).

Desjardins, T., *Un inconnu nommé Chirac* (Paris, Table Ronde 1983).

Desjardins, T., *Les Chiraquiens* (Paris, Table Ronde 1986).

Frémontier, J., *Les Cadets de la Droite* (Paris, Seuil, 1984).

Giesbert, F.-O., *Jacques Chirac* (Paris, Seuil, 1988).

Jouve, P., and Magoudi, A., *Chirac Portrait total* (Paris, Carrère, 1987).

Lallemand de Driesen, C., *A vous de jouer Jacques Chirac* (Paris, Bussac, 1983)

Nay, C., *La Double Méprise* (Paris, Grasset, 1980).

Nourissier, F., *Lettre ouverte à Jacques Chirac* (Paris, Albin Michel, 1977).

'Pouvoirs', *Le RPR,* no. 28 (Paris, PUF, 1984).

Schonfeld, W. R., *Ethnographie du PS et du RPR* (Paris, Economica, 1985).

Szafran, M., *Chirac ou les passions du pouvoir* (Paris, Grasset, 1986).

6 The providential loser: Raymond Barre

JOHN GAFFNEY

> 'I see my action as being of a different order from that of party leaders.'
> **Raymond Barre**

The development of presidentialism in the Fifth Republic has had two principal effects on the party system. The first is that individuals who are not in a strict relation to a political party can become serious contenders for the highest office within the polity. The second is that political parties or groupings of parties are themselves obliged to promote or support a presidential candidate in order to remain politically credible. Without a presidential contender, or association with a presidential contender, the political party is now in danger of being perceived as a spent political tradition which has lost its national calling.[1] The issue, therefore, is not that the UDF confederation allowed a 'lone' figure like Raymond Barre, Giscard d'Estaing's Prime Minister between 1976 and 1981, to represent its presidential interests in 1988, but that it simply *needed* a presidential candidate in order to avoid being dominated by its right-wing partner, the RPR.

Within the UDF itself, however, there existed many political, historical and cultural differences, many of which divided the UDF internally more than they distinguished elements within it from the RPR, or even from the Socialists, at one extreme, the *Front National* at the other. Between 1977 and 1981 Valéry Giscard d'Estaing was able to unite these disparities largely because he was the President of the Republic, offering the non-Gaullist right the possibilities of government and influence at all levels of the polity. In a word, the UDF was able to overcome its differences because the President offered it *success*. In 1988, therefore, and for as long as the UDF lasted, it needed a candidate, and Raymond Barre fulfilled this role partly because he was *not* the leader of any of its constituent, disparate and often rival elements.

Given these reasons and contexts, the fact that the UDF had a candidate, that the candidate was Raymond Barre, and that he was not powerful within the UDF itself, is, therefore, uncontentious and of limited interest. Our interest in Raymond Barre is that of establishing and appraising how a non-charismatic politician, whose style was that of someone as if uninterested in 'personality politics', if not in politics itself, was able to enter a charismatic political contest and exploit it, and for a long time remain the most formidable potential opponent to François Mitterrand for the presidency. We shall analyse here how an attempt was made to turn several disadvantages: his image of the *professeur*, of being intellectual to the point of being in no relation to the people or their perceptions, and his possession of no significant political base, to advantage, an advantage which was to make of him, after the 1988 elections, one of the main contenders for the leadership of the centre-right.

It is clear that it was Barre's having held office as Prime Minister (not simply any political outsider could make such a serious bid for the presidency) which was his major claim to national significance and his major political - perhaps, initially, his only - asset, although one which Barre himself had not seemed concerned to exploit during his period as Prime Minister.[2] Most former Prime Ministers of the Fifth Republic had exploited this political asset, and nearly all had entertained the idea of running for the presidency. Perhaps the only two not to have done so were Maurice Couve de Murville and Pierre Messmer (respectively, and briefly, de Gaulle and Pompidou's Prime Ministers), and Barre as Prime Minister was close to these two in his apparent lack of interest in a presidential career.[3] He was even less 'political' than these two in that they were both party men, Barre's reputation being based, as we have seen, upon a non-political image. The others (Debré, Pompidou, Chaban-Delmas, Mauroy and Fabius and, after the 1988 election, Rocard), though all servants of their President (Chirac is the exception to this convention), had a clear eye on the future. Raymond Barre, the professor, the economist, the workhorse, had, moreover, become Prime Minister in stark contrast to his careerist predecessor, Jacques Chirac. Like Debré or Pompidou, he had been an unerringly faithful Prime Minister but, unlike them, gave the impression that he was only barely aware of the existence of the political jungle - and that when he was, was impatient of it, so busy was he doing his job as 'France's best economist' (the expression was Giscard's). Barre, even though he had been European Commissioner and Minister for Overseas Commerce, had been nominated as Prime Minister by the President precisely because he was not associated with any political party, faction or clan, and therefore would rival the President's authority neither personally nor organisationally.

It is something of an understatement to say that, during his premiership between 1976 and 1981, Barre had been used as a buffer against damage to Valéry Giscard d'Estaing's popularity. All Prime Ministers in the Fifth Republic had played this protective role, but Barre particularly had drawn the nation's hostility away from the President to himself, his unpopularity becoming notorious. With Giscard's defeat in the presidential elections of 1981 it was generally assumed that Raymond Barre's political career was eclipsed. And with Valéry Giscard d'Estaing out of the way, Chirac's post-1981 strategy was based upon the idea that he would rapidly become the sole *présidentiable* on the right.

The bizarre twist, therefore, to the political trajectory of Raymond Barre is that his *traversée du désert*, unlike that of other contenders for power, de

Gaulle and Mitterrand especially, took place when he was in power rather than out of it. His retrospective claim to the *traversée* myth stemmed from his experience between 1976 and 1981 of being the Fifth Republic's most unpopular premier, and not from his period out of power after 1981 when his popularity came, for a time, to outstrip that of Jacques Chirac and to rival that of François Mitterrand. This subsequent popularity was based upon a generalised recognition that he may well have been right during his period of extreme national unpopularity. This is a first indication of how Raymond Barre's political fortune was acutely dependent upon public perceptions and upon the political conduct and fortunes of others.

In contemporary French political culture, moreover, only one real outsider, namely, de Gaulle, has ever been able to return to power from outside the party system itself, and this a) because of his former prestige, b) because the political system was in crisis, and c) because a large fraction of the ex-Resistance political elite was always ready to support him organisationally in any bid he might make for power. Pierre Mendès France was the only other comparable example to de Gaulle of a prestigious outsider, and he, after 1956, remained forever in the wings of history. Therefore, in spite of the strong focus upon the presidency in the Fifth Republic, and its encouragement both of individual figures and of the recapitulation of the de Gaulle myth, all contenders for power have needed the existing system (essentially political parties) in one form or another. Pompidou, Giscard d'Estaing, and Mitterrand were all in a relation of dominance to their own (or to both their own and other) political parties before they attempted to accede to the presidency. Jacques Chirac between 1976 and 1981, and François Mitterrand between 1978 and 1981 (these years being periods of vulnerability for each in terms of the viability of their potential national leadership) could bludgeon their parties into subservience and wait.[4] Raymond Barre, having no such political resource to see him through lean times, had, therefore, to make a virtue of his isolated position.

Recourse to *l'homme providentiel*, however, can only operate in one circumstance: a political crisis (or perceived crisis) which no figure from inside the prevailing institutional system is considered capable of resolving. We can see, therefore, that, because of his isolation, Raymond Barre had to develop into a national undertaking: first, the idea of his being 'outside' politics, or outside ordinary politics, and concerned only with 'real' politics rather than with the 'microcosm' (his own pejorative term for politics itself); and, second, the notion of an economic and/or institutional disorder, incapable of resolution by insiders, and the resolution of which was dependent upon his accession to power. He more or less succeeded in the first, and more or less failed in the second.

Certain elements of Barre's campaign were, therefore, paradoxical. He needed to cultivate the notion of being alone and outside politics. He needed also to remain politically relevant over a long period of time while cultivating the idea that he would simply be 'called' to power by both the 'non-political' and (elements of) the political communities at a particular moment. He also, however, needed to keep other rival leaders at bay, and, therefore, establish some form of relationship with the political parties while pretending to disdain them.

On the basis of these observations, let us divide our analysis into the four essential moments of the Barre campaign for the presidency of the Fifth Republic in 1988, four moments which correspond to challenges posed to a presidential undertaking of this kind, and which mix the mythical exigencies of a de Gaulle-like approach with the more 'microcosmic' exigencies imposed by the prevailing political system itself. They are: May 1981 - March 1986 (the restricted gathering of forces around isolated visionary leadership); March 1986 - September 1987 (the political organisation of the wider gathering); October 1987 - February 1988 (the attempt to reconcile the extra- and intra-system exigencies); February 1988 - May 1988 (the battle for leadership of the right).

May 1981 - March 1986

After Giscard's defeat in May 1981, Raymond Barre, on leaving Matignon, the Prime Minister's official residence, declared to the assembled journalists: 'Vous aurez l'occasion de me revoir'. Few took his claim to be anything more than the bravado of a lonely figure who had been rejected not only by the country but even by the President he had protected. As a result of Barre's unpopularity as Prime Minister because of his apparent coldness, his austerity measures, apparent defiance of public opinion and so on, he had, in 1981, been excluded from Giscard's presidential campaign. His total isolation and rejection in the aftermath of the 1981 elections were complete. From Matignon, he moved to a four room apartment in the Boulevard St-Germain. He retained the services of two secretaries, enjoyed the company of three or four close political friends (among them Pierre André Wiltzer and Jacques Alexandre), and returned to his studies and to teaching and lecturing.

Politically, two factors would be involved in any initial reversal of Barre's fortunes. The first was the need to justify retrospectively his premiership, in particular its economic and financial policy, and, therefore, transform his premiership into a kind of *traversée du désert*. This, in fact, was effected for him by the 'realism' imposed upon the post-1981 Socialist government, its u-turn on reflation, its own austerity measures, and the development not only of policies but also of a discourse similar to Barre's own no-nonsense economic and financial realism. The second factor was not provided for him but had to be developed and sustained, that of capitalising upon this relative reappraisal of his premiership and of projecting his national political relevance into the future so that his 'return' to power would not be seen as a return to the late 1970s, but as a move towards a new 'Barrist' France. Here myth and reality interweave and become the stuff of Barre's seven-year campaign for the presidency in 1988.

In the summer of 1981, a Dr Pierre Bocquet from Senlis wrote to Raymond

Barre, telling him that the country needed a figure like him to restore the nation's fortunes. In November, Barre attended a *dîner-débat* in Senlis attended by 80 or so people. There, he was pledged support akin to that offered to the inspired leader of a restricted, convinced community. This development was paralleled by a handful, later hundreds, finally thousands of letters, similar in intention to Dr Bocquet's. Associations of citizens in Bordeaux, Toulouse, Arras and, later, all over France, offered their support to Barre if he would respond to this national 'call' as they were urging him to.[5] The image projected was that of *la France profonde,* once again in its history, turning belatedly to a saviour.

Barre's provincial *dîner-débats* became weekly affairs, as one association after another pledged its support to him. The beginnings of a network of loyalists who, ostensibly, represented the French people themselves, and who would 'rise on the day', was being created. Barre began publishing (from November 1982) a monthly newsletter, *Faits et Arguments*, which was produced in copies of 20,000 and distributed to subscribers (and from 1986 sold through newsagents). By the end of 1982, the media began to take notice, treating Barre as a serious potential political force in the country, in this way responding to and enhancing the development of a national rally around the persona of Raymond Barre.

Two initial points can be made here in terms of Barre's political undertaking. First, although the political system encouraged individuals to contend seriously for the presidency, the continuing strength of the party system meant that individuals such as Barre were forced into attempts to create and subsequently detonate a rally of opinion from outside the formal political institutions which, organisationally, would rival the local and national power bases of the parties. Second, it was Barre's established reputation for economic soundness which enabled him subsequently to develop a stature which went beyond his earlier status and establish an institutional *prise de position* vis-à-vis the Republic itself. Barre's dual 'economic' past and future political potential, therefore, were designed to undermine symbolically not only those who had governed after him (the Socialists) but also the political dominance of the premier he had replaced in 1977, namely, Jacques Chirac. This brings us to the next phase of Barre's campaign, which was the *cohabitation* period which began after the 1986 legislative elections, and Chirac's return to power as Mitterrand's Prime Minister.

March 1986 - October 1987

This next phase of Raymond Barre's campaign was prefaced by two factors. The first was his unhappy descent into the 'microcosm' in March 1986. He was re-elected as an MP (he was first elected in 1978) but with a reduced majority which was attributed, probably accurately, to his asserted distance from the rest of the right, a distance he had to maintain in order to mark himself off from Jacques Chirac's leadership of the right.[6] This potential accusation of being a *diviseur* of the right was to shape and constrain his campaign thereafter. The second related and, again, constraining factor, was that the RPR-UDF national electoral coalition won the 1986 legislative elections by only a very slim majority. This meant that Barre, who was (somewhat incongruously as the post-1988 period would show) opposed to the right's *cohabitation* with a Socialist President, could not derive the benefit of rhetorical denunciations of it: if his rhetoric or his vote had brought the government down, he would have amplified his reputation as a *diviseur* and suffered accordingly, being seen not as the solution to the political crisis but as the cause of it.

It was also the case that Barre's hitherto purely economic discourse (or rather the public perception that his view was solely an economic one) had to be revised if he was to present himself as a *political* alternative to both Socialism and neo-Gaullism. His clear opposition to *cohabitation* as being antithetical to the Fifth Republic (though severely constrained by the fact that, like Chirac in the late 1970s, he had to avoid provoking a governmental crisis) reinforced the development of such an alternative position. The development of an institution-related discourse followed. And it is here that Barre's 'lone' campaign links up with the myth of de Gaulle, in terms both of his institutional critique of *cohabitation* (treating it as de Gaulle treated the Fourth Republic and, therefore, as a betrayal of the Fifth) and of his presentation of himself as the guarantor of a continuing Gaullian interpretation of the republiç (a strong, impartial President who was free of the political parties).

Faits et Arguments, Barre's monthly newsletter, became, in the *cohabitation* period, a parallel economic discourse to that of Chirac's government. In a typically Barre-like way it took on the aspect of the economics professor marking and correcting the government's initiatives in economic policy. More importantly, however, it also began to amplify the Gaullian aspect of Barre's campaign. Here is a typical example:

> L'observateur est conduit à se demander s'il ne s'agit pas d'une revanche, longtemps attendue, de la classe politique, et de tout ce qui gravite autour d'elle, sur la Ve République.[7]

Moreover, such a critique was not only an institutional one, its *personal* nature evoking memories of a de Gaulle criticising from outside the *régime des partis* of the Fourth Republic.

By the end of 1986, through provincial speeches, the diffusion (in their thousands) of the texts of speeches made at these, through *Faits et Arguments,* and, especially, through media reporting, Barre, without any major public interventions (although present in the National Assembly, especially on Wednesday afternoon at Prime Minister's question time, he never spoke), had not only established a series of publicly perceived attitudes to the predominant themes and issues of contemporary political life, but had also arranged these - and his relationship to them - in such a way as to suggest not only that he had an overall view of politics which went far beyond the purely economic, but that this world view, and the viewing associated with it, were quintessentially reminiscent of de Gaulle himself.

Barre consistently asserted, moreover, in a Gaullian manner, that he would make no promises to anyone or any interest group, while simultaneously developing his views on a whole series of issues: a *personnalisme social* reminiscent of de Gaulle's *participation* theme (and Mounier's), national defence, East-West relations, culture and the media, *les droits de l'homme*, and financial reform, and later, education and, finally, agriculture.[8]

Ironically, this period was called by the media Barre's 'year of silence' (March 1986-January 1987). In a sense this was true; Barre's interventions were quiet ones, usually made at provincial meetings, rarely national (Parisian) ones. It was as if Barre was continuing not only the developmental construction of his presidential persona, but also - through a breathtaking timetable of provincial meetings - the idea of the recreation and reactivation of a quietist *France profonde* which would, come the day, propel its champion to power. Nevertheless, Barre had, contrary to the media's assertion, been anything but silent. And there was, of course, an organisational complement to this development. During this 'year of silence', the developing army of Barre's collaborators was undertaking the coordination and development of the provincial associations which had expressed their support for him. Throughout the summer of 1986, two of Barre's closest collaborators, Charles Millon and Sylvie Dumaine, had toured France, laying the ground for what was to become a national, politically coordinated network of associational support for Barre's campaign for the presidency.

In the summer of 1986, Charles Millon created the organisation REEL (*réalisme-efficacité-espérance-liberté*) in order to coordinate the hundreds of pro-Barrist associations. This involved monthly meetings of between 12 and 80 local people, each chaired by a nationally known person. REEL established contact with groups in 85 departments, created a constant flow of information to them, established workshops on particular themes, and produced a bi-monthly bulletin, the first seven issues of which were printed at a rate of 35,000 copies (the figure was to rise considerably later).[9] In June 1987, moreover, REEL created four campaign-style departments concerned with *communication* (to develop coordination between the associations), *idées* (on the development of themes related to Barre's campaign), *terrain* (to address the problems and issues at the local level), and *accueil* (to recruit, inform and publicise).[10] At this time, REEL also created several subsidiary organisations in order to extend its influence: REEL *jeunes*, REEL *entreprises*, REEL *initiatives sociales*, and REEL *élus locaux*. Charles Millon had also created a twice-monthly bulletin of information and coordination of the associations related to the REEL network. Initially, these were printed at the rate of 40,000 copies. By December 1987, this had risen to 150,000 copies, and, from September 1987, between 500 and 1,000 new subscribers were being registered each week. In February 1988, *Faits et Arguments* became bi-monthly, and the campaign team also put out a weekly, *Barre Hebdo*.

Throughout this period, Barre continued his provincial meetings but added to these major rally speeches in, for example, Lille, 2 October 1986 (from where he went on to visit de Gaulle's birthplace), Roubaix, 3 October, Paris, 22 November, and Toulouse, 11 December. These speeches, normally devoted to one theme such as *participation, les droits de l'homme*, and *la défense nationale*, illustrate the developing image of Barre's national persona. Throughout this period, however, he maintained his silence, partly self-imposed and partly forced by the government's thin majority, on the 'small' questions concerning the daily politics and fortunes of *cohabitation*.[11] In early October a rally meeting of the traditional right in Vittel was staged. Chirac was present, but neither Giscard nor Barre attended.[12] Barre's absence - and by implication his distance from established politics - served his image well at this time: he remained as if above politics and yet still of potential significance on the political scene. His campaign was also able to imply by this time that significant elements of the political community and the country at large were being attracted to him as if to a magnet (one of the hallmarks of the visionary *recours*) while he himself was doing nothing to undermine the government or engineer his own political preeminence. By late 1986, not only was REEL becoming nationally established, but certain key personalities, Simone Veil, Christian Bonnet, Jean-Pierre Soisson, and to a less clear extent Giscard himself, were rallying to Barre to the point where a *mouvance barriste* seemed to be developing.[13] Moreover, certain link people were beginning to play the role of intermediary between Barre and Giscard, Barre and the UDF, and Barre and Chirac: Jean Lecanuet, Lionel Stoléru, Michel d'Ornano, among others, began acting in this way, drawing Barre closer to the established right. In October, Barre had his first significant meeting with Giscard since 1981 (and the following March the latter would declare that he would not be a candidate for the presidency). At the same time, it was estimated that 50 MPs inside the UDF were unequivocally committed to Barre. Circles of interest were established involving meetings of the dozen or so MPs closest to Barre, then meetings of locally-elected officials supportive of Barre, and finally meetings between the first two groups and potential converts of local significance. Barre began to issue to local people whose loyalty was unquestioned, a *carte de confiance*, a card of no statutory or other significance but which simply meant that the holder enjoyed a *compagnon de la première heure* status vis-à-vis Raymond Barre reminiscent of that enjoyed by de Gaulle's earliest supporters.

At the same time, and at the more profane level, Jean Lecanuet, the president of the UDF, partly in order to maintain the cohesion of the UDF, was negotiating both with the constituent elements of the UDF and with the RPR, in order to ensure that the UDF would field only one candidate in the 1988 presidential elections. The effect of this was to increase the momentum of UDF support for Raymond Barre without involving him directly in deals with the several factions within the UDF.[14] A concomitant development was taking place which involved the public presentation of the relationship between Jacques Chirac and Raymond Barre as being one between the two sole and equal presidential representatives of the right.

It was also clear that although Chirac could no longer ignore Barre's presence, Barre was himself being drawn necessarily closer to the 'microcosm' in an effort to a) derive support from the UDF, and b) ensure that his potential rivals (François Léotard in particular) were unable to impose themselves as the UDF's candidate. Chirac began to speak favourably of Barre at this point, and, in October, Barre met to discuss strategy with Edouard Balladur, Chirac's Finance minister (another meeting between Balladur and Barre took place in March the following year (and between Chirac and Barre in May) when the *code de bonne conduite* was formalised). This meeting was the first step in the establishment of the 'good conduct' rule, a modus vivendi which meant that Chirac and Barre (and their supporters) would avoid public attacks upon each other. The overall result of all these developments was the acceptance by the whole of the traditional right that Barre would be a candidate for the presidency alongside the RPR's candidate. We shall come back to the ultimate significance of these developments for Barre. We can say here that one of the effects of a good conduct code upon Barre's image, given that it drew him much closer to the 'microcosm' itself and involved him in objectively condoning or accepting *cohabitation* and the prevailing political establishment, while securing his unrivalled position as the UDF's candidate, was partially to withdraw from him the image of being a real *recours* on the margins of French political life.[15]

From this point, Barre's supporters, and especially his closest lieutenants, relatively secure in the belief that Barre would be the centre-right's only candidate, began to argue on every possible occasion that Barre was not a solitary figure but, on the contrary, had a great deal of clear, straightforward (non-mythical) support, and (often added as an afterthought, though the frequency of the assertion is an indication of the considered need to project the message) was very human, an ordinary family man who loved good food, had a great sense of humour, and so on.[16]

In terms of our overall analysis we should note here that the notion that the original depiction of Barre as a solitary figure was one which had to be subsequently corrected was something of a trompe l'œil. By 1987, Barre had been projected as alone yet not alone, aloof yet human, apart from the parties yet in some relationship to them. The real issue, therefore, was not whether Barre was or was not alone but that he was, simultaneously, both alone and not alone, that is, in terms of the Gaullist myth, *originally* alone and subsequently rallied to by a huge section of the population.[17] Such a consideration operated at *both* the mythical and the practical level and illustrates the true significance of Barre's attempt for the presidency in a presidential system in which the political parties exercise significant influence. In mythical terms, as we have suggested, Barre needed to be seen as both alone and rallied to; in a very practical sense he had to be, for the reasons we have discussed, both dissociated from any single component of the UDF and yet acceptable to the UDF as a whole in order that it could cohere around a candidate, thus enabling it to present itself as at least equal in political significance to its RPR partner.

1987 saw a further development in Barre's campaign, and a further development of his political image (and here we have a good illustration of the role of the media, and especially television, in the political processes of the republic). In January 1987, Barre's *rentrée politique* took the form of an appearance on *L'Heure de Vérité*, the popular television programme. As a result of this, the *national* reappearance of Raymond Barre (for nine months his political itinerary had been essentially provincial) was sympathetically received, and his popularity in the polls increased significantly.[18] This was also a time of extreme unpopularity for Jacques Chirac and his government (and to a lesser extent, for the President, François Mitterrand) because of student unrest (in response to proposed governmental policy on education), and an SNCF strike, both of which erupted at the end of 1986 and which seemed, moreover, to question the soundness of judgement of the Prime Minister and the credibility and viability of *cohabitation* itself. We can make two points here: 1) that public perception of Raymond Barre himself as a *recours* was crucial to his popularity, and; 2) as we have already seen, that his political fortunes, both good and ill, were in a systematic relation of dependence to those of Mitterrand, Chirac and *cohabitation* generally.

As has been stressed, however, in the introductory chapter of this volume, *cohabitation* itself, though never enthusiastically welcomed, was never unequivocally condemned, given that it was generally recognised as being the result of force of circumstance and not deliberately engineered by anyone specifically. The sympathy which could be generated for those involved in it who 'did their best' for the country was always a potential asset to them (and, of course, a potential handicap for Barre, as we have seen, in terms of his constant potential for being seen not only as a *diviseur* now of the right but as a threat to regime stability generally).[19] In this context, Barre, throughout 1987, could *only* continue to develop the '*grands thèmes*' of his enterprise (though often now through image-making international visits), and project his image in the media and through the intermediary of his entourage in the same way as he had since 1981, as *un homme de recours* who would not descend into the political arena. In spite of his inevitable association with the UDF on the one hand, and the exigencies of the presidential election campaign on the other, he did not deviate significantly from this attitude of preoccupied greatness right up until the first round vote of 24 April 1988.

One subtle change, however, involved Barre's developing a further aspect of the Gaullist myth. At the now traditional CDS *jeunesse* meeting at the beginning of September at Hourtin, Barre made the comment: 'j'aurai besoin de vous' to his audience. Most observers saw this as an indication of Barre the loner realising at last the need to win support and to refute his loner image. From our analysis we can see that this is not the point at all, nor is the observation strictly accurate, given, as we have seen, that this notion of the rallied-to loner had been developed for some considerable time. The widely-reported Hourtin declaration and speech involved the development of a very particular image of the leader and his relation to his following: the 'I need you' does not elevate the status of 'you' to that of 'I', but enhances the status of 'I', that is the 'I' of the providential leader recapitulating the Gaullist myth of the rally of the people.[20] From the *rentrée* of September 1987, therefore, what was being developed separately by Barre and by his supporters was the notion of a providential leader on the fringe of formal politics as if ready and waiting to be called forward by an awakening *France profonde* .

At a weekend meeting in Talloires on 12 October, Barre assembled his 25 most trusted MPs and gave them a series of prudential guidelines on how to go out and take his message (essentially an optimistic, humanist one) to the wider public. At the end of October, addressing the assembled delegates of REEL, Barre quoted de Gaulle:

> 'Je vous demande votre confiance car vous savez que vous pouvez compter sur la mienne'.

In November he imparted a similar confidence to 53 of his closest MPs, and at a well-attended meeting of supporters in Toulouse at the end of November he declared:

> Vous incarnez cette France calme et solide qui se détourne des agitations et des querelles.

What is interesting from these examples of a leader addressing his supporters is the *style* of address: its perpetual stress upon an almost sublime mission coupled with the quiet advice and reassurance of a towering figure; and its attempt to activate a further element of the de Gaulle myth, that of generalising from the more restricted rally of *compagnons* to the idea of a great national awakening.[21]

At the organisational level, the image of a gathering of ideas and an arousing of *la France profonde* was cultivated further. Colloquia were held on a host of 'themes', the results of which, like *cahiers de doléances*, were sent to Barre's headquarters in Paris. The symbolic reciprocal gesture took the form of large-screen televised addresses by Barre to the meetings organised in his support. At this point, the campaign began to focus specifically on the theme of the young. Practically speaking, this involved the creation of a Barrist appeal to the millions of young voters. Over and above this, however, was the enhancement of Barre's status as 'envisioning' a future society, and as representing a new generation of French men and women. The cycle which saw Barre's reputation transform itself from one based on past rectitude to that of a man preparing to be a representative of the future was complete.[22]

October 1987 - 8 February 1988

As the official campaign of the spring of 1988 approached, the contradictory nature of the relationship between the two main rightist candidates - whose political fortunes were based upon the necessary elimination of one of them - entered its most delicate phase. Even though Barre and Chirac's potential electorate were not identical, there was an enormous overlap between them. The problem was equally, however, one concerning symbolic personal status. If hostilities broke out between them in public, both would suffer in public opinion. This situation had never happened before, that is to say, two rival leaders appealing for the support of the same electorate and having to coexist peacefully over a long period of time.[23] The good conduct code was, therefore, maintained but in an increasingly artificial atmosphere. The two leaders were occasionally seen together at meetings and continued to meet, as did their lieutenants, privately, in order to avoid damaging public quarrels.[24] By this point, however, by the beginning of 1988, it was becoming clear that the good conduct rule meant that Barre could not attack Chirac, and that Chirac could ignore Barre.

However, for organisational as well as more symbolic reasons related to the fundamentals of his claim to the presidency, Barre's campaign strategy could not change. Whenever questioned by journalists in this period after the *rentrée politique* in October 1987, he always placed great emphasis upon work and travel as if he were as ever preoccupied with greater things, and with talking to the people of France, quietly, as if party to a secret with the silent majority. It is also true, however, that Barre's campaign was becoming paralysed by the several exigencies which gave rise to it on the one hand, and informed its continuing existence on the other, that is to say, the development of a political persona which refused the cut and thrust of political debate, and the 'fickleness' of changing opinion (as measured by polls). As the official campaign approached, Barre was reluctant to alter either the tempo of his campaign or its direction (he and Chirac had been likened respectively to the tortoise and the hare, though, in fact the tortoise ascription to Barre had begun when he was still Prime Minister in 1979). Given not only his character but the nature of his claim to the presidency, such an alternation was, in any case, impossible.

In this context, the problems for Barre on the question of the parties' support in the run-up to the elections were both practical and symbolic: practical, as we have seen, because the UDF parties had to be seen to be working for Barre rather than against him (actively or surreptitiously); symbolic in that their purely contractual support, though necessary, would not be sufficient to generate the *'on va gagner'* rally quality enjoyed by both Chirac and Mitterrand vis-à-vis their parties and devotionally displayed (especially in Chirac's case) by the dedicated activism of their members. However, purely contractual party support, and even much of that questionable, was all that Barre could attain, given, in the first place, the ambiguous position of the UDF vis-à-vis the Chirac government (many of the UDF's leading personalities were part of that government), in the second, the developing rivalries of its leaders, especially François Léotard (and to a more subtle extent Giscard d'Estaing), and their perception that they and their movements might profit less from a Barre first-round victory than from a Chirac one, and, in the third, Barre's fundamental hostility to the parties themselves, a sentiment not lost on many UDF activists and their party headquarters.

Of the several constituent elements of the UDF, all of which gave their formal support to Barre, none - with the possible exception of the CDS - gave it wholeheartedly. One after another in January 1988 the organised elements of the confederation gave Barre their official support: The *Clubs Perspectives et Réalités*; the CDS, the PR, the PSD, and the Radicals. In nearly all cases, however, the internal support was roughly 60:40 rather than the undisputed 100% support enjoyed by Chirac and Mitterrand in their own parties. And Barre's response to the parties' support, his thanks to them, his development of a *conseil politique* involving them, and, after the official declaration of his candidacy, his active collaboration with them by incorporating them - along with REEL - into *comités de soutien*, all had something about it which seemed to negate the whole seven-year strategy. Over and above this, the last-minute conflation of REEL with the party organisations into the support committees had no real campaign logic and in fact led to inaction and acrimony rather than to mobilisation.

The Election Campaign, 8 February-23 April 1988

It was generally assumed by Barre and his entourage, as well as by observers, that he would need, in the first round, to achieve a score of around 28% or else be at a distance of only 10% behind François Mitterrand in order to hope to win the election on the second round. His failure, therefore, to pull away from Chirac by February 8 when Barre declared his candidacy, three weeks after Chirac, was seen as an early indication of the failure of his bid for the presidency. An article in *Le Point*,[25] commenting on Barre's long, quiet, seven-year campaign made an apposite comparison of his campaign on the byways of politics about to meet the motorway juggernauts of the RPR.[26] Without having been able to outdistance Chirac significantly by February 1988, ten weeks before the first round of the election, Barre's official campaign needed, in order to create a dynamic for the *first* round of the election, to be a superb one in terms of the timed public intervention of himself and his lieutenants, his use of the media, his response to Chirac's interventions, the mobilisation of support, and his campaign publicity. And superb his campaign was not. After the first round, many commentators remarked that Barre's official campaign was an excellent illustration of how *not* to conduct a presidential campaign. Criticism was aimed at the chaos or inaction of the campaign network, the dullness of the campaign posters, at Barre's own apparent inaction, and at the machinations of the RPR. The reasons for the failure of Barre's campaign for the presidency in 1988 are, however, both simpler and more complex than these observations might lead us to believe.

Barre's campaign was essentially focused on the second round, and was fundamentally ill-equipped to respond positively to the first. It was, however, the nature of Barre's claim to the presidency - and not strategically misguided decisions - which brought this situation about. In terms of the media presentation of his personal image, Barre made all the correct interventions in early 1988, projecting a more 'human' personality while retaining his presidential stature. *Questions à domicile* (14 February), *Club de la Presse* (21

February), *Le Monde en Face* (17 March), and *L'Heure de vérité* (23 March) can all be measured as trials in which Barre acquitted himself more than adequately. Chirac's campaign, however, was fundamentally a first-round campaign directed, in spite of its ostensible targeting of Mitterrand, against Raymond Barre. Essentially, Chirac's campaign involved, in its first phase, the marginalisation of Raymond Barre, that is to say, the treatment of Barre as irrelevant. This took several forms. First, Chirac's team neutralised Barre by destroying his 'economic' difference from Chirac: Chirac's economic proposals (declared one month before Barre's candidacy) were very similar to Barre's (much to the impotent fury of the latter's supporters). After Barre's 8 February declaration, Chirac immediately affirmed that Barre's proposals were exactly the same, *mot pour mot*, as his own earlier proposals. Moreover, whenever Barre made an announcement, there was immediate media saturation by Chirac's lieutenants (for example by Juppé on RMC, Toubon on RTL, and Pasqua on *France-Inter* after Barre's *Questions à domicile,* involving their assertions that Barre's views were identical to the Prime Minister's own. We should also note the many interventions of Balladur which *stylistically* were very similar to Barre's own).

Barre's necessarily second-round strategy was being thrown into a first-round contest in which his adversary was not, in fact, François Mitterrand but Jacques Chirac.[27] Barre's continuing silence on Chirac's campaign, while he waited for his 'real' adversary, François Mitterrand, to declare his candidacy, added a further dynamism to Chirac's campaign and a further sense of irrelevance to the apparently inactive Barre. The one major attack by Barre and his lieutenants upon Chirac (presented to the press by Durieux at the end of January) involved criticism of the economic failures of the Mitterrand seven-year presidency, that is, the period which covered not only the Mauroy and Fabius governments, but also the *cohabitation* period.[28] This attack, however, simply resulted in the Barrists arguing in public with Chirac's supporters in what was called the *bataille des bilans* over the finer details of the 1981-1987 period as a whole. Over and above the image of bickering and point-scoring that this sole major attack generated, it threatened both the support of those UDF people who had participated in the 1986-1988 government, and, by extension, the potential RPR support in the second round.

As early as four days after Barre's declaration of his candidacy on 8 February the press and media were already claiming (and his entourage privately accepting) that Barre's campaign was thoroughly inadequate and that Chirac would beat him in the first round. In one of his few major interventions, to the 4,000 delegates at the National Council of the UDF on 13 February, Barre repeated, and was to repeat again, his Gaullian 'J'ai besoin de vous', and 'aidez-moi'. Now, however, such expressions carried with them less a tone of Gaullian authority, rather a note of desperation. From this point, his entourage was emphasising on every occasion that Barre was the best rightist candidate to face Mitterrand in the second round. This too was no longer simply an assertion but more like an increasingly desperate appeal to the electorate to allow Raymond Barre through round one in order that he could then reveal his undeclared potential. A campaign necessarily designed for the second round, which would include the television debate with François Mitterrand, and the confrontation of the nation's two heavyweights, was disintegrating before the first round had barely begun. Such developments reinforced the view held in political circles that when it came to 'real' politics, Raymond Barre was an amateur. The impression conveyed to the public was that Barre's 'waiting' for Mitterrand (who did not declare his candidacy until 22 March) demonstrated not only his refusal but his inability to respond to the dynamism of Chirac's campaign.

Barre's Minitel service and telephone answering service in which he presented his ideas alongside a personal profile, his long interview on the economy in *L'Expansion* (4 March), the publicising of the 80,000 *bulletins de soutien* received at party headquarters during February, and the creation of a weekly campaign paper, *Barre Hebdo*, were paltry manifestations compared to the national mobilisation of the RPR, and the timely interventions of Chirac's lieutenants at every opportunity.

By mid-March, Barre and Chirac were level in the opinion polls, the former on a downward trend, the latter on an upward one. By this time a kind of panic (similar to that within the British Conservative Party in the 1987 election when it feared it might lose) was gripping Barre's campaign team. The campaign posters were condemned as not persuasive and too bland. Even the split between the two-site headquarters in the Boulevard St-Germain was blamed. The older members of the campaign team were castigated, and the younger ones (Philippe de Villiers especially) were brought in on a daily basis to try to accelerate the campaign's momentum. Sympathetic MPs began talking of the need for a 'miracle' if the situation was to change. Barre, in the absence of Mitterrand as a candidate, continued his muted criticisms of the *cohabitation* period (e.g. TF1, 4 March), but by now the campaign had taken a different direction. Given that Chirac, and soon Mitterrand, would be campaigning on future-orientated tickets (in order to distinguish themselves from one another given their two-year association), attacks of this kind became increasingly irrelevant. In fact, neither Mitterrand nor Chirac were defending *cohabitation*, and only Barre was covertly criticising it. Moreover, two further and simultaneous developments took the headlines, both of which further marginalised Raymond Barre. The first was Chirac's flirtation with racist themes which seemed to make the choice as being that between Chirac and Mitterrand's world view. This was underscored when Mitterrand declared his candidacy on 22 March and also chose to emphasise the race issue, thus further suggesting that the fight was between him and the right/extreme right.[29] The second was Mitterrand's vigorous entry into the campaign which was based upon a surprisingly violent attack upon the 'cliques' and 'clans' as epitomised by the political parties, that is to say, not only a direct attack upon Chirac, but exactly the anti-party approach which had been adopted by Barre from 1981 onwards. Between them, therefore, Chirac (on the economy) and Mitterrand (on the institutions, and in fact, in terms of the appropriation of a Gaullian, disdainful, presidential *style*) stripped Raymond Barre of his exclusive status, and then went on to confront each other as if Barre did not exist. This was reflected in the media with Barre ending his campaign by limply complaining that it was being ignored. By mid-April Barre's opinion poll rating had fallen to 15%. A late rally to Barre was to occur, but his score of 16% on 24 April confirmed the failure of his campaign.

* * *

In terms of Barre's campaign for the presidency of the French Republic in 1988, we can make four concluding observations.

First, nowhere, in any of the ninety-six departments, did Raymond Barre beat Giscard d'Estaing's 1981 first-round vote. The circumstances, of course, were radically different. Nevertheless, the effect of such a failure to better Giscard's 1981 performance would enhance the latter's renewed claim to represent the centre-right after the 1988 elections, and thus counter Barre's pretensions to exclusive dominance of the centre-right in the late 1980s.

Second, Barre's campaign for the presidency of the Republic, if it had been successful (in either the first or second round), would have brought the Gaullist legend to its apogee, that is, the triumph of the individual leader over the party machines, the *féodalités*. From our analysis, however, we can see a) that the virtually total dependence of a personality upon extemporaneous factors meant that personal intervention and the ability to influence, even respond to, events, and, by extension, increase personal status, was seriously constrained, and b) that the existence of credible rival presidential figures *within* a system which encouraged presidentialism was a factor in the marginalisation of Barre's campaign because it questioned his relevance.[30] Related to this is the problem of the relation of such a presidential undertaking to the political parties themselves. Barre was unable to rally the unequivocal support of the UDF parties, either organisationally or symbolically, given that his claim to the leadership of the nation involved a repudiation of the parties' claims to political leadership. It is highly unlikely, therefore, given the mediocre UDF support, that he would have generated any significant mobilising support from the RPR were he to have got through to the second round.

Thirdly, on the question of Raymond Barre's image and projected personality, it is clear that his dependence upon the comportment of other candidates was total. In the event, Mitterrand stripped him of the claim to be the only guarantor of the institutions, Chirac (and others, Balladur and Rocard in particular) stripped him of his claim to exclusive economic preeminence. We can add to this that Le Pen (and the thin *cohabitation* parliamentary majority) also stripped him of his 'anti-system' stance.

Finally, and paradoxically, his own aloof campaign style, Chirac's low first round vote and Le Pen's 15% vote, actually enhanced Barre's political potential in the post-May 1988 period. His refusal to compromise and descend into the microcosm à la 'battling Jack', as some of the media described Chirac, became a sound asset, especially given Chirac's opportunist attitude to a strengthened extreme right. Moreover, Mitterrand's appeals to the centre, calls for *ouverture,* and the results of the June legislative elections, placed Barre in a nodal position in French politics (involving him in a clear rivalry with Giscard d'Estaing), making him, in the medium-term, a *recours* not in presidential but, once again, ironically, in prime ministerial terms.

All of these developments, the successes like the failures - all linked to Barre's demonstrable integrity - meant that, even though he did not get the chance to compete for the presidency against François Mitterrand, his political stature was further enhanced, projecting his presidential prospects forward to the next presidential contest. They also demonstrated how an individual in the Fifth Republic, without significant party support, could make and maintain a claim to national leadership, both before and after 1988.

NOTES

1. Linked to this is the fact that it is only the round-one constituencies, however small, which are considered significant in the electoral arithmetic of round two, that is to say, that to be credible, all political parties must be active throughout the presidential campaign.

2. It is possible that Barre's brief hospitalisation in Val de Grâce when Prime Minister (which saw his popularity rise significantly in the opinion polls) was an indication that, in spite of everything, his relation to Giscard's popularity was not a completely strict one but included a personal relation to the electorate.

3. Michel Rocard, appointed in May 1988, is an exception of a different kind in that public acknowledgement of his presidential potential pre-dated his premiership.

4. Such pre-eminence being itself not eternal even for such party leaders. If Mitterrand had lost the 1981 election, his position would most likely have become as delicate, vis-à-vis the PS, as Chirac's became after 1988, vis-à-vis the RPR.

5. Out of respect for a kind of political protocol, Barre did not create associations in Chirac's Limousin or Giscard's Auvergne.

6. Comparisons of the 1986 legislative election with others is, however, extremely difficult given the different electoral system used.

7. 'The observer is led to ask himself if it is not a question of a long-awaited revenge of the political class, and all that gravitates around it, upon the Fifth Republic.' Quoted in *Le Point*, 10 November 1986.

8. One of the factors of Barre's campaign which was to constrain its development in its later stages was the fact that none of his proposals could take a very concrete form for fear of appearing like the electoral promises of a 'microcosmic' candidate.

9. REEL eventually established itself nationally, developed computerised *fichiers* of supporters, systematic access to leading supporters, and coordination of the hundreds of associations supportive of Barre.

10. There were also extra sub-departments established concerned with France's overseas territories, the raising of funds, and the targeting of France's thousands of voters living

and working abroad.

11. Barre also took positions on certain other topical issues such as the Klaus Barbie trial, and the Aids issue, positions which were generally liberal, republican positions.

12. Interestingly, an earlier rightist convention which both Barre and Chirac attended was completely dominated by Giscard d'Estaing.

13. Opinion polls reflected and doubtless also contributed to the development of Barre's rising popularity.

14. This issue of the UDF's candidates flared up again the following April when it seemed that François Léotard, the leader of the UDF's main element, the PR, might run for the presidency. This issue, which dominated media reporting in April and May of 1987, became, however, a contest between Léotard and Chirac (whose Minister Léotard was) rather than one involving Barre. In September 1987, Lecanuet reaffirmed that the UDF would have only one candidate.

15. In fact the person to profit from Barre's abandoning his potentially anti-system stance was Jean-Marie Le Pen.

16. A good illustration of this supportive portrayal of Barre was Bernard Stasi's long interview in *L'Express*, 23 October 1987.

17. For an unusually early and perspicacious comment on this necessary duality in Barre's strategy, see article by Fabien Roland-Lévy in *Libération*, 14 January 1986.

18. An earlier *Heure de Vérité* appearance (January 1983) had not been a success.

It would be useful to give here a synthesis of Raymond Barre's fortunes in the opinion polls. It was from mid-1984 that Barre began to score well in the polls, and after January 1985 there was a significant increase in his popularity. With the legislative elections of March 1986 and the formation of the Chirac government, Barre's popularity began to fall. This fall continued until the end of the year when he had fallen below Chirac (although the latter never attained Barre's own earlier popularity rating (57% at its best)). Chirac's popularity was based not only upon his premiership but also upon a kind of national solidarity because of the spate of terrorist bombings in Paris through 1986. From late 1986, Barre's popularity began to rise steeply once more (this was the time of the student unrest and SNCF strike), overtaking that of Mitterrand for a time in January, and continued to remain strong throughout 1987 (and this in spite of the fact that many polls after march 1986, were only concerned with the popularity of *cohabitation* and, therefore, with Mitterrand and Chirac's popularity). In October 1987 (at the time of the Wall Street crash), there was another steep rise in Barre's popularity (paralleled, however, by that of Balladur). In November 1987, Barre was still 10% points ahead of Chirac. At the end of 1987, it still looked as if it would be a Barre/Mitterrand second round contest in the presidential elections. From January 1988 Barre started falling in the polls, Chirac rising. By February and March Chirac had overtaken him.

19. Barre was always vulnerable to this idea of being a *diviseur*. In early 1987, Gérard Longuet, one of Chirac's UDF ministers, even accused Barre of one of the most disparaging traits in French political culture by likening him to General Boulanger who had threatened the delicate stability of the Third Republic in the late 1880s.

20. This accentuation of the 'moi' in the moment of evocation and appeal to 'vous' had been a hallmark of de Gaulle's discourse particularly in moments of acute national crisis.

21. Barre's presidential stature was also enhanced at this time by several overseas trips, for example to Cairo in November, and Sénégal in December.

22. On 29 October Barre made a speech at the Catholic University in Lille to 3,000 students. Another significant Barrist appeal to the young was Phillipe de Villiers' *Lettres aux Jeunes* published in January 1988. It is worth stressing, moreover, that on the 24 April first-round vote Barre did capture a better youth vote than his rival Chirac.

23. The only comparable rivalry, in 1974, between Giscard d'Estaing and Chaban-Delmas was over a very short period. And, arguably, Giscard's work was done for him here by his then ally Jacques Chirac.

24. Given the underlying hostility, such coordination, however, was restricted largely to mutual accords concerning problems such as not pasting over each other's campaign posters.

25. *Le Point*, 30 November 1987.

26. Barre's declaration on 8 February was also a very down-beat affair, and his flimsy *Projet pour la France* did not appear until nearly two months later.

27. A further irony here is that, even after Mitterrand's declaration of 22 March, Barre's attacks upon Mitterrand were minimal.

28. Charles Millon also presented a 15-page document to the same effect on 18 March.

29. In organisational terms, too, Barre was further marginalised at this time by Edouard Balladur's unexpected declaration that, after the elections, the RPR and UDF might merge.

30. It is also worth pointing out here that the Wall Street crash of October 1987 did not produce any radical *mise en question* of the republic's ability to cope with the crisis.

INDICATIVE BIBLIOGRAPHY

Amouroux, H., *Monsieur Barre* (Paris, Laffont, 1986, and Hachette, 1988).

Barre, R., *Une politique pour l'avenir* (Paris, Plon, 1982).

Barre, R., *Economie Politique* (13e ed.) (Paris, PUF, 1983).

Barre, R., *Un plan pour l'Europe* (Presses Universitaire de Nancy, 1984).

Barre, R., *Réflexions pour demain* (Paris, Hachette, 1984).

Barre, R., *Au tournant du siècle* (Paris, Plon, 1988).

Barre, R., and Colombani, J., *Questions de confiance* (Paris, Flammarion, 1987).

Chamard, M., and Macé-Scaron, J., *La Galaxie Barre* (Paris, Table Ronde, 1987).

De Montvalon, D. and Pierre-Brossollette, S., *Le couple impossible* (Paris, Belfond, 1987).

Rémilleux, J.-L., *Les Barristes* (Paris, Albin Michel, 1987).

7 Campaigning from the fringe: Jean-Marie Le Pen

JAMES G. SHIELDS

'It is the reflection of an urbanised France in which the effects of economic recession coincide with the presence of large immigrant communities. What is remarkable about the election of 24 April, however, is that the FN gained ground throughout the length and breadth of France, exercising an appeal beyond the boundaries of its natural constituency.'[1]

French presidential elections, it is often observed, serve a dual function. In the first round, voters vent their feelings; in the second, they elect a Head of State. The elections of 24 April and 8 May 1988 proved no exception to this rule. In a first round which confirmed François Mitterrand and Jacques Chirac as the contenders-to-be in a second ballot run-off, almost 30% of the vote went to non-mainstream candidates. Such a proportion, though high, is not outstandingly so for an election in which there was no united front behind any single major candidate of right or left. In the 1981 presidential elections, with open rivalry on the right and only vestiges of 'union' on the left, the minor contenders (Communist, Radical, Green and smaller fringe candidates) together accounted for some 28% of the first round vote.[2]

Such superficial statistics aside, however, the election of 24 April 1988 is far from corresponding to any pre-ordained pattern. For the distribution of the first-round vote marks this presidential contest off from all that have preceded it under the Fifth Republic. With 14.4% of the votes cast, the support of some 4.4 million voters, the leader of France's far-right *Front National* (FN), Jean-Marie Le Pen, achieved a performance unrivalled by any extreme right-wing candidate in post-war France.[3] The perspective within which such a result is to be gauged is not difficult to establish. In the presidential election of 1974, when Le Pen was polling a miserable 0.7%, the Gaullist baron, Jacques Chaban-Delmas, attracted 14.6% of the vote.[4] In 1981, when Valéry Giscard d'Estaing and Jacques Chirac were disputing the right-of-centre vote, Le Pen was reduced to the role of spectator, unable to secure sufficient endorsement among elected officials to validate his candidature. Now, in 1988, some 5.5% behind outgoing Prime Minister Jacques Chirac and a mere 2% behind the magisterial Raymond Barre, Le Pen not only redrew the boundaries on the French right: he contributed to a dramatic shift in France's political balance overall. For the unprecedented success of the FN leader coincided with an all-time low presidential performance by the official Communist Party candidate, André Lajoinie. With a deplorable 6.8%, the latter could do little either to challenge Mitterrand's ascendancy on the left or to respond to an extreme right which has provided an altogether new focus for a protest vote once considered to be a Communist preserve. While Le Pen's increasing appeal to blue-collar workers put him on a par with the hapless Lajoinie and well in advance of the more marginal far-left candidates (demonstrating clearly that workers in hard-pressed industries no longer look solely to the left for their protection), his appeal to the unemployed was surpassed by that of Mitterrand alone.[5]

It is on the right, however, that the sharpest effects of Le Pen's relative success are to be measured. As recently as 1982, Paul Hainsworth described the 5.3% polled by Jean-Louis Tixier-Vignancour in the presidential election of 1965 as 'the high-water mark of extreme right-wing electoralism in the Fifth Republic.'[6] The turnaround in the fortunes of the far right in the few years since these words were written has been quite astonishing - the more so as Le Pen issues from a party which is far from geared to the launch of presidential candidates.[7] Chirac's humiliating 19.9% on 24 April stemmed in the main from his inability to offset the pressure exerted by Le Pen. The aggregate score of the three right-wing candidates gave the right a clear majority over the combined forces of the left. Yet the result which earned Chirac his place in the run-off against Mitterrand was lower than that of any leading right-wing or centrist candidate under the Fifth Republic, and only marginally better than that which saw him eliminated in the first round of the 1981 presidential election.[8]

By contrast, Le Pen exceeded even the most extravagant predictions to establish himself on an almost equal footing with Chirac's main rival, the sometime favourite of pollsters and presidential augurs, Raymond Barre. Squeezed between Barre and Le Pen, Chirac saw the Gaullist right severely debilitated at a moment when it should have been poised to reassert its hegemony. Whilst a contest between Chirac and Barre might have afforded enough latitude for an eventual victory over Mitterrand, a three-way split of the right and centre-right vote gave Chirac an insurmountable task. Though Giscard paid the price of fraternal rivalry in 1981, a pact with Barre could have limited the damage to Chirac's chances of harnessing the centre-right vote. Le Pen, however, presented a different challenge. An electorate as heterogeneous and as volatile as that of the FN was never to be wooed in the second ballot by a single mainstream candidate. From the moment Le Pen's 14.4% score was announced, the right's bid to unseat Mitterrand seemed fated to collapse.

That it did collapse, and with such emphatic statistics (54% to 46%), is a measure of Chirac's inability to be all things to all right-of-centre voters, to secure the middle ground while stretching his appeal to the far-right fringes so adeptly sequestered by Le Pen. Deeply damaging to his standing in the short term, Chirac's failure to mount an effective challenge for the presidency points up the problem confronting the French mainstream right as a whole. For the combined first-round vote of 36.4% achieved by Chirac and Barre was only marginally in advance of the 34% picked up by Mitterrand, leaving the right far short of its potential majority and confirming that the key to any victory over the left lay squarely with Le Pen's constituency.

What is above all remarkable about this constituency is its strikingly national character. The results of 24 April show a clear progression of the Le Pen vote throughout the length and breadth of France. In fully 76 of France's 96 *départements* Le Pen polled upwards of 10%; in eight of these *départements* (Alpes-Maritimes, Bouches-du-Rhône, Gard, Pyrénées-Orientales, Bas-Rhin, Haut-Rhin, Var and Vaucluse) his standing rose to between 20% and 30%.[9] Such statistics invite comparison with the results of Raymond Barre in particular. For if the latter fell below the 10% mark in only two *départements*, he exceeded 20% in no more than eleven.[10] Most ominously for the mainstream right, Le Pen emerged ahead of Barre and Chirac both, to become the major contender of the right, in all of nine *départements*, ranging from the industrial north-east to the Mediterranean belt. With 26.39% in the Bouches-du-Rhône, the leader of the FN came close to equalling the votes of Chirac (14.77%) and Barre (13.89%) put together, and fell only marginally short of Mitterrand's 26.96% in this traditional bastion of the Socialist left. In the bustling city of Marseille, capital of the Bouches-du-Rhône, Le Pen outstripped all candidates, including Mitterrand, with a spectacular 28% of the vote.

Having announced his candidacy in his native Trinité-sur-Mer in April 1987, Le Pen, the first of the presidential hopefuls to enter the race, embarked upon a long and exacting itinerary which saw him cover the length and breadth of France. In the first stage of his campaign in summer 1987, he conducted a *tournée des plages* reminiscent of the 'caravan' which he himself had orchestrated for Tixier-Vignancour in the 1965 presidential campaign. Speaking without notes from the podium in a giant marquee, and surrounded by the tricolour symbols and insignia of his movement, Le Pen displayed his considerable skills as an orator in a bid to keep the minds of the holidaying French fixed on the forthcoming election. Though the *tournée* met with mixed success, it allowed Le Pen to steal something of a march on his rivals and to maintain a constant public profile throughout the summer recess.

In its second phase, the campaign moved inland and indoors, as a succession of meetings and *dîners-débats* across France got underway with Le Pen as guest of honour. Presenting himself as the 'outsider' running against a field of worn-out nags, Le Pen sought to portray a purposeful image, that of a 'new man' and tribune of the people in the face of an inert political elite. As the first round of the election approached, the message was intensified through television appearances, radio broadcasts, articles in the far-right press and several waves of posters which served to keep Le Pen at the centre of national political attention. His campaign, financed in part by entrance fees at meetings

(30 francs) and in part through private donations, came to a close only as the ballot-boxes began to yield their first indications of what Le Pen described, on the evening of 24 April, as a 'political earthquake' and a radical transformation of the national political landscape.

If one considers the broad geographical profile of the Le Pen vote, it is clear that the gains of the previous four years were universally consolidated. As in the European elections of 1984 and the legislative elections of 1986, Le Pen was at his strongest in the built-up industrialised regions of the north and east, around the Parisian heartlands and along the Mediterranean coastline from the Pyrénées-Orientales bordering Spain through Hérault, Gard, Bouches-du-Rhône, Vaucluse and Var to the Alpes-Maritimes neighbouring on Italy. The highest concentrations of the Le Pen vote coincided once more with the presence of large immigrant communities in urbanised areas where problems of unemployment, housing and crime are particularly acute.[11] Along the Mediterranean belt, the leader of the FN's results appear to have been bolstered significantly by those French *colons* who were repatriated in the early 1960s following the granting by de Gaulle of independence to Algeria. For many such voters, Le Pen, with his history of active service in Indo-China and Algeria and his unrelenting nationalism, articulates a longstanding resentment against decolonisation and the subsequent recourse by France to immigration on a mounting scale during the 1960s and early 1970s.[12]

It would be a mistake, however, to seek in any single issue - immigration, unemployment, economic recession, law and order, nostalgia for *Algérie française* - the key to Le Pen's political success. The Le Pen phenomenon is tendrillous and cannot be easily unearthed from the soil in which it has taken root. To account for it with any accuracy, one would have to return to the establishment of the Fifth Republic and the years of Gaullist hegemony, the Giscardian transition of the 1970s, the accession to power of the left in 1981, and the vicissitudes of successive Socialist governments, culminating in a period of left-right *cohabitation* in office. Pierre Manent defines the FN quite emphatically as 'a *single issue party*'.[13] It may indeed be so in the perception of individual voters or groups of voters, motivated by a single factor in their support for the FN. Le Pen's, however, is no 'single-issue' party in objective terms. Nor can it rightly be defined, for that reason, as a 'multi-issue' party. Instead, Le Pen has crystallised support around a complex of issues and sub-issues which relate loosely to one another and which are easily, if at times spuriously, linked in the popular imagination. Immigration, law and order, and unemployment are no doubt the principal themes of Le Pen's political populism. Yet other 'issues', too, feature large. Conservatism in religion, the defence of traditional education, concern over moral standards and family values, the backlash against the perceived excesses of state *dirigisme*, opposition to prevailing tax structures, questions of national identity and of France's world role, apprehension over the implications for national character and individual well-being of the single European market of 1992, fear of AIDS and drug abuse, all are grist to the mill of a demagogue who promotes himself as a champion of the small man against an indifferent political establishment.

The need to define with care the nature of the FN's appeal is borne out by the fact that no movement has a broader socio-professional or 'ideological' base of support.[14] Le Pen may harvest his best results in those urbanised and industrialised areas where social and economic problems are at their most acute; but he is by no means bereft of support in regions where immigration, unemployment and crime are far from being foremost among voter preoccupations.[15] Nor is the electorate of any other party marked by the volatility discernible in the voting motivations of a constituency whose surface stability, as successive polls suggest, masks considerable evolution.[16] Support comes to Le Pen from across the political spectrum, his appeal being at its broadest in first ballots to which no clear risk attaches. While they may appear *prima facie* to confirm the view of the FN as a party which attracts disparate support around a single issue, these factors attest to the complexity rather than the simplicity of the motivations underlying the Le Pen vote[17] - a complexity that is further underlined by the ambiguities which lurk beneath the statistics. As John Frears points out, a very sizeable majority of those who voted for Le Pen on 24 April wanted to see *another* candidate elected to the Elysée.[18] More precise still on this point is Jérôme Jaffré, who estimates that as few as 17% of Le Pen voters considered the leader of the FN to be the most able candidate, while 28% only wished to see him elected President.[19]

It is important, therefore, to recognise in the Le Pen vote a strong element of protest which militates against the 'single-issue' label. Dissatisfaction with the political *status quo* takes many forms and covers a great deal of social, economic and ideological ground. Economic recession, unemployment, immigration, inner-city crime, while they provide a partial explanation only of Le Pen's political appeal, have proved nonetheless fertile ground for the populist politics of the FN. These are long-term issues which have exercised successive governments in the 1970s and 1980s and which, after the interregnum of *cohabitation*, weigh equally upon the prime ministerial endeavours of Michel Rocard. Le Pen's appeal on such issues is defined as much by what he rejects as by what he advocates. His presidential manifesto provided a distillation of the programme on which he and his party had campaigned from the moment they first arrived on the national stage in 1984.[20] Foremost among Le Pen's proposals were: a radical revision of the *Code de la Nationalité* and of the right of immigrants to accede automatically to French citizenship; the selective repatriation of certain groups of immigrants, such as illegal residents, those convicted of criminal offences and the unemployed; the practice of 'national preference' in the allocation of jobs, welfare benefits, housing and health care; the return of the death penalty; the promotion of the family through the institution of a maternal salary and an end to state-reimbursed abortion; the abolition of income tax, and the implementation of an unfettered popular capitalism. On all of these issues, Le Pen derives animus from his sustained opposition to the policies of *other* political leaders and parties. Even on the question that is considered to be the most important galvanising factor in the Le Pen vote, that of immigration, his appeal remains essentially negative. The systematic repatriation of immigrants is no more a panacea for France's socio-economic ills than the abolition of income tax or the restitution of capital punishment. What Le Pen offers on each of these issues in turn is a channel of discontent, a means not of advancing towards a positive solution but of signalling noisily that no clear solution has as yet been provided.

The nature of the favoured double-ballot system of voting in France has been of enormous statistical advantage to Le Pen in this respect. If the two-round system has kept his party at some remove from full participation in the processes of power, it has contributed *ipso facto* to his role as a repository of protest. Le Pen's success, however, his progression over seven years from zero to 14.4% in the presidential stakes, are not to be accounted for by the vagaries of first-round voting alone. Nor is support for the FN merely the expression of a protest vote which is calculated to stop short of granting anything more than symbolic influence to Le Pen and his party. When Mitterrand introduced proportional representation as a means of offsetting the projected gains of the right in the 1986 legislative election, he opened the way to 35 FN *députés*, voted into the National Assembly with the full endorsement of some 10% of the French electorate.[21]

Part of the difficulty implicit in reading the Le Pen vote of 24 April 1988 is that of determining in what proportion it is to be seen as an aberrational protest, and in what proportion it stands as an authentic statement of political preference. That as many as a quarter of Le Pen voters should have transferred their support to Mitterrand on 8 May is indeed remarkable, especially when set alongside the 13 or 14% of centrist Barre supporters who are estimated to have done likewise.[22] It is surprising, however, only if one takes no account of a similar transfer of votes in previous elections since 1981.[23] A comparable proportion of those who voted for Le Pen in the European elections of June 1984, for example, or in the legislative elections of March 1986, had given their support to Mitterrand in the run-off against Giscard d'Estaing in 1981.[24] Five years of Socialist government, a period of *cohabitation* between left and right, and the historic decline of the Communist Party have conspired, over the course of the 1980s, to inject an unpredictable element into the non-mainstream vote. What Le Pen benefits from above all in this context is, as Martin Schain observes, 'the inability of the established parties of the right to increase significantly their electoral support among registered voters in any recent election.' Instead, as Schain argues, there has been a tendency for 'unstable' voters to shift their support away from the established parties to Le Pen.[25]

This raises once more the question of the mainstream right's dilemma vis-à-vis Le Pen. The RPR and UDF alike remain seriously divided over the attitude which should be adopted towards the FN. The problem confronting Chirac in particular is as difficult to resolve as it is easy to comprehend. For the choice is one between a systematic ostracism which may do little to encourage Le Pen's supporters to return to the mainstream fold, and a conciliatory posture that could only place at risk the moderate centrist support without which no leader of the right can hope to command a majority. In the new climate of *ouverture*, the risks of reaching out to the radical fringe are indeed considerable. Nor is it at all clear what would be achieved by a policy of conciliation towards the far right. Two years of tough-minded government on law and order and immigration under the RPR Interior Minister, Charles Pasqua, may have succeeded in stemming a serious drain on the more authoritarian wing of RPR support as a result of Chirac's 'cohabitation' with Mitterrand; but they certainly did not provide any conduit for the return of wayward conservatives who had defected to Le Pen.

This is what makes the antics of the Chirac camp between the two rounds of the presidential election seem at once disconcerting and futile. Convinced of the need to mobilise the Le Pen constituency in Chirac's favour, Pasqua chose to insist upon the affinities, the 'common values', rather than the distinctions between the mainstream and far right.[26] While the gambit failed to bring anything but charges of cynical opportunism to Chirac's door, it was accompanied by a number of dramatic events which cannot be seen in isolation from the intention of appealing to the hard-right vote. The release of three hostages from Lebanon, the repatriation of the 'Greenpeace' saboteuse, Dominique Prieur, and the bloody storming in New Caledonia of a cave in which a number of *gendarmes* were being held captive by Kanak separatists can be seen as so many attempts to attract the Le Pen electorate without sacrificing the middle ground. That Chirac succeeded in securing the requisite support on neither flank may say something about the limits of barefaced opportunism as a political strategy. It certainly appears to confirm that the Le Pen constituency is more complex than is at times suggested, and not to be easily baited by overtures from the established parties, however populist or nationalistic in tone.

The mainstream right, however, is not alone in confronting a strategic dilemma. For Le Pen and the FN, too, have had to assess not only their impact upon the political establishment, but the means whereby such impact might be translated into more positive gains than hitherto. This, indeed, is where Le Pen's presidential bid is at its most revealing. For it raises the question of defining the FN not only in relation to other political parties of right and left, but in relation to the French right-extremist context from which Le Pen and his movement issue. Such a question is further prompted by the fact that, in a post-war Europe which has remained on the whole inimical to strident nationalist politics, Le Pen stands out increasingly today as an exception. As the single European market projected by the EEC for 1992 approaches, France's neighbours have every interest in assessing the nature and limits of the Le Pen phenomenon. What, then, are the lessons to be drawn from the vote of 24 April 1988?

In the first place, it can be said that the presence of an extreme-right fringe has nothing about it that is new to French political life.[27] The Poujadism of the 1950s gave renewed expression to a right-extremism which had seemed largely extinguished at the Liberation.[28] In the early 1960s, the OAS articulated a violent nationalism which found its focus in the Algerian crisis and in opposition to de Gaulle's policy of Algerian independence.[29] Since then, a myriad of extremist groups have come and gone on the outer reaches of the French right. Neo-fascism, monarchism, ultra-Catholicism, socio-economic populism, nostalgia for the armed forces and the colonies: such have been among the 'causes' espoused by a succession of movements which have never, under the Fifth Republic, been allowed a forum for the expression of their ideas.[30] Starved of the oxygen of political debate, such movements have tended to dissipate their energies in self-defeating internecine rivalry and to restrict their ambitions to the lowest rungs of political activism.

Le Pen and the FN have, in this respect, broken new ground for the far right. Yet this has been achieved only by renouncing the cruder trappings of right-extremism in favour of a more acceptable guise. Whatever Le Pen's ancestry, he has sought assiduously to campaign within the terms of the prevailing political context. This marks a most important departure by the FN from what might be understood to distinguish right-wing radicalism from conservatism. In a study of right-extremism in Europe, Klaus von Beyme defines thus 'the traditional criterion for differentiating between conservatives and reactionaries: conservatives try to maintain the status quo, right-wing extremists want to restore the status quo ante.'[31] While such a neat definition may be adequate to describe the royalists, fascist sympathisers and die-hard Catholic traditionalists who people tracts of the French far right, it fails to circumscribe Le Pen and his FN in any satisfactory way. For there is no clearly defined *status quo ante* to which the latter advocate a return, no past régime whose restoration is their goal. It is for this reason that labels such as '*héritier du vichysme*' remain much too restrictive to encapsulate Le Pen or his movement.[32] The Pétainist values of work, family and fatherland, nostalgia for a lost age of French greatness, the myth of a disappearing national and cultural homogeneity: these do not amount to a political programme, but are factors which, for all their importance as informing principles, fall some way short of qualifying Le Pen for the widespread appeal which he has been able to exercise.[33] Whatever suspicions one might entertain about a silent agenda behind the stated policies, one must recognise that these policies themselves, together with the language in which they are articulated, take Le Pen and his party far beyond the bounds of right-extremist politics as they have been known in post-war France, and as they continue to be manifest in less 'domesticated' segments of the French extreme right.[34]

To this extent, Pierre Manent seems founded in seeking to qualify the 'extreme right' label and to redefine Le Pen as 'a demagogue of the Right', a product of the modern French context who has little in common with those past traditions of 'royalists or fascists who wanted to replace the republic or democracy by another régime.'[35] Kinship between the extreme right and the more authoritarian wing of French conservatism is a well established feature of politics in the Fifth Republic. The right smothered the extreme right as much by integration as by proscription. Many respected members of the conservative mainstream 'served their time' among the right-wing activist groups and politico-intellectual coteries which flourished in the late 1950s and early 1960s,[36] just as a great deal of the FN's support has been drawn from the ranks of the 'classic' right, most notably Chirac's RPR. What is new is not the existence of political affinities - what Stanley Hoffmann calls 'the porousness of the borders' - between the right and extreme right:[37] it is the extent to which the latter, in the guise of Le Pen and his party, has been at pains to shake off a legacy of street politics and violent agitation in order to accede to full and legitimate participation in the national political process. Formed within the terms of a clear electoralist strategy in 1972, the FN campaigned in the wilderness for a decade before making its first inroads into the political landscape.[38] Its success in 1988 is testament to no long-term drift of the French voting public towards right-extremism, but rather to the success with which Le Pen and his party have *disengaged* themselves from the stereotypical image of the extreme right.

The measures of such self-conscious disengagement from his roots were not lacking in Le Pen's presidential campaign. No more for this ex-Poujadist *député* and 'para' the image of political pirate, complete with black eye-patch and beret, which he cultivated following the loss of an eye in a brawl with political opponents in the late 1950s. Instead, the gentrified leader of the FN deployed a fastidious attention to wardrobe, diet and hair-style in his campaign preparations. In like fashion, Le Pen's minders have discarded their military khaki for the more sedate garb of well-pressed suits and blazers. Such superficial indices, in an age of television politics, are not without significance. For Le Pen is above all anxious to strike a respectable posture and, by shaking off the image of an *épouvantail*, or scarecrow, to broaden his appeal among more moderate conservative voters.[39] His mastery of the television medium was a major factor in taking his message far beyond those who were willing to pay to witness his formidable skills as an orator. In a lacklustre presidential campaign, no candidate even came close to rivalling Le Pen's ability to inflame his audience at rallies or to boost the viewing figures during his periodic television appearances.

At the deeper levels of discourse and policy, there is similar evidence of a desire to succeed within the terms of the prevailing political context. Le Pen's much aired scorn for bureaucratic administration, his avowed desire to throw open the processes of government to wider popular participation through referenda, may have overtones of the anti-parliamentarianism endemic in certain currents of the far right. His, however, is no programme for the overthrow of the political establishment. Le Pen may not, in the words of René Rémond, embrace the Revolution; but he has long recognised the incontrovertibility of the Republic.[40] This is what must inform our interpretation of his campaign for the presidency. For there is implicit within it a very significant tempering of the aims, values and discourse of the far right as they are represented by Le Pen.[41] At all levels of political representation - local, regional, national and European alike - the strategy of Le Pen and his party has been to eschew what W. R. Tucker terms the extreme right's 'habitual tendency to refuse any approbation to the democratic process.'[42] Economic liberalism, moral regeneration, law and order, the defence of national and cultural identity, the ethic of individualist endeavour, all are themes that are common to UDF, RPR and FN alike. If Le Pen has captured the headlines on such issues, it is largely because he out-rights the right, not because he has anything intrinsically *different* to say. In this sense, Roger Eatwell is correct to question Monica Charlot's comparison of Le Pen to Enoch Powell. For while the latter, as Eatwell points out, 'sought to break an elite consensus of silence which subsequently remained largely unmoved', Le Pen exploits in immigration an issue which, over the course of the 1980s, has become part of mainstream political debate.'[43]

At the organisational level, too, the FN has slipped a number of its moorings on the far right. Unlike previous surge parties of the radical fringe, it has secured a broad membership, solid local implantation and a support base that has shown a remarkable capacity to adapt to the range of municipal, European, cantonal, regional, legislative and presidential elections in which it has made its mark since 1983. Le Pen's parliamentary group, formed in the wake of the 1986 legislative elections, appeared the very embodiment of political respectability. Far removed indeed from the traditional image of the extreme right, the group comprised eminent figures from a variety of professional fields whose urbanity, with few exceptions, seemed strangely at odds with the clamour surrounding the entry of this party for the first time into the National Assembly.

The contribution of the traditional right to this new-found respectability has been considerable. The emergence of the FN dates very clearly from the municipal by-election of Dreux in September 1983, when it was thought expedient by the UDF and RPR to join forces with Le Pen's party in order to defeat the incumbent Socialists. The unprecedented 16.7% polled by the FN was ascribed in that instance to the particular context of Dreux, with its high immigrant population and its worrisome unemployment and crime rates. Far from being an aberration, however, it was to mark the start of a pattern of local successes for the FN which were to force alliances and concessions from the mainstream right. In the elections to the Regional Assembly of Corsica in August 1984, and, much more significantly, in the country-wide regional elections of March 1986, similar tractations between the right and extreme right led to a number of *présidences* being bought for the UDF and RPR at the cost of sharing power with the FN. The legislative elections of June 1988 saw the continuation of this opportunistic policy in the hotly contested constituencies of Marseille. There a decision was taken by the URC (the joint UDF/RPR list) to withdraw candidates in those constituencies where the FN was better placed to carry the second round, a courtesy which Le Pen's party was only too willing to reciprocate.[44] In the event, none of the Marseille seats went to the FN, suggesting the difficulty which this party must inevitably confront when standing alone as the vehicle for the centre-right vote; but a similar arrangement in the third constituency of the Var *département* did secure the re-election of the Front's one surviving *député*, Yann Piat, in a run-off against the Socialist Gaston Biancotto, who had been ahead by a substantial margin in the first round.[45]

Though alliances and *désistements* of this sort have long been a feature of the so-called 'republican discipline' that obtains between Socialists and Communists on the left,[46] it is a new departure for a mainstream right still adjusting to the two major developments of the 1980s: the loss of its monopoly on power and the need to seek accommodation with a new and troublesome political neighbour. The schizophrenic attitude to which these developments have given rise - between a national leadership which obdurately refuses to countenance an accord with Le Pen, and a grass-roots willingness to enter into such deals - has served to damage the credibility of the mainstream right and to enhance Le Pen's claim to political legitimacy. The legislative elections of June 1988, with their return to the two-ballot majority voting system, saw the virtual elimination of Le Pen's party from the National Assembly. Yet the latter's showing of 9.65% in the first round - a replica, to the decimal point, of its 1986 performance[47] - was a clear signal that the FN remained a serious thorn in the side of the established right. That such a result in June 1988 could be viewed *not as a success but as a setback* - a *'recul général'*, as Pierre Servent put it in *Le Monde* [48] - speaks volumes about the evolution which French politics have undergone in the course of the 1980s. That the marginally better score of 11.3% for the French Communist Party in the same election could be deemed 'encouraging' tells the same tale from a somewhat different perspective.[49]

The 1980s will be viewed as the decade in which the Fifth Republic broke new ground. It is already being dubbed by some commentators as the end of the era instituted in 1958.[50] Yet reports of the impending demise of the Fifth Republic have, for several years, been greatly exaggerated. For the institutions of modern France have never given evidence of better health. The test of *alternance* has been passed, modifying the balance of power between right and left in potentially far-reaching ways. Socialism has shared the bed of power alternately with Communism *and* conservatism, without the predicted constitutional crisis in either case. *Cohabitation* may have pointed up the weaknesses in the Constitution; but it also reaffirmed some very substantial strengths. Lastly, but no less significantly, the mid-1980s saw the rise and participation in power at the regional, national and supranational levels of an extreme right which, for all its imprecations against the governing elites, operated, and continues to operate, within the strict norms of Fifth Republican democracy. Byron Criddle, in his article 'France: Legitimacy Attained', makes this point of the PCF and FN alike. 'The fact that they do not draw attention to their authoritarian predilections, through fear of electoral disavowal,' writes Criddle, 'confirms that a consensus on democracy does indeed exist and that even extremist parties have to respect it.'[51]

Respect the democratic consensus Le Pen perforce does. His ambition is to be admitted to the governing elite, to be permitted to wield a more than symbolic or spoiling influence in French political affairs. For this reason, his function as tribune is tightly circumscribed by an overriding imperative not to wave the spectre of constitutional upheaval. 'Dissatisfaction with the world as it is' remains, as W.R. Tucker observed in 1968, an abiding feature of French right-extremism.[52] If the mechanisms of the Republic - its institutions, parties, conventions - are the butt of Le Pen's censure, however, the *legitimacy* of the Republic itself is not overtly called into question. Le Pen's is, in this sense, less an ideological crusade than an opportunistic political movement which recognises its survival and future advancement to lie in its capacity to draw upon ever more moderate segments of the French electorate. A few of his more intemperate pronouncements aside, Le Pen's discourse is an object lesson in consumer-oriented political marketing, an appeal across the boundaries of class, ideology and narrow vested interest. His repeated calls for co-operation with the very party leaders he conspues is a further recognition that the FN can succeed only by escaping from its isolation on the far right and attaining the sort of legitimacy by association that has long been denied it.

Having reached the limits of what a place 'outside the system' can afford, Le Pen must either settle for his remarkable but short-lived gains to date, or hope that he can capitalise on his appeal among that segment of the right-wing electorate which, while flirting with the FN as a vehicle of protest, remains committed to the mainstream parties. There exists, in Martin Schain's expression, 'a reservoir of legitimacy for the National Front'[53] among voters who may never yet have accorded their support to this party. At the same time, however, those who do register support for Le Pen refuse in many cases to back their vote with the political conviction required to provide a disciplined and coherent electorate. The difficulty in taking the measure of the Le Pen phenomenon springs in part from the fact that he and his party are still relative newcomers to the political scene of the Fifth Republic. It also results from the uncertainty surrounding the precise character of the Le Pen vote, its stability from one election to the next and its potential durability. Added to such considerations is the fact, emphatically demonstrated in the legislative elections of June 1988, that FN support is distributed too evenly throughout the country for the party to translate votes into seats without the proportional representation from which it benefited in 1986. All of this amounts to a sizeable question mark over the long-term future of Jean-Marie Le Pen. What is certain, however, is that four and a half million votes are not easily to be written off among some 38 million registered electors. François Mitterrand's resounding 54-46% victory over Jacques Chirac on 8 May translated a difference of some two and a half million votes. The swing to the left which put Mitterrand in office and prefigured a landslide for the Socialists in 1981 was the result of a much smaller victory margin (little more than a million) over Giscard d'Estaing. Whatever Le Pen's fate in the wake of his presidential performance of 1988, those who voted for him on 24 April could be deciding France's political destiny, one way or another, well into the 1990s.

NOTES

1. 'C'est le reflet d'une France urbaine à forte population immigrée et frappée par la crise économique. Mais la nouveauté du scrutin du 24 avril, c'est que le FN mord partout et déborde le cadre naturel de son implantation.' 'La nationalisation de l'extrême droite',

L'élection présidentielle, 24 avril-8 mai 1988: Le nouveau contrat de François Mitterrand (Paris, *Le Monde: Dossiers et Documents*, May 1988) p. 34.

2. *Ibid.*, pp. 28-29. Cf. *L'élection présidentielle, 26 avril-10 mai 1981: La victoire de M. Mitterrand* (Paris, *Le Monde: Dossiers et Documents*, May 1981) p. 98. The 'Union de la Gauche', bringing together Socialists, Radicals and Communists in support of François Mitterrand's single candidature, makes the 1974 presidential elections a less ready model for the spread of voting which the two-ballot system permits.

3. For a comparison with Jean-Louis Tixier-Vignancour's performance in the presidential election of 1965, see W. R. Tucker, 'The New Look of the Extreme Right in France', *Western Quarterly Review*, 21, 1968, pp. 86-97.

4. See J. R. Frears, *Political Parties and Elections in the French Fifth Republic* (London, Hurst & Co., 1977) pp. 201-205.

5. See *L'élection présidentielle, 24 avril-8 mai 1988: Le nouveau contrat de François Mitterrand*, pp. 41, 44.

6. 'Anti-Semitism and Neo-Fascism on the Contemporary Right', in P. G. Cerny (ed.), *Social Movements and Protest in France* (London, Frances Pinter, 1982) p. 148.

7. As Criddle points out, all three of France's major party groupings - RPR, UDF, PS - have as their essential function to promote *présidentiables* and sustain them in office. See 'France: Legitimacy Attained', in E. Kolinsky (ed.), *Opposition in Western Europe* (London, Croom Helm, 1987) pp. 123-124.

8. See J. R. Frears, 'The 1988 French Presidential Election', *Government and Opposition*, 23, 3, Summer 1988, p. 284.

9. *L'élection présidentielle, 24 avril-8 mai 1988: Le nouveau contrat de François Mitterrand*, p. 34.

10. *Ibid.*, p. 32.

11. For an analysis of the FN's showing in the 1986 legislative elections, see J. Jaffré 'Front national: la relève protestataire', in E. Dupoirier and G. Grunberg (eds.), *Mars 1986: la drôle de défaite de la gauche* (Paris, PUF, 1986) pp. 211-229.

12. See G. P. Freeman, *Immigrant Labor and Racial Conflict in Industrial Societies: The French and British Experience, 1945-1975* (Princeton, Princeton University Press, 1979) pp. 281-283 *et passim*.

13. 'Two Views of the Mitterrand Presidency (1981-88)', *Government and Opposition*, 23, 2, Spring 1988, p. 191.

14. See J. Jaffré, 'Front national: la relève protestataire', in E. Dupoirier and G. Grunberg, *op. cit.*, pp. 211-229; G. Grunberg *et al.*, 'Trois candidats, trois droites, trois électorats', *L'élection présidentielle, 24 avril-8 mai 1988: Le nouveau contrat de François Mitterrand*, pp. 41-43; N. Mayer, 'L'"effet Le Pen" s'est nourri de l'"effet premier tour"', *ibid.*, p. 44.

15. For the remarkable geographical spread of the Le Pen vote on 24 April, see 'La nationalisation de l'extrême droite', *L'élection présidentielle, 24 avril-8 mai 1988: Le nouveau contrat de François Mitterrand*, p. 34; F. Platone 'Histoire de l'électorat Le Pen', *Le Journal des Elections*, 1, April-May 1988, pp. 23-24; P. Martin 'La droitisation de la droite', *ibid.*, 2, May 1988, p. 25.

16. See O. Duhamel and J. Jaffré, *Le nouveau président* (Paris, Seuil, 1987), p. 186; N. Mayer, 'L'"effet Le Pen" s'est nourri de l'"effet premier tour"', *L'élection présidentielle, 24 avril-8 mai 1988: Le nouveau contrat de François Mitterrand*, p. 44; F. Platone, 'Histoire de l'électorat Le Pen', *Le Journal des Elections*, 1, April-May 1988, pp. 23-24.

17. The question receives some discussion in S. Mitra, 'The National Front in France - A Single-Issue Movement?', in K. von Beyme (ed.), *West European Politics* (Special Issue: *Right-Wing Extremism in Western Europe*), 11, 2, April 1988, pp. 47-64.

18. 'The 1988 French Presidential Election', p. 285.

19. 'Le Pen, ou le vote exutoire', *Le Monde,* 12 April 1988. 26% of Le Pen voters, according to the same survey, wished to see a victory for Chirac, 16% for Barre, and 17% for Mitterrand.

20. *République Française: Passeport pour la Victoire*. Cf. *Pour la France: programme du FN* (Paris, Albatros, 1985); *Les Français d'Abord* (Paris, Carrère-Lafon, 1984); *La France est de retour* (Paris, Carrère-Lafon, 1985).

21. See J. G. Shields, 'Politics and Populism: The French Far Right in the Ascendant', *Contemporary French Civilisation*, XI, 1, Fall/Winter 1987, pp. 39-52.

22. See G. Grunberg *et al.*, 'La victoire de M. Mitterrand: une mobilisation tranquille', *L'élection présidentielle, 24 avril-8 mai 1988: Le nouveau contrat de François Mitterrand*, pp. 82-83; R. Cayrol, 'Ce qui a changé dans le paysage politique', *Le Journal des Élections*, 2, May 1988, p. 9.

23. Such volatility in the far-right vote is not, of course, restricted to the 1980s. The shift of support from extreme right to Socialist left has a striking precedent in the 1965 presidential election, where Mitterrand benefited substantially in the second ballot from those supporters of Tixier-Vignancour who, as Waterman puts it, were ready to endorse 'a man backed by the Communists rather than the man (de Gaulle) who had betrayed Algeria.' See *Political Change in Contemporary France: The Politics of an Industrial Democracy* (Columbus, Merrill, 1969) pp. 93-96.

24. See J. Lorien, K. Criton, and S. Dumont, *Le Système Le Pen* (Antwerp, EPO, 1985) pp. 222-223; M. A. Schain, 'The National Front in France and the Construction of Political Legitimacy', *West European Politics*, 10, 2, April 1987, p. 234.

25. 'The National Front in France and the Construction of Political Legitimacy', p. 234.

26. In an interview published on 2 May, Pasqua's attempt to throw out a bridge to Le Pen voters was transparent: 'Il y a sûrement au FN quelques extrémistes, mais, sur l'essentiel, le FN se réclame des mêmes préoccupations, des mêmes valeurs que la majorité. Seulement, il les exprime d'une manière un peu plus brutale, un peu plus bruyante. [...] Que les électeurs du FN soient préoccupés par les risques qu'une immigration incontrôlée fait courir à l'ordre public et à l'identité nationale me semble légitime, et nous partageons ces inquiétudes.' ('Charles Pasqua: "Les mêmes valeurs"', *L'élection présidentielle, 24 avril-8 mai 1988: Le nouveau contrat de François Mitterrand*, p. 61.) Such a pronouncement did little indeed to bear out Chirac's emphatic dissociation, throughout his campaign, from Le Pen and his movement. In stark contrast to Pasqua's remarks, moreover, was Raymond Barre's pledge to support Chirac in the second round on condition that he work for 'une société ouverte, tolérante, qui refuse la xénophobie, le racisme et tous les extrémismes.' ('Raymond Barre: "Une société ouverte"', *ibid.*, pp. 58-59.) Pasqua and Barre epitomised thus the poles between which Chirac would attempt so unsuccessfully to stretch his appeal.

27. For a review of the fortunes of the extreme right in the post-war years, see M. Anderson, *Conservative Politics in France* (London, Allen and Unwin, 1974) pp. 269-300.

28. See R. Eatwell, 'Poujadism and Neo-Poujadism: From Revolt to Reconciliation', in P. G. Cerny, *op. cit.*, pp. 70-93. For a detailed and authoritative study of Poujadism, see S. Hoffmann, *Le mouvement Poujade* (Paris, Colin, 1956).

29. See B. Brigouleix, *L'Extrême droite en France: les "fachos"* (Paris, Fayolle, 1977) pp. 60-75.

30. *Ibid.*, pp. 137-210; A. Chebel d'Appollonia, *L'Extrême-droite en France: de Maurras à Le Pen* (Brussels, Editions Complexe, 1988) pp. 274-332.

31. 'Right-Wing Extremism in Post-War Europe', in K. von Beyme, *op. cit.*, p. 1.

32. See S. Mitra, 'The National Front in France - A Single-Issue Movement?', in K. von Beyme, *op. cit.*, p. 48. Citing Alain Rollat's definition of the FN as a *'fourre-tout idéologique où se côtoient monarchistes, nostalgiques du pétainisme, catholiques intégristes, anciens de l'OAS, nationalistes révolutionnaires, néo-poujadistes...'*, Mitra argues that 'allegiance to the ideology of the extreme right' is common to all of the disparate elements that are brought together under the banner of the FN. This, however, is to take no account of the extent to which Le Pen's movement ranges *beyond* the narrow boundaries of the far right. Alain Rollat's profile of the movement, while it reflects something of the FN's ideological heterogeneity, can account for but a *fraction* of the support which Le Pen has attracted in the four years since the European elections of June 1984. .

33. Though the two perspectives may not be quite as easily distinguished as he suggests, Schain makes an important point when he asserts that 'support for the National Front comes far less from those who are most committed to traditional values of the past, and far more from those who are concerned with threats to the political community in the present.' ('The National Front in France and the Construction of Political Legitimacy', p. 247.) The substantial - and growing - proportion of young voters in the Le Pen electorate would seem to lend support to this interpretation. See on this point A. Gattolin, 'FN: stabilisation plus que reflux', *Le Journal des Elections*, 3, June 1988, p. 10.

34. On the breadth of the Le Pen electorate, see P. Perrineau, 'Le Front National: un électorat autoritaire', *Revue politique et parlementaire*, 918, July-August 1985, pp. 24-31; J. Jaffré, 'Front national: la relève protestataire', in E. Dupoirier and G. Grunberg, *op. cit.*, pp. 211-229; G. Grunberg *et al.*, 'Trois candidats, trois droites, trois électorats', *L'élection présidentielle, 24 avril-8 mai 1988: Le nouveau contrat de François Mitterrand*, pp. 41-43; N. Mayer, 'L'"effet Le Pen" s'est nourri de l'"effet premier tour"', *ibid.*, p. 44.

35. 'Two Views of the Mitterrand Presidency (1981-88)', p. 191.

36. See P. Hainsworth, 'Anti-Semitism and Neo-Fascism on the Contemporary Right', in P. G. Cerny, *op. cit.*, pp. 146-171.

37. See G. Ross, S. Hoffmann and S. Malzacher (eds.), *The Mitterrand Experiment: Continuity and Change in Modern France* (Oxford, Polity Press, 1987) p. 347. See also on this point A. Rollat, *Les Hommes de l'extrême droite: Le Pen, Marie, Ortiz et les autres* (Paris, Calmann-Lévy, 1985) pp. 157-162.

38. In contrast to Petitfils' judgment, as late as 1983, of the French far right as an electoral wasteland (*L'Extrême droite en France*, Paris, PUF, 1983, p. 123), Brigouleix

foresaw the possibility of a latter-day Poujadism in a new and updated guise. 'Poujade a incarné, et canalisé pour un temps,' wrote Brigouleix with some prescience in 1977, 'une forme de droitisme qui ne demande certainement qu'à se manifester de nouveau, fût-ce sur d'autres thèmes et sous d'autres chefs' (*L'Extrême droite en France: les "fachos"*, p. 201).

39. Le Pen's announcement of his campaign in his native Trinité-sur-Mer, rather than in his party base or Paris constituency, displays something of his readiness to play the game according to prevailing conventions. For the catch-all strategy required of presidential hopefuls imposes the need to mark a distance from narrow party political and sectarian affiliation. That his score in the presidential election far outstripped any comparable performance at the national level by his party - including that which followed in the June legislative elections - demonstrates the extent to which Le Pen's personal appeal carries beyond the boundaries of the FN electorate. One exit poll on 24 April showed that only 57% of Le Pen voters intended to support an FN candidate in the event of a legislative election. See P. Perrineau, 'Front national: la drôle de défaite', *Elections législatives 1988: résultats, analyses et commentaires* (Paris, *Le Figaro*/Etudes politiques, 1988) p. 30.

40. Cf. on this point M. Vaughan, 'The Wrong Right in France', in E. Kolinsky, *op. cit.*, pp. 311-312.

41. The very title of Le Pen's campaign manifesto - *République Française: Passeport pour la Victoire* - should not go unremarked in this respect. For such anodyne language, with its noteworthy gesture to 'the Republic', could have served as the rallying cry for *any one* of the major candidates, right and left alike.

42. 'The New Look of the Extreme Right in France', p. 87.

43. 'The French General Election of March 1986', *The Political Quarterly*, 57, 3, July-September 1986, p. 320. Cf. Schain, 'The National Front in France and the Construction of Political Legitimacy', p. 237: 'The social issues that define the political space into which the National Front has moved were first defined and legitimised as *political* issues by established party élites.'

44. The significance of such co-operation between the mainstream right and the FN in a parliamentary election should not be underestimated. Until now, Le Pen's prospects for collusion have been restricted to municipal and regional elections. The eight Marseille constituencies in which the URC, under the auspices of Jean-Claude Gaudin, formally withdrew its candidates in favour of a better placed FN challenger took Le Pen and his party one step closer to the 'normalisation' which they seek in their relations with the mainstream right.

45. Piat was later expelled from the FN for failing to toe the party line on a number of issues. This left Le Pen's movement once more bereft of representation in the National Assembly and returned it to the extra-parliamentary status beyond which it had progressed in 1986.

46. The disparity between the FN's one seat and the Communist Party's twenty-seven in the June legislative elections (bearing in mind that the former picked up 9.65% of the first-round vote, the latter 11.3%) can be ascribed to the more effective distribution of the PCF vote and, not least, to its electoral co-operation with the Socialist Party.

47. See *Les élections législatives du 16 mars 1986: Le retour de la droite* (Paris, *Le Monde: Dossiers et Documents*, March 1986) p. 67; *Les élections législatives, 5-12 juin 1988: Une majorité à inventer*' (Paris, *Le Monde: Dossiers et Documents*, June 1988) p. 30.

48. 'Recul général', *Les élections législatives, 5-12 juin 1988: une majorité à inventer*, p.

38. The FN's result on 5 June appears to have been adversely affected by the inordinately high abstention rate. See P. Perrineau 'Front national: la drôle de défaite', *Elections législatives 1988: résultats, analyses et commentaires*, p. 30.

49. See Fawcett's 'Close-up' on Georges Marchais in *Marxism Today*, July 1988, p. 48.

50. 'With hindsight,' writes Manent, 'we can see that the election of François Mitterrand marked the end of the Fifth Republic' ('Two Views of the Mitterrand Presidency (1981-88)', p. 186).

51. 'France: Legitimacy Attained', in E. Kolinsky, *op. cit.*, p. 118.

52. 'The New Look of the Extreme Right in France', p. 88.

53. 'The National Front in France and the Construction of Political Legitimacy', p. 236.

INDICATIVE BIBLIOGRAPHY

Anderson, M., *Conservative Politics in France* (London, Allen and Unwin, 1974).

Brigouleix, B., *L'Extrême droite en France: les "fachos"* (Paris, Fayolle, 1977).

Chebel d'Appollonia, A., *L'Extrême-droite en France: de Maurras à Le Pen* (Brussels, Editions Complexe, 1988).

Chiroux, R., *L'Extrême droite sous la Ve République* (Paris, Librairie Générale de Droit et de Jurisprudence, 1974).

Criddle, B., 'France: Legitimacy Attained', in Kolinsky, E. (ed.), *Opposition in Western Europe* (London, Croom Helm, 1987).

Jaffré, J., 'Front national: la relève protestataire', in Dupoirier, E. and Grunberg, G. (eds.), *Mars 1986: la drôle de défaite de la gauche* (Paris, PUF, 1986), pp. 211-229.

Le Journal des Elections, 1, April-May 1988: *5 Clés pour le 2e tour*; 2, May 1988: *Les marges de manœuvre du président*; 3, June 1988: *Les surprises d'un scrutin qu'on disait sans surprise*.

Le Monde: Dossiers et Documents - May 1981: *L'élection présidentielle, 26 avril-10 mai 1981: La victoire de M. Mitterrand*; June 1981: *Les élections législatives de juin 1981: La gauche socialiste obtient la majorité absolue*; March 1986: *Les élections législatives du 16 mars 1986: Le retour de la droite*; May 1988: *L'élection présidentielle, 24 avril-8 mai 1988: Le nouveau contrat de François Mitterrand*; June 1988: *Les élections législatives, 5-12 juin 1988: une majorité à inventer*.

Le Pen, J.-M., *Les Français d'Abord* (Paris, Carrère-Lafon, 1984).

Le Pen, J.-M., *La France est de retour* (Paris, Carrère-Lafon, 1985).

Le Pen, J.-M., *Pour la France: programme du Front National* (Paris, Albatros, 1985).

Le Pen, J.-M., *République Française: Passeport pour la Victoire* (presidential manifesto, 1988).

Lorien, J., Criton, K., and Dumont, S., *Le Système Le Pen* (Antwerp, EPO, 1985).

Petitfils, J.-C., *L'Extrême droite en France* (Paris, PUF, 1983).

Plenel, E. and Rollat, A., *L'Effet Le Pen* (Paris, La Découverte/*Le Monde*, 1984).

Rémond, R., 'The Right as Opposition and Future Majority', in Ross, G., Hoffmann, S., and Malzacher, S. (eds.), *The Mitterrand Experiment: Continuity and Change in Modern France* (Oxford, Polity Press, 1987) pp. 128-139.

Rollat, A., *Les Hommes de l'extrême droite: Le Pen, Marie, Ortiz et les autres* (Paris, Calmann-Lévy, 1985).

Schain, M. A., 'The National Front in France and the Construction of Political Legitimacy', *West European Politics*, 10, 2, April 1987, pp. 229-252.

Shields, J. G., 'Politics and Populism: The French Far Right in the Ascendant', *Contemporary French Civilisation*, XI, 1, Fall/Winter 1987, pp. 39-52.

West European Politics (Special Issue: von Beyme, K. (ed.), *Right-Wing Extremism in Western Europe*), 11, 2, April 1988.

8 His master's voice?
André Lajoinie

GINO RAYMOND

'One must not play with history.'
André Lajoinie

'I am committed to a different kind of history.' **Pierre Juquin**

The presidential elections of 1988 created a new situation for the Communist movement in France. In addition to his traditional right-wing opponents, André Lajoinie, the candidate of the *Parti Communiste Français* (PCF), had to face a former high-ranking member of the PCF hierarchy, Pierre Juquin, who had decided to present himself as a presidential candidate on behalf of the Communist *rénovateurs* : those who had decided to break with the PCF in pursuit of what they advocated as a reconstructed form of Communism. In the event, Juquin obtained only a modest 2.10% share of the votes cast in the first round on 24 April 1988. His challenge, nevertheless, had been taken very seriously by the PCF leadership during the period of campaigning before the first ballot, and his decision to stand as a candidate reflected serious strands of discontent at grassroots level in the PCF.

In another respect, however, André Lajoinie faced the same obstacles in his presidential campaign as other Communist candidates who had stood for the presidency during the life of the Fifth Republic: a constitutional obstacle, in that his party disagreed with the definition of the office to which he hoped to be elected; and a party political one, in that his Socialist rival was supported by a party that had shown itself more willing and more successful in adapting to the exigencies of presidentialism in the Fifth Republic.

The extent of the powers which the constitution of the French Fifth Republic confers on the President was something with which the PCF had disagreed from the outset. The banner headline on *L'Humanité* on 29 September 1958 was 'La Constitution monarchique adoptée', and disapproval was voiced by the PCF inside and outside parliament regarding what it saw as the arbitrary and quasi-monarchical powers of the French President under the new constitution. As the years progressed, the PCF found ways of working within the constraints of the constitution, and via ideological accommodations such as its development of State Monopoly Capitalism Theory (SMC) which enabled it to envisage the left coming to power and engaging in a revolutionary transformation of society while at the same time maintaining the fundamental nature of the constitutional division of power under the Fifth Republic.

With the inclusion of four Communist ministers in the second government of Pierre Mauroy, the Socialist Prime Minister, in 1981, the PCF's accommodation with the Fifth Republic became concrete as, for the first time in the existence of this Republic, it became a party of government. As the life of the government progressed, however, the PCF found it increasingly difficult to give its wholehearted support to the policies of the Socialists, especially the package of austerity measures, the 'plan de rigueur' of 1982. The European elections of June 1984 represented a serious setback for the left, in spite of the record number of abstentions (43%) which, rather than a switch to other parties, was almost the exclusive cause for the drop in the number of votes cast for the PCF. The PCF's score of 20.5% in the 1979 European elections fell to 11.3% in 1984. This was interpreted by the party leadership as a serious warning. At the central committee meeting on 26 and 27 June the government was criticised for its failure to halt unemployment and increase the purchasing power of the people. For its part, the central committee decided that the future for the party lay in the restoration of its Communist vigour and identity, in order to make it more attractive to the workers and the young. A few days after the election result President Mitterrand replaced Mauroy with the right-wing Socialist, Laurent Fabius. At a central committee meeting on 19 July the decision was taken to try and obtain a pledge from Fabius to boost investment and employment. This commitment not forthcoming, the Communist ministers were withdrawn from the government.

The explicit criticism voiced by the PCF of the Socialist government after its withdrawal, was supported by a return to Communist criticism of the constitution from which it derived its powers. The resolution adopted at the PCF's 25th congress in 1985 marked an end to the strategy that had characterised its attitude to governmental office for the preceding quarter century. Cooperation with the *Parti Socialiste* (PS) which had brought the left to power had, according to the resolution, been a mistake and had resulted in too many compromises at the expense of the PCF. The party's political activity would therefore be marked, after the congress, by autonomous action among the masses, with a view to creating a *nouveau rassemblement populaire majoritaire*.[1] In his report to the congress, the General Secretary, Georges Marchais, made explicit condemnation of the way he believed that the constitution of the Fifth Republic permitted the concentration of power in the hands of one individual. Calling for a democratisation of the institutions created by the constitution, Marchais outlined five objectives: a parliament with greater power over legislation, notably its inception; a more powerful Prime Minister, and therefore greater independence of the government from the President; a less direct role for the President in the exercise of power, and a greater definition of his role as a ceremonial guardian of the Republic's institutions; real decentralisation; and effective debureaucratisation. These objectives were supported by nine specific proposals which included a non-renewable seven-year term for the President, a change in the voting system to allow any candidate with more than 10% of the vote in the first round to stand in the second round, a more narrowly defined presidential right to dissolve parliament, and more power for parliament to decide the order of business.[2]

Marchais' proposals for the reform of the presidency notwithstanding, the 1988 presidential campaign would place the PCF in the situation of promoting its candidate for an office which it believed to be ill-defined constitutionally, and against - apart from its traditional adversaries on the right - a Socialist incumbent which it accused of adopting right-wing policies, and an erstwhile PCF member who, it claimed, was surreptitiously supported by the Socialists and by the media in an effort to damage the credibility of the PCF.

External and Internal Challenges

The 6.76% of the votes cast for André Lajoinie in the first round of the presidential elections on 24 April 1988, marked the weakest performance at the polls by the PCF since its formation in 1920. In the eyes of many political observers this result appeared to confirm a trend that had developed over the preceding two decades each time the PCF was faced with a major electoral challenge; a trend which suggested an ineluctable decline in the PCF's ability to win the confidence of the French electorate. As the following figures show, the electoral fortunes of the Communists between 1969 and May 1988 had suffered a virtually continuous decline, and one which was particularly marked in the decade prior to the presidential elections of 1988:

Electoral Performance of PCF since 1969[3]
(percentage of PCF vote at first ballot)

Type of election	Year	Vote
Presidential	1969	21.5
Legislative	1973	21.4
Legislative	1978	20.7
European	1979	20.6
Presidential	1981	15.6
Legislative	1981	16.2
European	1984	11.3
Legislative	1986	9.8

The result of the presidential contest of 1988 seemed to justify the view that the PCF was a party whose political prospects had been damaged because of its intellectual and organisational rigidity,[4] and which could not be confident of retaining the fidelity of its own members unless its conception of change was broadened and adapted to include non-economic issues of concern to individuals and not only the economic issues that concerned the class it represented.[5] Analyses of the PCF's own figures, made in the months preceding the presidential campaign, suggested that it was unable to increase its total number of members and add to a solid grassroots membership. In spite of the 45,000 new members the party claimed to have recruited by the end of 1987, the total figure of paid-up party members in December 1987 was virtually equivalent to the total established for the previous year, which led some of the party's critics to the conclusion that the 45,000 new members who joined in 1987 merely replaced those who had left. Moreover, an analysis of the financial statement produced by the central committee at the party's 26th congress in December 1987 revealed a serious discrepancy between the total number of party members and the funds available to the party, suggesting that a considerable number of subscriptions were not being renewed and that the official number of party members was inflated.[6]

This concentration by PCF critics on the factors inhibiting the reversal in the decline of the PCF's fortunes as an electoral force, however, helped to create the misleading impression of a party that seemed indifferent to the need for change and disinclined to pursue electoral success. The unanimous decision of the political bureau on 18 May 1987 to propose André Lajoinie to the PCF central committee as the party's candidate in the presidential elections, and the subsequent ratification of his candidacy, expressed in fact the willingness of the party to learn from previous experience and adapt its tactics to ways which it believed would bring greater electoral benefits.

The view that prevailed among the PCF's critics regarding the choice of Lajoinie, was that he was the undistinguished but faithful party man who would enable Marchais to avoid shouldering the blame for the party's defeat at the polls. As both General Secretary of the PCF and its candidate in the presidential elections in 1981, Georges Marchais was doubly vulnerable to criticism provoked by the PCF's disappointing share of the vote in the first ballot. The suggestion that the decision of the General Secretary not to put himself forward as a presidential candidate in 1988 was simply to protect the leadership from blame in case of failure, did not, however, take into account a certain consistency in what had motivated the choice of presidential candidate to represent the PCF in both 1981 and 1988. Both occasions signified an attempt by the PCF to enhance its image as a credible electoral force. In 1965 and 1974 the PCF had supported François Mitterrand as the single candidate representing the left, and agreed to Duclos' candidacy in 1969 only because the Socialists had not accepted a joint candidate. The decision of the PCF national conference in October 1980 to put up Georges Marchais as the Communist candidate for the April 1981 presidential election was therefore the first step of its kind, signifying an attempt to end the perception of the PCF's electoral strategy as purely defensive. The choice of André Lajoinie in 1988 expressed the PCF's hopes of attracting an electorate that would regard its candidate as a credible alternative to what the PCF regarded as the growing concern with image over substance in the exercise of presidential power, and the shift of the Socialists to the right.

By 1981, the PCF had come to the conclusion that backing a Socialist candidate from the first round had resulted in a measure of self-effacement which undermined its credibility as anything other than a contributor to a left-wing alliance which, even if successful, would be disinclined to implement Communist policies. Marchais' candidacy, according to the PCF leadership, was compatible with the tactic elaborated at the 23rd congress in 1979, of fulfilling the party's ambitions step by step through a series of battles. The presidential campaign was to be but one of the battles to be fought in the struggle to mobilise the masses. Its essential purpose was to secure a number of votes for the Communist candidate in the first ballot that would be high enough to force a victorious Mitterrand to enter into a genuine coalition with the Communists, and one that might result in what the Communists would consider as meaningful reforms.

The PCF's campaign in 1981 was led vigorously by Marchais and focused powerfully on him, especially as he was both the party's General Secretary and its presidential candidate. Marchais' high-profile campaign had to demonstrate to, and convince, the electorate that the rationale put forward by the party for voting Communist in the first ballot was a valid one: a strong vote for the Communist candidate would show which policies people really liked, so that even if he had to stand down for the left-wing candidate most likely to be elected in the second ballot, the latter would have to take account of the wishes expressed by the Communist vote in the event of him being elected President.

The strategy behind the PCF's presidential campaign and its style, which gave considerable prominence to the candidate, did not bring the results that the party had hoped for. Communist expectations were greatly disappointed when it was revealed that Marchais' share of the vote at the first ballot on 26 April, was only 15.3%. This disappointment was exacerbated by the fact that the opinion polls had shown that Marchais might take an 18% or 19% share of the vote. Furthermore, in terms of the attendance and his reception at meetings, Marchais had fought a good campaign. The reaction of the party and its leadership was to recognise the need for a more effective way of soliciting the votes of the French electorate. In the debates during and around the PCF's 24th congress in February 1982, there was a general acceptance of the criticism that the party had, from 1956 onwards, lagged behind the very considerable changes in French society, failing, for example, to adapt with sufficient speed and flexibility to the fact that the majority of French men and women had become salaried workers. Among the principal themes which Marchais developed in his address to the congress, was the need for the party to develop a new and broader dimension which would accommodate a new style of contact with the people at large, and to follow a path characterised by positive proposals rather than just criticism.[7]

Marchais' address to the PCF's 24th congress expressed an awareness, on the part of the leadership, of the pressure to succeed that was building up on two fronts. On the one hand, the leadership had to project the party and its ideology into the political arena and in a way that convinced the electorate of the viability of its bid for power; especially presidential office. On the other hand, the PCF leadership had to manage the dissent and criticism that emanated from within the party about the way it managed the party's affairs, and defined the party's ideological orientation and political strategy. Success on one front could not be divorced from success on the other. The PCF leadership had, therefore, to take account of those who posed a challenge from inside as well as from outside the party.

Contestataires and Rénovateurs

The PCF leadership had had to face criticism from within party ranks during the years immediately preceding the presidential elections of 1981 as well as after. Considerable criticism followed the failure of the Common Programme of Government which the PCF had signed with the Socialists in 1972 and which effectively had ended in September 1977. The legislative elections six months later, in March 1978, resulted in the defeat of the left, but were notable in that, for the first time in France's post-war history, the Socialists had taken a larger share of the vote than the Communists: the outcome of the first ballot gave the PS 22.6% of the vote and the PCF 20.7%. The debate within the party concerning the leadership's electoral strategy, and particularly its relationship with other left-wing parties, grew in scope to include the issue of democracy within the party.

The desire by some party members to see these issues discussed in the party press as well as at branch level was frustrated, but the voices of those challenging the leadership's handling of the party's affairs, the *contestataires*, continued to be heard, most notably in the form of an open letter carrying a thousand or so signatures and emanating from the PCF university branch at Aix, criticising the way the leadership had handled the party's relationship with the PS and the *Mouvement des Radicaux de Gauche* (MRG). A significant number of critical books and articles appeared, written by Communists who disagreed with the leadership but who affirmed their desire to remain within the party, aspiring to change it from within. Notable contributors to this literature were the Communist intellectuals Louis Althusser and Jean Elleinstein.

The PCF leadership demonstrated its recognition of the need for debate by organising, in a manner which had not been seen for a number of decades, a series of discussion meetings on 9 and 10 December 1978, at which four hundred intellectuals were invited, including some of the party's liveliest critics. It was, in the judgement of *Le Monde*, a forum in which disagreements were aired but one where the PCF leadership was supported with regard to the essence of its policy.

Some of the *contestataires* remained, nonetheless, unwilling to be placated, particularly those among the party intellectuals in the Paris area. Notably outspoken was Henri Fiszbin, the former Paris district secretary who had resigned from the central committee in 1979 and who, in May 1981, together with François Hincker, founded *Rencontres communistes*, a group comprised of PCF dissidents and some others. Both figures were expelled from the PCF in October of that year, the reason given by the party being that they had published their criticisms in the bourgeois press instead of the party press. Two other notable departures from the party in that year were Elleinstein and another prominent critic, Etienne Balibar. A further focus of discontent was established in the creation of *Union dans les luttes*, a body set up by Socialist and Communist intellectuals with the purpose of restoring the unity of the left to the top of the agenda and of refuting the PCF's claim that the PS had shifted to the right.

The criticism of the party that was expressed after the 24th congress differed, however, from the kind that was expressed after the disappointment of the legislative elections of 1978 and which culminated in the debates in December of that year, in that it contained a strand that could not be counted on to agree with the leadership on the essence of party policy. It was a critical element in the party that was not only reformist but also *rénovateur*, i.e., that was prepared to advocate a renewal of the party's appraisal of its aims through, if necessary, a radical overhaul of some of its fundamental assumptions, e.g. regarding democratic centralism. In a speech in Limoges in June 1984, Pierre Juquin, then still a member of the PCF central committee, expressed his belief in the need for a debate within the party about the way it was run, a debate which would not treat any subject relating to the party as taboo. Furthermore, Juquin added that the democratic centralism in the party could be modified for the better.

This criticism became overt at the party's 25th congress in February 1985. It was in this forum that Juquin made his call for a 'PC rénové', a reconstructed Communist Party in which democratic centralism would be informed by the will to self-management. The reaction of the party leadership was to reach a pact with the *rénovateurs,* as a result of which Juquin was not reelected to the political bureau of the party but was reelected to the central committee, together with two other members of it who sympathised with his viewpoint, Marcel Rigout and Félix Damette.

There was a resurgence of criticism of the leadership by PCF members after the party's poor result in the legislative elections of 1986, when it obtained 9.8% of the votes cast. This criticism found focal points in the *cercles marxistes*, the communist discussion groups which were formed, according to one *rénovateur*, in at least ten towns to discuss the issues raised by *rénovateur* criticism of the leadership.[8] The reaction of the party leadership to the growing strength of this criticism from within, was to take the offensive. In an interview on the television channel, *Antenne 2*, on 14 January 1987, Georges Marchais accused the *rénovateurs* of being the *liquidateurs* of the party. In a written statement, Marcel Rigout declared that Marchais' condemnation of the *rénovateurs* was a publicly delivered blow against the unity of the party, and on 27 January, Rigout resigned from the central committee of the PCF. On 31 January, *rénovateurs* from fifteen departments met in Paris and established themselves organisationally by forming a *collectif de coordination*. The basis now existed for an unprecedented challenge to the PCF leadership.

Pierre Juquin had signalled his challenge to the leadership of the PCF in November 1986, when he declared the intention of the *rénovateur* group within the PCF to change the party from within and from below. This ambition was to prove harder to fulfil than they had imagined, and as the presidential election drew closer Juquin marked an increasing distance between himself and the leadership. In May 1987, he was absent from the central committee meeting that approved unanimously the choice of Lajoinie as the party's presidential candidate, and in June he announced his resignation from the central committee. On 12 October, he announced his decision to stand as a candidate in the presidential election and on 14 October, he was excluded from the party.

The organisational backing for Juquin's candidacy began to take concrete form on 24 October when the national coordinating committee of the Communist *rénovateurs* (*COCORECO*) met in Paris. It elected at its head Claude Llabrès, who was among the group of Communists from Toulouse to be excluded from the PCF. Llabrès had been a member of the central committee but had resigned in September 1987, arguing in a newspaper interview and in terms made familiar by Juquin, that the PCF had lost touch with French society. This was a familiar argument in the early months of Juquin's candidacy, which developed against a background of notable discontent within the PCF. The divisions in the PCF from which Juquin's campaign might hope to profit were well illustrated by the problems that surfaced in Claude Llabrès' home base of Toulouse, in October and November of 1987, and where the local Communists came under the regional authority of the federation of Haute-Garonne. The exclusion of the local communist, Serge Diaz, for 'factional activity' elicited a reaction among PCF members in Toulouse which revealed not only that friction existed between *rénovateur* sympathisers like Diaz and officials like Emile Ochando, who defended the party orthodoxy, but that there was another disaffected group which wanted to remain within the party but which was highly critical of PCF management and strategy, led by Daniel Garipuy. These *contestataires* argued that from being a federation with 11,000 members in 1979, Haute-Garonne now had no more than 3,500;[9] a figure disputed by the officials of the federation but which nonetheless suggested the potential for Juquin's candidacy to rally more than the declared *rénovateurs* among the Communist electorate. This was a potential underlined by the resignation, in early November, of Marcel Rigout and eighteen other *contestataires* who were members of the party's federal committee in Haute-Vienne and who cited the national leadership's inability to tolerate differences as the principal factor forcing their decision to resign.

The freedom to express individual differences was one of the values that featured in the book by Juquin which appeared in 1985 and which defined his understanding of the challenges facing the Communist movement and the changes it had to make.[10] The way Communists envisaged the purpose of their movement, according to Juquin, had become reliant on terms that had become ideologically frozen, such as 'the masses' and 'the class struggle', and which led to a conception of society in which the individual was indistinguishable from the mass. For Juquin, the class struggle led by the Communist movement should be perceived in a fresher light as aiming ultimately to allow the human person to assume its individuality. The way for the Communists to secure the liberation and fulfilment of this individuality would not be through an exclusive preoccupation with economic change, but through profound cultural change. In his book *Fraternellement libre*, published shortly before the start of his campaign, Juquin returned to this conception of Communism as being, above all, a project to transform society's values.[11] And this concern would be translated in the way Juquin defined his electoral programme.

The Presidential Challenge

Georges Marchais' decision, announced at a central committee meeting on 12 May 1986, to exclude himself from the choice of possible candidates to represent the PCF in the presidential elections of 1988, and his subsequent characterisation of André Lajoinie's campaign, expressed his awareness of past mistakes and of the immediate challenges facing the party in the run-up to a crucial test of its continuing viability as an electoral force in the Fifth Republic. Marchais' high-profile campaign had failed to bring the PCF the success hoped for in the presidential elections of 1981. This time, the party professed its refusal to compromise with the tactic it condemned in the other parties of concentrating on an American-style packaging of their candidates in order to achieve maximum impact in the media at the expense of a proper examination of the programmes they were supposed to be advocating. According to Marchais, the image of the party would not be portrayed in the person of one individual during the campaign, but in the collective identity of its members.

The distinction between the nature of Lajoinie's presidential campaign and that of the other candidates was of fundamental importance to the preservation of the PCF's ideological integrity. It enabled the PCF to participate in the pursuit of presidential power while at the same time not relinquishing its condemnation of presidentialism in the Fifth Republic, which it believed to run contrary to the interests of democracy.

The reasoning behind the decision to place the onus for the success of Lajoinie's candidacy on the party as a whole, was made explicit in Marchais' report to the PCF's 26th congress in December 1987.[12] He condemned the American-style focus of the media on politics as a form of showbusiness, regarding it as an attempt by bourgeois forces to stifle real debate and the spirit of critical analysis. According to Marchais, the PCF was laying the grounds for its success in the presidential election by genuine discussion with the people about the issues that mattered to them. Lajoinie alone could not succeed in making France receptive to the ideas and policy proposals of the Communist Party, Marchais affirmed. The success of the Communist candidate's campaign would depend on the ability of every party member to convey the party's ideas to the people around him or her in all aspects of everyday life and persuade them that the only way to make themselves heard would be to vote for Lajoinie in the first round. Such a dialogue, initiated by all party members, could not be stifled by the media. This, therefore, was the professed purpose behind the style of the campaign. But in addition to the need to renew the appeal of the PCF's presidential candidate to the French electorate as a whole in 1988, there were additional and difficult considerations in the choice of candidate and the management of his campaign: the need for a candidate both acceptable to the party at large and one on whom the leadership could rely in the case of continuing criticism of it from within the party, and one who could be seen to maintain the delicate line which the PCF had to tread if it was to be considered as committed to the accession of the left to power but not merely subordinate to the Socialists; i.e., reverse the role of political bridesmaid destined always to help the PS into office and never to enjoy it herself.

In contrast to his Socialist rival in the presidential campaign, Lajoinie was chosen to represent the qualities that were antithetical to those displayed by the kind of candidate whose personality and ideas could come to dominate the party he was supposed to represent. Rather than set up a pole of attraction that could compete with the party and relegate its leadership to a secondary role, Lajoinie's appeal was to be an integral aspect of the appeal of the PCF as a whole, and of its message. In the PCF's portrayal of him, André Lajoinie was the type of candidate who would eschew the ego-building and political manœuvrings of his rivals in order to project the policies determined by a political collectivity for the collective benefit of French society. Hence the prominent role played by Georges Marchais throughout the presidential campaign.

In a very important respect, the PCF was represented by two figures during the presidential campaign. Whereas André Lajoinie was the *présidentiable* who, if elected, would assume the office of President, Georges Marchais was the figure who defined the terms for the PCF's participation in the elections. In his report to the PCF's 26th congress, Marchais referred directly to the institutional obstacles Lajoinie would face. In his opinion, the presidential election would reinforce the anti-democratic and monarchical nature of executive power. The presidency was beginning to resemble an elected monarchy not only because of the power concentrated in the hands of the President, but also because of the fact that since the President's mandate is obtained directly from the people, Marchais argued that this had led to the widespread belief that the office of President conferred a legitimacy that could not be challenged by any other democratic institutions. Therefore, in deciding how to vote, the French electorate were guided above all by the choice of individual rather than policy. Furthermore, Marchais asserted, the logical consequence of the form of electoral choice with which the French people would be faced would put them under extreme pressure to make their votes count, the *vote utile*. The electors would be under pressure to cast their first-round votes, not for the candidate who expressed their views, but for the one most likely to obtain an absolute majority in the second round: they would be discouraged from voting for the candidate with whom they identified in favour of the possible winner least unacceptable to them. Such a system, Marchais concluded, was an obvious handicap to any candidate and party advocating radical change.

Marchais rejected, however, the suggestion that the outcome of the election was a foregone conclusion and defined in unequivocal terms what a vote for the Communist candidate could achieve, how his campaign could be justified, and its success measured. In Marchais' opinion, Lajoinie's candidacy would rally all those wishing to register their disagreement with the policies of the government, and the weight of their votes for him in the first round would influence the final outcome and the subsequent decisions of the newly elected President. A good result for the PCF candidate in the first round would be a measure of the desire for change in French society, and, in Marchais' view, would be the only new and significant event that would distinguish the election.

Marchais' representation of Lajoinie's candidacy in the terms outlined above is what enabled the PCF to reconcile two conflicting terms in the equation expressing their participation in presidential elections. By portraying Lajoinie as the candidate who embodied the consultative and collectivist virtues that would check the drift to right-wing presidentialism, the PCF leadership could deny the legitimacy of presidential power and its manifestations while, without apparent contradiction, putting forward a candidate in the presidential elections.

André Lajoinie's Campaign

André Lajoinie was chosen to run as the PCF candidate in the presidential election in preference to better-known Communist figures like Georges Séguy, the former General Secretary of the CGT trade union, and Anicet Le Pors, who had been one of the four communist ministers in the cabinet of the Socialist Prime Minister, Pierre Mauroy. Lajoinie's progress in the party and his service to it, however, are an indication of the social and political qualities that made him appear an appropriate choice to the party leadership as the most reliable candidate in the attempt to balance the factors outlined above. Born of peasant stock in the Corrèze in 1929, Lajoinie reflected the simplicity and solidity that characterises the support on which the party can rely in certain agricultural areas, and it was through service to the party's agricultural concerns that he rose in the organisation. Lajoinie first gave dramatic proof of his commitment to the party and its beliefs during the campaign against the French colonial war in Algeria, when he was seriously assaulted and injured in a demonstration in May 1958. Lajoinie progressed through the courses organised for party members, and in 1976 became responsible for the Communist weekly journal for farmers, *La Terre*. In 1978 he was elected as a member of parliament representing a constituency in the department of Allier, and joined the central committee of the party in February 1982 on the occasion of its 24th congress. By his own description, one of Lajoinie's chief qualities was his capacity for quiet diligence, and his preferred activity was to meet the people where they lived and worked and to discuss their problems with them in a way which eschewed hedging or rhetoric, using the straight talking (*parler direct*) which he believed was most effective in reaching people.[13]

The PCF leadership had shown its support for André Lajoinie when almost all the members of the party's political bureau and three of the four former Communist ministers in the Socialist government were present in the studio on Lajoinie's first major appearance on television, on 19 October 1987, to present himself and his programme as the Communist candidate in the forthcoming presidential election. During the course of the programme, *l'Heure de vérité,* on *Antenne 2,* Lajoinie elaborated on the themes, political and personal, that would recur during his campaign.[14] This broadcast, together with another keynote interview given to the media by Lajoinie in early November 1987, illustrated the nature of Lajoinie's campaign and the policy concerns that characterised it.

On the programme, Lajoinie began by outlining what his first three priorities would be should he be elected President. Firstly, a raising of the minimum wage to 6,000 francs, increases in low and average incomes, and an amnesty for all union activists unfairly penalised by the law. Secondly, he would call a meeting of the captains of industry in the public and the private sector in order to find ways of creating employment and raising industrial output. Thirdly, he would find ways of taxing income from financial transactions and of reducing the military budget. In view of the febrile state of the Paris stock exchange at that juncture, Lajoinie argued that he was the only candidate to have a programme with specific provisions for resolving the problems being encountered there, including: the protection of France from the vagaries of the American-dominated world financial system through exchange control, taxes on the export of capital, and incentives to production instead of speculation; an end to privatisation and some nationalisations; and the withdrawal of France from the European Monetary System.

Regarding relations between the PCF and the PS, Lajoinie argued that whereas in 1981 there was some common ground between the parties, the gap between the two parties towards the end of 1987 had become enormous. While refuting the likelihood of the PCF participating in another Socialist dominated government, Lajoinie did not exclude permanently the possibility of cooperation with the Socialists with regard to the exercise of governmental power in the distant future. Describing himself as a revolutionary candidate in the deepest sense of the word, Lajoinie declared that his principal adversaries were the right and the capitalist forces in French society. He affirmed his belief that the millions of Communist votes cast in the first round would weigh more heavily on the outcome of the second round, and its aftermath, than they did in 1981. As for the support shown by some Communist mayors for Pierre Juquin, who had entered the presidential race and been excluded from the party earlier in the month, Lajoinie dismissed the number of mayors as less than a handful and accused Juquin of dishonesty in his dealings with the PCF.

As for the management and style of his campaign, Lajoinie revealed that this was entrusted to a commission headed by the political bureau member, Pierre Blotin. The image that best represented him as an individual candidate in human terms, Lajoinie believed, was one of a plain and simple man of the people, capable of appreciating popular tastes, like pop music, while avoiding some of the more frivolous preoccupations to which it could give rise.

Lajoinie's television performance was a successful one judging by the audience reaction. He began with the lowest rating of any guest on the programme, scoring only 14% in favour of him in a survey of viewers' attitudes carried out during the broadcast. At the end of the broadcast, the number of viewers expressing a favourable opinion of Lajoinie had risen to 33%, one of the most marked progressions registered by any guest on the programme.

Outside of the television studio and vis-à-vis the French electorate as a whole, the percentage of electors inclined to cast their vote for Lajoinie in the first round was 5%, the same as in July, according to a poll carried out by *Paris Match*-BVA in early October.[15] Vis-à-vis the rank and file of his own party, however, Lajoinie's campaign was unfolding against a background of increasing dissatisfaction. Juquin announced his decision to stand for the presidency on behalf of the *rénovateurs communistes* on 12 October and, with the exception of Félix Damette, the central committee voted to exclude him from the party on 14 October. Nationally, in places like Isère, Meurthe-et-Moselle, Pays-Haut and Hérault, Juquin's departure from the party and his candidacy exacerbated the tensions between local *rénovateurs* and their more orthodox comrades, and the party's central organisation.

In November, Lajoinie returned to the fray in a major interview with a panel of journalists on the broadcasting platform provided by the *Forum RMC-FR3*.[16] In response to a question referring to Juquin as the other Communist candidate, Lajoinie argued that such a description of a candidate was impossible because he (Lajoinie) had been approved unanimously by the party as its candidate. Furthermore, he asserted that there was an orchestrated attempt by some sections of the press and those with an interest in preserving the economic and social status quo, to use Juquin's candidacy to damage the PCF. In his opinion, the Juquin candidacy would not have seen the light of day were it not for the support of the media, the other political parties and even the banks who had agreed to provide Juquin with a substantial advance in order to finance his candidacy. In contrast to what he implied was Juquin's artificial candidacy, Lajoinie underlined his own progress in making the French electorate listen to him.

A reference by a journalist to the willingness expressed by the Socialist, Jacques Delors, to serve as Prime Minister under Raymond Barre, should he be elected President, allowed Lajoinie to develop the PCF position regarding the posture of the PS. Lajoinie described Delors' offer as the tip of the iceberg, arguing that it expressed the fundamental inclination of the PS to cooperate with the right, which it called the centre. Delors had simply jumped the gun, as the policy of *cohabitation* between the Socialists and the right, resulting from the majority that eluded them in the legislative elections of 1986, was the prospective basis for an alliance with the right. As evidence of this, Lajoinie cited the agreement between the Socialists and the right over economic austerity measures, defence expenditure and, as he put it, the integration and subjection of France to the interests of European and American capital.

Resulting from his interviews with the media in October and November of 1987, Lajoinie's campaign was defined by four principle themes: a certain notion of how presidential office should be perceived, embodied in his person as a type of presidential aspirant; his programme; what the candidacy of Pierre Juquin really represented; and the drift of the Socialists, led by François Mitterrand, towards compromise with the right.

According to the *Paris Match*-BVA poll published in mid-November, Lajoinie's campaign was meeting with some sympathetic reaction among left-wing voters as a whole. Asked to decide who, between Delors, Fabius, Lajoinie, Mauroy, Mitterrand and Rocard would be the best candidate to represent the left, 14% of left-wing voters chose Lajoinie, as opposed to 9% in response to the same question in September. The responses to questions regarding first round voting intentions, however, suggested that Lajoinie was making little progress in convincing the electorate of his genuine credibility as a presidential candidate. Asked who they would vote for in the first round of the presidential election were it to be held on the following Sunday, 5% of the entire cross-section of voters surveyed chose Lajoinie; the same percentage as for September.[17]

By the end of November, Lajoinie was committed to a busy schedule of meetings and was drawing audiences of between 1,200 (Castres) and 4,000 (Toulon) on the departmental campaign trail. The PCF congress in December allowed Lajoinie to define himself as the candidate who was legitimately chosen by the party (in contrast to Juquin who Lajoinie called 'self-proclaimed'), and outline how his campaign fitted into the overall objectives of the party. During the open discussion on 4 December, Lajoinie dismissed any suggestion that Juquin could be regarded with any seriousness as the second Communist candidate in the race for the presidency, referring to him instead as the second Socialist candidate. Lajoinie underlined his support for the positions of the party leadership as had been expressed in Marchais's report to the congress, and reiterated the three key themes in the PCF programme: justice, liberty and peace. It was only through the Communist vote in the forthcoming election, Lajoinie asserted, that these objectives could be pursued successfully. And this point was made by Marchais in the opposite way, by affirming that a vote for any candidate other than Lajoinie in the first round would be a vote for the policies of austerity, authoritarianism and excessive arms spending that the party judged to be currently in place. In contrast to what could be interpreted as a vote of no confidence in the leadership by the *rénovateurs* of Haute-Vienne in November, at the end of the PCF congress in December, Georges Marchais was returned to office for the fifth time as the party's General Secretary. The *rénovateur* Félix Damette was not, however, reelected to the central committee of the party.

To what extent the PCF conference influenced the French electorate's perception of the party and its presidential candidate would be very difficult to judge accurately. It would nonetheless be safe to say that it had little success in enhancing it, to judge by the opinion polls. When asked by the *Paris*

Match-BVA survey of mid-December what their voting intentions were for the first round, the respondents gave Lajoinie the same score as in the previous month, 5%. There was, however, a change in the percentage of left-wing voters willing to regard Lajoinie as the best candidate to represent the left. This dropped from 14% to 11%.[18]

The tone was set for the continuation of Lajoinie's campaign in 1988 by the contents of the report presented to the central committee by Pierre Blotin of the political bureau, and which was unanimously adopted by it on 6 January 1988. Blotin outlined a programme of 50 meetings to be held by Lajoinie, 17 of which would be attended by Georges Marchais, in the 15 weeks that remained of the presidential campaign. The burden of the party's hopes, however, would be carried equally by its membership and its candidate. The report called for a harnessing of resources at the level of party cells, through an effort to find and contact absent members and encourage them to participate in the success of the PCF's campaign. This had to be achieved against what the report deemed to be a background of collusion between the right-wing and Socialist press aimed at creating, on the one hand, a feeling of anti-communism among the electorate at large, and on the other, a feeling among the potential voters for Lajoinie that the outcome of the election was a foregone conclusion. The PS and the President were also the subjects of 38 denunciations for their betrayal of former commitments and their acceptance of right-wing policies. Whatever their preferences in the second round, the report maintained that those desiring changes in government policy had no option but to vote for Lajoinie in the first round. Pierre Juquin was dismissed as a candidate put up by the PS and the report also recorded the decision of the PCF not to ratify the election of the *rénovateur,* Martial Bourquin, to the post of secretary to the Communist federation in Doubs because, according to the report, the party could not ratify the election of someone who advocated policies that differed from those advocated by the party at national level.

Lajoinie's campaign faced a more serious obstacle posed by the *rénovateurs* as January wore on. In an interview to the daily newspaper, *Libération,* on 15 January, Juquin asserted that during the presidential campaign of 1981, Marchais had expressed a preference for seeing Communists vote for the right-wing candidate in the second round rather than see them help install a Socialist President in office. Lajoinie counter-attacked in an interview on the radio station, *Europe 1,* on 17 January, denying that there had been any preference shown by the leadership for a 'revolutionary vote for the right' (*le vote révolutionnaire à droite*) in 1981. He further accused Juquin of cowardly dishonesty since the latter, according to Lajoinie, had declined Georges Marchais' challenge to justify the charge with explicit proof. In spite of the vigorous denials of the PCF leadership and Lajoinie's attempt to portray Juquin as an individual lacking in integrity, Juquin's claim did detract from the PCF's attempt to build an image of itself as a party above unprincipled political machination. The credibility of Lajoinie as a *présidentiable* suffered as January progressed and in the *Paris Match*-BVA survey published at the end of the month, the number of respondents willing to cast their votes for Lajoinie in the first round had fallen from 6% at the end of December 1987 to 4.5%. The number of left-wing voters who considered him as the best candidate to represent the left had also fallen to 10% over the same period.[19]

During the course of a press interview dealing with the central committee meeting in early February to review the progress of Lajoinie's campaign, Marchais revealed the organisational concerns of the party leadership. The central committee had become aware that a significant number of party members were not participating actively in the campaign.[20] To counter the possibility of resignation and sectarianism within the party, Lajoinie and Marchais began the month by reiterating the idea that a vote for Lajoinie in the first round did not preclude the possibility of waging an effective fight against the right in the second round. However, in order to placate those sectarian Communists who might be inclined to obstruct the election of Mitterrand in the second round, the party leadership remained disinclined at this juncture to declare itself unequivocally in favour of a vote for Mitterrand in the second round.

As the month of February progressed, Lajoinie's candidature received the support of the *contestataires* who had remained within the party. In a declaration entitled 'Malgré tout, mais avant tout, votons André Lajoinie', signed by the philosopher Henri Lefebvre and other notable *contestataires*, the point was made that in spite of the failings of the party leadership, the PCF remained the best defence against capitalism and preserved the honour of the left. In an indirect reference to Pierre Juquin's campaign, the declaration stated that a Communist tradition could not be established within the space of a few months, and could not rest on a basis of well-meaning but vague notions. The PCF leadership, criticised by the *contestataires*, was not unaware, however, of the need to inject the party's image and its candidate's campaign with more appeal and vigour. To this end, therefore, the leadership began to draw attention to the 'meeting points' (*points de rencontre*) set up by local party members outside factories, offices, supermarkets etc., and which gave the public the opportunity to meet and discuss with party representatives.

On 21 February, Lajoinie was the presidential candidate invited to discuss his views in a broadcast on the radio station RTL. During the course of the discussion he declared that the PCF was for the unity of the left, as long as it resulted in a change of policies. Lajoinie described a vote for him in the first round as the only one possible for anyone wishing to see a brake applied to the slide to the right in French politics. He expressed his belief that his share of the vote in the first round would exceed the result obtained by the PCF in the legislative election of 1986 (i.e., 9.8%). As to which candidate the PCF would support in the second round, this would be formally declared on the Wednesday following the first round. Lajoinie was categorical in rejecting the prospect of Communists once more accepting ministerial posts in order, as he put it, to implement the policies of the right. On the question of exclusions from the party, Lajoinie denied that any had occurred for political reasons, arguing that they followed from the fact that some members had acted in ways that were irreconcilable with the party's way of life. In dealing with the inevitable question of Juquin's candidacy, Lajoinie's criticism of the PS became very pointed. He described Juquin's candidacy as an anti-communist one which would not have been viable without the support of the PS. Lajoinie hinted that the support given by the PS might cost it dearly, but did not go into detail. As for the viability of Lajoinie's own candidacy, by the end of February he was polling 5.5% of the first round voting intentions of those interviewed in the *Paris Match*-BVA survey.[21]

It is safe to assume that Lajoinie's modest and generally unchanging performance in the polls was a consideration in the party leadership's review of the campaign in early March and helped inject its conclusions with a measure of urgency. A central committee meeting which took place on 8 March was expanded to include all the leaders from the departments as well as the national leadership and lasted for two days (as opposed to one day at the equivalent juncture in the 1981 presidential campaign). By this point in the campaign, Lajoinie's inability to poll more than 5 or 6% of voting intentions was of grave concern to the party leadership, given the fact that François Mitterrand had not yet officially declared his intention to run for a second term of office. The possible scenario which most concerned the PCF leadership was the one in which Mitterrand's long-awaited entry into the race released so much momentum for the Socialist candidate that it swept away all the other left-wing candidates.

Georges Marchais' contribution to the central committee meeting was marked by the assertion of his authority over the party and aimed at overcoming the two dangers which threatened to undermine Lajoinie's campaign. The first danger was the insufficient mobilisation of party members in support of André Lajoinie's campaign. The secretary responsible for party organisation, Jean-Claude Gayssot, had identified a 35% deficit in the number of party members who should have been engaged in promoting Lajoinie's campaign. Marchais stressed the need, beginning with central committee members and the secretaries of Communist federations across the country, to make a greater and more sustained commitment to working for the success of Lajoinie's campaign and the realisation of the goals it represented. The second danger identified by Marchais was the threat posed by the resort by Communist voters to the *vote utile* in the first round. On this issue, Marchais had to resolve the misunderstanding, underlined by one central committee member, which had arisen in the party regarding the PCF's position over the second ballot. Some members had concluded that *désistement* in favour of Mitterrand had already been decided. Marchais made clear what he believed could be the consequence of such a misunderstanding. The largest vote possible had to be mobilised for Lajoinie in the first round in order to prevent Mitterrand achieving what Marchais asserted had been his ambition since assuming the leadership of the PS in 1971: a presidential majority in the first round of elections for the presidency and thereby a crucial undermining of the PCF as a credible left-wing alternative to the PS. Marchais therefore reiterated the position of the PCF regarding the second round of voting, which had been determined at the party's 26th congress in December 1987. The central committee, after consultation with the federal committees, would decide which candidate it would support in the second round at a meeting on the Wednesday following the first round.

Lajoinie's appearance on *L'heure de vérité* on 23 March, came shortly after François Mitterrand had announced his decision to seek a second term as President, and reflected the concerns that had come to the fore in his (Lajoinie's) campaign in the period before the final weeks leading up to the first ballot. Lajoinie outlined the principal policy objectives that defined his campaign: the minimum wage raised to 6,000 francs, the transfer of 40 billion francs from the defence budget to education, the commitment to public sector industries which would be well-funded and *autogestionnaires*, a determination to prevent the single European market of 1992 operating against the interests of the workers, the fight against racism and the extension of voting rights to immigrants, and the protection and extension of the liberties of the citizen in general. In addition to these familiar objectives, however, Lajoinie showed his concern to distinguish his campaign from those of his left-wing rivals and the parties supporting them. Lajoinie criticised Mitterrand's pronouncement in favour of the single European market envisaged for 1992 on the same grounds that he questioned Mitterrand's declared pursuit of social harmony: both pronouncements masked the intention of the Socialists to facilitate the exploitation of the workers by right-wing economic interests. Regarding Mitterrand's commitment to disarmament, Lajoinie reminded the viewers that the PCF was the only party that had refused to vote for increases in the defence budget. As for his *rénovateur* rival, Lajoinie stressed that Juquin's was a candidacy inspired by the PS and designed to split the Communist vote. Lajoinie emphasised the importance of a first round vote for him as the only genuine vote for a left-wing alternative to the policies of the right and, in keeping with the PCF's attempt to portray him as the antithesis of an autocratic presidential figure, Lajoinie reiterated the PCF's commitment to a non-renewable mandate for the President. The telephone poll conducted immediately after the broadcast showed that 3% more of the viewers had found Lajoinie convincing than had done so after his appearance on the programme in October 1987. The *Paris Match*-BVA survey published two days later showed Lajoinie polling 6.5% of voting intentions in the first round.[22]

The Final Weeks

The final weeks of the campaign began with some unwelcome news for André Lajoinie. At a meeting of the Communist Party in the French overseas department, La Réunion, on 4 April, the decision was taken to make their votes count from the first round by casting them for Mitterrand. This decision was clearly contrary to the warnings issued by the PCF leadership regarding the damage the *vote utile* could do to the party, and it was severely criticised in the final meeting of the PCF central committee on 7 April. In the report presented by Roland Leroy, the *Parti Communiste Réunionnais* was described as an undemocratic group dominated by a clan. As well as castigating the Réunionnais Communists for acting against the interests of the PCF, Leroy's report also identified the two factors outside the party that the leadership believed were operating against the success of Lajoinie's candidacy: the institutional obstacle faced by the PCF, and a Socialist candidate inclined to ally himself with the right against the Communists.

Published in *L'Humanité* on 8 April, the report underlined the leadership's belief that the presidential election was the most undemocratic envisaged by the country's constitution, and, therefore, the most detrimental to the Communist Party. François Mitterrand, as the Socialist incumbent who had shown his ability to adapt to the constitution of the Fifth Republic and (as was shown by *cohabitation* with a right-wing Prime Minister) to use it to preserve Socialist interests, was the target of severe criticism. Leroy's report condemned the statement of aims contained in Mitterrand's recently publicised *Lettre à tous les Français* as constituting a platform for an alliance with the right. The report condemned as a 'vulgar trap' what it deemed to be Mitterrand's attempt to persuade the electorate to vote for him in order to prevent a Chirac presidency. It argued that the duel with Chirac was being used as a means of obscuring the issues really at stake, and marked a profound disrespect for democracy. Quoting from words Mitterrand himself had written in 1964, the report denounced him for resorting to the personalisation of power that he himself had once condemned.

In a television interview on 11 April, Lajoinie underlined the importance of a first-round vote for the PCF candidate as the only point at which voters would be able to express their objection to the alliances Mitterrand was planning with the right. Notwithstanding the frequent repetitions of warnings of this kind, during the week beginning Monday 11 April, 41 current and former prominent members of the CGT trade union launched a written appeal against what they regarded as the unfair pressure placed on the members by the union leadership to vote for Lajoinie (see Chapter Ten). In a major interview on the radio station *France-Inter* on 13 April, Lajoinie returned to the offensive by warning the voters against what he argued was the manipulation of the electoral process by those in power, and re-emphasised the importance of the first round vote for him as a way of halting the extension of right-wing policies and asserting the desire of the electorate for a left-wing alternative.

For his part, as General Secretary of the PCF, Georges Marchais attempted to add to the credibility of the PCF candidate's campaign by a systematic refutation of the contents of Mitterrand's *Lettre à tous les Français*, in an interview on the *Europe 1* on 15 April. In addition to the familiar arguments concerning the Socialists' compromises regarding economic and social policies, Marchais criticised the President's failure to make concrete plans to extend voting rights for immigrants; something Mitterrand had declared himself to favour. While, on the one hand, Marchais sometimes clarified and generally helped facilitate the public understanding of the PCF policies expressed by Lajoinie, on the other, he perhaps added to the public's perception of Lajoinie himself as not being a *présidentiable*. Marchais' frequent appearances in the media and his scheduled presence at almost a third of the campaign meetings programmed for Lajoinie, created a situation in which two figures appeared to be carrying the banner for the PCF into the presidential election, rather than the single figure who had been chosen as the PCF candidate.

Lajoinie returned to the theme of racism at a meeting in Marseille on 16 April, where Georges Marchais was also present on the platform. Lajoinie condemned Mitterrand and Chirac for using and allowing themselves to be used by the leader of the racist *Front National* party, Jean-Marie Le Pen. Marchais accused Le Pen of persistent dishonesty in describing the PCF's commitment to justice for immigrants, condemning it as an attempt to discourage potential PCF voters. In spite of the increased and visible presence of a new generation of French young people born of immigrant parents, the turn-out at the meeting was small, and local party leaders suggested that the Communist candidate would be unlikely to obtain the 25% share of the vote that he had obtained in 1981.

An appeal by the political bureau of the PCF to the party to mobilise appeared in *L'Humanité* on 18 April. Seven days before the first round, the appeal maintained that the outcome was not a foregone conclusion and that there were still many voters to be won over to the Lajoinie candidacy, as the one representing the only genuine vote for the left and for change. Speaking on RTL on 20 April, André Lajoinie expressed optimism about his candidacy. He believed that the PCF had regained much of the influence it had lost over recent years and expressed the wish to see the PCF share of the vote equal or exceed that obtained in the 1986 legislative elections. While expressing his hopes, Lajoinie did not forego the opportunity to give voice once more to PCF misgivings about the undemocratic nature of the election. Regarding Mitterrand, Lajoinie argued that his *Lettre à tous les Français* could well have been signed by Raymond Barre or Jacques Chirac, so clearly did it reflect Mitterrand's adoption of right-wing policies. Nonetheless, Lajoinie insisted that the PCF remained favourable to the unity of the left, particularly with regard to the municipal elections to come in 1989. Two days later, the *Paris Match*-BVA poll showed a small increase in the percentage of respondents expressing an inclination to vote for Lajoinie in the first round: 7.5% as opposed to 6% at the beginning of the month.[23]

Pierre Juquin's Campaign

On 9 January, the *rénovateurs* held their first conference, at Villeurbanne, in the Rhône, attended by several hundred delegates. As these Communists were defining their distinctness organisationally from the PCF, so their candidate distanced himself from the PCF candidate. In November and December, Juquin had been on the campaign trail in regions like Finistère, where the *rénovateur* movement was strong, but had avoided overt attempts to undermine Lajoinie's campaign. Assisted by David Assouline, the student leader, and Khaïssa Titous, the vice president of *S.O.S.-Racisme*, Juquin's message was simple and idealistic. He declared himself to be a feminist, for voting rights for immigrants, for self-management (*autogestion*), and against the nuclear deterrent. Juquin called on his listeners not to relinquish their dreams and spoke of his own dream in which three million people expressed the will to marry morality with politics.

In the daily newspaper, *Libération,* on 15 January, however, Juquin made an assertion that could not fail to be interpreted as purposely detrimental to the credibility of the PCF candidate. He maintained that, in 1981, a majority of the members in the political bureau of the PCF believed that Mitterrand would be beaten in the presidential elections, and that they should help ensure this result. Furthermore, he cited a statement made by Georges Marchais at the time, to the effect that success for Mitterrand would result in an experiment in social democracy that could damage the PCF, and that therefore it was better for the right to obtain power.

Notwithstanding the apparent damage to the PCF, the benefits of this episode for Juquin's candidacy were not evident in the polls. The *Paris Match*-BVA opinion poll at the end of January 1988 gave him the same modest share of voting intentions as in the previous month; 2%. Juquin's opportunity to convince the electorate of his credibility would come with his first appearance on the television programme, *L'Heure de vérité,* on 2 February. The constitutional barrier to the viability of Juquin's candidacy had been overcome shortly before this major test, with the promise by 500 elected representatives in French local and regional government to sponsor his candidacy; a fact which Juquin used to underline his credibility. Presenting himself as the candidate who was 'free' of party ties, Juquin expressed his hope of rallying a very diverse electorate. He was, nonetheless, a man of the left and stated clearly that he would advocate support for the Socialist candidate in the second round of the election. Juquin outlined the principal planks of his campaign with regard to social and economic policy: the reduction of the working week to 35 hours without any reduction in pay, an increase in the minimum wage to 6,000 francs and much greater resources for education.

The social changes advocated by Juquin expressed his belief in a more just and egalitarian society, racially and sexually. He argued on the one hand for the right to self-determination for the Kanaks, the indigenous people of France's troubled overseas territory of New Caledonia, and on the other for the extension of voting rights to immigrants in France and the creation of a more integrated society. In keeping with his declared sympathy for feminism, Juquin argued that measures needed to be taken to ensure that half the representatives in France's elected assemblies were women. Juquin's was a programme for a new kind of society and he wanted to build it with what he declared was a new movement comprised of new people, and not a pale imitation of the PCF.

As the first round approached, and in addition to the *rénovateurs*, Juquin could rely on support provided by Alain Krivine and his group, the *Ligue*

Communiste, the *Parti Socialiste Unifié* (PSU), the *Parti pour une alternative communiste* (PAC), and the *Fédération de la gauche alternative* (FGA).[24] The left-wing votes that Juquin could hope to win over would be from the Communist *contestataires* who wanted to change the party but had opted to do so from within, and from Socialists who were marginalised and dissatisfied by the 'tontonmania' which the PS had given itself over to.

As he had suggested on *L'Heure de vérité,* Juquin's aspirations went further. Much impressed by the Green movement in West Germany and its fusion of ecological issues with radical politics, Juquin, as the campaign progressed, injected his speeches with expressions of strong concern for environmental issues. The new movement for a new society of which Juquin had spoken, would, to judge by his campaign, be one that could pursue sexual and racial equality, and ensure employment and fair conditions of employment for the workers, while at the same time safeguarding their natural environment. In the weeks following his first major appearance on television and prior to the first ballot in the elections, the polls suggested that Juquin's project to transform society was failing to convince the electorate. His share of voting intentions in the *Paris Match*-BVA polls during that period remained stubbornly between 2% and 3%. The accuracy of the projections were proven when the results of the first ballot on 24 April became available.

First Round Results

Judged by the hopes he had expressed before the first ballot, of seeing the party equal its performance in the 1986 legislative elections, André Lajoinie's 6.76% share of the vote must be regarded as disappointing.[25] A comparison with the performance of the PCF in 1981 makes its performance in 1988 seem more modest still. The 2,055,995 votes cast for André Lajoinie represented less than half the total cast for Marchais in 1981. In only one department, Allier, which he represents as an MP, did Lajoinie poll more than 15%. He polled between 10% and 15% in 14 departments, between 5% and 10% in 51 departments and less than 5% in twenty-eight. The decline of the Communist vote was also marked in the communist heartland of the 'terres rouges': Corrèze (13.66% against 21.85% in 1981), Creuse (11.18% against 20.32%), Haute-Vienne (11.36% against 24.27%), Cher (11.78% against 20.25%), Val-de-Marne (11.03% against 21.37%), Bouches-du-Rhône (11.19% against 25.55%), and Seine-Saint-Denis (13.50% against 27.27%). Out of the 151 Communist municipalities of significant size, the Communist candidate was beaten in 145 by François Mitterrand and in 79 by Jean-Marie Le Pen. The Parisian 'red belt' also failed to contain the slide in the Communist vote. Lajoinie was beaten into second place by Le Pen in many of the constituencies of the red belt, and the share of the Communist vote in Paris dropped to less than 4%; barely a point more than Juquin's.

This last fact, however, added to Juquin's modest performance nationally, showed that the PCF did not suffer a massive transfer of loyalties to the *rénovateur* candidate. The performance of the PCF candidate was a disappointment compared to 1981. On the other hand, it was a source of considerable relief that it was substantially better than Juquin's. The PCF leadership was aware of how fatal the implications would have been for the future viability of the party if Juquin's share of the vote had approached or exceeded Lajoinie's. The failure of Juquin's experiment was more important to the preservation of the PCF's position as the only party offering a genuine and credible left-wing alternative in French politics, than the defeat of François Mitterrand. In the event, Juquin had failed to create a new movement and the PCF had survived to contest future elections.

Further comfort could be derived from the fact that although the level of abstentions nationally was similar to that in 1981, the proportion of abstentions among Communist voters had increased significantly compared to 1981, particularly in areas of the Parisian red belt, where the increase in Communist abstentions reached, in some cases, 8%. This, however, did not explain entirely the decline in the Communist vote compared to 1981. During the week after the first round results became known, Georges Marchais argued that André Lajoinie's share of the vote was so modest because many PCF voters had exercised what they had been persuaded was the *vote utile*, contrary to the advice of the PCF leadership. Looking ahead to the second and decisive round of voting, Marchais advocated a vote for François Mitterrand, but this in order to stop the right-wing candidate rather than out of any enthusiasm for what the Socialist candidate represented. Marchais expressed confidence, however, that Communist voters who had opted for the *vote utile* in the first round of the presidential elections of 1988 would revert to their Communist loyalties in the municipal elections that would take place in 1989. The rejection of Marchais' explanation of Lajoinie's low score by some observers and the announcement of the PCF's death as an electoral force was indeed shown to be premature by the PCF's performance in the unscheduled legislative elections of June, when it polled 11.31% of the votes cast.[26] Marchais' argument that many PCF members had chosen to vote usefully from the first round of the presidential ballot was, in fact, shown to have some substance by the fact that the PCF bastions which appeared to have failed to support Lajoinie were the ones responsible for the revival in the party's fortunes in the legislative elections.

The *vote utile* was one factor among several behind Lajoinie's modest showing. The mobilisation at the grassroots which the PCF had called for was not totally successful, and the campaign waged by 600,000 committed members in their everyday lives to make the electorate aware of the real Communist programme did not fully materialise. For his part, André Lajoinie failed to emerge as a candidate who was truly *présidentiable*. From the moment of his choice as the PCF candidate for the presidential elections, some observers chose to portray Lajoinie as the figure who would pursue the strategy determined by Marchais, and over whose campaign the shadow of Marchais would always loom.[27] As the presidential campaign developed, it became clear that Marchais, as well as Lajoinie, would assume the responsibility for articulating the PCF position on major issues. The ability of the electorate to focus positively on one presidential figure from the PCF was made more difficult by the high profile assumed by the General Secretary of the party. During the month of February, it was noted in *Le Monde* that Georges Marchais made five major appearances on television whereas André Lajoinie made only two. This tendency for Marchais to eclipse Lajoinie was of fundamental importance in creating the impression, which persisted throughout the campaign, that the choice of Lajoinie as the PCF's presidential candidate had not diminished Marchais' role as the real guiding force within the party. This duality, uncontentious in itself, nevertheless underscores the fundamental difficulty a party such as the PCF faces when confronted with an institution like the French presidency.

Pierre Juquin's 2.10% share of the votes cast in the first round testified to his failure to rally the support he had hoped for. Throughout his campaign the polls had suggested that Juquin's message lacked a clear cutting edge and was unable to carve out a space on the terrain of electoral politics in which his movement might take root. In some of the departments where *rénovateur* dissatisfaction with the PCF had been strongest, Juquin obtained a share of the vote that was higher than his share nationally, as in Finistère (2.77%), Haute-Garonne (3.02%), and most notably Haute-Vienne (4.05%). But the modest nature of these increases and Juquin's performance overall showed that he had failed to rally disenchanted PCF members in sufficiently large numbers to make the alternative he was proposing, viable. The fact that Juquin's score was surpassed by that of the ecologist, Antoine Waechter (3.78%), and that his share of the vote in 48 departments was lower than his share nationally, suggested that the environmentally aware, disenchanted Socialist voters, and the new electorate he dreamed of as wishing to marry morality with politics, were not persuaded of the credibility of his candidacy, and, besides, in Waechter, they already had such an alternative candidate to vote for. Juquin had gambled on a promise of change based on a union of green and red values, but, as was consistently suggested by the opinion polls leading up to the first ballot, the electorate were disinclined to believe in it as a realistic option.

In the aftermath of the first round, the recriminations among Juquin's supporters suggested a general disappointment with the way his programme had been defined and his potential constituency targeted. Gilbert Wasserman, responsible for the periodical 'M', which provided a forum for the *rénovateurs,* expressed regret at what he affirmed he had foreseen as the failure of a movement with a muddled and derivative programme based on red and green policies. A common view among observers outside the group of *rénovateurs* who had backed Juquin was that his campaign had, to too great an extent, been an effort improvised around symbolic notions of a new society and inclined to drift in the direction of utopian socialism. One of the most succinct and penetrating comments on the stillborn nature of Juquin's enterprise came from the political scientist Yves Roucaute, who had served for a time on Juquin's campaign staff. He suggested that Juquin would have taken 2% of the votes cast in the first round even if his campaign had not taken place, so negligible was its impact.[28]

* * *

André Lajoinie's share of the vote in the first round of the presidential elections was a disappointment, but did not mark the inevitable long-term demise of the PCF, and the collapse of Juquin's aspirations to create a new movement on the left allowed the PCF to preserve its role as the only standard bearer for the Communist cause with a mass party base and members in parliament.

André Lajoinie's challenge for the presidency had been faced with a number of important obstacles. On the one hand, the PCF had made clear its belief that the nature of the presidential election was undemocratic, but saw no alternative to putting up a candidate to contest it. Once committed to the presidential campaign, the PCF found itself faced with a left-wing rival, the PS, which had adapted well to the electoral system and seemed prepared to sacrifice the shibboleths of the left in order to respond to the changing attitudes of the electorate. Unlike the PCF, the PS was not averse to adapting its message and presenting its candidate in a way that enabled it to enjoy the benefits of a successful media campaign.

Instead of negotiating these obstacles through compromise, the PCF attempted to distinguish itself from the other parties fielding candidates by attempting to overturn these obstacles through adherence to its principles. The undemocratic nature of the election and the way it discriminated against the Communist candidate remained a theme that surfaced throughout Lajoinie's campaign. His candidacy was presented by the PCF leadership, not as a compromise, but as the only way of halting the extension of right-wing policies, which it accused the PS of assisting. Juquin's candidacy was depicted as a spoiling tactic devised by the PS, and abetted by the press, in an attempt to split the Communist vote. The PS itself was accused of sabotaging debate through an American-style focus on personalities rather than issues, and its candidate of planning to collude with the right in the event of his re-election. However true such accusations might be, they were clearly not a recipe for success in a presidential contest.

A key feature in Lajoinie's appeal was meant to rest in his campaign's rejection of presidential image-building and of the transformation of the election into a competition between personalities rather than programmes. Consequently, the PCF leadership adopted the strategy of explicitly laying the foundation for the success of Lajoinie's campaign as much on the efforts of the mass membership as on the efforts of the candidate himself, in what it wished to portray as a collective effort to install a President committed to a genuine left-wing alternative to the right-wing policies then being pursued. Furthermore, the elaboration of the Communist programme for change was a task that was also shared, between the General Secretary of the party and its presidential candidate. As a result of this strategy, André Lajoinie's profile as a *présidentiable* failed to develop in a convincing manner, and his campaign sometimes assumed the negative nature of a rearguard action designed simply to preserve the PCF as an electoral force in French politics. The PCF's overt ambition of taking the political high ground through the election of André Lajoinie to the presidency was manifestly unsuccessful. Its endeavour to preserve its viability as an electoral force, however, was not as unsuccessful as many observers asserted in the aftermath of the presidential elections. As was shown by the results of the legislative elections which followed in June 1988, the PCF's fate remained uncertain rather than clearly sealed and, to a certain extent, dependent once more upon the way the party, its leadership and its membership responded to the challenges it confronted.

NOTES

1. G. Lavau, 'Le parti communiste: un congrès de survie', *Revue politique et parlementaire*, 914, January-February 1985, pp. 6-15.

2. P. Bauby, 'Le révisionnisme institutionnel du PCF', *Revue politique et parlementaire*, 919, September-October 1985, p. 97.

3. E. Dainov, 'Problems of French Communism 1972-1986', *West European Politics*, 3, July 1987, p. 375.

4. M. Naudy, *PCF le suicide* (Paris, Albin Michel, 1986) p. 171.

5. M. Cardoze, *Nouveau voyage à l'intérieur du parti communiste français* (Paris, Fayard, 1986) p. 324.

6. R. Milon, 'Le PCF est toujours un parti passoire', *Est et Ouest*, 50, January 1988, p. 29.

7. Marchais' report was published in *L'Humanité*, 4 February 1982.

8. M. Cardoze, 'PCF: le destin du courant critique', *Revue politique et parlementaire*, 927, January-February 1987, p. 48.

9. M. Samson, 'PC: divorces à la toulousaine', *Libération*, 31 October 1987.

10. P. Juquin, *Autocritiques* (Paris, Grasset, 1985) Chapter Nine.

11. P. Juquin, *Fraternellement libre* (Paris, Grasset, 1988) p. 28.

12. Published in *L'Humanité*, 3 December 1987.

13. A. Lajoinie and R. Passevent, *A cœur ouvert* (Paris, Messidor, 1987) p. 170.

14. O. Biffaud, 'M. Lajoinie se définit comme un "candidat révoutionnaire" ', *Le Monde*, 21 October 1987.

15. *Paris Match*, 9 October 1987.

16. Reported in *L'Humanité*, 16 November 1987.

17. *Paris Match*, 13 November 1987.

18. *Ibid.*, 11 December 1987.

19. *Ibid.*, 21 January 1988.

20. M. Samson, 'Marchais: communistes, encore un effort pour être mobilisés', *Libération,* 11 February 1988.

21. *Paris Match,* 26 February 1988.

22. *Ibid.,* 25 March 1988.

23. *Ibid.,* 22 April 1988.

24. Small left-wing groups existing outside the two major left-wing parties.

25. All statistics taken from *Le Monde, Dossiers et Documents: l' élection présidentielle,* May 1988.

26. *Le Monde, Dossiers et Documents: les élections législatives,* June 1988, p. 33.

27. D. Jeambar, 'Présidentielle: l'ombre de Marchais', *Le Point,* 25 May 1987, p. 68.

28. P. Krop, and M. Szac-Jacquelin, 'Même Juquin n'a pas pu ressusciter le PC', *L'Evénement du Jeudi,* 28 April 1988, p. 52.

INDICATIVE BIBLIOGRAPHY

Adereth, M., *The French Communist Party: a critical history (1920-1984)* (Manchester, Manchester University Press, 1984).

Becker, J-J., *Le Parti Communiste veut-il prendre le pouvoir? : La stratégie du PCF de 1930 à nos jours* (Paris, Seuil, 1981).

Burles, J., *Le Parti Communiste dans la société française* (Paris, Editions Sociales, 1981).

Burles, J., Martelli, R., and Wolikow, S., *Les communistes et leur stratégie* (Paris, Editions Sociales, 1981).

Cardoze, M., *Nouveau voyage à l'intérieur du parti communiste français* (Paris, Fayard, 1986).

Elleinstein, J., *Le PC* (Paris, Grasset, 1976).

Fauvet, J., *Histoire du Parti Communiste Français* (Paris, Fayard, 1977).

Gaffney, J., *The French Left and the Fifth Republic* (London, Macmillan, 1989).

Gaudard, J.-P., *Les Orphelins du PC* (Paris, Belfond, 1986).

Juquin, P., *Autocritiques* (Paris, Grasset, 1985).

Juquin, P., *Fraternellement libre* (Paris, Grasset, 1988).

Kriegel, A., *Les communistes français* (Paris, Seuil, 1970).

Lajoinie, A. and Passevent, R., *A cœur ouvert* (Paris, Messidor, 1987).

Laurens, A., and Pfister, T., *Les nouveaux communistes aux portes du pouvoir* (Paris, Stock, 1977).

Lavau, G., *A quoi sert le PCF ?* (Paris, Fayard, 1981).

Pronier, R., *Les municipalités communistes* (Paris, Balland, 1983).

9 Business as usual: the employers

GEORGE JONES

> 'As far as business is concerned, our impression is that this election won't have much effect'.
> **François Vivien**, president of the Wirth and Gruffat machine-tool company.

On 11 May 1981, trading on the Paris stock exchange was suspended, so great was the volume of sales in a market where no buyers were to be found. At the same time, the franc fell to its 'floor' within the European Monetary System (EMS) and had to be rescued by the combined efforts of the Bank of France and the Bundesbank.

Different indeed was the situation seven years later. Share prices rose as soon as the market opened on 9 May 1988, the morning after President Mitterrand's reelection. The financial press continued to report that threatened rises in German and American interest rates were a source of greater concern to French investors than the outcome of the presidential election.[1] The franc slipped a little against the deutschmark but after modest support from the central bank managed to end the day only 0,55 pfennig down against a stronger deutschmark, and unchanged against the dollar.

Partly, this sang-froid was due to the fact that so clearly had the polls pointed to a Mitterrand victory that the markets had already discounted its effect; partly it was because financial markets and the business community in general expected the effect to be slight.

Twelve years before, at a celebrated 'Forum' organised by *L'Expansion*, François Mitterrand and several leading Socialist politicians met representatives of industry. A poll conducted by the magazine showed that 45% of company chairmen believed that the Communist Party was more powerful than the Socialist, 51% felt that a future left-wing government would 'go much further' than the then Common Programme, and 66% believed that the Socialist party, even without the Communists, would be incapable of running the French economy.[2]

In the event, fears of Communist domination proved grossly exaggerated, but the years 1981-1983 remained a disagreeable memory for the business community. In addition to the nationalisations and the unwelcome extension of the power of organised labour, there had been the government's efforts to widen the tax base. Corporation tax, it is true, remained at the same level (50%), but a variety of activities found themselves the target of new taxes: these included employment agencies, oil companies, insurance, finance companies, and television advertising. A (most unwelcome) tax on business entertaining was introduced. Higher rates of VAT were imposed on luxury hotels, diamonds and fur coats. Personal income tax was increased and, to complete the assault on the fur-coated classes, the Finance Law for 1982 brought in a wealth tax. At the outset, the rates were fairly low, but the resentment was none the less great.

The story of the change to a different policy has been told elsewhere.[3] Suffice it to say that the decision to remain in the EMS and reject a policy of competitive devaluation made it imperative to find other ways of cutting industrial costs, including wage costs. Indexation of wages to the rate of inflation had not been a legal right in France, but had become part of established wage bargaining in many industries (the negotiators assumed from the outset that employees were entitled to be compensated for inflation; increases beyond that depended on the relative bargaining strength of the parties). The then Finance Minister, Jacques Delors, was determined to put an end to this de facto indexation, and began by discouraging index-linked pay deals in the nationalised industries. By the end of 1983, wages were failing to keep pace with inflation, particularly in manufacturing industry. Company profits, which had been falling since 1979, began to revive, and there was a sharp recovery in business confidence. In December 1983, only 4% of company chairmen interviewed by the polling organisation, SOFRES, were optimistic about the coming year. By December 1985, the proportion had risen to 36%.[4] The years 1983-1985 also saw a shift of public opinion, which became more kindly disposed to business and more inclined to believe that 'there was no alternative' to promoting the health of French companies, 62% questioned in a poll in October 1983 believing this to be the only way out of the recession.[5]

Pierre Bérégovoy replaced Jacques Delors as Finance Minister in May 1984; the following year, he brought in the first reduction in business taxation since the Socialists had come to office: corporation tax was brought down from 50% to 45% (on undistributed profits), the intention being to raise investment. The efficacy of such measures was to be a subject of debate during the period of *cohabitation* (1986-1988), and during the subsequent presidential election campaign.

The Employers and the *Cohabitation* Government

The right-wing government which came to power in March 1986 embarked on a programme of deregulation and tax-cutting without parallel in French history. Taking deregulation first, it should not be forgotten that, in 1986, ministers were still equipped with powers to regulate the price of anything and everything. The source of these powers, *Ordonnance* 45-1483 of 30 June 1945, had originally been an attempt to deal with post-war black marketeering, but had remained in force as an instrument of counter-inflation policy and corporatist control. Although many prices had been freed, many others were still regulated, notably the price of many basic foods. These controls came to an end with *Ordonnance* 86-1243 of 1 December 1986.

Exchange controls were progressively dismantled: by May 1987, companies could invest abroad freely, decide whether and when to repatriate foreign currency earnings, and operate freely on the foreign exchange markets, including forward cover of exchange risks.

The burden of business taxation was reduced, corporation tax being brought down from 50% to 45% on all profits (whether re-invested or not),[6] and then further reduced to 42%.[7] The tax on business entertaining was abolished, as was the wealth tax on personal fortunes.[8]

The abolition of price controls had long been a demand of French industrialists. It was Raymond Barre, as Prime Minister, who had begun the process of liberalisation when he had removed the controls on the price of industrial goods in 1978. One of Barre's leading supporters, Gérard Pellisson, joint chairman of the Accor catering group, singled this out as one of his main reasons for backing the former Prime Minister in the 1988 campaign. Yet a policy favouring greater competition contains within it a contradiction. Edouard Balladur, Finance Minister in the *cohabitation* period, might write that 'whenever a ferment of competition has been brought into our economy, the economy has emerged stronger'[9] but is the entrepreneur moved mainly by concern for the strength of the national economy? Some, such as prospective entrants to newly contestable markets, may genuinely welcome competition. Others may pay lip-service to it as a national interest, but in practice find it unwelcome when applied to themselves. Those who seek to promote more competition cannot expect to be universally popular in the business world, as Balladur himself knew: 'Market freedom does not simply mean freedom to increase prices to consumers … . Competition is a demanding discipline, hence the temptation to escape from it … . We are the country of *corporations* (guilds) and the tradition has, in many ways survived. More than other countries, we have long been sheltered from the force of international competition … .'[10]

Moreover, the satisfaction of one demand of business may add to problems and cause increased complaint in another area. The abolition of exchange controls was generally welcomed for its savings in administrative time and because it permitted more efficient company treasury management. Yet a persistent source of complaint at the time of the 1988 election was that French interest rates were excessively high.[11] The high rates, however, were in part a product of government policy. In March 1988, Balladur admitted[12] that such high rates were necessary to protect the franc: 'we are still suffering from our own past reputation. We have to show that we are determined to defend the franc/deutschmark exchange rate, by every possible means'. However, the government's abolition of exchange control, which had been applauded by business, made the task harder. The 'Lettre de conjoncture de la BNP' (January 1988) estimated that there were now 60, 000 million francs worth of currency held outside France by French residents (mainly companies), and available for speculation against the franc, making the task of managing the French currency much harder than it had been when strict capital controls had been in force.[13]

The Employers' Organisations and the 1988 Election

It had become a tradition that before a presidential election the largest representative organisation of French business, the CNPF (*Conseil national du patronat français*), and its rival in the small business sector, the CGPME (*Confédération générale des petites et moyennes entreprises*), should produce a policy document setting out each organisation's claims on behalf of its members.

The CNPF was circumspect, declaring itself neutral - in contrast to 1981 when its president had warned that France faced a stark choice between 'a society based on freedom of initiative' on the one hand, and 'a programme which would take France along the road to collectivism' on the other. At the 1987 annual conference of the CNPF, François Perigot, president since December 1986, had demanded that 'business should not be a political football in the election campaign'. However, he then entered the political arena himself by claiming that 'companies are convalescing. Any radical change of policy will produce a relapse', and then added without apparent irony 'the important thing is that whoever is elected should pursue the policy which I ask of him, in the name of business'.[14] Two months later, the CNPF produced its official pronouncement on the campaign, the 'Resolution in favour of a society based on freedom and responsibility'.[15] It was a turgid and wordy document which, by its prose style alone, could be seen to be the work of long hours spent in committee. The nub of its argument was that companies had regained four essential freedoms: the freedom to determine prices, to move money in and out of the country, to fix staffing levels, and to deploy the staff as they saw fit. Companies, the document promised almost apologetically, would 'use responsibly' the new freedoms which they had been given, 'But' and here followed the most naive and implausible of the document's suggestions 'in order for there not to be the slightest risk [to the four freedoms], the CNPF asks that these economic freedoms should, like political freedoms, be guaranteed by the Constitution'. One is baffled to know whether the CNPF really thought they could persuade one of the candidates, if victorious, to introduce a constitutional amendment forbidding exchange control. The document was also markedly corporatist in tone: it was necessary to 'associate civil servants and trade unionists with the drive for competitiveness'. Indeed, the policy of the CNPF had a pleasantly old-fashioned flavour in the new free-market climate. On another occasion, François Perigot made it clear that he had not abandoned the long-standing CNPF request for a stimulation (*réactivation*) of the economy[16] - basically a Keynesian reflation not unlike that of 1981-1982, except that it would have relied more on public investment and less on the stimulation of private consumption. Interestingly, a survey of 450 industrialists regularly polled by *L'Expansion* gave this idea the thumbs down, but there was, as we shall see, no shortage of industrialists willing to plead in favour of increased public expenditure in their own sector.

Very different in tone from the CNPF document was the 'White Paper' (*Livre blanc*) produced on the same day, 17 February, by the CGPME. The relationship between the two bodies is complex: the CGPME remains, technically, an affiliated member of the CNPF, but has never concealed its view that the CNPF is a stodgy, bureaucratic and wishy-washy organisation. 'The CNPF', said the CGPME vice-president, Jean Bruet 'is only just starting to take up some of the points we were making twenty years ago'.[17] The White Paper was a short document written in a simple, punchy style. It conceded that 'since March 1986, decisions have gone our way' but denounced the government's reform of the competition law (see above) as too weak. Yet the enthusiasm for competition was limited in scope: the CGPME demanded more protection, under the 'Royer' law of 1974, against the establishment of supermarkets. The number of approvals given had, it claimed, been 'grossly excessive'. It demanded an end to what it described as the 'discrimination' against small and medium-sized businesses (PME) in the granting of credit: they paid, it was said, 1.5% more on average for long-term loans and 3-4% more for short term loans than did large companies. These figures are borne out by the Bank of France study of the industrial sector of small/medium sized business which found these firms paying 2.5% more on average for all types of loan than did the large firms.[18] Yet what solutions were the CGPME, champions of freedom, actually proposing? Why, after all, should the banks not offer better rates to the larger customers who are often a lower risk and whose accounts, if withdrawn, would be a more important loss to the bank?

The CGPME document contrasted sharply with the corporatist tone of the CNPF 'Resolution'. No cosy get-togethers with civil servants and trade unionists! Trade unions were denounced as 'alien, politicised bodies which are being foisted on companies'. The new government should give equal rights to company unions, and cut down the amount of time which union representatives can spend on union business. The right to strike should be abolished in the public services; elsewhere, industrial action should be subject to a compulsory secret ballot. The president, René Bernasconi, had none of Perigot's carefully contrived neutrality. He was for a Socialist defeat. Hedging his bets, however, he joined the campaign committee both of Barre and of Chirac.

There were in fact inconsistencies in the positions both of the CNPF and the CGPME. The CNPF, strongly marked by the corporatist tradition and still seeing itself as the privileged interlocutor of government, was anxious not be at odds with whichever government might emerge from the elections. The decision to back one presidential candidate against another in the 1981 election was widely believed within the organisation to have been an error which had cost the CNPF influence with the new government and even cost Giscard votes. Yvon Gattaz, a member of the executive council in April 1981 and president of the CNPF from December 1981 to December 1986, claimed that the factor which swung the council in favour of committing itself to Giscard was fear of being upstaged by Bernasconi who, in 1981 as in 1988, had come out firmly against the Socialists.[19] Yet it was far from clear what was the best tactic to pursue in 1988. The problems for the CNPF were as challenging in 1988 as they had been in 1981: Bernasconi and his CGPME were as assertive as ever; gratitude for the 'four freedoms' was mixed with the fear that they might be taken away: they needed to be defended, but in a way which could be presented as 'non-political', hence the nonsense about writing them into the Constitution; finally, there were two leading right-wing candidates not one, leading to the embarrassing possibility that when they disagreed, the CNPF might have to choose between them. The CGPME, although it preached an aggressively free-market philosophy, did not hesitate to demand the intervention of government to protect its members against the rigours of market forces. However, in its uncertainties towards the market principle, the organisation reflected an attitude widespread in French business, and not only in the small business sector.

The Economic Policies of the Candidates

The polls indicated that the only candidates who could hope to reach the second ballot were Mitterrand (or if he declined to stand, another Socialist candidate) and either Chirac or Barre. Employers worked, planned and lobbied on the assumption that one of these three would choose the next Prime Minister and determine the political, legal and, above all, fiscal environment of business for the next seven years.

At the centre of the economic programme of all three leading candidates was tax. They sought to respond to the main arguments of the business community which were, in essence, that the total burden of taxation was still too high, that too great a proportion of government revenue was raised from business rather than personal taxpayers and that the structure of taxation penalised both employment and investment.

Before studying the proposals of the candidates, it is worth examining briefly the main characteristics of the French tax system.

Let us consider first the proportion of government revenue raised, in various industrial countries, by different forms of taxation (see table 1, p. 192 - the figures are for 1986).

What stands out here is the low proportion of the French government's tax receipts which comes from personal income tax, and the very high proportion which comes from 'social security'.

The latter is made up of the employer's and employee's contributions to the various funds (*caisses*) which insure the employee against sickness and unemployment and provide his or her old-age pension and family allowances (the employer's contribution is more than double that of the employee). In addition, both employer and employee have to contribute to a fund which provides insurance against accidents at work, and to another which pays the wages owed to the staff of failed businesses. Nor is that all: the employer pays into a staff housing fund, and helps to finance the city transport system (in Paris, he also meets half the employee's transport costs).

	Taxes on personal income	Taxes on company profits	Social Security	Taxes on wages, payable by employers	Taxes on personal capital	Taxes on goods and services	Others	Total
France	13.0	5.2	42.7	2.0	4.8	29.4	2.9	100
Belgium	33.7	6.7	33.6	-	1.9	24.0	0.1	100
Italy	28.0	9.9	34.3	0.5	2.7	24.6	-	100
West Germany	28.5	6.0	37.2	-	3.1	25.2	-	100
Netherlands	20.3	7.3	42.5	-	3.6	26.0	0.3	100
Sweden	38.0	4.7	25.0	4.5	2.8	24.8	0.2	100
USA	35.4	7.0	29.8	-	10.3	17.5	-	100
UK	27.9	10.3	17.9	-	12.9	30.9	0.1	100

Source: Ministry of Finance, based on OECD statistics.

The employer's contributions are calculated as a percentage of gross wages paid, resulting in an addition of more than 40% to wage costs (over 46% in the case of management staff).

It is interesting to compare the position of a French and a British employer who might wish to offer a similar wage to an employee:

Clerical worker, (France, Central Paris)		Clerical worker, (United Kingdom)	
Gross pay per month	8 000 ff	Gross pay per month	£800.00
Total of all payroll taxes due from employer	3 359 ff	Employer's National Insurance Contribution	£ 83.60
Total cost to employer	11 359 ff	Total cost to employer	£883.60

Figures are for 1988.[20] The figure for 1985 (the last complete year of socialist rule) would have been 11.239 ff.[21] The French figure excludes employer's contribution to employee's transport costs. The British figure assumes the employee is 'contracted-in' to the state occupational pension scheme.

The Chirac government was under intense pressure to reduce these payroll taxes. It tried in the run-up to the election campaign to accommodate this pressure by making modest reductions in the employer's contribution to three of the minor funds, but rising unemployment forced it to put the 'unemployment' contribution up, so the net benefit to employers was nil.[22] But if, as the CNPF requested, employers should bear a lower share of the burden, who was to pay more in their place? Even Raymond Barre, whose programme was the most comprehensive, never really addressed this question. When he pointed out, without drawing a clear conclusion, that most of French income tax is raised from only 15% of households, Chirac, in the television programme, *Questions à domicile*, on 14 February 1988,[23] hit back by accusing him of wanting to tax people on low incomes, and Barre backed off.

The French reliance on a multiplicity of social insurance funds and levies on employers as a means of financing social expenditure is a 'high visibility' form of taxation which inevitably serves as a rallying point for political protest. In economic terms, the objections to the system are not without merit: the French employer can point out that he pays large sums in payroll taxes simply because he employs staff, and whether or not he makes a single centime of profit.

Equally difficult to reform, and also a target of the employers' dislike, was the *taxe professionnelle*. Mitterrand could take pleasure in recalling on *Antenne 2*[24] that he had called it a 'stupid tax' when the Chirac government (not that of 1986-1988, however, but that of 1974-1976) had introduced it. All Mitterrand could offer, however, was a 'remodelling' of the tax - plus a reminder that during his presidency the burden of the tax had been reduced by a quarter (this was true, but most of the reductions had taken place after 16 March 1986!).

What, then, is the *taxe professionnelle*? Chirac's reform of 1975 had preserved the principle of the earlier *'patente'*, a tax dating back to revolutionary times, which stipulated that the local authorities (*communes*) should be able to tax economic activities taking place on their territory. The base for the *taxe professionnelle* is, firstly, the imputed rentable value of a firm's land, buildings and equipment situated in the local authority's area, and, secondly, 18% of the value of the wages it pays to those employed in the same area. Once these two values have been determined, the rate of tax to be levied on them is a matter for the local authority to decide. The same rate of tax will yield vastly differing amounts of revenue from one local authority to the next, depending on the number and size of firms operating in the area. To help the weaker authorities, the Socialists had introduced a 'national compensation fund' (*fonds national de péréquation* (financed by a further levy on employers!)). In response to pressure from employers, governments both of the left and of the right had made a number of concessions. The Socialists had stipulated that the rises in the *taxe professionnelle* should be linked to rises in other local taxes, which were payable mainly by households, in order to prevent local authorities from transferring too much of the burden away from personal taxpayers and onto business.[25] Raymond Barre's government had agreed that the *taxe professionnelle* payable by a company should not exceed 8% of the added value which the company produced,[26] and subsequently reduced this to 6%.[27] Pierre Bérégovoy brought it down further to 5%.[28] Raymond Barre's election programme for 1988 proposed that this maximum should be reduced again, to 3.5%, and that responsibility for fixing the rates of the *taxe professionnelle* should be taken away from the *communes* and given to the next tier of local government, the *département*, a reform which was scarcely popular with the *communes*.

The base of the tax (equipment and wages) was simply wrong, but to abolish the *taxe professionnelle* altogether would have cost the local authorities, on average, a quarter of their income. The argument was destined to go round in circles unless or until there was a thorough reform of local finance. Such a reform might upset personal tax payers, the local authorities, or business, or possibly all three, and was not, therefore, a likely prospect at election time.

Uncertain how to proceed, Balladur had, in March 1987, formed a committee under Senator R. Ballayer which was to put forward proposals for reform of the tax. Although Balladur received the committee's report just before the election, he did not publish it until just afterwards (in fact, the changes it advocated were fairly modest). In the meantime, the fact that the committee was at work enabled Chirac to agree that the base of the tax should be changed, but without saying how.[29]

Were there any significant differences between the tax programmes of Barre, Chirac, and Mitterrand? For both Barre and Chirac, the tax reductions begun in 1986 were to be continued. Barre claimed it was possible to find 130 billion francs of reductions over 7 years by reducing VAT, redistributing income tax and reducing corporation tax. Chirac's programme offered 45 billion francs over 3 years, again by reductions in corporation tax as well as by a more generous tax treatment of savings. Both candidates undertook to reduce the budget deficit, which implied that spending must fall faster than taxes but both were vague on the economies they would propose.

The most conservative of the three front-running candidates was Mitterrand who advocated what amounted to a standstill in the tax field. VAT would be reduced 'but only to the extent a margin of manœuvre in the budget might allow' (*Lettre à tous les Français*). Mitterrand was against an all-round reduction in corporation tax but in favour of reverting to the arrangement made in 1985 by Pierre Bérégovoy - i.e. a more favourable treatment of reinvested profits, as well as the use of tax credits as an incentive to investment. Here Mitterrand joined Barre, but was opposed to Chirac. Chirac and Balladur had begun in 1986, as we have seen, a policy of reducing corporation tax. At the same time, industrial subsidies were cut by 17%. In other words, companies would keep more of their own money to spend as they pleased.

The principle of government aid to industry is not new in France. No less than seven different schemes were in operation between 1966 and 1986. Chirac's objection to Barre's proposal was that it had been tried before and was quite simply ineffective, because firms responded by bringing forward investment projects they would in any case have carried out, in order to collect the subsidy.[30] In his interview with *Le Nouvel Economiste* of 18 December, Perigot had seemed to go as far as he could - granted his ostensible neutrality - towards supporting Barre's view rather than Chirac's (whilst dressing it up as a concern for small business). Interestingly, 61% of industrialists polled in a survey in *Le Monde* on 26 April were in favour of ending state aids to industry, so it may well be that Chirac's view was more in tune with business opinion than Barre's or Perigot's. The *Conseil des Impôts* had studied investment incentives in detail, and had concluded that in order to have any impact on investment decisions, the tax reductions would need to be very great - and so very costly to government.

Moreover, investment incentives needed to be maintained over a long period 'whereas in France they have always been instruments of short-term economic management'.[31] The report came down in favour of tax reductions for all businesses rather than specific investment incentives. Although it supported Chirac's point of view rather than Barre's, the latter would certainly have agreed that France needed a long-term tax reform: 'Too many changes in the past have come from considering the circumstances of the moment rather than taking an overall view'.[32] The code-word for this attack on the government was 'pointilliste' ('des mesures pointillistes et ponctuelles'). What, however, could be more 'pointilliste', said the Budget Minister, Alain Juppé, picking up Barre's expression and throwing it back, than concentrating on investment incentives rather than on all-round measures to raise business profits?[33]

Don't Rock the Boat

In the election of 1981, said Balladur in March 1988, the illusion was still current that governments could increase the purchasing power of the population.[34] However, answering the implied suggestion of the interviewer that wage inflation was still too high in France, Balladur let slip the interesting admission that 'it is better to have half a percent more on purchasing power if it avoids a wave of industrial unrest (*une crise sociale*)'. The government was very anxious indeed to avoid any confrontation with labour in the pre-election period, even though it faced continuous, if not united, pressure from the employers over wages, dismissals, and the rights of staff representatives. In 1987, 60% of employers polled by SOFRES wanted the Socialist government's Auroux laws on staff representation to be abolished altogether, while just over a quarter (26%) wanted to see the end of the national minimum wage (SMIC).[35] Responding to pressure from members, the CNPF had renewed a long-standing request that the national minimum wage should be increased only once a year (rather than quarterly), but the Minister for Social Affairs, Philippe Séguin, had refused. The CNPF admitted that the government had done a great deal for employers in the matter of flexible working practices and the right to hire and fire. These were two of the 'four freedoms' mentioned in the CNPF 'Resolution in favour of a society based on freedom and responsibility.' But, said Perigot, 'the actual application of the [reforms] does not match their objectives, particularly in the matter of dismissal.'[36] This was a reference to employers' frustration at the operation of the law of 3 July 1986: by this reform, employers were freed from the necessity of obtaining the approval of the Ministry of Labour inspectors before making workers redundant. Much rejoicing. The government seemed to have accepted the CNPF's argument that if such rigidities in the labour market could be removed, more employment would be created. In fact, a study of the operation of the earlier legislation showed that 46% of employers' applications were approved at once; the number of approvals rose further (though by how much is disputed) after renegotiation and appeals.[37] Even if the application was finally accepted, what rankled with employers was the time-consuming procedure, including the 'cooling-off period' which had to elapse before any redundancies could be implemented. The 1986 reforms provided that the 'cooling-off period' would be retained, but would be reduced to a period varying between 30 and 60 days, depending on how many jobs were to be lost. However, the provisions which required the staff representative committee (comité d'entreprise) to be consulted were unchanged, as was the right of this committee to demand an accountant's report on the company's financial position before beginning to negotiate redundancy terms. Deprived of the possibility of blocking the redundancies altogether by an appeal to the labour inspectorate, the unions seized on the accountant's report as a way of gaining time. To the fury of the employers, the courts ruled that the 'cooling-off period' could not begin to run until the accountant's report had been received, or alternatively that the unions could demand the accountant's report even when the 'cooling-off period' was almost over. Throughout the autumn of 1987, the CNPF had pressed Séguin to do something, and he had agreed to sponsor an amendment to the law which would have had the effect of setting an upper limit to the delays, but with the approach of the elections this was judged too 'hot', and the matter was shelved. In continuing to press for changes, Perigot insisted that 'we are not calling into question the social achievements of the Republic. Our aim is better management, in the interest of all'.[38] The same language had been used by Pierre Guillen, president of the Industrial Relations Committee of the CNPF, who at the annual conference a few days earlier, had said that the CNPF was not calling into question the system of staff representation but wanted abuses to be corrected.[39] Perigot said that many employers felt that strikes in the public services were 'intolerable' but declined to say whether they should be banned or not: 'The employers have no wish to promote a change in the law on strikes'.[40]

The CNPF leadership was treading on thin ice and knew it. When Perigot had taken over as president, it was not surprising that, after years of in-fighting, only 37% of the members had confidence in the leaders of the organisation. After a year in office, Perigot had raised this to 46%. To adopt the demands of the more extreme members would not only have been politically unwise, it would have ruined the dialogue which Perigot had been trying to build up with the unions (the government, too, had held out high hopes that such contacts might find a solution to the dispute over the delays in implementing redundancies, thus obviating the need for legislation). Equally, to do nothing, or to seem too passive, was to risk renewed dissatisfaction amongst the membership, or even the defection of some of the smaller firms to

Bernasconi's CGPME, with its simpler, clearer and more robust programme.

For Chirac, a period of silence on the part of the more strident employers would have been more than welcome. In a speech to the Forum de l'Expansion on 7 January 1988, Chirac had warned that employers should not 'indulge in irresponsible whims which would call into question the social security system'. In the last days of the campaign, interviewed by *Les Echos*, Chirac was at pains to stress that the social security system was safe with him. Questions about the abolition of the Auroux laws were simply sidestepped.[41] The Prime Minister's combative image was a mixed blessing among the electorate as a whole. Substantial numbers of electors were said to think him aggressive and intolerant,[42] whereas tolerance was seen as one of Mitterrand's greatest virtues.[43] The more extreme demands of some employers were an embarrassment which it was better to ignore for the sake of his appeal to a wider electorate even if it meant a few more first-round votes for Le Pen from disgruntled small businessmen.

There was even some anxiety amongst the employers at the consequences of a Chirac victory, although whether this was directed against Chirac personally or the right in general is difficult to say. Seven months before the election, an IPSOS poll carried out for *Le Monde* among senior managers of large companies, both public and private, had found that 80% thought a left-wing President would be more successful in avoiding industrial unrest, while 49% felt he would be more successful than the right in controlling wage inflation. When in April 1988, Chirac was matched against Mitterrand, the results of a poll amongst a similar group show that, in these larger organisations at any rate, the fear of conflict with the unions if Chirac won was a real one:

In which three of the following areas would you have the highest hopes - if Jacques Chirac is elected? - if François Mitterrand is elected?

	Jacques Chirac	François Mitterrand
Industrial relations	4	55
Wages and salaries	6	19
Social Security	9	28
Prices	19	15
Employment	41	24
Payroll taxes	47	11
Growth	64	12
Value of the currency	17	5
Balanced budget	43	7
Balance of payments	18	5
None of these	1	13
Don't know	8	11
Total	*	*

* Total less than 300: some respondents gave less than three answers.

Source: IPSOS, *Le Monde*, 26 April 1988.

In which three of the following areas would you have most fear - if Jacques Chirac is elected? - if François Mitterrand is elected?

	Jacques Chirac	François Mitterrand
Industrial relations	72	8
Wages and Salaries	23	20
Social security	29	19
Prices	14	17
Employment	16	20
Payroll taxes	10	49
Growth	7	26
Value of the currency	13	30
Balanced budget	14	48
Balance of payments	23	29
None of these	5	2
Don't know	11	8
Total	*	*

* Total less than 300: some respondents gave less than three answers.

Source: *ibid.*

Even if there was a substantial degree of convergence on some subjects, notably prices, the images were clear: Mitterrand for peace and quiet (even if he is spendthrift); Chirac for economic growth.

Vested Interests

Lower taxes, less bureaucracy, fewer restrictions on hiring and firing - these are objectives which almost any business would urge upon government. But that is where agreement ends. Thereafter, sectional interests take over, often defended in France by trade associations of great vigour and effectiveness. One might have thought, for instance, that the government scheme for giving work experience to unemployed young people (SIVP), started by the Socialists and maintained by Chirac, would have met with universal approval. This was not so, for example, in the case of the National Association of Temporary Work Agencies (UNETT) whose members had been doing very nicely from the employers' fear of those restrictive labour laws which Chirac had attempted (however inadequately, some said) to reform. The art of the lobbyist, when he takes his campaign to the public, is to convince that the sectional interest coincides precisely with the public good, or alternatively, that it assists a vulnerable group (the elderly, the handicapped, the unemployed) who are objects of public sympathy. Thus UNETT pointed out[44] that 40% of those who sought work through its member firms were unskilled; SIVP trainees would now take their jobs, so, by implication, unemployment among the unskilled would rise (the possibility that more of the unskilled might find work without going through UNETT members was not raised). For the construction industry, represented by the *Conseil national de la construction*(CNC), the public interest lay in building more houses - such at any rate was the conclusion of a report it produced in January 1988 and sent to all candidates (*Pour une reprise durable de la construction: relancer la relance*). To this end, restrictive planning laws about maximum densities should be relaxed and capital gains tax abolished on property sales, provided the gains were reinvested in more property. The report was inspired by Michel Pelège, chairman of the Pelège construction company and of the National Federation of Property Developers, and a supporter of Raymond Barre. Just as the competing claims of interest groups divided the politicians, so the rivalries of politics might divide the interest groups: one of the member groups of the CNC, the FNB (National Federation of Builders), declined to endorse the report: the policy depended essentially on state stimulation of investment in the building sector, which it found too corporatist.

The lobbies for the road transport industry, the *Conseil national routier* and the *Fédération nationale des transporteurs*, were both frightened of the competition which would follow if the government implemented its plans to deregulate the industry, and took advantage of the electoral period to press the government for six months delay and 'further study'.[45]

The small shopkeepers, still numerous, embittered and well-organised, stepped up their rearguard action against the advance of the multiples, with the Minister of Commerce, Georges Chavannes, left awkwardly in the middle. The Royer law of 1974 provided that approval for opening a supermarket[46] had to come from a special committee in each *département*, and ultimately from the Minister himself. To the supermarket owners, it appeared that Chavannes had more than kept his promise to reduce the number of approvals granted;[47] to the president of the Union of Associations of Shopkeepers (SNAC) it appeared that he had granted far too many.[48]

The pharmacists, in their battle against the multiples, had an extra weapon at their disposal: their professional status as dispensers of medicines. Barre's electoral material assured his electors that 'only pharmacists should be allowed to dispense medicines', which might seem unexceptional, but in fact it begged the question: what are medicines? Large numbers of over-the-counter drugs sold in supermarkets in Britain or the US are a pharmacist's monopoly in France; yet in the more competitive climate introduced by Balladur, the pharmacists were on the defensive. The new *Conseil de la concurrence* (Competition Council) found that the pharmacists' cosy understanding with certain manufacturers of cosmetics (that these products would be available only in pharmacies) was an anti-competitive practice, and levied heavy fines on the pharmacists' professional associations.[49] However, thanks to the presidential elections, the pharmacists were able to counter-attack and regain some lost territory. No law said that baby milk was to be sold only through pharmacies, but in practice it was unavailable elsewhere. Readers may wonder why the producers should wish to limit their outlets in this way. The answer is that they did not, but they feared a boycott by the pharmacies of all their other health products, including those which were legally a pharmacist's monopoly.

As long ago as 1969 this tactic had been used with great success against Nestlé, which had been forced to withdraw its *Pelargon* brand from the supermarkets. However, just after the elections of 1986, Nutricia broke ranks with its competitors, started to distribute through the Mammouth hypermarket chain, and was duly boycotted by the pharmacies. Balladur decided to refer the whole question of the baby milk market to the *Conseil de la concurrence* for an advisory opinion. It reported in June 1987[50] and found that the distribution of baby milk exclusively through pharmacies was an anti-competitive practice which should be outlawed. Politically this was a very inconvenient verdict. The pharmacists could see their position crumbling all around them; they had votes, however, and were determined to use them. Between the two rounds of voting, the government caved in and produced a statutory instrument (*arrêté*)[51] which gave legal backing to the pharmacists' monopoly.

Although it might seem to be an advantage for the Prime Minister that he could satisfy an interest group in this way, it was also a misfortune for Chirac and his ministers that, being in government, they found themselves in situations where it was difficult to avoid choosing between rival interests. The surrender to an electorally powerful group such as the pharmacists brought not only indignation from the losing party but ridicule in some sections of the press (and damage to the Prime Minister's 'strong man' image). Such were the perils of *cohabitation*, as Barre had warned. Small wonder that ministers increasingly took refuge in delay, as when a dispute blew up in March about the opening of a new paper mill in Lorraine, which would have the effect of ... closing one down in Alsace. Faced with the clamour from east of the Vosges, the government retreated, commissioned a study of the feasibility of having a paper mill in each of the two provinces, and awaited the report - which was due after the elections.

Barre's campaign strategy was to be above all this. Returning to the subject of tax changes, he claimed that hitherto, French tax reforms had been '*clientélistes*' (that is, favouring particular interest groups), and went on to ask 'Are the French adult or not?'[52] Later in the campaign he asked: 'If you vote for me only because I can do something for you, how can you expect me to take an objective view of the state of the country?'[53] The problem with this approach was that it was not easy to be olympian and have a policy about absolutely everything. Here once again was demonstrated the superiority of the wily Mitterrand who, when challenged by the professor of economics, replied that he declined to be drawn into a battle of figures - and who would never have dreamed of having a policy about paper or baby milk.

Europe

Only an elector determined to ignore the campaign altogether could have failed to hear the words 'Europe', '1992', and 'Single market'. The theme was used by both Mitterrand and Chirac to rally national unity around themselves. For Chirac: 'France can and must win the European battle in 1992. To do this we have to mobilise all the economic and social forces of the country - this is an objective which surpasses all political divisions'.[54]

For Mitterrand, the need to rally France for the Single market meant that the thorny question of nationalisation could be elegantly sidestepped as an outmoded distraction from national unity:

> Nationalisations and privatisations: so much upheaval in so short a time, and yet we are entering a period, between now and 31 December 1992, which will see the creation of a single internal market between the twelve - a formidable rendezvous to which I myself agreed, on behalf of France, in 1985. This requires such energy, such a pulling together, such unity, that I don't think we should get into another battle about nationalisations... we also need to end this... contagion of privatisations... . Neither of these reforms is appropriate at the present time... . If we are asking the French people to really devote themselves to their entry into the common internal market, we need a national mobilisation.[55]

For the CNPF, if Europe had not existed, it would have been necessary to invent it. For years, the CNPF had sought, in the best traditions of the lobbyist, to present its members' claims as a national rather than a sectional interest. The day that the election result was announced, Perigot declared that 'the most important thing at stake now is the preparation of France and its companies for 1992. This is the only way to ensure growth and bring down unemployment... . Success is in sight, and companies owe it in large measure to their own efforts and those of their managers and staff. But it is also due to the reductions in the burdens of taxation and the increased freedom to manage which they have gradually won.'[56] The traditional CNPF demands could now more than ever be presented as a patriotic necessity which would help France defeat the foreigners.

On behalf of the CGPME, Bernasconi said much the same. The priorities for the incoming government should include 'the reform and harmonisation of our tax system for the opening of the single internal market.'[57] This was easier said than done. The two main areas of taxation where France was out of line with the other Community countries were payroll taxes (as we have seen) and VAT. The government had reduced some of the higher rates of VAT, notably on records and motor vehicles.[58] It was widely, if erroneously, believed both among politicians and business people that the single market would be impossible if VAT rates were different in the member states, or, alternatively, that French industry would be gravely handicapped if French rates remained higher.[59] Balladur had decided against a harmonisation of VAT rates, and said, quite correctly, that it was unnecessary.[60] It might not be unkind to suggest that in a pre-electoral period, an announcement that VAT would have to come down could only lead to the question of which tax would have to go up.

Few in the business community challenged the principle of the Single European Act to which the politicians had put their signatures. The public consensus among employers was that 1992 (or, more correctly, 1993) was a challenge, an opportunity, and for France as a whole, generally A Good Thing.

But genuinely to welcome it for one's own company or industry was a different matter. '1992 - year of take-off or suicide?' wondered the editorialist in one trade magazine.[61]

The Chamber of Commerce at Châlons-sur-Marne found a certain amount of apprehension and a good deal of ignorance in December 1987 when it carried out a survey of small and medium-sized firms in its area (which has a fairly diverse economic base and no special reason to fear the future). 53% of respondents admitted to knowing little about the Single European Act. It was generally seen as 'an opportunity' but 50% feared increased competition, particularly from Germany, Italy and Spain. 14% expected to lose ground on the French market, while 25% thought it would make no difference; 8%, it must be said, expected to do better in France (they were not required to state why), whilst 53% simply had no idea. Granted that, as we have seen, the government's measures to promote more competition within France had a mixed reception, there was no reason to expect that increased competition on a Euro-scale would be universally popular, and accusations of unfairness and bad faith were only to be expected.

On 15 February, a delegation from the Association of Chambers of Commerce and Industry complained to Chirac about excessive industrial subsidies in the southern European countries. On the same day, Balladur was lobbied by the Association of French Lending Institutions (AFEC), basically the bankers' trade association.[62] He was told by its president, R. Pelletier, that France was ill-prepared for the total abolition of capital controls in 1992. The banks were penalised by unfair taxation, such as the tax payable by the bank on credit granted to customers,[63] the special tax on the expenditure of financial institutions,[64] and the tax on wages.[65] The delegation was also worried about how they would compete when French residents were free to invest abroad directly; at present such investments can be made only through an approved French intermediary, usually a bank or a stockbroker, who has to report the transaction to the French tax authorities. In the future, what was to stop the customer dealing directly with the foreign bank, reducing not only the profits of the French banks but the tax collected by the treasury? Moreover (M. Pelletier was clearly a master of the lobbyist's art), would it not be more difficult for French industry to finance itself if a large volume of domestic saving went abroad?[66]

In road transport, too, there was anxiety; as we pointed out earlier, government plans for encouraging more competition between French firms were unpopular enough; in a poll organised by a trade magazine, 50% of road hauliers interviewed admitted to being worried about the prospect of increased foreign competition after 1992.[67]

The longstanding protection accorded to the sugar industry was about to end. The law of 30 March 1902 forbade the use in France of any artificial sweetener more powerful than sugar. By the 1980s, this had the effect of excluding from France a range of 'diet' drinks readily available in Europe, and which were now to be admitted. However, as a parting shot, the defeated sugar lobby had managed to insert in the draft of the new legislation a clause which prevented French products containing artificial sweeteners from being described as 'sugar-free', to the dismay of the Federation of Chocolate and Sweet Manufacturers, who told *L'Expansion*: 'We'll be done for if we don't get control of our domestic market before it's invaded by foreign products which say "sugar free" ' (a selling point).[68]

On 21 April, the CNPF held a one-day conference devoted to 1992. The representatives of the textile, motor vehicle, and electrical industries wanted national quotas to be maintained on the import of these products into the Community. Otherwise, it was argued, how was the European quota to be divided up? What was to stop, say, an Italian importer from grabbing the quota of cheap Taiwanese tee-shirts and re-exporting the whole lot to France? 'We need a period of transition to allow the French textile companies and distributors to strengthen their position', said Thierry Noblot, the economic director at the Textile Industries Association. The meeting ended with some sharp disagreement between, on the one hand, the delegates and, on the other, the representative of the European Commission, who could see the 1992 deadline receding into the distance once there was talk of 'transitional periods'. There would be no single market, he told them, if national quotas were maintained and industries started asking to be made an exception.

The Response to Mitterrand's Victory

When it was known that Mitterrand had won, Perigot made a lengthy and verbose statement to the press: 'The French people have made their wishes known. It is not for the CNPF to make a judgement on their choice...' and so on and so on. He then made, in essence, the point which we have noted above, namely, that the recovery of French business was due in part to the reductions in taxation and increased freedom to manage, and that any change of policy would destroy the 'élan' which had been built up.

Bernasconi's statement was in an altogether simpler style, and in a few short sentences restated the four main points of the CGPME credo, namely:

- the government should recognise that management was entitled to hire, fire and run the business as it saw fit.

- tax should be harmonised with Europe for 1992.

- there should be 'non-discriminatory' interest rates for small firms.

- there should be a tightening of competition law to strengthen small firms against the large.[69]

Employers willing to be questioned were generally very calm. G. Tollès, chairman of the Bidermann textile firm, said: 'The left doesn't have the same image as it had in 1981. There is every reason to think that it will carry on along the same lines as it did after 1983, i.e. with a policy of 'rigueur'... . There's a consensus nowadays that social measures and employment can only come through the firm... .'[70] This was the attitude adopted by nearly all the business leaders contacted by *Les Echos* and *L'Expansion*. 'The left had power, they lost it. now they're back. It's a change of government without a change of society', said Jean-Louis Pétriat, chairman of FNAC.[71] If there was to be no change of society, business leaders could still try to work out how, if at all, the new government could be of use to them. 'This government took a step in the right direction when it brought down VAT on records from 33% to 18%. The left ought to take the next step', said M. Pétriat.[72] For others, it was a question of personalities. 'The important thing is to get a Minister of Industry who knows about industry', said Claude Perdrillat, chairman of Goupil computers. 'We could never communicate with Edith Cresson. Alain Madelin was even worse' (respectively Socialist and *cohabitation* Industry Ministers). A textile company chairman who declined to be named confided to a journalist that 'I'm sure I'll get my business done quicker with the new government than with the old lot. Their preferred style, particularly at Finance, was a sort of bumbling interference.'[73] Balladur, who had made many enemies, would certainly not be missed. Although only 9% of the panel of business leaders regularly polled by *L'Expansion* went so far as to say that his replacement by Bérégovoy was a good thing; 67% described it - perhaps even more hurtfully - as 'an event of no great consequence.'[74]

But there was one cloud on the horizon - personal taxation. 'If they want to favour enterprise, they have to be careful not to follow a tax policy which ruins the entrepreneur. The danger is that at the beginning they'll go in for symbols.'[75]

This was aimed at the one measure of increased taxation which plainly was coming: the restored wealth tax, which even Bérégovoy had recognised was 'a symbol', albeit one 'intended to mobilise the French people for the modernisation of the economy.'[76] The indefatigable M. Pelège, whose efforts on behalf of the construction industry will be remembered, now stood ready to launch a lobbying campaign about the wealth tax: 'If we have to have it [the wealth tax] then we've got to get something in return, such as a massive reduction in transfer tax or inheritance tax. Otherwise the revival in the building industry will be threatened... .'[77]

Perhaps those who were in the most fortunate position were those who felt (or at least claimed to feel) that it did not make a scrap of difference who was in power: 'What matters to a drinks company,' said Patrick Ricard of Pernod Ricard, 'is sunshine, not government.'[78]

* * *

The presidential election of 1988 was the first since 1969 in which there was no candidate with a serious chance of being elected who proposed major changes in the ownership and control of business. No more nationalisations. No more Auroux laws. Moreover, this was an election at which even the leading candidate of the left agreed that 'the burden of taxes and social security contributions has reached the point where it takes away the will and the means to be an entrepreneur'. (François Mitterrand, *Lettre à tous les Français*). Nor was this a sudden pre-electoral conversion: Mitterrand's acceptance of what had for years been a central argument, indeed *the* central argument, of the employers, may be traced back to his speech at Figeac on 22 September 1983. Yet would the will and the means exist, after the election, to help business by a fundamental reform of the tax system? It seemed doubtful. Mitterrand had fought on a programme which aimed not to offend, rather than to initiate radical, and inevitably divisive, change. The same was to a considerable extent true of Chirac - and even of Barre, in spite of his protestations to the contrary. A classic example of this caution was the consensus among the three leading candidates that the *taxe professionnelle* should not be abolished. Although this tax was not as onerous as employers liked to claim, it was quite unsuited to twentieth-century business practice. In 1791, when its predecessor the *patente* had been introduced, most business undertakings consisted of a single establishment. Nearly two hundred years later, in a world of multi-branch businesses, taxing a firm's equipment at site involved the application of complex rules to ensure that, for instance, the owners of fleets of lorries did not underpay or, conversely, that a single small *commune* could not cream off the entire benefit of having the Crédit Lyonnais computer centre located on its territory.

The presidential candidates could have put forward a radical solution to the problem of the *taxe professionnelle* but chose not to. In the matter of investment, they had put forward a solution of a sort but could only *hope* it would work. It was common ground among the three that business investment was too low. Yet, whether or not the Chirac approach (continued reductions in corporation tax) or the Mitterrand/Barre scheme (which favoured specific investment incentives) was adopted, there could be no certainty that firms would invest one extra centime, either wisely or at all. Similarly, it was common ground that research should receive favourable tax treatment, but there could be no certainty that a single worthwhile innovation would result. It is important to bear in mind these limitations on the power of government in a market economy, given the emphasis often placed in studies of French business on the role of the state. It is true that France has used public investment far more decisively than has, for instance, the United Kingdom: energy and transport are two examples of the contrast between French planning on the one hand and the piecemeal and incoherent UK approach on the other. It is also true that certain French companies have benefited from the strong home base which public investment projects have provided, and have used the proven success of their products on the domestic market to win valuable export orders in fields such as railway technology.

Nonetheless, it is equally important not to neglect the numerous successes of French business which owe nothing to state initiatives. An example would be the family-owned 'Cristallerie d'Arques' glass manufacturer, which exports 75% of its production, and owes its performance to a correct perception of the customer's needs, the correct application of technology, and clever marketing.

The congress (or so-called Estates-General) called by the CNPF at Villepinte in December 1982 attracted 28,000 employers who unanimously adopted 'Eight proposals for the survival of business'.[79] Central representative organisations such as the CNPF tend to gain in relative importance at times of crisis when it is believed, rightly or wrongly, that the fundamental interests of all business are at stake. Yet even in 1982 most of the government-business dialogue was concerned, as always, with matters which affected only one industry or service.

The *arrêtés* which pour out of the ministries (not to mention the regulations made by the European Community authorities in Brussels) concern such apparently arcane subjects as health standards in dairies, permissible grades of flour, the specifications of shatterproof glass, sales outlets for baby milk, and the use of saccharine in lemonade. An unfavourable decision or the exclusion of one's own product can lead to huge financial loss.

Firms look to their own efforts, and above all to those of their trade associations to defend their interests in such cases. When contact is at ministerial level, what matters to the firm is not that the minister comes from one political party rather another, but that he is well briefed, has understood the problem correctly, and has the power or influence to do something about it. This is true of all advanced Western economies. In France, the intensity of government-business contact is increased by the strength of the state tradition, which extends public regulation into minutely detailed areas of the national economic life. (Returning for a moment, by way of example, to the pharmacists: even in the deregulatory climate of 1986-1988, *arrêtés* were still being produced which specified, inter alia, what densities of population in rural areas should justify the opening of new pharmacies, and how many assistant pharmacists should be on duty whenever the shop was open). To business, the strong presence of the state as regulator was alternatively welcome and unwelcome; the state was a powerful enemy, but it might also be enlisted as a powerful friend, to block the progress of an importunate competitor.

On the morning of 9 May 1988, it was indeed 'business as usual'.

NOTES

1. *Les Echos*, 10 May 1988; *Financial Times*, 10 May 1988.

2. Reported in 'Les Socialistes face aux patrons', *L'Expansion*, Paris 1977.

3. Notably by P. A. Muet and A. Fonteneau in 'La Relance contrariée' and 'Vers le nouvel équilibre', *Les Cahiers français*, no. 218, October 1984.

4. SOFRES, *L'Etat de l'Opinion* (Paris, Seuil, 1987) p. 218.

5. Cf. Fontaine, 'Les Français ont viré leur cuti' in *L'Express,* 12 October 1983. See also: J. Jaffré, 'Le Retournement de l'Opinion', *Le Monde,* 1 January 1984.

6. Supplementary Finance law of 11 July 1986.

7. Finance law for 1988: law of 30 December 1987.

8. Supplementary Finance law of 11 July 1986.

9. E. Balladur, *Une France plus forte* (La Documentation française, Paris 1987) p. 46.

10. E. Balladur, speech on the inauguration of the Competition Council, 20 February 1987, in 'Conseil de la concurrence - Premier rapport d'activité', *Journaux officiels* (Paris, 1988) pp. 22-23.

11. See, for instance, J.-M. Vittori, 'Des taux d'intérêt absurdes pour une France qui va mieux', *L'Expansion,* 22 January 1988; or see CNPF 'Resolution'.

12. Interview in *L'Expansion*, 4 March 1988.

13. The efficacy of French captial controls has been demonstrated in S. Collins, 'Exchange rate expectations and interest parity during credibility crises: the French Franc, March 1983', Harvard University, Mimeo, 1984, and in F. Giovazzi and A. Giovannini, 'Capital controls and the European Monetary System', Euromobiliare Occasional Papers, no. 1, Euromobiliare, Milan, 1985.

14. *Les Echos*, 16 December 1987.

15. The text was published in *Les Echos,* 17 February 1988.

16. Interview with *Le Nouvel Economiste*, 18 December 1987.

17. *Les Echos*, 17 February 1988.

18. Bank of France statistics in Ministère de l'industrie, *L'Etat des PMI* (Paris, 1988).

19. Y. Gattaz, *Les Patrons reviennent* (Paris, Laffont, 1988) p. 64.

20. *Fiscal 1988* (Paris, Editions F. Lefebvre, 1988).

21. *Fiscal 1985* (Paris, Editions F. Lefebvre, 1985) p. 1105.

22. *Les Echos*, 8 January 1988.

23. Reported in *Les Echos*, 15 February 1988.

24. Reported in *Le Monde*, 24 March.

25. Law of 28 June 1982.

26. Law of 3 January 1979.

27. Law of 10 January 1980.

28. Law of 29 December 1984.

29. Speech to the Chamber of Commerce of the Yvelines, 7 February 1988.

30. *Ibid.*.

31. Conseil des Impôts, *9ème rapport au Président de la République, relatif à la fiscalité des entreprises* (Paris, Journaux Officiels, 1987) pp. 196-204.

32. Interview on *Club de la Presse, Europe I*, 28 February 1988.

33. Interview in *Les Echos*, 19 February 1988.

34. Interview with *L'Expansion*, 4 March 1988.

35. SOFRES, *L'Etat de l'Opinion* (Paris, Seuil 1988) p. 214.

36. Interview with *Le Nouvel Economiste*, 18 December 1987.

37. M. Elbaum, G. Cornilleau and A. Fonteneau, 'La question de la suppression de l'autorisation administrative de licenciement: des emplois ou des chômeurs?', *Observations et diagnostics économiques* (Lettre de l'OFCE), no. 31, 22 January 1986, in *Problèmes économiques*, no. 1963, 26 February 1986.

38. Interview with *Le Nouvel Economiste*, 18 December 1987.

39. *Les Echos*, 16 December 1987.

40. Interview with *Le Nouvel Economiste*, 18 December 1988.

41. *Les Echos*, 29 April 1988.

42. IPSOS poll in *Le Monde*, 5 March 1988.

43. SOFRES poll in *Le Monde*, 19 February 1988; IPSOS poll in *Le Monde*, 24 March 1988.

44. *Les Echos*, 2 February 1988.

45. *Les Echos*, 18 February 1988.

46. Although a solecism, the term is used here to include hypermarkets.

47. *Libre-service actualités*, 1988, no. 1, January 1988, Institut français du libre service.

48. *Les Echos*, 25 January 1988.

49. Decision 87-D-15, *Bulletin officiel de la concurrence de la consommation et de la répression des fraudes*, no. 15, 17 June 1987. Decision upheld by the Paris Court of Appeal, 28 January 1988.

50. Opinion 87-A-02, *Bulletin officiel de la concurrence, de la consommation et de la répression des fraudes*, 1987, no. 13, 2 June 1987.

51. *Arrêté* of the 28 April 1988.

52. Speech at Yssingeaux, 27 January 1988.

53. *Le Monde*, 23 April 1988.

54. Interview with *Les Echos*, 29 April 1988.

55. Interview on *A2*, 22 March 1988, reported in *Le Monde*, 24 March 1988.

56. *Les Echos*, 9 May 1988.

57. *Ibid..*

58. Finance Law for 1988: law of 30 December 1987.

59. As an example, see the article of R. Leduc, president of the trade association for the perfume industry (FFIPPBT), in the association's journal, *Parfums, cosmétiques et arômes*, no.88, February-March 1988.

60. Interview with *Les Echos*, 14 April 1988.

61. Title of the leading article by S. Némon in *La Vie du cuir*, no. 8801, January 1988.

62. *Les Echos*, 16 February 1988.

63. 0.1% or 0.15% of the sum advanced; dates from 1979, now incorporated in the *Code général des impôts*, art. 235.

64. A Socialist innovation dating from 1982, now incorporated in the Law of 29 December 1984, art. 21: 1% on general management expenses.

65. *Code général des impôts*, art. 231. A long-established tax. For a bank, a typical rate would be approximately 2,5% of the remuneration paid.

66. In a truly free market, the solution to the latter difficulty would be for French industry to borrow more abroad - quite possibly at a rate of interest lower than that offered by M. Pelletier's members.

67. *L'Officiel des transporteurs*, February 1988.

68. 'La bataille du sucre', *L'Expansion*, 18 March 1988. This is probably a misunderstanding. Even if the effect of the French regulation had been, paradoxically, to discriminate against the French product, the Federation would have stood a good chance of challenging it before the European Court of Justice.

69. *Les Echos*, 9 May 1988.

70. *Ibid.*.

71. *L'Expansion*, 20 May 1988.

72. *Ibid.*.

73. *Les Echos*, 9 May 1988.

74. *L'Expansion,* 1 July 1988.

75. G. Tollès in *Les Echos*, 19 May 1988.

76. Broadcast on RMC, reported in *Les Echos*, 14 December 1987.

77. *Les Echos*, 10 May 1988.

78. *L'Expansion*, 20 May 1988.

79. Text in Gattaz *op. cit.*, pp. 266-268.

INDICATIVE BIBLIOGRAPHY

Balladur, E., *Vers la liberté* (Paris, La Documentation française, 1987).

Balladur, E., *Une France plus forte* (Paris, La Documentation française, 1988).

Bauchard, P., *La crise sonne toujours deux fois* (Paris, Grasset, 1988).

Brault, D., *L'Etat et l'esprit de concurrence en France* (Paris, Economica, 1987).

Cerny, P. G. and Schain, M., (eds.), *Socialism, the State and Public Policy in France* (London, Pinter, 1985).

de Fourcade, J.-B., *La fin du social-colbertisme* (Paris, Belfond, 1988).

Gattaz, Y., *Les patrons reviennent* (Paris, Robert Laffont, 1988).

Machin, H. and Wright, V., (eds.), *Economic Policy and Policy-making under the Mitterrand Presidency 1981-1984* (London, Pinter, 1985).

Muet P.-A. and Fonteneau, A., *La Gauche face à la crise* (Paris, FNSP, 1985).

Weber, H., *Le Parti des patrons: histoire du CNPF, 1946-86* (Paris, Seuil, 1986).

Zysman, J., *Governments, Markets and Growth* (Ithaca, Cornell University Press, 1983).

10 Guardians of the Republican tradition? The trade unions

SUSAN MILNER

'Even if, today, our voice is drowned out by the noise of the elections, we must rediscover the real questions. We should gather our forces to put pressure on those who will be in office. Only the trade union movement can do this; and this only if it preserves its freedom of movement and shows itself to be capable, at the right moment, of questioning any decisions likely to go against the interests of the weakest sections of society.'
Claude Pitous (*Force Ouvrière*)[1]

'There is a fundamental difference between the function of a trade union and that of a political party. It is absolutely essential that this difference is respected. Having said that, we cannot remain silent over the great problems of our country. Politics is important in order to mobilise energies against unemployment, for job creation and for the defence of freedoms.'
Edmond Maire
(*Confédération Française Démocratique du Travail*)[2]

The nature of the presidency in France makes presidential elections a major, if not *the* major forum for public political debate. Social actors such as the French trade unions are not directly involved in presidential elections: as we shall see, the distinction made between political parties and labour organisations, which helps the trade unions to define their role in society, distances them, at least in theory, from all political elections. In addition, the main French trade unions, basing their claim to a place in society on the republican tradition of democratic pluralism, have viewed presidentialist trends in the Fifth Republic with suspicion. In practice, however, the distinction between 'social' and 'political' actors frequently becomes blurred, and the relationship between the trade unions and political actors means that the former have been forced to adapt to changes in the political environment since 1958. An examination of the position of the trade unions in the 1988 presidential campaign therefore reveals much not only about the place of trade unions in French political life but also about the constraints posed by the presidential nature of the French Fifth Republic.

The attitude of the main trade unions - the *Confédération Générale du Travail* (CGT), the *Confédération Française Démocratique du Travail* (CFDT), *Force Ouvrière* (FO), the *Confédération Générale des Cadres-Confédération Française de l'Encadrement* (CGC-CFE), and the *Confédération Française des Travailleurs Chrétiens* (CFTC) - towards politics is complex. Republican tradition, to which trade unions are firmly attached, dictates that only directly elected representatives, repositories of popular will, may participate in the legislative process. For this reason, labour organisations have always been very careful to draw the line between their social function and the legislative process to which national elections pertain. Added to this basic principle there has traditionally been a certain distrust by labour organisations of 'politics' in its negative sense (the quest for political office). At the beginning of the twentieth century this distrust inspired the famous proclamation of trade union autonomy known as the *'Charte d'Amiens'*.[3] Yet the Amiens Charter was itself also a *political* document; it defined the long-term objective of trade unionism as complete emancipation of the working-class through expropriation, and viewed trade union activity as the sole means of achieving this end. Today, French trade unions lay claim to the Amiens Charter as an assertion of autonomy, yet only a tiny minority would agree that trade unions alone can realise the transformation of society. What is important is that French trade unions, despite, or perhaps because of, their professions of political independence, have always reserved the right to define their own set of political ideas and demands, and thus to enter the political sphere.

In particular, French trade unions have always considered it a right and a duty to express their opinion on political events and decisions, and even on the working of political institutions. After the Second World War, the place of trade unions in democratic society, enshrined in the Constitution of 1946, was defined as being that of an essential intermediary between state and citizen. Since then, the trade unions have jealously preserved their right to act as a counter-balance within democratic society and as guardians of the republican constitution, a role which has allowed them to lay claim to a representativeness which went beyond their official membership numbers.[4] On a more practical level, the dividing-line between trade unionism and politics is further blurred by an erratic industrial relations system which historically has depended on the state to create the conditions for bargaining and arbitration, and even to impose legislative solutions. The state, the trade unions and the employers are therefore 'social partners' on a national level. Moreover, in modern industrial society, conflicts easily spill out of the strict confines of the workplace and become issues of national political importance. For these reasons, trade unions are 'condemned to politics'.[5]

In order to represent and negotiate on behalf of the workforce, the trade unions must adapt to the prevailing political circumstances. As we shall see, the Fifth Republic has provided the trade unions with a severe test of their role within the polity. Since 1958, the three major trade unions (the CGT, FO, and the CFTC, which became the CFDT in 1964 - leaving behind a minority CFTC *maintenue*) have had to adapt to a political framework which they have often criticised. The following sections look at the way in which the trade unions reacted to the Gaullist presidency and right-wing domination of the state apparatus from 1958 to 1981 and to the political change-over after 1981. We shall then examine the role of the trade unions in the presidential election campaign of 1988.

Trade Unions and Presidentialism in the Fifth Republic

THE TRADE UNIONS AND GAULLISM

The revolt of the generals in Algiers on 13 May 1958, which signalled the end of the Fourth Republic, shook the French trade union movement. Not only did the major trade unions wish to defend the parliamentary regime of the Fourth Republic,[6] they were also alarmed at the prospect of losing the place in society which that regime had given them. The trade union response to the May 1958 events was, however, weak and uncoordinated, partly because of internal divisions over the question of Algeria, but mainly because the non-communist confederations feared involvement in joint activities with the CGT, which was still seen during this period as the 'transmission belt' of the *Parti Communiste Français*. Ultimately, French workers did not share the trade unions' desire to save the Fourth Republic.

The trade unions' attitude towards Charles de Gaulle was ambivalent. They supported the General insofar as he seemed to offer the only solution to the Algerian war and the political crisis it had produced in France. Eugène Descamps, an opponent of Gaullism who was to become General Secretary of the CFTC, later admitted:

> Only General de Gaulle and Pierre Mendès-France, because of their character and their way of rallying the country behind them, possessed the means of stopping this war. The other political leaders were too sensitive to outside pressures.[7]

On other aspects of Gaullist policy, however, particularly on economic and social policy, there were violent disagreements between the General and the trade unions. Moreover, significant sections of the trade union movement questioned the constitutionality and the democratic nature of the Gaullist regime. The CGT openly opposed Charles de Gaulle, whom they described as authoritarian, and the CFTC warned against the personalisation of the political framework and the by-passing of parliament. On 2 June 1958, the day after de

Gaulle's appointment, the CFTC's Confederal Bureau issued a statement which criticised:

> the insurrectionary events which set off and marked the course of the crisis, [and] the unusual procedure, with strange and sometimes worrying developments, used to put an end to it.[8]

FO too warned against the prospect of a presidential regime, but committed itself to support General de Gaulle insofar as it considered his appointment strictly legal. Above all, FO's actions were limited by the fear of communism. In a telling article published in 1962, FO General Secretary Robert Bothereau explained his confederation's position:

> Gaullism is a phenomenon which is necessarily limited in space and time, whereas communism is a real organisation supported by international horizons. That is why, in spite of the victory of the former, we should fear even more the coming to power of the latter.[9]

The CGT, which organised demonstration after demonstration against the General, had not yet emerged from the 'transmission belt' era, and indeed played the PCF's game by prioritising political activity. Weakened by its own divisions, the trade union movement was unable to divert popular support away from Gaullism. Only the CGT and a minority of the CFTC urged outright rejection of the constitutional referendum in September 1958, whilst FO and the CFTC majority remained neutral. The CGC, on the other hand, publicly, if cautiously, supported the new constitution.

The trade unions' energetic response to events in Algeria over the next few years, however, allowed them to both regain some popular support and unite in opposition to the new regime. The campaign in 1962 against the right-wing terror group, the *Organisation de l'Armée Secrète,* generated a mass movement in which the CGT and CFTC held a key place, and opened up a political space which later allowed the formation of a movement of opposition to the Gaullist regime. Broad opposition to the presidential regime was revealed by the campaign against the constitutional amendment providing for direct election of the President, put to referendum in Autumn 1962. Along with the CGT, some federations of the CFTC were active in the anti-amendment campaign. Developments within the trade unions themselves helped them develop their capacity to respond to the challenges of the new Republic. Within the CFTC, the minority, eager to experiment with new tactics and to cast off the confederation's Catholic-conservative image, was rapidly gaining strength, a process which was to result in the 'deconfessionalisation' of the organisation in 1964. The CGT, after years of being the 'transmission belt' of the Communist Party, entered a period of 'relative autonomy' which divided more clearly trade union activity from political work, without nonetheless cutting the ties between union and party.[10]

If the major confederations had been caught on the defensive in 1958, after 1963 they were able to consolidate their position and capitalise on an upsurge in workers' unrest.[11] Not only were the trade unions now in a better position to voice their opposition to Gaullism; the success of the constitutional amendment providing for direct election of the President transformed the political framework and encouraged the unions to develop new political strategies in response to the Fifth Republic.[12] Paradoxically, because of the political constraints created by the presidential regime of Charles de Gaulle, presidential elections logically became the forum in which trade union opposition to the regime was articulated.

The 1965 presidential election campaign provided the unions with the chance not only to make their views known, but to legitimate their presence on the political scene. The non-Gaullist candidates appeared to attach as much if not more importance to the unions' support as to that of political parties.[13] The CFTC began experimenting with a political strategy whose aim was to encourage left unity around a candidate able to contest General de Gaulle's position, and became involved in discussions on the possible candidacy of the centre-left Gaston Defferre (see Chapter Two). Defferre's plans failed, but the CFTC's involvement in the initiative, which allowed François Mitterrand to step forward subsequently as the left candidate, signalled its recognition of the need to push for political change by means of the presidential elections. In 1965, the newly-named CFDT gave no specific voting instructions, but made it plain, in the words of its General Secretary, Eugène Descamps, that 'one cannot be a trade unionist and Gaullist'.[14] The CGT was more explicit: it urged workers to vote for François Mitterrand. Significantly, the CGT made a distinction between the institution and the office-holder, claiming that a republic led by François Mitterrand would be different from one headed by de Gaulle. By rallying to the left candidate, the CGT not only explicitly recognised presidential elections as a potential agency for change, but also defined its view of trade unions as central actors in the political process.

The failure of the Defferre candidacy put a stop to any chance of *Force Ouvrière* moving in the same direction. Had Gaston Defferre stood for the presidency, his 'third-force' strategy (grouping of the non-communist left and centre-left forces) could have pulled FO into the political sphere.[15] Instead, the alliance of Socialists with Communists around François Mitterrand ensured that FO kept its distance from the 1965 presidential elections. This was to remain the pattern over the following years, as the CGT and CFDT became ever more identified with the left opposition. The bipolarisation of political life, caused by the adversarial nature of the all-important presidential elections and by the need for political parties to form 'majorities', also had effects on the trade unions.

A joint platform of basic demands was agreed by the CGT and CFDT in 1966. In the talks between the two confederations, however, it became obvious that the CGT saw trade union activity as a means of generating political opposition; in the words of its leader, Georges Séguy, the CGT's strategy was that of 'the transmission belt in reverse'.[16] For the CFDT, too, the trade union movement had a role to play in the reconstruction of the left, but the CGT's ties with the PCF made it wary of the project.

The events of May-June 1968 pushed the trade unions to the front of the political stage, when a massive strike movement, coupled with student revolts, seriously threatened the stability of the Gaullist regime. The CGT's intentions now became transparent, as the confederation sought to channel the protest movement into a political alliance led by the PCF. The CFDT, for its part, became involved in behind-the-scenes negotiations in May 1968, with a view to persuading Pierre Mendès-France of the *Parti Socialiste Unifié* (PSU) to stand as candidate in a presidential election which seemed increasingly imminent. Although CFDT leaders were also in contact with François Mitterrand who, on 28 May, declared his intention to stand in the hypothetical election, Mendès-France, with his particular brand of moderate 'realism' and modernism, was seen as the man most likely to win the support of both trade-unionists and students. These plans came to nothing when the political vacuum was filled by Charles de Gaulle's dramatic re-entry on the scene. What is significant is that, at a time when trade union action, and not political opposition, seemed likely to bring the Gaullist regime to a close, both the leading labour confederations looked to political, and more specifically, *presidential* initiatives as the solution.

LEFT UNITY 1972-1977

If the events of May-June 1968 temporarily disrupted the tentative moves begun in 1966 towards an alliance between the CGT and the CFDT, they nonetheless confirmed a growing politicisation of the action of the two confederations which later found expression in the 'unity of action' of the 1970s. After the resignation of Charles de Gaulle in 1969, an eventual left-wing succession seemed possible. The CGT threw itself wholeheartedly into support for the Common Programme of Government signed by the left parties in 1972, and sought to persuade the CFDT to do likewise. Guided by its new ideological beacon of *'autogestion'* (workers' self-management), the CFDT remained true to the 1966 alliance with the CGT but stopped short of endorsing the Common Programme, believing that its content marked too heavy a reliance on state intervention. Despite its refusal to sign the Common Programme, the CFDT openly supported the left and endorsed François Mitterrand's candidacy in 1974. The CFDT leadership saw the confederation as a force for the elaboration of new strategies on the left, and the 1974 presidential elections created the dynamic for such initiatives. In 1974, the CFDT was actively involved in moves to bring the PSU into the new *Parti Socialiste*,[17] and many CFDT members joined the PS around this time. During this period, local workplace conflicts and negotiations were relegated to the background, and priority was given instead to national mobilisation.

Such an overtly political stance was not wholly beneficial to the labour confederations. Surveys showed the public's disaffection from the CGT and the CFDT from 1973 onwards, coupled with a widespread identification of the two confederations with the left, whilst those confederations not heavily identified with any political party or grouping increased their public support.[18] In a poll carried out by IFOP in October 1979, 21% of non-trade union members and 31% of ex-members cited excessive politicisation of the trade unions as their reason for not joining or for having left unions.[19] Moreover, the priority given by the CGT and CFDT to high-profile, national events meant that other unions, FO in particular, were able to gain full credit for agreements which they signed but which had often been obtained because of the left unions' mobilisation. By pinning all their hopes on political change, the left unions allowed the 'reformist' confederations to occupy the trade union territory they had left behind.

THE TRADE UNIONS RETURN TO THE DEFENSIVE

As left unity disintegrated in the autumn of 1977 (when negotiations between the PS and the PCF to update the Common Programme broke down) and the chances of a left government diminished, the CFDT saw the advantages of the CFTC's and FO's policy. As well as the effects on the image of the confederation, the CFDT risked internal division because of its involvement with the political left. The CFDT leadership attempted to repair the damage in 1975 by reasserting complete autonomy of thought and action. In 1977, the CFDT began a process of 'recentrage' or 'resyndicalisation': henceforth, priority would be given to workplace activities over national political concerns. Instead of unity of action with the CGT, the CFDT drew closer to FO and, in a deliberate emulation of FO's tactics which shocked the political world, General Secretary Edmond Maire made a point of visiting President Giscard d'Estaing after the defeat of the left in 1978. At a meeting of the CFDT National Council in April 1978, Edmond Maire laid down 'six commandments' for future activity, one of which stated categorically that the CFDT should refuse 'especially in the period to come, to place its collective action in would-be preparation for 1981 [the presidential election] or any foreseeable legislative elections.'[20] Edmond Maire further distanced the confederation from the political left by stating, in an interview published on 6 December 1979, that:

> The way things are now, in the absence of any dynamic, of any political perspective, of popular confidence, whoever the candidates or candidate of the left are, they will fail. I'd go so far as to say that, if a left-wing president was elected in these conditions, it would still be a failure.[21]

Despite the CFDT leader's explanations that his statement was meant as a sympathetic warning, the left saw it as a betrayal.[22]

Within the CGT, the disintegration of left unity caused dissension. The leadership's condemnation of the PS, in line with PCF policy, shook the confederation, which was still theoretically committed to the Common Programme. When Georges Séguy publicly urged workers to vote Communist in the 1978 legislative elections (a position justified by the General Secretary on the rather unconvincing grounds that he was speaking as an individual), the ensuing uproar forced the CGT to embark on a period of internal reflection and self-criticism.

The left unions were not alone in facing disarray over their presidential election strategy. The CGC, already divided ideologically between an old-style corporatism and a modernist, more open style of unionism, was wracked by internal conflicts under the leadership of Yvon Charpentié (1974-1979). After 1976, the CGC's strong support for President Valéry Giscard d'Estaing was strained by Giscardian economic policy, which threatened to erode the *cadres'* economic position. Politically, however, the CGC had nowhere to turn, since its fear of the left (particularly of the PCF) was greater than its mistrust of the right. Yvon Charpentié, seen as too indulgent towards the President of the Republic, was replaced in 1979 by Jean Menu, whose strategy of hardening opposition to political measures fell into line with the general evolution of the confederation and brought the CGC closer to the other unions.

With the approach of the 1981 presidential elections, the CGC, bereft of a clear strategy because of its refusal to support either left or right, made a curious choice: it decided, in December 1980, to present its own candidate in the elections. The project was short-lived, since the dangers were all too obvious, but it revealed the dilemma facing the CGC.

Paradoxically, then, the 1981 presidential elections, which were to result in the victory of the candidate who had represented the left unions' hopes since 1965, found the trade unions once again locked in their defensive positions. Let us now examine how each of the major confederations reacted to the new challenge of the first François Mitterrand presidency.

1981-1986: The 'President's Men'?

THE CFDT

Despite the CFDT's earlier attempts to distance the confederation's activities from the perspective of the presidential elections, the CFDT called on workers, before the first round of the elections, to vote for the left in order to help build 'a more genuine and more responsible democracy, a socialist society based on self-management (*autogestion*)'.[23] The statement masked a basic contradiction. By calling on workers to vote for the left, the CFDT was acknowledging implicitly that such a vote could bring real change, and yet CFDT ideology rested on the necessity of change from below: 'Centralism is always to be feared, whatever its positive achievements'.[24] The contradiction was all the more apparent in the context of presidential elections, which underlined the concentration of political power in the hands of one individual.

On the whole, the CFDT welcomed the chance of a Socialist President, but warned that the election of François Mitterrand would not in itself bring change, and that the CFDT would continue to exercise pressure on the new incumbent. The election of François Mitterrand, and subsequently of a Socialist majority in the National Assembly, forced the CFDT to embrace the chance for reform. Not only did several leading CFDT members join the new presidential and government cabinets,[25] the CFDT offered its research and proposals to the new government and was later rewarded by the Auroux laws on workplace negotiation and democratisation of the public sector, and the promise of measures on job sharing and new forms of employment (a theme developed by the CFDT since its Brest congress in 1979). Nevertheless, friction was evident at an early stage. In October 1981, several members of the CFDT National Bureau spoke of the need to rid the confederation of its image as a 'government trade union'. Around the same time, the CFDT leadership had a series of public clashes with presidential policy on nuclear energy policy and on nationalisations, followed in February 1982 by a row over the reduction of working hours without loss of wages.

The dangers of appearing to be the 'President's men' increased after the dramatic return to economic austerity in June 1982. The CFDT's reactions to the change in government economic policy were, as might be expected, mixed. On one hand, the CFDT leadership rejected the social market strategies promoted by the CGT and urged François Mitterrand to be realistic in his economic and financial choices, for instance over social security funding and the need for economic austerity. On the other hand, the CFDT could not abandon the wage demands its own members were making. The difficulties of such a strategy became apparent when FO pushed the CFDT out of its customary second place at the elections to social security administration committees in March 1983.[26] Drawing the obvious conclusion, Edmond Maire attributed the CFDT's poor performance in the Social Security elections to its identification with political power.[27] After 1983, the CFDT was therefore forced to harden its criticism of the government's industrial policy partly in order to quell internal dissent. Strong identification of the union confederation with a Socialist President and government, particularly with a President and government associated with economic austerity, was, despite the reforms which the CFDT acknowledged to be a positive result, damaging to the CFDT's internal cohesion and image among workers.[28]

The CFDT leaders therefore determined to revert to the strategy already decided before 1981. In the run-up to the legislative elections of 1986, the CFDT attempted to distance itself from the electoral process and from the debate on political institutions (the '*cohabitation*' debate) which, it insisted, had nothing to do with the people's real preoccupations.[29]

In a book published in 1987, Edmond Maire delivered a damning judgement on the years of Socialist presidency. Whereas the CFDT had been able to ally itself with the left parties before they came to power, he argued that, after 1981, the PS 'is not, cannot be equally a party for society and a party for the state [...]. The logic of the state and the logic of society cannot be the same.'[30] His reasoning was clear: the institutions of the state make identification of trade unions with Presidents or governments in power impossible.

By 1987, the CFDT had returned ostensibly to a position of non-intervention in presidential or legislative elections, without, however, renouncing its right to develop its own projects on economic and social issues, or indeed to express opinions on political decisions.

THE CGT

The CGT's dilemma in 1981 concerned the nature of the relationship between the confederation and the PCF. After the defeat of the left in the 1978 legislative elections, the CGT was forced to begin a singular process of self-criticism. At the confederation's 1978 congress, the CGT leadership decided that, instead of relying on political change or on purely defensive unionism, the confederation should open out activities at the base and develop alternative proposals for industry, in response to the deepening global crisis of the capitalist economy. The 1978 congress therefore promised to open a new phase of offensive unionism independent of political developments.

The CGT was, however, far from unanimous in its interpretation of the 1978 congress decisions. The National Confederal Committee, meeting in December 1980, interpreted them to mean that the CGT should work not for Socialist victory in the 1981 presidential election but for reinforcement of the Communists' power base. In other words, 'autonomy' meant mobilising for a communist victory. The decision led to protests from within the confederation. In the event, it was not until after the first round that the CGT called upon its members to vote for the Socialist candidate.

From June 1981, the CGT's ties to the government and President it had eventually helped to elect were strengthened by the appointment of four Communist ministers. Yet the positions elaborated by the confederation since 1978 went directly against close collaboration between the CGT and a government forced of necessity to 'manage the crisis'.

The first major internal conflict erupted in October 1981 when two members of the Confederal Bureau, Christiane Gilles and Jean-Louis Moynot, resigned their positions, claiming that the CGT leadership still had done nothing to realise the changes decided by the 1978 congress. After the defeat of the dissidents at the 1982 congress and the replacement of Georges Séguy by Henri Krasucki (who had been less than enthusiastic about the changes brought about in 1978), the CGT pursued its strategy but found it increasingly difficult to defend in the context of increasing pressure on wages. The result was an erosion of the CGT vote at the *prud'hommes* elections of December 1982[31] and the Social Security elections of April 1983.

After the withdrawal of the PCF from government in July 1984, the CGT was free to criticise the government's economic measures, but faced the danger of being used by the PCF as a political tool against the PS in government. The CGT found itself unable to channel popular discontent into organised action; its mobilisation against austerity in 1984-1985 found only a limited response among workers, and membership continued to decline. The lesson for the CGT of the 1981-1986 period was therefore twofold: firstly, the nature of government, particularly in the context of the world economic crisis, was such that left victory was no guarantee of success for trade union demands; secondly, the PCF's blatant attempts to use the CGT after July 1984 to discredit the Socialist government forced the confederation, in the words of Henri Krasucki, to 'cultivate [its] trade union garden'. At its 1985 congress, the CGT declared its intention not to tie the confederation to any political agenda. Again, however, this policy was used by some to boost the PCF at the expense of the PS, whose policy CGT leaders equated with those of the right.[32] Whereas, in theory, the CGT moved to a position of greater political independence after 1984, its political stance was effectively dictated by the needs of the PCF.

THE 'REFORMIST' TRIO: FO, THE CFTC AND THE CGC

In relation to the experience of the CGT and CFDT, FO's scrupulously kept distance from the Socialist President paid off. Its General Secretary, André Bergeron (himself a long-time member of the PS), insisted that he regarded François Mitterrand in the same light as any other President of the Republic.[33] Nevertheless, FO's vociferous protests against the inclusion of Communists in the second Mauroy government, coupled with scathing criticisms of François Mitterrand's analysis of the economic situation, placed FO with the CFTC and the CGC in the 'opposition' camp, at least in the public's perception. FO complained loudly that the CGT and the CFDT received privileged treatment under François Mitterrand; André Bergeron's special status as negotiator, acquired under right-wing Presidents, was threatened. In response to the new situation, FO moved closer to the CFTC and the CGC, and in March 1982, shortly before the departmental council elections, the three 'reformist' unions held a joint meeting (the third of its kind since 1979) where they sharply criticised the government.[34] The election of a Socialist President thus appeared to reinforce the bipolarisation of the 1970s, with the CGT and CFDT seen as 'pro-Mitterrand' and FO, despite its professions of neutrality, seen as 'anti-Mitterrand'. Indeed, the RPR actively attempted to capitalise on FO's disaffection with the left; by speaking favourably of the confederation, it hoped to boost its own standing and to embarrass the Socialists.

Despite such moves, however, FO managed to retain a largely non-political image, thanks partly to the plurality of political sympathies within the confederation, but mainly to the determinedly 'bread-and-butter' preoccupations which continued to guide its activities. FO's score in 'social' elections continued to increase slowly but steadily.

For its part, the CFTC in general tried to avoid direct confrontation with the left government, but several public clashes (notably over private education in Spring 1982, and later over wage controls) underlined the ideological gap separating the confederation from the Socialists. Like FO, the CFTC had some difficulties steering between a left-wing government, whose policies it often opposed, and the right parties determined to profit from the situation, as seen by the latters' exhortations to their voters to support the CFTC in the 1983 Social Security elections. The CFTC attempted to demonstrate its neutrality by contrasting its activities with those of the CFDT, seen as too closely involved with the new President and his entourage. For FO and the CFTC, their ability to oppose a left-wing government and at the same time fend off approaches from the right was the ultimate test of the 1981-1986 period, but it was during the 1986-1988 period that the test reached its final stage. Both confederations kept their distance from the political world during the 1986 legislative election campaign, although the CFTC's publication of the programmes of the main parties showed it to be closer to the right than the left.[35] But if the CFTC criticised the Socialist presidency, it did not spare the right-wing government after March 1986.

The CGC, which had suffered divisions under right-wing Presidents, attempted to repair unity under a Socialist President. In a key document of October 1982, the CGC abandoned the adjective 'apolitical', which had, in the past, given rise to accusations of a 'soft' attitude towards Presidents and governments because it implied a refusal to comment on political actions and a lack of political proposals. Instead, the CGC adopted the mantle of 'independence', which would allow it to be critical of all political administrations.[36]

From 1982, however, the CGC's mobilisation against the left corresponded to the confederation's ideological return to the right. Indeed, the CGC did not spare its criticisms of the left in government, publicly insisting on Prime Minister Pierre Mauroy's departure in 1983, as part of its campaign for the Social Security elections. In response to accusations of partisan conduct, the CGC asserted that the distinction between left and right was a 'false debate' and that the confederation classed itself neither on one side nor the other. Nevertheless, the CGC's political 'independence' came across as a rejection of the left and, therefore, as support for the right. Despite its proclamations of independence, the CGC, after Paul Marchelli took over as president in May 1984, moved closer to its traditional allies, the Gaullists. In 1986, the themes chosen by the CGC - modernisation, competition, flexibility - corresponded to those put forward by the RPR-UDF. Without actually calling on its members to vote for the right, the CGC endorsed the RPR-UDF electoral platform.

In theory, therefore, the major union confederations moved closer together after 1981 by stressing trade union activity at the expense of political commitment. In practice, the trade unions' attitude towards the presidency and presidential elections varied greatly according to each confederation's ideological and tactical priorities.

Let us now turn to the trade unions' response to the presidential elections of 1988.

1988: The Trade Unions' 'non-campaign'

The presidential elections of 1988 took place against a backdrop of increasing concern regarding the place of trade unions in French society and their right to represent the workforce. The continuing debate on the representativeness of trade unions, fuelled by an abstention rate of over 50% at the *prud'hommes* elections of December 1987[37] and by public speculation about membership figures,[38] made it all the more important for the trade unions to think carefully about their role in political elections. For the trade unions as well as for the politicians, the stakes were very high.

By the end of January 1988, all the major confederations had announced that they would remain independent and would not issue voting instructions to their members for the presidential elections. Nevertheless, all the trade unions were present in the presidential elections, not least because the idea of 'independence' implied the capacity to criticise all political proposals and to put forward trade union counter-proposals. This was true even in the case of the CFTC, a confederation known for its traditional refusal to become involved directly in political elections. As in 1986, the CFTC contented itself with publishing answers from the presidential candidates to questions of policy.[39] In addition, the CFTC publicised its own list of priorities (economic growth, increased dialogue between employers and workforce, social protection, wages) and allowed its members and the wider public to compare the responses of the candidates with the confederation's demands. At the same time, and perhaps more importantly, the CFTC was laying down a set of demands and proposals which might serve as a basis for talks after the election of the President of the Republic. The CGC also published a list of the candidates' positions on questions which the confederation considered important.[40] Like the CFTC, the CGC wished to avoid damaging its public image by identifying itself strongly with specific political groups or leaders,[41] but also saw the presidential elections as an opportunity to present its proposals, knowing that the post-electoral period would allow it to mobilise for them. Paradoxically, then, the trade unions' 'independence' implied a certain detachment from the presidential election (in terms of choosing between the candidates), but also a reinforcement of the trade unions' political presence (in terms of offering political comment and proposals).

The distinction between these two forms of political activity remained, however, blurred, particularly in the case of the three major confederations, whose role in the presidential election campaign will be examined here in turn.

THE CGT

The CGT's 1985 congress decision not to tie its activities to political objectives did not prevent the confederation from organising in 1987 a series of demonstrations and protests which had clearly political implications; the largest of these, which took place in October 1987, denounced government 'attacks' on the Social Security system, and was followed by several demonstrations in November and December in defence of trade union rights.[42] Some of the CGT's activities were geared specifically towards the presidential elections: on 27 January 1987, the CGT mobilised for an explicitly political demonstration, organised in conjunction with the PCF, against what they saw as the media's legitimation of presidential candidate, Jean-Marie Le Pen. On 29 January, however, the CGT announced the results of its National Confederal Committee's deliberations on the subject of the presidential elections: the confederation would not commit itself to any candidate's campaign.

As in 1981, the concept of 'non-commitment' was open to interpretation by the CGT leaders. Already in January, conflicts within the CGT over the question of support for the PCF candidate were apparent. On 6 January, a report given to the PCF's Central Committee stated the PCF's belief that CGT members could not vote other than for the Communist candidate, André Lajoinie. Significantly, François Duteil, a member of the PCF's Political Bureau and at that time tipped as future General Secretary of the CGT, responded by declaring the confederation's complete independence, but added that CGT activists could appeal in a personal capacity for members to vote for Lajoinie. The CGT decision of 'non-involvement', announced on 29 January, therefore took place amidst disagreements between those supporting François Duteil's interpretation of independence and those such as André Deluchat, a member of the PS, who condemned the idea of CGT support for the PCF.[43] François Duteil's point of view prevailed, as General Secretary Henri Krasucki's statement to the press showed: 'We will be neither indifferent, nor neutral, nor dumb'. On the right-wing candidates, Henri Krasucki was explicit: 'they are our enemies'. As for François Mitterrand, his term of office had, according to the CGT leader, disappointed workers.[44] The CGT therefore concluded that the only suitable candidate was the PCF's André Lajoinie whose proposals, including that for a minimum wage of 6,000 francs, exactly mirrored those put forward by the CGT. In fact, Pierre Juquin, the dissident Communist candidate, proposed a similar series of measures, including a minimum wage of 6,000 francs. Indeed, Juquin's candidature had already attracted some CGT federations and members. The CGT leaders refused, however, to accept any electoral programme except that of the PCF candidate, and the 'convergence' of the PCF's and the CGT's views became a major theme of the latter's public statements.

The PCF, for its part, saw the individual support of trade union leaders as central to its campaign strategy. At a meeting of the PCF's Central Committee on 9 February, a report by Madeleine Vincent called upon leading trade union activists to make an appeal, in a personal capacity, on behalf of André Lajoinie. The party's General Secretary, Georges Marchais, defined the role of Communist CGT members in the campaign in a key statement on 8 March: each Communist should make a personal effort to win over voters; in the case of union leaders and activists, that meant 'hundreds, if not several thousands' of votes.[45] The CGT leaders were not slow to respond. On 8 March, the Communist daily L'Humanité published an interview with Henri Krasucki in which he confirmed his choice in favour of André Lajoinie. On 16 March, a 'National appeal for André Lajoinie', published in *L'Humanité*, contained the signatures of Henri Krasucki, his second-in-command, Louis Viannet, and other leading CGT figures, and in the following weeks, *L'Humanité* presented example after example of trade union members, branches and federations committing themselves to vote Communist.

Georges Marchais's statement of 8 March also demanded that the Communist members of the CGT use trade union activity to focus on the reasons for voting for the PCF candidate, that they demonstrate that 'each demand constitutes a good reason to vote for André Lajoinie'. The CGT could therefore play an important role in the *political* campaign by stepping up its *trade union* activities. From the CGT's point of view, this strategy was convenient because the confederation could argue that it was not straying from its traditional role. CGT discourse during the presidential campaign therefore focused on the need to develop a parallel, *economic* struggle which would constitute the 'third round' of the elections. The idea was given concrete form by several strike movements supported by the CGT, notably at Michelin and SNECMA, which took place during the presidential campaign and presented the traditional, 'industrial' face of trade unionism. The CGT was, therefore, able to present its activities 'before and after' the elections as part of the same process.[46]

In reality, few saw the CGT's pronouncements and activities as anything but direct intervention on behalf of the Communist candidate. Despite the leadership's claims to respect the 'diversity' of opinion in the confederation, the CGT's increasingly explicit support for André Lajoinie caused a rift within the organisation. On 6 April, the Executive Commission adopted a resolution which stated specifically that only the PCF candidate stood for the CGT's demands. Without actually calling for members to vote for André Lajoinie, the text asked members to 'reflect' upon the similarities between the CGT's and the PCF's proposals and to do their duty.[47] The leadership's indirect but, nonetheless, obvious call for workers to vote Communist was, however, contested by a significant section of the confederation, not because the dissenters wished to observe political neutrality, but because of the PCF's increasing marginalisation. In order both to ensure the defeat of the left and to avoid joining the PCF in the political wilderness, this section of the CGT argued that the confederation should encourage support for the wider left.

Their argument was all the more significant because the CGT's support for the PCF often took the form of an unequivocal attack on the *other* left candidates, particularly François Mitterrand. From the PCF's point of view this was vital because, while it was clear that most CGT members would vote for the left, the threat of the right made the best-placed left candidate (François Mitterrand) more attractive to undecided trade unionists. One of the CGT's major contributions to the PCF campaign consisted, therefore, of a denunciation of the 1981-1988 presidency, which became a theme of CGT activities.[48] The PCF for its part took CGT support for granted.

The first round of the presidential elections showed that CGT support of the

PCF candidate was not enough to stop the party's decline. A poll conducted by CSA-*L'Evénement du Jeudi* indicated that the proportion of CGT members who voted for the Communist candidate, usually just above 50%, had dropped slightly to 50%.[49] According to the same poll, as many as 38% of CGT members had voted for François Mitterrand, which, given the confederation's strong criticism of his term in office, left doubts about the efficacy of the CGT's message. Nevertheless, the CGT proved itself once again to be a reliable electoral ally for the PCF. Questioned by IFOP about the reasons for their first-round choice, a significant number of Lajoinie voters replied: 'Because I'm in the CGT, and [André Lajoinie] is close to the CGT.'[50] Once the first round was over, and the Communist candidate eliminated, the CGT's direct involvement in the campaign was apparently finished.

THE CFDT

In an interview in November 1987, Edmond Maire set the tone for the CFDT's deliberations on the presidential elections, declaring that:

> There is a fundamental difference between the function of a trade union and that of a political party. It is absolutely essential that this difference is respected. Having said that, we cannot remain silent over the great problems of our country. Politics is important in order to mobilise energies against unemployment, for job creation and for the defence of freedoms. [51]

In other words, the CFDT leader was differentiating between an apolitical stance, which would imply a rejection of politics, and an independent stance, which would allow the confederation to enter the political sphere, without tying itself to any one candidate. Having made this distinction, he went on to criticise the lack of social dialogue under the Chirac government, while hastening to point out that this was not an electoral standpoint. The CFDT leader also spoke out on a theme which was to dominate the confederation's attitude during the campaign: the nature of the campaign itself. According to Maire, the candidates were so preoccupied with an ideological clash over privatisation, that essential questions, notably employment, were neglected. Since the campaign proper had not started when the CFDT leader said this, his words may be interpreted as a warning to the left (as in 1979-1980) to focus policy on questions which were of interest to the trade unions (employment and social protection). In addition, he claimed that, since both right and left were elevating their policies to holy writ, the duty of trade unionists was to show 'disrespect': 'On these occasions, if the trade unionists weren't there to speak plainly, who would?' The CFDT leader thus claimed for his organisation the role of popular representative, the intermediary voice between the politicians and the people.

Edmond Maire's declarations of 'non-commitment' were confirmed when the National Council issued a statement on 29 January 1988 announcing its decision (by 68.5% to 23.75%) not to call for a vote in any candidate's favour. In order to emphasise its non-partisan position, the CFDT reaffirmed its rejection of 'both economic liberalism and statism'. Nevertheless, it spoke out against attacks on the right to strike, racism and the exploitation of people's fears, and in favour of social dialogue. Given the CFDT's previous condemnations of the lack of consultation and the erosion of trade union rights under the Chirac government, the statement could be interpreted as a loose message of support for the (left) parliamentary opposition. And in terms of economic policy, the mixture of planning and decentralised negotiation proposed by the CFDT recalled François Mitterrand's own ideas.

For some within the CFDT, the implicit support for François Mitterrand contained in the National Committee statement did not go far enough. The opposition of around a quarter of the National Committee members to the decision not to issue voting instructions revealed strong differences of opinion within the confederation. Some of the key arguments were reproduced in the confederal press. Some activists, like Bernard Henry of the Pays de Loire federation, argued that the CFDT's duty was to ensure the defeat of the right, and that support for the left should be explicit. In response, Edmond Maire spelled out the reasons for 'non-commitment'. Firstly, he cited the damage suffered by the confederation as a result of its identification with the presidency between 1981 and 1986. Secondly, he argued that public opinion rejected the excessive politisation of trade unions (as the abstention rate at the 1987 *prud'hommes* elections had shown). The CFDT leader claimed, therefore, that the only position true to CFDT principles was one of non-involvement in the electoral sphere but increased involvement in the trade-union sphere. This did not, however, imply an apolitical stance. Maire pointed out that the role of trade unions should be not to command workers but to 'teach' them.[52] The CFDT therefore interpreted its role in political elections as a pedagogical one, in a double sense: firstly, its job was to 'advise' the presidential candidates by communicating popular demands; secondly, its comments on the candidates' response to these demands would enable the electorate to make a choice.

The National Council of 12-14 April confirmed that the CFDT's decision not to issue voting instructions did not preclude evaluation of the relative merits of individual presidential candidates' policies. At a press conference following the National Council, Edmond Maire criticised explicitly Chirac's remarks on immigration, and reiterated his disapproval of the low standard of political debate in the campaign. In an editorial in the last issue of the CFDT weekly *Syndicalisme* before the first round of the elections, National Secretary Jean-François Troglic strongly condemned the Justice Minister for 'debasing the image of justice', and the government collectively for interfering in broadcasting freedom and for undermining the right to strike in the civil service.[53]

From 14 April, after all the presidential candidates had presented their policies, the CFDT ran a comparative dossier explaining its own positions on the most important questions.[54] The overall effect of the CFDT's pronouncements was to point its members, without making an explicit statement of support, towards the candidate who best matched the confederation's positions, namely, François Mitterrand.

Over and above the reasons cited by Edmond Maire to justify the CFDT's position, the confederation's refusal to endorse directly François Mitterrand reflected the union's original reservations concerning the democratic nature of presidential campaigns and, particularly, their inevitable personalisation of power. In March, for instance, the confederal press attacked François Mitterrand for delaying his decision to stand in the elections. According to Jean-François Troglic, François Mitterrand's tactics had not only reinforced the 'excessive personalisation' of the campaign and obscured the essential political issues, they had also allowed the right, particularly the far right, to monopolise the political scene.[55] Moreover, the CFDT claimed that without the pressure of the trade unions as popular representatives, politicians would soon forget their electoral promises once in power. The role of trade unions was therefore to set the political agenda and to ensure that the politicians kept to it, both during the campaign and after the elections.[56] As in the case of the other union confederations, this idea showed that the CFDT was thinking of the post-electoral period as much as of the campaign itself. In this general sense, the CFDT's position revealed its conception of the role of trade unions as guardians of democracy.

Despite the absence of specific voting instructions, CFDT members responded to the confederal leadership's analysis of the campaign by voting massively in favour of François Mitterrand. According to the CSA-L'Evénement du Jeudi exit poll immediately after the first round, a staggering 70% of CFDT members voted for the Socialist candidate on 24 April.[57] The crucial difference between the situation in 1981 and that in 1988, from the CFDT's point of view, was that the choice was based not on CFDT sponsorship of the candidate, but on agreements in policy which would not exclude, or be invalidated by, any future disagreements.

FORCE OUVRIERE

In the case of FO, the question of support for presidential candidates was settled by tradition. In an interview in November 1987, General Secretary André Bergeron categorically ruled out any electoral stance on the part of his union: 'The election of the President or of deputies is a matter for the citizens alone. The trade union movement should not get involved in the political debate'. Over and above the basic democratic principle, Bergeron saw another reason for non-commitment: 'We have to negotiate with all governments, and God knows I myself have known a few'.[58] Apparently, therefore, FO's position was straightforward enough. Nevertheless, the campaign began on a sour note for FO when Jacques Chirac used, on his early election posters, a remark made by André Bergeron (in the same interview), to the effect that '[Jacques Chirac] has always been extremely fair, and to me, fairness is very important'. Extremely sensitive to accusations of support for the RPR, Bergeron insisted, with some anger, that the references be removed. The incident revealed not only what influence the 'elder statesman' image of André Bergeron had on the right, but also the importance attached during the election campaign to judgements made by trade unions.

Like the CFDT, FO also emphasised from the start of the campaign the democratic need for a high-quality and fairly fought campaign. In January 1988, Claude Jenet, Confederal Secretary, commented in the organisation's weekly paper *Force Ouvrière* on a competition run by *Paris-Match* to guess the date of François Mitterrand's announcement of his candidacy and the final election result. Political manœuvring had reduced the presidency of the Republic to a game, complained Jenet: 'The institutions, the politicians themselves bear a large part of the responsibility for this continual deterioration'.[59] André Bergeron took up this idea in an editorial at the end of January which laid down FO's line on the presidential elections. Commenting on the series of political 'scandals' which had surfaced, the FO leader emphasised 'how damaging that could be for our democracy in as much as public opinion would end up losing confidence in those who direct, and to some extent uphold, the Institutions of the Republic'.[60] The theme ran constantly through the pages of *Force Ouvrière*. Like the CFDT, FO was determined to occupy the moral ground by presenting itself as the upholder of democratic republican institutions.

Implicit in this conception of the role of trade unions was the idea of trade union independence, which would allow FO to transcend the political debate (by not committing itself to any candidate) whilst at the same time retaining its capacity to criticise (thereby, paradoxically, becoming involved in the debate itself). Claude Pitous (one of two rival candidates for the succession of the leadership of FO) summed up the confederation's position: 'Even if, today, our voice is drowned out by the noise of the elections, we must rediscover the real questions. We should gather our forces to put pressure on those who will be in office'.[61] FO's pronouncements, therefore, echoed those of the CFDT.

This role entailed some evaluation of the candidates' economic policies. Without directly criticising Jacques Chirac, the confederal press voiced its disapproval of the prevailing economic climate.[62] It did not, however, express any preferences. The results of the CSA-*L'Evénement du Jeudi* exit poll on the first round of the presidential elections suggested that the confederal press mirrored the views of FO membership. The findings reflected FO members' criticisms of the 1986-1988 government (Jacques Chirac received only 8% of FO members' first-round votes), but showed no clear-cut preferences among the other presidential candidates. According to the poll, 35% of FO members voted for François Mitterrand in the first round, 26% for Raymond Barre, and 20% for Jean-Marie Le Pen.[63] The relative fragmentation of the FO vote mirrored the political divisions within the confederation (which includes elements as disparate as Trotskyists and Gaullists). In order to unite this politically diverse membership, FO has traditionally emphasised political independence laced with a strong dose of anti-communism. In 1988, the high proportion of votes accorded to the *Front National* leader by FO members pointed perhaps to the dangers of a lack of clear political direction, indicating as it did a rejection of mainstream political parties which FO, by its emphasis on political independence, has perhaps encouraged, or at least reflected, over the years.

Jean-Marie Le Pen's score in the first round of the presidential elections held implications not only for FO but for all the trade unions which saw themselves as upholders of republican democracy. The first-round result brought the trade unions, whose attempts to distance themselves from the presidential campaigns up until 24 April had in any case been ambiguous, back onto the forefront of the political stage.

THE TRADE UNION AND THE 'REPUBLICAN FRONT'

The question of the trade unions' involvement altered dramatically between the two rounds of the elections, largely in response to the first-round score of Jean-Marie Le Pen. With, according to some surveys, more than 20% of workers voting for Le Pen in the first round,[64] the trade unionists asked themselves whether they had been too complacent about the far right. The CFDT set up a Minitel hot-line to ask members what to do about the FN vote. The poll which showed that 20% of FO members voted for Le Pen indicated that, in the case of FO at least, trade union members had not responded to the far right in a significantly different way from workers in general, which threw into question the unions' perception of themselves as the most advanced section of the workforce (though it, perhaps ironically, underlined their representativeness).

Apart from the long-term question of how to respond to workers' discontent, as expressed in first-round electoral support for the FN candidate, the trade unions faced the immediate threat of far-right domination of the political scene. With the debate now polarised over fundamental questions of political allegiance (racism, citizenship, the nature of democracy) as a result of the importance of the FN in second-round calculations, and in response to the clear signals from the left parties in favour of a 'republican front' against the far right, the trade unions stepped up their activities.

The result was the most impressive May Day rallies for years. Faced with the threat of a hijacking of workers' day by the FN (which had conveniently moved the Feast of Joan of Arc back to 1 May), the CFDT, the teachers' union the *Fédération de l'Education Nationale*, and the *Fédération Générale Autonome de Fonctionnaires* organised a joint demonstration, together with students' unions, on the morning of 1 May, which took as its theme the need to counter the far right. For the CFDT, which, until the shock of the first-round result, had not planned to demonstrate on 1 May, the move represented a 'burst of indignation at what is in danger of happening to workers and to this country, if we don't find the way to link the action of democratic, trade union forces and of associations with the situation people are living in'.[65] Questioned about the

CFDT's participation in a political demonstration, Edmond Maire stressed that the dangers posed by the far right made it 'necessary to modify our habits'.[66]

For the CGT, which organised a separate demonstration in the afternoon of 1 May, the need to combat the FN formed only part of a wider struggle against capitalism. The objectives of its May Day demonstration therefore stretched beyond countering the FN rally to encompass 'demands for improving the life of workers, those in unstable employment, the unemployed, [and] the struggle against hatred, racism and division'.[67] In addition, the CGT saw the demonstration as an opportunity to step up its mobilisation in order to put pressure on the future President (since its own candidate was no longer in the running). Given such a fundamental difference between the aims of the two demonstrations, it was not surprising that they failed to present a united trade union front, and the press made much of the division. Nevertheless, some attempt was made to bridge the two demonstrations, and, more importantly, both constituted a show of strength for the trade union movement (the first demonstration rallied an estimated 20,000 people, whilst the CGT brought at least twice that number of marchers onto the streets of Paris in the afternoon).

Meanwhile, overt support for François Mitterrand grew within the confederations between the two rounds of the elections. Within the CGT, CFDT, and FO, individuals and federations took an independent stand for François Mitterrand. Several hundred trade-unionists from various unions, uniting under the title 'Unité 88', launched an appeal for a vote for the left. Finally, on the eve of the second round, the CGT's Executive Commission appealed to its members to vote against Jacques Chirac, without explicitly recommending a vote for the Socialist candidate. (The PCF had already on 27 April called on workers to vote for François Mitterrand in the second round). The other confederations refused to endorse a candidate officially, but the trade union response to the threat of the far right was sure to work in favour of the left. All the unions in their respective journals reflected on the FN issue, conceding that, in the words of André Bergeron:

> Those who suffer the consequences of difficulties of all sorts end up feeling that no-one is listening. And that's how they lose confidence in the traditional political parties and, to some extent, in the trade union movement.[68]

The trade unions concluded that, instead of becoming involved with individual candidates, they and the political parties should work together immediately to improve the quality of life, remove injustices and inequalities, and renew social dialogue. In other words, the trade unions pursued their theme of the 'third round', which would enable them, as trade unions and not as political support groups, to work on concrete proposals for change. Claude Pitous of FO, in an article which rejected the suggestion of a 'third round' in the sense of an all-out mobilisation (as the CGT clearly intended), spoke, nevertheless, of the need for renewed trade union activity in order to fulfil the promise of social and economic change.[69] In this sense, the trade unions were contesting the ability (or the will) of the presidency to act for change, and were reaffirming the need for the trade unions to play an economic role. Paradoxically, however, their contributions to the political, economic and social debates surrounding the elections ensured their political presence and, at the same time, implied a recognition of presidential elections as a major focus for those debates.

In 1988, the trade unions were unanimous in acknowledging the importance of the presidential elections as a vehicle for change, because of the nature of the powers conferred on the President by the Constitution of the Fifth Republic.[70] In this sense, the trade unions have accepted the institutions of the Fifth Republic as the framework for political activity, and have sought to use those institutions to press forward their demands. At the same time, the trade unions made it clear in 1988 that, in their view, the importance of the presidential elections stemmed not only from the nature of the political institutions but also from the nature of their economic circumstances. Because of this distinction between the economic and the political, the trade unions claimed their right to intervene in the presidential campaign and to put forward comments and proposals. The distinction was crucial because it sought to justify the role of trade unionism in society. However, if trade unions acknowledged, by their political conduct, that political institutions constituted the only means of change, they would lose one of their most powerful arguments for membership of a trade union, and would limit their role to one of simple defence. This was precisely the trap that the CGT and the CFDT had fallen into in the 1970s, with disastrous results for membership numbers and their own public standing.

* * *

In 1988, the trade unions sought to reinforce their role as forces for economic and social change by placing emphasis on their proposals concerning such issues as employment and training, collective bargaining and social protection, as a means of both commenting on the elections and preparing the ground for negotiation after the elections. The trade unions interpreted their political role as that of intermediary rather than actor: by claiming to act as a channel between the political leaders and the people, they attempted to avoid involvement in party politics and, at the same time, stake their claim to popular representation.

In order to maintain their distance from the electioneering aspects of the campaign, the trade unions developed a discourse based on the defence of democratic values, a discourse which allowed them to go beyond criticism of individual candidates. The CGT, the CFDT and FO all posed as defenders of the Republic in denouncing the personalisation of the presidential campaign, the use of immigration as a propaganda tool, and the key position given to the FN candidate by the right's need for alliances. Between the two electoral rounds, the trade unions mobilised explicitly on this theme in response to the first-round score of Jean-Marie Le Pen. In the case of the CFDT and, to a lesser extent, the CGT, the republican discourse and the trade unions' response to the rise of the far right helped them to move into the political mainstream.

The debate on the FN candidate's first-round score placed the trade unions in an awkward position, however. Although the trade unions positioned themselves at the forefront of opposition to the far right, they were also forced to admit that they bore some responsibility for the far right's appeal to workers. The trade unions, like the political parties, had failed to convince workers of the possibility of change.[71] Far from legitimising the trade unions' place in society, the debate caused by the rise of the far right served to question further the trade unions' capacity to respond to workers' needs.

In particular, the debate posed the question of trade union unity. Despite the common aims of the trade union mobilisation against the far right, the two biggest union confederations were unable to unite their May Day demonstrations in a combined show of strength against the FN. More generally, the trade union movement remained divided between those who felt the need to make a strong statement of support for the left as a means of undermining the far right and those who saw complete political independence as the best solution. The attempt by individuals from the various confederations to launch a united appeal for François Mitterrand in the presidential election served only to emphasise those divisions. Once again, the CGT's exclusive support for the Communist candidate constituted a major stumbling-block to trade union unity.

Paradoxically, however, the various trade unions' priorities and demands in 1988 were remarkably similar. In the ideological battle which separated left candidates from right in the presidential elections, trade union views converged on questions which divided the political world: immigration, social cohesion, consultation and negotiation. After the election, the unions were unanimous in their demand for wage increases, even the traditionally conservative unions joining the drive for improved living standards.

The place of the unions in workplace and national bargaining received a boost in the presidential campaign. For once, the trade unions' demands - on employment, training, the need for new forms of consultation, and social protection - were reflected in the candidates' programmes, and matched the mood of the campaign, which at least paid lip service to social concerns, despite being dominated by talk of economic constraints. This provided the unions with the chance to put forward their demands in the name of social justice. The task of trade unions was to draw from the campaign debates and promises the basis for future negotiation, or *'grain à moudre'*, to use the phrase associated with André Bergeron.

One of the major themes of the election campaign, the need for social dialogue, should serve as a pointer for future trade union activity. The trade unions, by distancing themselves from the electoral candidates, emphasised that real change would come not from the elections but from the struggles and negotiations which followed. The CGT, whose activities were bound up with the Communist electoral campaign, also pursued this line, but this precisely because the candidate it supported stood no chance of election. In this case, the emphasis on economic action could be interpreted as an admission of political impotence as much as a declaration of strength in the workplace. By recognising the limitations of the state's role - a radical change since 1981 - the trade unions, during the 1988 presidential elections, staked their claim to a place in the Republic and to a place in the negotiation process. The trade unions' dilemma concerning their role in helping to effect political change and their attitude towards the institutions of the Fifth Republic was not solved during the 1988 presidential elections, but the alternatives were perhaps more clearly outlined than ever.

NOTES

1. *FO-Hebdo,* 10 February 1988, p.7.

2. Interview with Edmond Maire, *Le Point,* 2 November 1987, p.42.

3. *15e Congrès national corporatif (9e de la CGT) tenu à Amiens du 8 au 16 octobre 1906. Compte rendu des travaux* (Amiens, 1906) pp.170-171. The text, a basic document of the French trade union movement, is reproduced in many books on the history of the labour movement: for example, J.-D. Reynaud, *Les Syndicats en France* (2 vols.) (Paris, Seuil, 1975), Vol. II, pp. 26-27.

4. The latest figures from INSEE indicate that trade union members constitute less than 13% of the French workforce. French trade union membership, which has never gone beyond 25% of the workforce, is thus one of the lowest, if not the lowest, among the industrialised nations (see *Le Monde,* 31 May 1988). Recent studies have suggested that the membership rate is even lower: for example, Pierre Rosanvallon has put the figure at 9% (see Jacques Julliard in *Le Nouvel Observateur,* 22 January 1988, p.23). According to Rosanvallon, of the largest unions, the CGT has 600,000 members, FO and the CFDT 400,000 each. In the sense of regularly subscribing members, the French trade unions are extremely weak. Their weakness is compensated to some extent by participation in various state bodies (adminstration boards of Social Security funds, joint employer-employee industrial tribunals known as *conseils de prud'hommes,* training and employment committees) and in workplace representation (consultative boards known as *comités d'entreprise* or *d'établissement,* workforce delegates or *délégués du personnel*). Membership of these boards and appointment to the position of workforce delegate are decided by elections in which the trade unions have a special place. Any evaluation of the strength of the trade union movement must therefore consider the results and the effects of these 'social' elections as well as straight membership figures. The trade unions can therefore claim to represent a much larger proportion of the workforce than their membership figures would suggest.

5. R. Mouriaux, *Syndicalisme et politique* (Paris, Editions Ouvrières, 1985) p. 164.

6. The position of CGT, which, like the PCF, had been hostile to the Fourth Republic, was rather difficult, but it rallied to the Republic in response to the threat from the right.

7. L. Rioux, *Clefs pour le syndicalisme* (Paris, Seghers, 1972) p. 159.

8. H. Hamon, and P. Rotman, *La Deuxième Gauche* (Paris, Seuil, 1984) p. 112.

9. Quoted in A. Bergouniaux, *Force Ouvrière* (Paris, Seuil, 1975) p. 154.

10. See G. Ross, *Workers and Communists in France: from Popular Front to*

Eurocommunism (Berkeley, University of California Press, 1982) pp. 113-114.

11. The dramatic intervention of the Elysée in requisitioning striking miners in March 1963 not only helped to show the President as authoritarian, it also increased public support for the strike and, by extension, the standing of the trade unions.

12. This was stated explicitly in a note to the Confederal Council in February 1963: 'insofar as political life revolves around the election of the President of the Republic, it is up to the CFTC to follow the moves towards a gathering of forces which are taking place in accordance with that event'. M. Branciard, *Syndicats et partis: Autonomie ou dépendance* (2 Vols.) (Paris, Syros, 1982), Vol. II (1948-1981) p. 142.

13. G. Lefranc, *Le Mouvement syndical de la Libération aux événements de mai-juin 1968* (Paris, Payot, 1969) p. 191.

14. Lefranc, *Le Mouvement syndical,* p. 192.

15. See Bergouniaux, *Force Ouvrière,* p. 157.

16. Hamon and Rotman, *La Deuxième Gauche,* p. 188.

17. The CFDT was actively involved in the organisation of the *Assises du Socialisme,* a meeting of the various forces of the Socialist left, in 1974. For the CFDT leaders and the PSU, the aim was to bring the PSU, and with it its ideas, into the new *Parti Socialiste* and thus to stimulate the renewal of the left. The initiative failed because of mutual distrust between the PS and the PSU, but Michel Rocard and his allies in the PSU did move across to the PS. Another result of the initiative was that it brought the CFDT closer to the PS. Within the confederation, the CFDT leaders' involvement with the political left gave rise to fierce criticism.

18. O. Duhamel, and J.-L. Parodi, 'Images syndicales', *Pouvoirs,* no.26, 1983, pp.158-163.

19. *Notes et documents du BRAEC*, no.21, September 1982, p. 75.

20. Hamon and Rotman, *La Deuxième Gauche,* p. 310.

21. The relevant section of this interview, published in *Le Républicain lorrain* on 6 December 1979, and Edmond Maire's explanation of his words, published in *Le Monde,* 10 December 1979, are reproduced in E. Maire, *Reconstruire l'Espoir* (Paris, Seuil, 1980) pp. 181-188.

22. In addition, far from distancing the confederation from politics, Edmond Maire's remarks were interpreted by some commentators as a criticism of François Mitterrand and a move in favour of his challenger for the PS candidacy in the presidential elections, Michel Rocard. See Hamon and Rotman, *La Deuxième Gauche,* p. 334. Maire, for his part, insisted that his objective was to warn against internal wrangling in the party over the choice of presidential candidate, which he saw as a liability.

23. *Syndicalisme,* 16 April 1981, p. 17.

24. *Syndicalisme,* 7 May 1983, p. 3.

25. The most notable of these were Jeannette Laot, who became a member of the presidential entourage, Hubert Lesire-Ogrel, René Decaillon and Hubert Prévost, who joined ministerial cabinets.

26. The CGT obtained 28.19% of the votes, FO 25.17%, the CFDT 18.38%, the CGC

15.93% and the CFDT 12.30%. In previous elections, the CFDT had always obtained more than 20%, and FO well under 20%. The elections were therefore widely interpreted as a major setback for the CFDT and a boost for FO. However, the results are subject to the important qualification that Social Security elections are less representative than elections taking place in the workplace or *prud' hommes* elections because they exclude around half the workforce, whilst including other groups such as students and pensioners. See J.-P. Aujard, and S. Volkoff, 'Une Analyse chiffrée des audiences syndicales', *Travail et Emploi,* no.30, December 1986, p. 47.

27. *Syndicalisme,* 27 October 1983.

28. The CFDT published a comprehensive study of the trade unions and public opinion in 1983, taking particular note of the strong identification of the CFDT with the new President. *CFDT-Aujourd' hui,* no.61, May 1983, pp. 48-59.

29. *CFDT-Magazine,* no.103, March 1983, p. 4. This argument, based on the CFDT's conception as its role as upholder of democracy, was also to be important in the 1988 presidential elections.

30. E. Maire, *Nouvelles frontières pour le syndicalisme* (Paris, Syros, 1987) pp. 29-30.

31. *Conseils de prud' hommes* are industrial tribunals composed of an equal number of elected employers' and employees' representatives. The elections, held for the second time under new voting conditions in 1982 and thereafter every five years, are generally held to be the most representative of the 'social' elections (covering 13.5 million employees in 1982). The CGT's share of the vote in the employees' section dropped from 42.09% in 1979 to 36.81% in 1982, with the smaller unions (the CFDT and the CGC) and the tiny independent unions being the principal beneficiaries of the CGT's losses.

32. See, for example, the CGT's Louis Viannet in *Le Monde,* 4 June 1986: 'The expression 'more of the same' isn't the CGT's. But, it's true, the Chirac government has found, in the most important areas, ground which has been prepared for them by the preceding government. That's the reality of the situation'.

33. See A. Bergeron, *1500 jours* (Paris, Flammarion, 1984). Significantly, Bergeron's book, essentially of FO's dealings with the early Mitterrand presidency, begins in 1980, thus establishing a certain continuity between the Giscard presidency and its successor.

34. The text of the joint statement issued after the meeting was published in *Le Monde,* 17 March 1982.

35. See 'Dossier: la CFTC interroge les partis politiques', *Syndicalisme CFTC,* March 1986.

36. The document is reproduced in Mouriaux, *Syndicalisme et politique,* p. 104.

37. Only 45.96% of enfranchised employees in metropolitan France exercised their right to vote. Of those who voted, 36.34% chose the CGT, 23.05% the CFDT, 20.49% FO, 8.3% the CFTC and 7.43% the CGC.

38. The debate was sparked off by the latest figures from the INSEE (see footnote 4) and a book by Pierre Rosanvallon, which put the overall membership rate at 9%. P. Rosanvallon, *La Question syndicale* (Paris, Calmann-Lévy, 1988).

39. Published in *La Lettre confédérale* of 12 April 1988. See *Le Monde,* 24 April 1988.

40. *Encadrement,* no. 13, April 1988, pp. 13-42.

41. The CGC's poor showing in the 1987 *prud' hommes* elections was seen by many as the result of its support of the Chirac government. See *Le Monde,* 11 December 1987.

42. On 21 November 1987, a tribunal at Bobigny ruled that notices of impending strike (a legal requirement for public employees) lodged by unions representing Air Inter pilots and mechanics were 'unlawful' because they were likely to lead to unlawful disturbance. This followed a similar ruling in July, at Bobigny, to the effect that the unions' claims were unreasonable. The management therefore obtained injunctions against the unions to prevent strikes in support of three-man crews. The trade unions reacted strongly to what they saw as an attack on the right to strike, some unions, notably the CGT, linking the judicial decisions with statements made in right-wing circles about the need to curb strike activities. On 27 January 1988, the Paris Court of Appeal decided that the Créteil and Bobigny tribunals had exceeded their powers in ruling against the strikes. The right-to-strike issue was therefore looming in the background during the election campaign.

43. *Le Monde,* 30 January 1988.

44. *Le Monde,* 31 January 1988.

45. *L'Humanité,* 8 March 1988.

46. See, for example, confederal Secretary Michel Warcholak in *L'Humanité,* 18 March 1988: 'If the President of the French Republic is elected for seven years, the same is not true of the CGT which continues before, during and after (the elections)'. See also Henri Krasucki's editorial, 'Tout passe par la lutte', in *Le Peuple,* 19 May 1988, pp.3-4.

47. *Le Peuple,* 14 April 1988, p. 6.

48. See, for example, the 6 April statement by the Executive Commission, reproduced in *Le Peuple,* 14 April 1988, pp. 5-6.

49. See *L'Evénement du Jeudi,* 28 April 1988, p. 13.

50. *Libération,* 30 April 1988.

51. *Le Point,* 2 November 1987, p. 33.

52. *Syndicalisme,* 11 February 1988, pp. 8-9.

53. *Syndicalisme,* 21 April 1988, p. 3.

54. *Syndicalisme,* 14 April 1988, pp. 4-7.

55. *Le Point,* 23 November 1987, p. 33.

56. See *Syndicalisme,* 14 April 1988, p. 1.

57. *L'Evénement du Jeudi,* 28 April 1988, p. 13. This figure is all the more noteworthy when compared with the figure of 45% put forward as the proportion of British Trades Union Congress members who voted for the Labour Party in 1987, that is, in a situation where party and trade union are officially linked. Of course, the comparison has limited value because of the difference in numbers of trade unionists involved in the two cases (the TUC had 8.8 million members in 1988), but it does help to emphasise the overwhelming nature of the CFDT vote for François Mitterrand. This trend began at

the 1974 presidential elections, when 74% of CFDT members voted for the left candidate (see Branciard, *Syndicats et partis,* p.275). The figures help to explain the CFDT's attempts to influence PS policy and strategy, particularly in the 1970s; the confederation felt that, since its membership was actively helping the party, its contribution should be recognised.

58. *Le Point,* 23 November 1987, p. 33.

59. *Force Ouvrière,* 20 January 1988, p. 2.

60. *Force Ouvrière,* 3 February 1988, p. 1.

61. *Force Ouvrière,* 10 February 1988, p. 7.

62. See, for example, *Force Ouvrière,* 17 February 1988, pp. 3-6.

63. *L'Evénement du Jeudi,* 28 April 1988, p.13. *L'Evénement du Jeudi* later commented that the figure of 20% for Le Pen could have been slightly exaggerated, but was more or less accurate.

64. Another survey, carried out by the CNRS and the BVA, put the number of workers voting for Le Pen at 16%. However, this survey was much more detailed than the CSA-*L'Evénement du Jeudi* exit poll, which presumably included in its 'worker' section other categories such as unemployed workers (19% of whom voted for Le Pen, according to the CNRS-BVA survey) and white-collar workers in the commercial sector (21% of whom voted for the *Front National* candidate in the CNRS-BVA survey). If these differences are taken into account, the figure approaches the 20% put forward by the CSA -*L'Evénement du Jeudi* exit poll.

65. Interview with Edmond Maire in *Libération,* 29 April 1988.

66. *Libération,* 2 May 1988.

67. *L'Humanité,* 29 April 1988.

68. *Le Monde,* 7 May 1988.

69. *Le Monde,* 12 May 1988.

70. Even the CGT, the most vociferous trade union opponent of the institutions of the Fifth Republic in the early years of the Republic's existence, acknowledged this explicitly in an interview given by Henri Krasucki in *L'Humanité,* 8 March 1988.

71. See two very critical articles which focus on the trade unions' response to the far right: P. Eliakim, 'Les Syndicats dans la tornade politique', *L'Evénement du Jeudi,* 26 May 1988, pp. 94-9, and H. Gibier, 'Syndicats: pas de pause électorale', *Le Nouvel Economiste,* 29 April 1988, pp. 16-17.

INDICATIVE BIBLIOGRAPHY

Adam, G., *Le Pouvoir syndical* (Paris, Dunod, 1985).

Bergeron, A., *1500 jours* (Paris, Flammarion, 1984).

Bergouniaux, A., *Force Ouvrière* (Paris, Seuil, 1975).

Branciard, M., *Syndicats et partis: Autonomie ou dépendance* (2 vols.) Vol. II, 1948-1981 (Paris, Syros, 1982).

Grunberg, G. and Mouriaux, R., *L'Univers politique et syndical des cadres* (Paris, Fondation Nationale des Sciences Politiques, 1979).

Hamon, H., Rotman, P., *La Deuxième gauche* (2nd ed., Paris, Seuil, 1984).

Krasucki, H., *Un Syndicat moderne? Oui!* (Paris, Messidor, 1987).

Lefranc, G., *Le Mouvement syndical de la Libération aux événements de mai-juin 1968* (Paris, Payot, 1969).

Maire, E., *Nouvelles frontières pour le syndicalisme* (Paris, Syros, 1987).

Mouriaux, R., *Les Syndicats dans la société française* (Paris, Fondation Nationale des Sciences Politiques, 1983).

Mouriaux, R., *Syndicalisme et politique* (Paris, Editions Ouvrières, 1985).

Reynaud, J.-D., *Les Syndicats en France* (2 vols.) (Paris, Seuil, 1975).

Rioux, L., *Clefs pour le syndicalisme* (Paris, Seghers, 1972).

Rosanvallon, P., *La Question syndicale* (Paris, Calmann-Lévy, 1988).

Ross, G., *Workers and Communists in France: from Popular Front to Eurocommunism* (Berkeley, University of California Press, 1982).

Notes on Contributors

David Bell   is a lecturer in politics at Leeds University. He obtained his DPhil from Oxford University. He has written and researched on various aspects of French and Spanish elections in the 1970s and 1980s. He is the author (with B. Criddle) of *The French Socialist Party* (OUP, 1988) and joint editor of *The Biographical Dictionary of French Politicians since Napoleon III* (Harvester/Wheatsheaf, 1989). Along with John Gaffney, he is the editor of the quarterly journal on European political issues and policies, *Contemporary European Affairs*.

Alistair Cole   graduated with a degree in Government and History from the LSE. He subsequently obtained his DPhil from Oxford University. He has written on the French Socialist Party and elections in France. He is the joint author with P. Campbell of *French electoral systems and elections since 1789* (Gower, 1989). He is currently working on a study of the French party system.

John Gaffney   obtained his DPhil from the University of Sussex. His research interests are French and British politics, in particular, the relationship between language and political practice. He has written on political leadership, political culture and the inner-city riots in Britain. He is the author of *The French Left and the Fifth Republic* (Macmillan, 1989), and *The Language of Political Leadership in Contemporary Britain* (forthcoming). He is joint editor, with David Bell, of the journal, *Contemporary European Affairs*.

Susan Hayward   obtained her PhD from Exeter University. She has taught in both Britain and the United States. She has published widely on French Cinema in American and British journals. She is the co-author and joint editor with Ginette Vincendeau of *French Film: Texts and Contexts* (Routledge, 1989). She has written on French and British television and her articles include analyses of the relationship between the state and television, television as a popular cultural medium and television genres.

George Jones graduated from Brasenose College, Oxford, in Modern History and Modern Languages. He taught in Universities in London and Paris before joining the European Business School, London, in 1983 as Head of the Department of French Studies. His interests lie in the field of government-business relations, and in business law. He is currently writing a book on the reform of competition policy in France. He contributes on the subject of British and European business environment to periodicals in the United Kingdom and continental Europe.

Susan Milner obtained her PhD from Aston University. Her doctoral research examined the theory and practice of internationalism in the labour movement before 1914, and particularly the role of French syndicalism in the development of international labour organisation. A book on this subject is due to appear in 1990 (Berg Publishers). She has written on the relationship between the labour movement and the state in the French Fifth Republic, and is currently researching into labour organisation and social policy in the context of European economic integration.

Gino Raymond has a PhD from Cambridge University, for his thesis on the inter-relationship between politics and myth in the novels of André Malraux. He has taught at a number of institutions in England and France. His research interests encompass both politics and literature. He has written on the Communist Party in France, the dilemmas faced by committed writers in France, and is presently working on a study of the cultural assumptions behind the French presence in Vietnam.

James Shields graduated with an MA in French and Hispanic Studies from the University of Glasgow. He has taught in several institutions in Britain and France. He is currently completing a PhD on Stendhal. His areas of research interest are French philosophy and politics. He has published on Stendhal and on the politics of the contemporary right and extreme right in France. He is working at present on a study of the French right in opposition.